DOM. GEORGE WILHELM MANCIUS
(1706—1762)
Co-Pastor with Dom. Petrus Vas at Kingston Dutch Church, 1732.
Missionary to the Minisink District

Minisink Valley Reformed Dutch Church Records, 1716-1830

The New York Genealogical and Biographical Society

HERITAGE BOOKS
2008

HERITAGE BOOKS
AN IMPRINT OF HERITAGE BOOKS, INC.

Books, CDs, and more—Worldwide

For our listing of thousands of titles see our website
at
www.HeritageBooks.com

Published 2008 by
HERITAGE BOOKS, INC.
Publishing Division
100 Railroad Ave. #104
Westminster, Maryland 21157

Copyright © 1913 The New York Genealogical and
Biographical Society

In Cooperation with The Genealogy Society of Sussex County, New Jersey

All rights reserved. No part of this book may be reproduced or transmitted in any form or by any means, electronic or mechanical, including photocopying, recording or by any information storage and retrieval system without written permission from the author, except for the inclusion of brief quotations in a review.

International Standard Book Numbers
Paperbound: 978-1-559613-556-9
Clothbound: 978-0-7884-7107-0

Minisink Valley Reformed Dutch Church Records

OFFICERS AND COMMITTEES OF THE SOCIETY
FOR 1913

President,	Clarence Winthrop Bowen
First Vice-President,	William Bradhurst Osgood Field
Second Vice-President,	William Isaac Walker
Secretary,	Henry Russell Drowne
Treasurer,	Hopper Striker Mott
Historian,	William Austin Macy, M. D.
Necrologist,	Winchester Fitch
Registrar of Pedigrees,	Winchester Fitch

Executive Committee

Abraham Hatfield, Jr., *Chairman*

William Bradhurst Osgood Field	Henry Pierson Gibson
George Austin Morrison, Jr.	Hopper Striker Mott
Clarence Winthrop Bowen	William Isaac Walker

Trustees

Howland Pell	Gen. James Grant Wilson
Henry Pierson Gibson	William Isaac Walker
Samuel Reading Bertron	Tobias Alexander Wright
Ellsworth Everett Dwight	Henry Russell Drowne
Clarence Winthrop Bowen	George Austin Morrison, Jr.
Thomas Townsend Sherman	John Reynolds Totten
Abraham Hatfield, Jr.	Hopper Striker Mott

William Bradhurst Osgood Field

Committee on Publication

Hopper Striker Mott	Josiah Collins Pumpelly
George Austin Morrison, Jr.	John R. Totten
Royden Woodward Vosburgh	Tobias A. Wright
Capt. Richard Henry Greene	William Alfred Robbins

William Becker Van Alstyne, M. D.

RECORDS

Minisink-Machackemeck Church Record.

	Pages
Baptisms by Dom. Petrus Vas, 1716 to 1719,	97 to 98
Baptisms and Births, 1737 to 1803,	98 to 219
Marriages, 1738 to 1797,	265 to 278
Church Members, 1745 to 1791,	281 to 285

Minisink Church Record.

Baptisms and Births, 1805 to 1816,	219 to 230

Machackemeck Church Record.

Baptisms and Births, 1803 to 1827,	231 to 264
Marriages, 1804 to 1825,	278 to 280

Walpeck Church Record

Baptisms and Births, 1741 to 1830,	1 to 92
Marriages, 1741 to 1769,	92 to 94

With Portrait of Dom. George Wilhelm Mancius

EDITED, WITH AN INTRODUCTION, BY
ROYDEN WOODWARD VOSBURGH

NEW YORK
PRINTED FOR THE SOCIETY
1913

LIMITED EDITION

100 numbered and signed copies

No._____

New York Genealogical and Biographical Society

Henry Russell Drowne
Secretary

INTRODUCTION

It is not within the limits of this introduction to recite in detail the story of the earliest visits of the Dutch, in the region generally termed as the Minisink valley. The first occupation was for the purpose of conducting mining operations. It is probable that these operations were commenced during the time of the Dutch occupation of New York; and they may have been continued secretly for a time, after the colony was transferred to the English. It seems quite clear that the first occupation has no connection with the settlement of the valley, by the way of Kingston, which commenced about the year 1690. We quote here from Eager's History of Orange County, giving the recollections of some of the settlers, who were old men in 1787; as a whole, we believe this to be as authentic a story of the earliest history of the region as can be briefly presented.

"We place before the reader a copy of a letter from Hazard's Register, written by Samuel Preston, Esq., which will throw much light upon the point of early settlement in the Minisink country, by whom and when made, and be far more satisfactory than anything we could say. * * *

Copy of Letters from Sam'l Preston, Esq., dated Stockport, June 6 & 14, 1828.

MINISINK, MINEHOLES, &C.

In 1787 the writer went on his first surveying tour into Northampton County; he was deputed under John Lukens, Surveyor General, and received from him, by way of instructions, the following narrative respecting the settlement of Minisink on the Delaware, above Kittanny and Blue Mountain:

That the settlement was formed for a long time before it was known to the Government in Philadelphia. That when the Government was informed of the settlement, they passed a law in 1729 that any such purchases of the Indians should be void; and the purchasers indicted for forcible entry and detainer, according to the law of England. That in 1730 they appointed an agent to go and investigate the facts; that the agent so appointed was the famous Surveyor, Nicholas Scull; that he, James Lukens, was N. Scull's apprentice to carry chain and learn surveying. That as they both understood and could talk Indian, they hired Indian guides, and had a fatiguing journey, there being then no white inhabitants in the upper part of Bucks or Northampton County. That they had very great difficulty to lead their horses through the water gap to Minisink flats, which were all settled with Hollanders; with several they could only be understood in Indian. At the venerable Depuis's they found great hospitality and plenty of the necessaries of life. J. Lukens said that the first thing which struck his attention was a grove of apple-trees of size far beyond any near Philadelphia. That as N. Scull and himself examined the banks, they were fully of opinion that all those flats had at some very former age been a deep lake before the river broke through the mountain, and that the best interpretation they could make of Minisink was, *the water is gone.* That S. Depuis told them when the rivers were frozen he had a good road to Esopus, near Kingston, from the

Mineholes, on the Mine road, some hundred miles. That he took his wheat and cider there for salt and necessaries, and did not appear to have any knowledge or idea where the river ran—Philadelphia market—or being in the government of Pennsylvania.

They were of opinion that the first settlements of Hollanders in Minisink were many years older than William Penn's charter, and that S. Dupuis had treated them so well they concluded to make a survey of his claim, in order to befriend him if necessary. When they began to survey, the Indians gathered around; an old Indian laid his hand on N. Scull's shoulder and said, "Put up iron string, go home." They then quit and returned.

I had it in charge from John Lukens to learn more particulars respecting the Mine road to Esopus, &c. I found Nicholas Dupuis, Esq., son of Samuel, living in a spacious stone house in great plenty and affluence. The old Mineholes were a few miles above, on the Jersey side of the river by the lower point of Paaquarry Flat; that the Minisink settlement extended forty miles or more on both sides of the river. That he had well known the Mine road to Esopus, and used before he opened the boat channel through Foul Rift, to drive on it several times every winter with loads of wheat and cider, as did also his neighbors, to purchase their salt and necessaries in Esopus, having no other market or knowledge where the river ran to. That after a navigable channel was opened through Foul Rift they generally took to boating, and most of the settlement turned their trade down stream, the Mine road became less and less traveled.

This interview with the amiable Nicholas Dupuis, Esq., was in June, 1787. He then appeared about sixty years of age. I interrogated as to the particulars of what he knew, as to when and by whom the Mine road was made, what was the ore they dug and hauled on it, what was the date, and from whence, or how, came the first settlers of Minisink in such great numbers as to take up all the flats on both sides of the river for forty miles. He could only give traditionary accounts of what he had heard from older people, without date, in substance as follows:

That in some former age there came a company of miners from Holland; supposed, from the great labor expended in making that road, about one hundred miles long, that they were very rich or great people, in working the two mines,—one on the Delaware where the mountain nearly approaches the lower point of Paaquarry Flat, the other at the north foot of the same mountain, near half way from the Delaware and Esopus. He ever understood that abundance of ore had been hauled on that road, but never could learn whether lead or silver. That the first settlers came from Holland to seek a place of quiet, being persecuted for their religion. I believe they were Armenians. They followed the Mine road to the large flats on the Delaware. That smooth, cleared land suited their views. That they bona fide bought the improvements from the native Indians, most of whom then moved to the Susquehanna; that with such as remained there was peace till 1755.

I then went to view the Paaquarry Mineholes. There appeared to have been a great abundance of labor done there at some former time, but the mouths of these holes were caved full, and overgrown with bushes. I concluded to myself if there ever had been a rich mine under the mountain it must be there yet in close confinement. The other older men I conversed with gave their traditions similar to N. Dupuis, and they all appeared to be grandsons of the first settlers, and very ignorant as to dates and things relating to chronology. In the summer of 1789 I began to build on this place; then came two venerable gentlemen on a surveying expedition.—They were the late Gen. James Clinton, the father of the late De Witt Clinton, and Christopher Tappan, Esq., Clerk and Recorder of Ulster County.—For many years before, they had both been surveyors under Gen. Clinton's father, when he was surveyor general. In order to learn some history from gentlemen of their general knowledge, I accompanied them in the woods. They both well knew the Mineholes, Mine road, &c., and as there were no kind of documents or records thereof, united in the opinion that it was a work transacted while the State of New York belonged to the government of Holland; that it fell to the English in 1664; and that the change in government stopped the mining business, and that the road must have been made many years before such digging could have been done. That it undoubtedly must have been the first good road of that extent made in any part of the United States."

The "Minisink country" consists of the valley of the Neversink, west of the Shawangunk Mountains, and the Delaware valley, as far as the Delaware Water Gap. The first settlements of which authentic knowledge can be ascertained were made about 1690, at what was later called the Upper Neighborhood, near Cuddebackville. A few years later more families came, and the settlements stretched further down the Neversink valley, to the junction with the Delaware; in later years the valley between Huguenot and Port Jervis was known as the Lower Neighborhood. The Neversink river was then called the Machackemeck, and the valley between Cuddebackville and Port Jervis was often spoken of as Peenpack. The earliest Patents in this neighborhood were the Waghaghkemeck* Patent, Oct. 14, 1697; the Minisink Patent, Aug. 28, 1704, which confirmed the Indian deed of 1702, and several other patents of less importance, which need not be enumerated here. The Waghaghkemeck* Patent was granted to Jacob Cuddeback, Thomas Swartwout, Anthony Swartwout, Bernardus Swartwout, Jan Tys, Peter Guimar and David Jamison. The settlers in the Minisink valley were Dutch, French Huguenots and English.

The first minister of the Gospel among the settlers in the Minisink was the Rev. Petrus Vas, of Kingston. The earliest baptisms that he administered will be found in the records of the Kingston Dutch Reformed Church. Sixteen of the baptisms administered by Vas will not be found in the Kingston record. They cover the years 1716 to 1719, and were obtained from some source (probably from Vas) by Domine Johannes Casparus Fryenmoet, and recorded by him on page 15 of the Minisink-Machackemeck record in the year 1745 and numbered by him as baptismal entries 206 to 221. When George Wilhelmus Mancius arrived in the Province of New York, excepting a short stay in New Jersey, he took up work in the congregations of Ulster county, and soon he became the colleague of Vas, at Kingston and its allied churches. His scholarly accomplishments which enabled him to speak Dutch, French, English and German, were of great advantage to him in his labors in the Minisink. He was the prime mover in the religious work, which resulted in the establishing of four Dutch Reformed churches in the Minisink

---

* Or Maghaghkemeck.

valley. A part of the records of three of these churches has been transcribed in this volume. And it is our purpose here to outline the history of these four churches, to show the sites that they have occupied, and to cite briefly the group of secondary churches that have grown out of them.

THE MINISINK CHURCH.

The first entries in the Minisink-Machackemeck record are in the handwriting of the Rev. George Wilhelmus Mancius. They extend from Aug. 23, 1737, to Sept. 19, 1740, occupying pages 3 to 10 in the original record, and being numbered as baptismal entries 1 to 102; see pages 98 to 103 in this volume. The title page of the Minisink-Machackemeck record, which should be on page 97 of this volume, is as follows:

*Kerkelyk protocoll voor de gemeente van Menissing beginnende met den jaar 1737 d. 23 August.

Kerken Boek Van Den gemeenten Van Minissink en Magagkamack.

The Property of the Prot. Refd. Dutch Church Deer Park, Classis of Orange, N. Y. July 1844. Geo. P. Van Wyck, Pastor.

The first title was written by Domine George Wilhelmus Mancius; the second by Domine Johannes Casparus Fryenmoet. The facts brought out by the title page and by the handwriting on it, seem to be sufficient to warrant the supposition that the Minisink church was the senior of the four churches, and for this reason it is taken up first. The only act of Consistory recorded in the hand of Domine Mancius is generally supposed to have been passed at the first meeting, when the organization of the churches was effected. A translation of it follows:

"Whereas, some among us are unwilling to remunerate the minister who is coming to officiate among us and yet wish to avail themselves of his services, it was approved and resolved by the Consistory: That every one dwelling among us requiring the services of the minister shall pay for the baptism of a child six shillings, and those who live without our bounds shall pay for the baptism of a child three shillings. Signed in behalf of others.

GEORG WILHELM MANCIUS.

Done in Consistory, August 23, 1737."

It should be noted that the name Machackemeck does not appear in this record during the ministry of Domine Mancius.

---

*Translation: Ecclesiastic record for the congregation of Menissing, beginning with the year 1737, the 23rd of August. Church Book of the congregations of Minissink and Magagkamack.

The Minisink church was about eight miles below Port Jervis, on the Old Mine Road, in the present township of Montague, Sussex county, N. J. The name Minisink was applied locally by the settlers to the tract of land in the vicinity of this church, extending principally to the southwest. It was also known as the Nominack or Namanach church, deriving this name from the parsonage, which was located about three miles below it on the Old Mine Road. The site of the church was about abreast of the northernmost point of Minisink island, where the Delaware river forks. It is about a quarter of a mile below the cross roads where an old building stands, formerly a store kept by Judge Stull and now a tavern known as the "brick store." There is a sharp bend in the road, which swings from a southeasterly to a northeasterly direction, and on the river side sloping down towards river bed, lies the land once occupied by the ancient Minisink church and burying ground. The ground is thickly wooded with trees of between fifteen and twenty-five years' growth, and is overgrown with dense underbrush. The site would hardly be discernible in passing along the road, were it not for one or two badly neglected modern gravestones, which lie at the turn of the road, so near the highway that they might easily be taken for milestones. Further back among the trees some twenty rough field stones remain, marking as many graves. They are flat stones, probably from the river bed, and the traces of inscriptions are only evident on one or two of them. There are also in this graveyard about six modern marble stones, bearing dates 1824, 1825 and 1853. A considerable number of the legible gravestones, formerly here, were transferred to the newer cemetery behind the present church, in Montague village, which is about three quarters of a mile along the road, in a northeasterly direction. Among the stones transferred to the newer cemetery, are a number of Westbrook family stones, bearing dates shortly after 1800.

It is difficult to fix the date when the old Minisink church ceased to be used for the purpose of Divine service. On two occasions the Minisink congregation petitioned the New Jersey Legislature for permission to hold a lottery to raise money to pay off the indebtedness upon their church, resulting from repairs to the church edifice and parsonage. The first petition was dated Oct. 16, 1795, Thomas Kyte being allowed £1 :05 :09, in the Donation Account of the Minisink Corporation under date of Oct. 31, 1795, "to go to Trenton to advocate a petition for a church lottery before the Assembly to pay the arrears of the church building and parsonage, &c." The second petition was dated Oct. 9, 1804. It would appear that a number of years intervened between the time that the old church became untenantable, by reason of age and want of repair, and the time that the second church was erected in about the year 1827. Information concerning the date of the erection of the second church very indefinite; however the county records of Sussex county were not examined. It seems quite certain that during this interval this congregation worshiped in the Shapanack church.* The minutes of the Minisink Consistory contain nothing definite about the date of the erection of the second church, although the date of the sale of the old church is mentioned. There are no minutes between Sept. 5, 1797, and July 14, 1816.

The first book of the Minisink church record was also used by the Machackemeck church. The baptisms appearing in this book are transcribed in this volume, covering pages 97 to 230; the marriages, covering pages 265 to 278. For additional items not included in this volume, see translation of this record by Rev. J. B. Ten Eyck, published by W. H. Nearpass, Port Jervis, N. Y., 1877. Abstract of items omitted in this volume:

    Minutes of Consistory, Aug. 23, 1737 to Feb. 16, 1792.
    Act of Subordination, signed by Church Officers, Apr. 16, 1745 to Apr. 19, 1755.
    Members of Consistory, 1741 to 1750.
    List of members received in Machackemeck church by Rev. Elias Van Bunschooten, on Oct. 12, 1787, from a piece of paper, not a part of the record book.

The proper title of this book should be the Minisink-Machackemeck record, as it was the joint record of the two churches, from 1741 to 1803; from 1805 until it ends in 1816, it is the record of the Minisink church alone. The last meeting of the Consistory recorded in Low Dutch in this book, is translated by Ten Eyck as follows:

"The Reverend Consistory being assembled together in fear of the Lord, February 16, 1792, at the house of Joannes D. Westbrook, after prayer it was resolved to become incorporated in pursuance of the Act of the State of New Jersey, and for this end that we unanimously sign a short application to be enrolled in the Register Book of the County of Sussex, in the above mentioned State."

The second book of records of the Minisink church (now the only one in their possession), was the minute book of the Corporation and Consistory, and was commenced in the year 1792. The following extracts are copied from this book:

"Records of the Elders and Deacons of the Church of Menesing incorporated the first day of March 1792 as may be seen in the Records in Clerk's Office in the County of Sussex   Rhodes Clk.   as also may be viewed in the church records of Menesing dated February 16, 1792."

---

* For Shapanack church see page xix.

"Succession of Consistory and their Acts. There has been a succession of Elders and Deacons in the Church of Menessing from August 23, 1737 to May the 11, 1785 when the combined Consistories of Walpeck, Menesing, and Magagkameck, viz.

Isaac Van Campen
Joannes Decker
Hendrick Wm. Cortrecht
Joannes C. Westbrook
Hendericus Decker
Jesias Cortrecht
William Ennes
Frederick Van Demerck
J. R. Dewitt
Simon Westfall
Harmanus Van Emwigen
Jacob D. Gumaar
Elias Cortrecht
Thomas Kyte

made a Call on the Rvd. Elias Van Bunschooten then Minister of the Gospel of Schachtkook who accepted of the Menesing Call the 9th of July next following and was installed by the Revd. Jacob R. Hardenbergh the 29 of August 1785 and also at the same time by the above mentioned Consistories received as their lawful Minister of the Gospel as may be seen in Menesing church records."

"On a meeting of the Consistory of Menesing Church the 16 February 1792.

Present
Elias Van Bunschooten
Joannes D. Westbrook
Gysbert Sutfin
Joannes Van Etten
Abraham Westfal
Cornelius Cole
Benjamin Fisher
Gedeon Cole
Jeremiah Van Demerck

After calling on the name of God they thought for several reasons that it was best to be incorporated: and for that purpose, at the same time, signed a certifacate which is recorded by Rhodes Clerk of the County of Sussex of the State of New Jersey the 1st of March, 1792."

"July 14th, 1816 the surviving members of the Consistory together with the male members of this Congregation met at the house of Mr. Stool* the meeting was opened with prayers by the Rev. Charles Hardenbergh.
Whereas it Appeared that there were only two members remaining in Consistory Viz Abraham Westfall Elder and Joseph Ennes Decon it was
Resolved that the meeting proceed to the Election of church officers when the following persons were only chosen Viz

Abraham Westfall and } Elders
Joseph Ennes
Peter Vannest and } Decons
Benjamin Depui

the Elders and Decons Elect After having been published to the Congregation were Installed In there respective offices.
At the same time Also Elizabeth Ogden wife of Samuel Depui on making a satisfactory confession of her faith was received as a member in full Communion with the church.
Q T CHARLES HARDENBERGH Pres."

"September 8, 1829.
The Consistory, trustees of the Minisink Congregation having previously consulted with most of the owners of the seats in the old meeting house, and having given public notice of the meeting this day with the owners of seats to see if there were any objections to selling the old house, the proceeds thereof to be applied by the Consistory for the use and benefit of the congregation.
This day accordingly a number of the inhabitants met with the consistory & no one objecting to said sale the Consistory resolved to sell said

---

* James Stoll.

house, & gave public notice of such sale on the 26th of September inst. at the old house.

September 26, 1829, the sale of said house was postponed untill Saturday October 11th, 1829.

C. C. ELTING, Prest & Clk of Consistory."

The old church was finally sold on Nov. 7, 1829, the fund arising from the sale amounting to $148.33.

Abstract of contents of second book, Minisink record:

Baptisms, June 14, 1817 to Jan. 18, 1903.
Marriages, Oct. 5, 1817 to Dec. 17, 1902.
Minutes of Consistory, Feb. 16, 1792 to Sept 8, 1866. "The minutes are continued in the new book procured for the purpose November 1866."
Communicants, July 14, 1816 to Dec. 5, 1879.
Donation account, Dec. 15, 1792 to Nov. 25, 1798; salary receipts, etc.

THE MACHACKEMECK CHURCH.

The Machackemeck Church stood on the Old Mine Road, about one quarter of a mile above the point where it crossed the Neversink. This site is at the junction of East Main Street and New Jersey Avenue, in the City of Port Jervis; it is on the opposite side of East Main Street from the old Machackemeck burying ground, and is at present occupied by a public school. The first church was probably built in the year 1743. We quote the documentary evidence, from the minutes of the Consistory, in the Minisink-Machackemeck record, which concerns the building of this church as well as the first Minisink church.

"The Reverend Consistories of the two churches met together March 7th, 1742, and executed the following:

VIII. Having approved of the object by collection to aid and build up the Low Dutch churches in the States of New York and New Jersey, and that for this object suitable persons should be chosen by Consistories and Justices in these churches.

IX. The Reverend Consistory chose Jan Van Vliet, William Cool, Hannes Westbroeck, Hendrick Kortrecht. Besides, his Majesty's Justices chose Salomon Davids, Peter Keuikendal, William Kortrecht. The following persons were appointed Collectors, viz. Jacobus Swartwood, Jan van Vliet, Hendrick Kortrecht and Derrick Westbroeck.

August 21. The Collectors reported that they had collected £13, 9s. od. Their expenses were £2, 0s. 4d.

January 7, 1743. The Reverend Consistory resolved that of the money collected each church should retain half. That the money should be appropriated for the upbuilding of one church should they agree to build together, and if not, then each church should retain the amount collected in their bounds. And if it should occur that they should both build, and any money should remain over, it should be used for the benefit of both churches, and if more money should be collected, it would be subject to the above conditions.

I testify to the above minute in behalf of the Consistory of both churches.

JOH: CASPARUS FRYENMUTH.

Done in Consistory January 7th, 1742/3."

The first church remained standing until it was burned to the ground, with a good part of the surrounding settlements, by the Indians under Brandt, on the night of July 20, 1779. The second church was probably erected about the year 1786, as various sums of money and some building material were donated in the spring and summer of that year, as it appears in the church record. It occupied the same site as that of the first church. The third church was built in 1833, on the main street of the Village of Port Jervis, about a mile north of the first site. The fourth church was built in 1868, upon the site of the third church. The church of 1833 was then moved to the new cemetery at Carpenter's Point, about one quarter of a mile below the site of the first church, where it now serves as a chapel for conducting funeral services, and for a Sunday school.

When and how the Minisink-Machackemeck church record was secured by the Reformed Dutch Church of Deer Park, we are unable to state, but it is evident that the Rev. Geo. P. Van Wyck thought it prudent to settle any question of ownership, by his writing on the title page in July, 1844. It seems likely that when the Rev. Samuel B. Ayers became pastor of the Minisink church in 1838, that the Rev. Cornelius C. Elting, who had previously been pastor of both churches, retained for the Port Jervis church the old Minisink-Machackemeck record. As stated before, this record was used exclusively by the Minisink church, from 1805 to 1816. What is now known as the second book of the Machackemeck church record, but what was really the first book belonging to that church exclusively, contains the following title page, which should appear at the top of page 231.

"Magagkameck church Record bought of Solomon Smith for s16 by Elias Van Bunschooten in A. D. 1795."

Abstract of contents of this book:

Baptisms, June 19, 1803 to Nov. 4, 1871.
Marriages, Feb. 8, 1804 to Feb. 7, 1872.
Minutes of Consistory, 1817 to 1858.
Communicants, 1817 to 1871.

From the Trustees' record book of the Machackemeck church commenced in the year 1789, by the Rev. Elias Van Bunschooten, we copy a part of the records relating to the incorporation of the church, as they were written in his hand.

"It appears from the church record of Menessing and Magagkameck dutch reformed protestant churches, that there were in the church of Magagkameck regular ecclesiastical officers in August 23th 1737 and that their succession has continued till May 11th, 1785 at the time last mentioned the Elders, Jacob R. Dewitt, Symon Westfaal, Harmanus Van Emwegen and Deacons Jacob Dewitt Gumaar, Thomas Kyte, together with the Elders and

Deacons of the Churches of Walpeck and Menissing made a regular call upon the Revd. Elias Van Bunschooten which call the said Minister accepted the 9th day of July 1785 and was installed by the Revd. Jacob R. Hardenbergh the 28 day of August the same year, and in the said Hardenbergh's presence, the said Elders and Deacons of the said united churches received and accepted the said Bunschooten for their regular and lawful Minister of the Gospel according to the discipline of the dutch reformed protestant Church in America.

Moreover it appears from the abovesaid church records, that a regular succession of Elders and Deacons of said church of Magagkameck has been continued from the 11th day of May 1785 to the 14th day of March 1789. On the said 14 day of March 1789 a certificate formed according to the laws of the State of New York for religious incorporation passed the 7th day of March 1788 and the 6th day of April 1784 as may be seen in the preceeding copies of the said acts, was signed by the Minister, Elders and Deacons viz

Elias Van Bunschooten
Solomon Kuikendal
Benjamin Depuy
Wilhelmus Cole
Samuel Depuy

Wilhelmus Vredenburgh
Jacobus Swartwout
Simeon Westfal
Joannes Decker

and according to law the said Sertificate was Acknowledged and recorded the 9th day of June 1789 as may be seen in the said Sertificate.

* * * * * * *

A copy of the first return March 29, 1793.

An account and Inventory of all the Estate both real & personal with the annual Revenue arising thereon belonging to the Dutch reformed Church of Magagkameck in the county of Orange.

One acre of ground with the Church on it without any annual income from the seats.

The third part of twenty-three acres and some parts of an acre of ground, with a house and barn on it, which the Minister possesses for the time being as part of his salary.

Between forty-four and forty-five pounds subscribed yearly to be paid to the Elders and Deacons of said Church, and by them to be paid unto our present Minister while he resides among us.

One Bible, One Psalm-Book, One Book of Records, Sabbath-Day Collection in Bank, two pounds, fifteen shillings and nine pence, One little Trunk.

This is to certify that on the 29th day of March 1793 the within account and inventory was exhibited on oath to William Wickham one of the Judges of the Court of Common Pleas for the County of Orange by the Subscribers being a majority of the Trustees of the Church within named.

Sworn the 29th day of
March 1793 before me
WM. WICKHAM

BENJAMIN DEPUY
HARMANUS VAN EMWEGEN
JOANNES DECKER
WILHELMUS COLE
MARTEINUS DECKER."

The church was first incorporated as the "Reformed Dutch Church of Mahackamech." In 1838, by an Act of the Legislature, the name was changed to the "Reformed Protestant Dutch Church of Deerpark."

THE WALPECK CHURCH.

The site of the first church of the Walpeck congregation was within the Walpeck Bend of the Delaware, about a mile west of the present village of Flatbrookville, in the township of Walpack, Sussex county, N. J., near the fork of the road leading down to Rosencrantz ferry. This site was upon the Old Mine Road. *"The original deed for the ground (containing four acres), upon which the church was erected, was made by Thomas Brink and Nicholas Schoonhovan, in the tenth year of His Majesty, King George, February 1st, 1737. This deed was never recorded, and on February 26th, 1744, another genuine deed was made and recorded, a note of which is made on the Church Records. The church edifice was erected prior to 1741 (though its exact date is not known), since Rev. Mr. Fryenmoet was preaching in it at that time. * * The second church edifice of Walpack was built a half-mile further up the river road, near where Jacob Smith now lives. The date of its erection is unknown, but it was previous to 1800. In this building Rev. Mr. Van Benschoten and Rev. Mr. Force preached. It was occupied down to 1816, when the third edifice was erected, on the original foundation. * * * This third building was erected by the German Reformed people, who had at this time a church organization there. It was dedicated on Christmas day (1819), the services being conducted in both German and English. After its erection, the Reformed Dutch congregation, on account of their own building having become old and dilapidated, purchased one-half of the edifice built by the Germans. The two congregations occupied it on alternate Sabbaths. Soon after the commencement of Mr. Pitts' labors, the members of the German Church mainly united with the Reformed Dutch Church. The Germans however continued to own a half interest in it so long as it stood. Two Trustees were chosen biennially, to have charge of their half of the building."

The above is quoted from Dr. Mills' Discourse, because as much reliable information is not available at present. The occupants of the Jacob Smith farm now are Isiah and Elijah Gariss; their mother was a relative of Jacob Smith and they have lived on this farm for the past thirty years. The house occupied by Jacob Smith is three-quarters of a mile north of the original site of the Walpeck Church, on the river side of the road. About two hundred yards north of the Smith house, on the opposite side of the road, and some distance back from it, are the foundations of an old building. So far as the recollections of the Gariss brothers can be relied upon, this building was a house and never a church. It is probable that Dr. Mills drew some of his information from the Trustees' book of the Walpeck

* See Historical Discourse of Reformed Dutch Church of Walpack, by Rev. S. W. Mills, pp. 23-24.

church, of which further mention will be made. The fourth church was built on the original site, in 1855. The corner stone was laid August 22nd, 1855, by Rev. Robert Pitts; the church was dedicated on Dec. 20, 1855, the Rev. David A. Jones, of Montague, preaching the sermon. This church supplied the needs of the congregation until 1897, when the fifth church was erected in the village of Flatbrookville, about a mile east of the original site. The land for the present church was given by John S. Smith. The Flatbrookville congregation still uses the old burying ground, conveyed by the deeds of 1737 and 1744. At the present time it occupies less than two acres, bordering on the side road leading down to Rosencrantz ferry. There are a few very old gravestones in the graveyard, but all traces of inscriptions have vanished long ago. The oldest stone with an inscription shows the date 1793; nothing more. Another reads "M. W. B. May 2, 1795."

The only book of records at the present time known to exist, concerning the Walpeck congregation, is transcribed in this volume, covering pages 1 to 94. The parts of this record not printed are the Minutes of the Consistory, 1741 to 1793, which are not very complete, and a small list of members admitted, covering the years 1745 to 1827. We quote from this record, written in the hand of the Rev. Elias Van Bunschooten, the following relating to the incorporation of the church:

"Dec. 14, 1793. The Rev. Consistory, meeting in fear of the Lord, after calling upon God's name, have deemed it proper and resolved to be incorporated and therefore signed a certificate, December 14, 1793.

The same was registered, through Jacobus Cermer and Andries Dingman Jr. by Chas. Rhodes Clerk on Dec. 26, 1793.

The above matter has been noted in the Corporation book, dated February 14, 1795."

When the Minisink, the Machackemeck and the Walpeck churches were incorporated, the duty of making proper records of incorporation fell to the pastor at the time, the Rev. Elias Van Bunschooten, and a more painstaking and accurate recorder could not have been found, as the Trustees (or Corporation) books of the Minisink and of the Machackemeck congregations bear witness. He bought at least four durable record books, of uniform size, bound in full calf. Two of these books are now in the possession of the Port Jervis church. The third is the principal record now in the possession of the Minisink church. And the fourth was probably in the possession of the Walpeck church, up to the year 1902. This fourth book is referred to a few lines above as "the Corporation book." It was undoubtedly consulted by Dr. Mills, when he wrote his historical discourse on the Walpeck churches; it is probably referred to by Mills, when he mentions that a note of

the deed of 1744 "is made on the Church Records." It is reported
that this book was burned at Flatbrookville, in the year 1902, in a
fire of the store of John S. Smith, who for many years had been
Treasurer of the Lower Walpack congregation, and who had in his
possession almost all of the papers and records of both the Upper
and Lower Walpack congregations. This book probably contained,
in addition to the Corporation records, the baptisms, marriages, etc.,
beginning at the time the first book of records was completed. The
present records of the Lower Walpack churches will be found abstracted under the heading of the Bushkill Church, see page xxii.
Nathaniel Van Auken, living about two miles north of Flatbrookville, on the river road, has in his possession some unimportant
Sunday school records of the Flatbrookville church, covering about
twenty years, commencing about 1865.

THE SMITHFIELD CHURCH.

As the records of the Smithfield church do not appear in this
volume, it has not been thought necessary to give much information
concerning it, beyond what appears in Dr. Mills' Historical Discourse on the Walpack church, pages 22 and 23, a copy of which
follows:

"Before speaking of the Church edifices in the bounds of the Walpack
Church, it may not be amiss to allude to the Old Log Church, in which the
Smithfield congregation first worshiped. This was, so far as we can learn,
the first house of worship of any description erected in this region of country. It was built below the 'Mine Holes', on the Pennsylvania side of the
Delaware, opposite Tock's Island, near the present village of Shawnee.
It is supposed to have been built about the year 1725. It was probably
erected for the purpose of furnishing the miners, and those settled around
the mines, with a place for holding religious services, while as yet there
was no Church organization. When the Smithfield Church was organized
(in 1737), they worshiped in this Log Church, and for many years subsequently. The evidence, from the original Records of the Reformed Dutch
Churches of Machackemeck and Menissinck, during the ministry of Fyrenmoet, is clear and decisive that this Smithfield Church was Reformed Dutch,
with its Consistory composed of Elders and Deacons, the names of whom
from time to time are recorded in that Book, with those of the three other
Churches. We deem it important to state this, since the intimation has
been made, in a History of the Shawnee Presbyterian Church (by Rev. J.
Kirby Davis), that this was originally a Presbyterian Church; they are called
'Dutch Presbyterians', i. e., Presbyterians using the Dutch language. The
Church first in existence known as the Smithfield Church, at what is now
called Shawnee, was Reformed Dutch, and not Presbyterian. Its officers
signed the 'Act of Subordination to the Classis of Amsterdam', with those of
the other three Churches, April 19th, 1746. Their names were, Benjamin
Depuy and Moses Dupuy, Elders, and Lambart Brynck and James Hyndshaw,
Deacons.
This Church continued in connection with the other three Churches in
enjoying the services of the same minister, as before remarked, until about
the year 1753, when it withdrew. The cause leading to this withdrawal was
probably the erection of a 'Presbyterian Meeting-House' there in 1752,

the land for which had been given by William Allen, in 1750. This was a stone building (known as the Old Stone Church), and after its erection was occupied by various denominations—Presbyterians, Reformed Dutch, and Lutherans. Notwithstanding the Smithfield Dutch Church withdrew from the other three Churches, still Fryenmoet and Romeyn both preached from time to time in this Stone Church, which was now used by the Dutch congregation, on account of the Old Log Church having become unfit for use. But while the Presbyterians had their house of worship, it appears from the History by Mr. Davis, just referred to, that there was no organization of a Presbyterian Church until 1816, when the Rev. John Boyd ordained the first Elders. Previous to this, Presbyterian ministers preached here occasionally to those preferring that form of worship and organization. Meantime the Reformed Dutch Church, having no house of worship of its own, declined and at length died out, and those who had been connected with it fell in with the Presbyterian Church when its organization was effected."

The Smithfield Presbyterian church was organized before 1816. Mr. Samuel Turn of Bushkill, Pa., has in his possession the original subscription list, to raise money for the calling of the Rev. John Boyd. It is dated November 4, 1813, and commences as follows:

"Whereas the Honorable Mr. John Boyd of the State of New Jersey has offered his Services to preach the Gosple in Middle Smithfield and Lower Smithfield, * * *"

The organization of the Presbyterian church was effected on Jan. 3, 1814, as it appears in the church record. The minutes of the Consistory as recorded in the Minisink-Machackemeck record, contain a number of references to the Smithfield church, before it withdrew from the other three churches. The withdrawal of this church did not mean that it ceased to exist as a Dutch Reformed church. After the separation of the churches, the Smithfield church sold their rights in the parsonage occupied by Domine Fryenmoet. Mention of this will be found in the Acts of the Coetus of Oct. 7-14, 1755, an extract from which follows:

*"5. James Hyndshaw, elder at Smithfield, and Johannis Westfael elder at Minnesink, presented to our Assembly for our consideration and our decision, a certain difficulty existing between the Consistory of the three churches of Rev. Fryenmoet, and the Consistory at Smithfield. This arose out of a misunderstanding about certain ecclesiastical action taken by the Rev. Consistory of the four churches on April 16, 1750. Both sides have promised to acquiesce wholly in our decision to be given thereon.

The Rev. Assembly, having heard the reasons for and against, and having carefully considered the action itself, found itself in conscience bound to give the following unanimous decision: That, whereas it appears that the church of Smithfield has been legally and ecclesiastically separated from the three other churches, the Rev. Consistory of Rev. Fryenmoet's three churches are, according to the contents of the aforesaid action, obliged to pay to the Rev. Consistory at Smithfield thirty pounds. It will have to make every effort to secure that amount from the churches; and, should anything be lacking, to supply the deficiency out of the elders' treasury. Whereupon both parties thanked the Assembly for this decision."

For further particulars concerning the Smithfield church, see History of Wayne, Pike and Monroe counties, Penn., page 1096.

---

* See Ecclesiastical Records of the State of New York, page 3598.

Abstract of contents of the Smithfield record:
Baptisms, May 22, 1741 to July 1, 1807.
Marriages, July 4, 1742 to Feb. 16, 1752.
Minutes of Consistory, Record of Resolutions, and Record of Church Councils.
Members admitted, by confession and credentials.
Record of Expenditures.

THE PARSONAGE AT NAMENACK.

Within a few years after Domine Fryenmoet was settled as pastor of the four congregations, arrangements were made to secure him a suitable parsonage. The site of the parsonage was selected so as to be as nearly central as possible for the four congregations. It was in the present township of Montague, about three miles below the Minisink church, on the Old Mine Road, opposite Nominack Island and near the old Nominack Fort, which was erected during the French and Indian War. The land was originally owned by the Westbroecks. At the present time the land is a part of a farm owned and occupied by James B. Fuller, the son of Eli Fuller. The old building and well were not far from the present Fuller house, and one of the stones now in the foundation of the Fuller house was once the corner-stone of the parsonage. It has carved upon it the monogram of Domine Fryenmoet, in fac-simile of his handwriting. As the nearest church to the parsonage was the Minisink church, it was sometimes known as the Nominack church. The Consistory frequently met at the parsonage, and the words "Done in Consistory at Namenack," often appear in the minutes as recorded in the Minisink-Machackemeck record. We quote from this record as follows:

"February 4, 1745. The Reverend Consistories of the four churches, assembled together, passed the following resolutions: * * *

3. The Consistory of the three churches have resolved to provide a suitable dwelling house for their minister so soon as practicable, and for this end have appointed Derrick Westbroeck as Superintendent. They have fixed the first Monday in April to begin the work, or sooner. For this purpose he should notify the people to aid in the work, and those who did not do work should pay money. The Superintendent should provide all the materials; he should keep a true account of the same, which should be repaid to him by the Consistory of the four congregations, to which, by their signatures, they have bound themselves. Each Consistory shall bear the fourth part of the expense."

The minutes of the Consistory as recorded in the Minisink-Machackemeck record, contain frequent reference to the Domine's house and repairs for it. On April 16, 1750, a resolution in Consistory was passed to the effect that, if any of the four congregations wished to separate from the others, the fourth part of the house and lot should be purchased by the remaining congregations, or sold at auction. It was also resolved that "by the present dwelling of the

Domine there shall be built of stone another house twenty feet long and twenty broad, or the same breadth of the present house with a cellar underneath and a study above." It is probable that the cornerstone, referred to above, is from this stone house.

The parsonage and twenty-three acres of land, belonging jointly to the congregations of Minisink, Machackemeck and Walpeck, was sold in 1800, and the sale was duly recorded in the Trustees' book of the Machackemeck church as follows:

"Peter Vannoy a trustee of the Mahakkamack Congregation Sold there part of the personage house and Lot for 442 Dollars and Seventy Cents and Received the First payment may 1st 1800 Which is to be paid in three Eaqual payment.
Peter Vannoy paid two Dollars of Sd. money to Mr. Kuyte for Writing the Deed for our Share."

According to the Machackemeck Trustees' book, the final payment was received on June 7, 1802.

THE SECONDARY CHURCHES.

THE CLOVE CHURCH.

In the month of August, 1756, it is supposed that Domine Fryenmoet was forced to abandon his congregations, on account of Indian massacres in this section, brought about by the French and Indian War. A number of the settlers, after the burning of their homes, sought a more protected spot than the Peenpack valley. They removed "over the mountain" about fifteen miles southeast, and settled in the Clove. According to the petition, which is quoted on the next page, the settlement commenced about 1747; probably there were one or two families there some years before, although the principal influx of settlers occurred during the French and Indian War. Among the early settlers were the Deckers and the Ditsoorts (now Titsworth). The Clove church stood about three miles north of Deckertown up the Clove valley, in the township of Wantage, Sussex county, N. J. An ancient burying ground marked the spot until about twenty years ago, when the remaining stones were pulled up by William Wilson, at that time the owner of the farm upon which they stood. At the present time the field is ploughed over and used as a meadow, and all traces of the graveyard have disappeared; Horatio Hill is the present owner of the farm. The second Clove church stood about one-half a mile south of the first site, on the left hand side of the road leading to Deckertown; immediately opposite this site is the old church graveyard. The third Clove church now stands about 200 yards north of the second site, on the same side of the road. This church is now known as the First Presbyterian

Church of Wantage. The records of the church are in the possession of Wallace W. Titsworth, who also has the original petition to the Classis of New Brunswick, for the organization of the church. The petition is dated Aug. 21, 1787, and is signed by fifty-eight inhabitants of the Clove; in part it reads as follows:

*"Our Ancestors, a few in number, who formerly belonged to the Low Dutch Reformed Church, settled our country about forty years since. During part of that time, the Rev. Thomas Romine, by permission of his Church-Council and people of the Minisinks, preached some of his time amongst us. By his leaving there we again became destitute, till the Rev. Mr. Bunschooten was installed in Minisinks congregations, who labored some time amongst us; and whose labor, to appearance, has been attended with the blessings of God, so as we have upwards of thirty communicant members amongst us."

The Rev. Elias Van Bunschooten was pastor of the Clove church until 1812. He settled there in 1792 and owned a farm and mill; he died there on Jan. 10, 1815.

Abstract of records of the First Presbyterian Church of Wantage:

Vol. I. Clove Dutch Reformed church organized, Apr. 16, 1788. Presbyterian church organized, Nov. 24, 1817; Trustees sworn in Dec. 7, 1817.
Baptisms, Oct. 22, 1785 to Oct. 25, 1818.
Marriages, Sept. 2, 1798 to Sept. 19, 1812.
Members, from organization to March 28, 1816.
Minutes of Consistory, Nov. 24, 1798 to Feb. 20, 1812.
Minutes of the Presbyterian church from organization to 1835. Church accounts.
Vol. II. Missing.
Vol. III. Baptisms, July 3, 1835 to Apr. 29, 1843.
Vol. IV. Commences 1873.

The Sussex County Historical Society has the marriage records of the Rev. Sylvester Cooke, kept while he was pastor of this church, probably for the years intervening between Vol. III and Vol. IV.

THE WESTTOWN CHURCH.

A few years after the Rev. Elias Van Bunschooten began preaching at the Clove church the congregation found that they were unable to pay his salary, that had been agreed upon. Accordingly they united with the church at Westtown, in order to divide the expense. The Dutch Reformed Church of Westtown was probably located in the present village of Westtown, in the town of Minisink, Orange county, N. Y. It is about eight miles east of Port Jervis and northeast of the Clove church. The union of the Clove and the Westtown churches commenced in 1791 and ended in September, 1799. But according to the records of the Clove church, Van Bunschooten continued to serve the Westtown church, after the separation and at least until May 4, 1802, when the parsonage jointly owned by the

---

* See Historical Discourse of Reformed Dutch Church of Walpack, by Rev. S. W. Mills, page 30.

two churches was sold. The church was organized as a Presbyterian church, on March 10, 1803. No examination was made of the records of this church. For further particulars, see Clove church record and Ruttenber and Clark's History of Orange county, page 667.

THE CUDDEBACKVILLE CHURCH.

Cuddebackville, in the town of Deer Park, Orange county, N. Y., is about eight miles northeast of Port Jervis, in the Neversink valley. The first settlement was made there in 1690. For many years it was a preaching station of the Machackemeck church. On Aug. 6, 1844, a committee consisting of the Rev. George P. Van Wyck, Benjamin Cuddeback, Philip Swartwout and John P. Whitaker, was appointed for the purpose of organizing a church at Cuddebackville. The effort was not successful, but the church was finally organized in the spring of 1854. The records of this church were not examined.

THE HAINSVILLE CHURCH.

The village of Hainsville is about three miles southeast of Montague, in the township of Sandyston, Sussex county, N. J. This church, known as the North Dutch Church of Sandyston, was erected in 1855, at a cost of $850. It is within the bounds of the Minisink congregation, and under the control of the Minisink Consistory, as a branch church. It was erected through the efforts of the Rev. David A. Jones, while pastor at Montague, and all the steps leading to its organization will be found fully recorded in the minutes of the Consistory of the Minisink church. On May 4, 1855, at a meeting of Consistory in the church at Montague, it was "Resolved, First, that it is very desirable & important to erect a Church in Sandyston in connection with the R. P. Dutch Church of N. America. Second, That as a Consistory, we will cordially cooperate in the attainment of this object." On June 25, 1855, a meeting was called at the house of Amos Van Etten in Sandyston, and it was determined to solicit subscriptions for the new church, in both Sandyston and Montague. On July 7 another meeting was held, when it appeared that $680 had been subscribed. A Building Committee was appointed, consisting of Joshua Shay, C. W. Brodhead, Samuel Clark, John Kyte, Abraham Credmore, John D. Everitt and James Bennet. July 14, the Committee reported at a meeting of the subscribers, and the land offered by Abraham Bennet was selected as the site of the church. This land, comprising one-quarter of an acre, was adjoining the turnpike in Sandyston, near the Stone School House, in which there had been preaching for many years, in connection with the Dutch Church of Minisink. Abraham Bennet gave the land for the use of the church, with the provision that, if the church ceased to exist as a Dutch Church, the land should revert to himself or his heirs. July 23, the bid of Jacob Wainwright of the Clove, Montague, to put up the building for $850 was accepted. Sept. 20, the corner-stone was laid by the Rev. David A. Jones, with suitable ceremonies. The new church was dedicated on Tuesday, Dec. 11, 1855. "The following was the order of the service: Invocation, Salutation and reading portions of the Scripture, as Psalms 122 & 132 & Kings 8: 54 to close; Rev. Robert Pitts of Walpack. Prayer; Rev. S. D. Beegle, Methodist Minister of Hainsville. Sermon; Rev. Dr. McLaren of Newburgh, N. Y. from Rom. 1: 16. Dedicatory Prayer; Rev. D. A. Jones, Pastor of the Minisink Church. Benediction; Dr. McLaren." On Jan. 1, 1856, a Sociable was held at the house of Amos Van Etten, to aid in furnishing the church, which netted $83, which was expended for blinds, stove, etc.

For many years the church at Hainsville was occupied jointly by the Dutch Reformed and the Methodist Episcopal denominations, and it was known as a Union church. But under the terms of the deed of gift of the land, and by numerous resolutions of the Consistory of the Minisink church, it is evident that the ownership remains solely Dutch Reformed. In consideration of the fact that the Methodists had assisted financially, in the building of the church, permission was granted them to use the church for their services. A few years ago the Methodists built a new church, opposite the old church, and since that time the church has been unoccupied by either denomination. The records of this church (if any exist) were not examined.

THE SHAPANACK CHURCH.

This church, although included with the secondary churches, was so closely identified with the original four churches, that it might well be treated as one of them. It stood on the Old Mine Road, about thirteen miles below the site of the Minisink church and seven miles above the site of the Walpeck church. The Shapanack tract of 962 acres of land was deeded by John Crook, Jr., to Alexander Rosenkrans and Frederick Schoonmaker, on March 16 and 17, 1729. Col. John Rosenkrans, the son of Alexander, gave the land for the site of the Shapanack church and burying ground, with the provision that it should revert to the donor, when no longer used for religious purposes. The site of the church is about 400 yards north of Col. John Rosenkrans' dwelling which was a part of the old Shapanack

Fort, of Revolutionary fame. The church stood on a knoll on the east side of the river road, almost opposite the head of Shapanack Island. *"The exact date of the erection of the church is not known, but it is supposed to have been before the Revolutionary war, during the Pastorate of Rev. Mr. Romeyn. It was built of logs and was octagonal in form. Some of the logs, and even the foundation, were to be seen" as late as about the year 1860. The Shapanack church was in use until about the year 1825, but was vacant after the stone church at Peters' Valley was erected. For a time at least, after the first Minisink church had fallen into decay and before the second church was erected, it was the only church where Divine service was held, between the Machackemeck and the Walpeck churches. The farm upon which this church stood is now owned by Mr. Joseph Hull, an Elder of the Lower Walpack congregation. Elder Hull states that this church was in use as late as about the year 1825. That he knew an old lady who died about twenty-five years ago, who had told him that she used to go to the church, when she was a girl; that she rode to the church on horseback, from the brick store at Montague, a distance of about thirteen miles. And that at that time there was no other church where services were held, below the Machackemeck church. Elder Hull well remembers the site of the church, which is now in a ploughed field; it is about fifty feet back from the road. A knoll about 100 feet north of the church site, surmounted by several trees, contains about a dozen gravestones lying flat on the ground. One is the gravestone of William Clark, who died Aug. 10, 1795, AE. 45 y. 5 m. 3 d. On a higher knoll across a deep gully, and about 200 feet further north, is what appears to be the oldest graveyard. On a little plateau on the top of this knoll, stretching from one edge to the other, is a row of unmarked graves, supposed to be Van Campens. No records of the Shapanack church are known to exist; this church was within the bounds of the Walpeck congregation, and was probably under their jurisdiction.

THE PETERS' VALLEY CHURCH.

The ancient Walpeck congregation is still one civil corporation. It now consists of two separate congregations, each with their own church officers and pastor, the separation having taken place about 1860. The Upper Walpack congregation has two churches, one at Peters' Valley (Bevans P. O.) and the other at Dingmans. The Lower Walpack congregation also has two churches, one at Flat-

---

* See Historical Discourse of Reformed Dutch Church of Walpack, by Rev. S. W. Mills, page 25.

brookville and the other at Bushkill. Peters' Valley is in the southern part of the township of Sandyston, Sussex county, N. J. About the year 1825 a stone building was erected there, which was used both for a church and a school-house. In 1838 this building was sold at Sheriff's sale and purchased by Robert Stoll and used for a time as a store. Within a few years it became a tavern, for which purpose it serves at the present day. The present church edifice at Peters' Valley is about 100 yards below the tavern, in a southerly direction. It was erected in 1838, at a cost of $1,400, by James C. Bevans, contractor. It was dedicated on the last Thursday in May, 1839. The records of this church have always been kept with the records of Dingmans church.

THE DINGMAN'S FERRY CHURCH.

The village at present known as Dingmans is in the township of Delaware, Pike county, Pa., about three miles northwest of Peters' Valley. The church is about one-quarter of a mile north of the village on the east side of the river road, leading to Milford, Pa. It was erected in 1850, at a cost of $1,300. The Building Committee consisted of John I. Westbrook, Albert S. Stoll and John Van Gorden; the contractor was W. F. Brodhead. For some time before the erection of this church services had been held in the school-house, nearly opposite the church and just below the cemetery. The Dingmans cemetery lies north-west of the church, on the west side of the road leading to Milford, and extends back up on the mountain. This cemetery was in use at an early date, as the Dingman family burying ground. At the present time there is no evidence of the burying ground having been used before 1820, although some of the gravestones being rudely carved and "home made," have a similar appearance to the early pioneer stones in the Machackemeck and the Minisink burying grounds. The records of Dingman's Ferry and the Peters' Valley churches are in the possession of Mr. Frank Stoll, the Clerk of the Consistory of the Upper Walpack congregation. They were commenced by the Rev. Harmon Van Slyke Peeke, in the year 1892, while he was Student Supply to this congregation; since that time they are far from complete. A memorandum by the Rev. Mr. Peeke states that the list of members, which commences on Jan. 1, 1862, was taken from the minute book of the Consistory; and that no knowledge of older records could be obtained in the year 1892. With the exception of the list of members, all records commence in the year 1892. Mr. Frank Stoll states that all the records of the Peters' Valley church were kept in the Dingman's Ferry book.

He has in his possession a letter from the Rev. Gilbert S. Garretson, who was pastor of the Upper Walpack congregation from 1863 to 1884, in which he says that the older records of this congregation were borrowed by the Lower Walpack congregation and were never returned. If such is the case, it is possible that they were destroyed in the burning of the store of John S. Smith, at Flatbrookville, already referred to.

THE BUSHKILL CHURCH.

At the present day the Bushkill church is much stronger than the other church of the Lower Walpack congregation, at Flatbrookville, already described under the heading of the Walpeck church. The village of Bushkill is in the township of Lehman, Pike county, Pa. The site of the church is on the east side of the road leading to Dingman's, just above the railroad crossing. The church is about one and a half miles south-west of the site of the first Walpeck church. It was erected in 1832, largely through the efforts of the Rev. David Cushing, who was Stated Supply to the Walpeck congregation at this time. The land was given by Henry Peters. The Building Committee consisted of Simeon Schoonover, John M. Heller and James Nyce; the edifice cost about $2,000. The corner-stone of the present church edifice was laid July 11, 1872, by the pastor, the Rev. John F. Shaw. The first Building Committee was Henry M. Labar, J. M. Swartwood and P. J. Guillot. A new Committee was appointed on Aug. 20, 1873, consisting of Jacob Nyce, William Schoonover and John Heller; they served until the building was completed, and employed Edward Burch, as contractor. The edifice cost $5,359.95. *"It was dedicated January 13th, 1874, when the Historical Discourse * * was preached in the morning by Rev. S. W. Mills, of Port Jervis. Rev. E. P. Rogers, D.D., of New York, preached the dedication sermon in the afternoon, from Ps. lxxxiv, 1; after which the form of dedication was read by the Pastor. Rev. J. H. Bertholf, of New York, preached in the evening." The corner-stone of the present edifice bears the following inscription: "R. C. A. Built 1832. Rebuilt 1872." The cemetery adjoining this church is not so large as the Dingmans cemetery, but at the present time it contains evidence of more older gravestones. The oldest one at present legible shows the date of death as 1795. The records of this church are largely destroyed or missing. Commencing with June, 1909, complete records have been kept by the present Stated Supply, the Rev. William Schmitz.

---

* See Historical Discourse of Reformed Dutch Church of Walpack, by Rev. S. W. Mills, page 32.

Abstract of contents of records of the Lower Walpack churches:
Vol. I. Members, from 1878 to present. Dismissals, deaths, marriages and baptisms, 1909 to present.
Vol. II. Minutes of Consistory, 1878 to present.
Vol. III. Record of Elders Meetings, of Bushkill and Flatbrookville, kept separately.

THE GERMAN REFORMED CHURCH AT FLATBROOKVILLE.

The Walpack Union Congregation (German Reformed) was incorporated April 15, 1820. The trustees were John Bergstracer, Lewis Trauger, Philip Smith, Leonard Gariss and George Crisman. This congregation was absorbed by the Walpeck congregation in 1841. No church records of this congregation are known to exist.

In describing the secondary churches, it should be understood that the only ones listed are those of the Reformed Dutch denomination, as originally constituted.

JOHANNES CASPARUS FRYENMOET.

Johannes Carparus Fryenmoet was the first settled pastor of the Minisink congregations. He was born in Switzerland, about 1721. When sixteen years of age he came to this country and settled in the Minisink.* He was ordained in the spring of the year 1741 by Rev. Peter Henry Dorsius, who was minister of the congregations in Bucks county, Penn. He was probably installed as pastor of the Minisink congregations in the month of May, 1741. His first baptisms were administered at Smithfield, on May 22, 1741; he commenced the church record at Walpack, on May 31, 1741; and on the following Sunday, he recorded his first baptisms in the Minisink-Machackemeck record. The validity of his ordination by Dorsius

---

* Extract from the letter of the Consistories of Machackemeck, Minisink and Walpeck, to the Classis of Amsterdam, dated May 3, 1743; see Ecclesiastical Records of the State of New York, pages 2801-3.
* * "In the same way there was urged upon us a man by the name of Johannes Casparus Fryenmoet. He had studied a little in Zurich, Switzerland. On coming over here he was hired out to service to somebody. He however gave evidence of an excellent character, and lived an edifying life. In the course of time he came in contact with Rev. Dorsius, who agreed to educate him for the ministry on condition that we should pay him for it. We did not question his right to ordain him. Meanwhile we were supplied by Rev. (G. W.) Mancius. When we came to feel that our congregations ought to have a minister of their own we were deceived in our judgments by that pretended authority; and with deplorable thoughtlessness we neglected to ask advice from his Rev. (Mancius) who had so faithfully ministered among us. A while after, when Fryenmoet had been fulfilling the office of minister among us in all its parts, we understood that other ministers, your High Revs. Correspondents, denied the legality of the power which Revs. Dorsius and Frelinghuysen were exercising; also that Rev. Freeman was among the first who questioned their authority.
When those gentlemen were asked for a proof of their authority, the Rev. Dorsius, who figured as the principal actor in this affair, declined to show his authority. * * * He declared that it was sufficient that his Rev. had signed the Certificate of Ordination; that, if anyone wanted proof of his authority, he must either be good enough to come down to see him, or make complaint against him before the Synod. However urgently they begged of him to show them his authority, that the distressed churches might be relieved of their anxieties, inasmuch as they were in great distress about the validity of the administration of the Sacraments; — for they were devoted to the observance of our Reformed Church-Order, conformable, as it is to the Word of God—was all in vain. We were refused. * * "

was soon questioned. The Classis of Amsterdam censured Dorsius for ordaining Fryenmoet and John Henry Goetschius, as he had acted without their authority. The Consistory of the four Minisink churches applied to Vas and Mancius for advice about the matter; subsequently it was also submitted to Boel. At the suggestion of these ministers the whole matter was referred to the Classis of Amsterdam. Boel and Mancius mention it in their letter to the Classis, dated Aug. 9, 1743 (2813)*. The Consistory of the Minisink churches sent a letter to the Classis, dated May 3rd, 1743, in which they asked for a ratification of Fryenmoet's ordination; Fryenmoet joined in this request. The letter recites that in the fall of the year 1742 it was learned that Dorsius was not authorized to ordain (2802). That immediately it was agreed that Fryenmoet should cease administering the Sacraments, until the case was decided.

All baptisms administered by Fryenmoet prior to this time and entered in the records of the Minisink churches, have been crossed off by Fryenmoet, as is shown in the photographic reproduction, opposite page 2. The crossing off of these baptisms reveals an error in dating in the transcript of the Minisink-Machackemeck record, as printed in this volume, on pages 106 and 107. In the original record, *from which these observations are made,* the eleven baptisms from "Debora Schoonhoven" to "Lydia Vredenburgh," are recorded without year date; Jonathan Decker and Lydia Vredenburgh are recorded as being baptized on December 6th. It is evident therefore that the year in which these baptisms took place was 1742 and not 1743, as it is printed. The note on page 106 was made by a person having no knowledge of the facts, and even without an examination of the original record. It is true that the baptisms as designated in the note, were crossed out. The other baptisms marked *"onwettig,"* and also crossed out in the record, as illustrated by the photograph, extend from "Hermanus Brinck," on page 103, to "Angontje Kermer" on page 105. The baptisms on page 105, taking place on May 3, 1743, were administered and recorded by Domine Mancius. The baptisms on page 106, dated "April 23" and "April 26" are without year date in the original record, but to anyone *with the original before them,* it is obvious that they are a continuation of the baptisms of April 23, 1744, written in the hand of Fryenmoet, as are the other baptisms of that date.† The dates on which Mancius administered

---

* All numbers following in parenthesis are page numbers referring to the Ecclesiastical Records of the State of New York.
† If further confirmation as to the correct year is desired, it is suggested that the record of baptisms in the families involved, be worked out.

baptisms are therefore May 3, 1743; Oct. 17, 1743; Oct. 18, 1743; April 23, 1744, and April 26, 1744. All the baptisms recorded in the Walpeck record, up to "Eva Dingenman" on page 2, were crossed out by Fryenmoet, but no explanation was given in that record, and they were not marked *"onwettig."*

In their letter of May 3rd, 1743, the Consistory and Fryenmoet avow that it would be very desirable, if time and money were available, for him to complete his studies in Holland, and to appear before the Classis for examination and ordination, in the usual way (2802). But, as Fryenmoet had already married, and as his services were constantly needed by the congregations, they begged the Classis to accept his written Confession of Faith, which was sent with the letter, instead of a personal appearance (2803). The letter was acted upon at a meeting of the Classis of Amsterdam, held on May 4, 1744. The Classis gave permission to the ministers neighboring on Fryenmoet, to examine him and to ordain him, in the name of the Classis (2839). A letter to this effect was dispatched to the Consistory of Minisink and Machackemeck, dated May 30, 1744 (2843). A meeting was held at Kingston, on Dec. 16, 1744, by the Consistory of Minisink*, and the Revs. Vas, Mancius and Weiss. These ministers accepted Fryenmoet's written Confession of Faith, instead of holding an oral examination, and questioning him upon Theological Doctrines. On that day Fryenmoet was ordained validly, with the laying on of hands by the Rev. Petrus Vas; he was also legally installed as pastor of the Minisink congregations. A full account of the proceedings of the previous day was dispatched to the Classis of Amsterdam, in a letter dated Dec. 17, 1744 (2862-64), which was signed by the members of the Consistory of Minisink* and Fryenmoet, Vas, Mancius and Weiss. All these transactions are fully confirmed and corroborated by an entry in the minutes of the Consistory, as recorded in the Minisink-Machackemeck record, dated April 16, 1745, which follows:

"The Consistories of the three churches—Menissinck, Walpeck and Machackamech—assembled together, transacted the following, viz:
 1. They have looked over and confirmed the following classical letters, viz: The letter to Classis, dated May third, 1743, and the answer to it by the Rev. Classis of Amsterdam, May 30, 1744. The reply to the Reverend Classis, dated December 17, 1744."

The failure to hold an examination at the time of Fryenmoet's ordination at Kingston and the matter of rebaptism of the children was the subject of further correspondence with the Classis of Am-

---
* Through some error, made either by the scribe of the Classis, or by the translators, the letter to the Classis of Amsterdam, dated Dec. 17, 1744, and the reply from the Classis, dated June 6, 1746, both mention the Consistory of *Kingston*, instead of the Consistory of *Minisink*, as it should be.

sterdam (2909). In his letter of July 18, 1747, to the Classis, Fryenmoet mentions the hardship that will fall upon the minister, in case his congregation join the Coetus, on account of the expense and difficulties of the journey to New York; also that his two most distant congregations are about fifteen Dutch miles (sixty English miles) from each other. He states that the congregation have accepted "with great pleasure and satisfaction" the decision of the Classis declaring invalid the baptisms administered by him, before his valid ordination at Kingston, and that "therefore most of the children have again been baptised, excepting those who have died or have removed away" (2963-64). There is no evidence of the rebaptism of these children as far as the records are concerned; the names have been crossed off as illustrated, but they are not re-entered in the records. The Classis of Amsterdam replied to Fryenmoet's letter, on May 5, 1749. They "heartily wish and earnestly request" that the Consistory of Minisink will join the Coetus, "now established" (3060). This recommendation was accepted as is shown by the minutes of the Consistory in the Minisink-Machackemeck record.

"October 15, 1749. In an ecclesiastical assembly of the four united churches of Smithfield &c., assembled together, the following was transacted:
1st. A letter was read from the Reverend Classis of Amsterdam. It was specially agreed to take it into consideration the next morning at eight o'clock, for which purpose the former Consistory, October 16, again assembled and transacted the following: The whole Consistory were unanimously agreed, pursuant with the desire and request in the letter for us to join the Coetus, which desire and request was complied with and is adopted."

Domine Fryenmoet sent a letter to New York expressing his willingness to join the Coetus; it was read at the meeting of the Coetus held on Nov. 7, 1749 (3098). At the meeting of the Sixth Coetus, held Sept. 11, 1750; the minutes read as follows (3132):

"1. New Members.—Domine Fryenmoet, minister at Minisink, with his elder, Benjamin De Puy, were affectionately received as members of the Assembly."

Fryenmoet continued his pastoral relation with the Minisink congregations until August, 1756, when it is supposed that he was obliged to leave, on account of the incursions of the French and Indians. The last baptisms recorded by him in the Minisink-Machackemeck record, during his pastorate, took place on August 22, 1756. Several references to his flight from Minisink are quoted below, and from them it would appear that the reason why Fryenmoet left his congregations is not clearly stated. From letter of the Conferentie to the Rev. Classis of Amsterdam, dated Nov. 9, 1756 (3679).

"4. * * * Raritan congregation * * * A great part of the congregation was induced to call Dom. Fryenmoet, (a fugitive minister, who had been compelled to leave his place through danger of the public foe;) but a committee or Circle of the Coetus was called in who did what they could to remove him, and now have succeeded, * * * "

From letter of the Coetus to the Rev. Classis of Amsterdam, dated Oct. 3, 1758 (3719).

"The churches being vacant, Rev. Casparus Fryenmoet went to live there, under pretext of having been obliged to flee from the enemy. Thereupon a dispute arose in the only recently united churches, about calling him. * * * At last Rev. Fryenmoet himself, seeing that no urging on his part could well bring it to a (unanimous) call, consented to accept a call that came to him from Livingston Manor, Claverack and Kinderhook."

From letter of the Conferentie to the Rev. Classis of Amsterdam, dated Oct. 12, 1758, mentioning the trouble at Raritan and its associated congregations, Readington, Harlingen and Bedminster, N. J. (3722).

"* * * Complaint of a committee from the North Branch portion of the congregation at Raritan, * * *
2. Dom. Fryenmoet, fleeing before the public enemy, came to North Branch, and was several times asked by the Consistory there to officiate, which he did with so much acceptance that many members of the four united congregations requested that he might preach in all the churches; but the Consistory in the other three villages refused, no doubt because of their engagements to a certain Hardenberg, who had married the widow of Dom. Frelinghuysen."

LIST OF PASTORS OF THE FOUR MINISINK CONGREGATIONS.

Minisink, Machackemeck, Walpeck and Smithfield.

GEORGE WILHELMUS MANCIUS, Aug. 23, 1737, to Sept. 19, 1740.

JOHANNES CASPARUS FRYENMOET, May 22, 1741, to Aug. 22, 1756.

THOMAS ROMEYN, April 20, 1760, to Sept. 22, 1771.

Minisink, Machackemeck and Walpeck.

ELIAS VAN BENSCHOTEN, May 11, 1785, to Aug. 28, 1797.
The second date marks the expiration of his second call, although he supplied the churches occasionally, in later years.

Minisink.

JOHN DEMAREST, 1803 to 1806.

CORNELIUS C. ELTING, Jan. 30, 1817, to Oct. 16, 1837; installed Feb. 26, 1817.

SAMUEL B. AYERS, Mar. 24, 1838, to April 20, 1841; installed June 28, 1838.

JACOB BOOKSTAVER, Oct. 25, 1841, to March, 1847; installed Jan. 12, 1842.

JAMES G. MORSE, Presbyterian Supply, Aug. 21, 1848, to 1849.

JOHN T. DEMAREST, April 8, 1850, to May 12, 1852; installed May 14, 1850.

DAVID ADKIN JONES, Nov. 26, 1852, to Sept. 26, 1858; installed May 17, 1853.

CORNELIUS GATES, April 10, 1860, to March 17, 1862; installed May 16, 1860.

WILLIAM CORNELL, July 10, 1862, to April 16, 1863; installed Sept. 2, 1862.

WILLIAM S. MOORE, April 18, 1864, to July 19, 1869; installed June 29, 1864.

N. ELMER, Supply, 1870.

WILLIAM J. HILL, Student Supply in Summer 1871.

WILLIAM E. TURNER, May 21, 1872, to 1875.

P. F. WYCKOFF, Supply 1877 to 1879, but never ordained.

THOMAS FITZGERALD, April, 1879, to April, 1881.

JOHN L. STILLWELL, May 28, 1882, to May 4, 1884.

JOSEPH MILLETT, 1887 to July, 1890; installed July 19, 1888.

GILBERT LANE, May 21, 1893, to April 27, 1896.

ANDREW J. MEYER, 1900 to 1904.

Machackemeck.

JOHN DEMAREST, 1803 to 1806.

CORNELIUS C. ELTING, called Nov. 16, 1816; installed Jan. 25, 1817; died Oct. 24, 1843.

GEORGE P. VAN WYCK, Feb. 29, 1844, to May 19, 1852.

HIRAM SLAUSON, Feb. 22, 1853, to Oct., 1857.

SAMUEL W. MILLS, called Dec. 16, 1857; installed Feb. 22, 1858; to Nov., 1871.

SAMUEL J. ROGERS, called Feb. 15, 1872; installed April 2, 1872; to May, 1876.

HENRY M. VOORHEES, March, 1877, to 1879; installed May 10, 1877.

GOYN TALMAGE, 1879 to 1887.

LIVINGSTON L. TAYLOR, 1887 to 1891.

xxix

AME VENNEMA, 1892 to 1895.
THOMAS H. MACKENSIE, 1896 to 1905.
WILLARD CONGER, 1905 to ——.

Walpeck.

JAMES G. FORCE, Nov. 15, 1808, to 1827; installed Nov. 17, 1811.
ISAAC S. DEMUND, called Oct. 15, 1827; installed Dec. 2, 1827; to June 13, 1829.
DAVID CUSHING, Oct., 1831, to July, 1832, Stated Supply.
GARRET C. SCHENCK, Feb. 23, 1834, to March, 1835; installed April 6, 1834.
JAMES B. HYNDSHAW, called Oct. 26, 1835; installed Jan. 17, 1836; to Oct. 9, 1839.
ROBERT PITTS, April 21, 1841, to 1860, Stated Supply.

Lower Walpack.

ALEXANDER McWILLIAM, Nov., 1860, to May 17, 1870; installed June 1, 1861.
JOHN F. SHAW, Oct. 1, 1870, to 1877; installed Dec. 8, 1870.
HENRY L. REX, Feb. 1, 1878, to April 15, 1888.
ELIAS W. THOMPSON, Student Supply in Summer of 1889 and 1890.
FRANK DeW. TALMAGE, Student Supply in Summer of 1891 and 1892.
CHARLES H. WHITAKER, Dec. 10, 1893, to April 13, 1900.
JOSEPH R. BEALE, April 15, 1904, to Oct. 15, 1905 (or later?).
WILLIAM SCHMITZ, June 1, 1909, to —— ——. Stated Supply.

Upper Walpack.

NATHAN W. JONES, Stated Supply, 1861 to 1862.
GILBERT S. GARRETSON, March, 1863, to 1884; installed May 19, 1863.
JOHN M. ALLEN, 1888 to 1892.
HARMON V. S. PEEKE, Student Supply in Summer of 1892.
GEORGE HAWS FELTUS, Student Supply in Summer of 1893.

WILLIAM GUTHRIE MYLES, 1894 to 1897.

JOSEPH ADDISON JONES, Student Supply in Summer of 1897 and 1898.

GEORGE ALBERT LUCKENBILL, April, 1899, to Oct., 1899.

J. W. LOUDEN, April, 1900, to July, 1901.

ALONZO A. RANSON, Student Supply in Summer of 1903.

JOHN D. GRULL, Oct. 16, 1903, to April, 1905.

N. I. M. BOGERT, Student Supply in Summer of 1905 and 1906.

FRANK E. MASON, Student Supply in Summer of 1909 and 1910.

J. H. RENDALL, Student Supply in Summer of 1911.

Walpeck Church Records

# KERCKENBOECK VAN DE GEMEYNTE WALPECK
BEGONNEN MET DEN PREDICKDIENST VAN
JOH. CASPARUS FRYENMUTH
PREDIKANT ALDAER A. D. 1741 MAY 31.

Translation

CHURCH REGISTER OF THE WALPECK CONGREGATION.

COMMENCED WITH THE PASTORAL SERVICE OF JOH. CASPARUS FRYENMUTH. PREACHER THERE, MAY 31, 1741.

DATE	PARENTS	CHILD	WITNESSES
1741.			
—— 31.	Gerrit Brinck Maria Ditsoort	Stephanus	
	Johannes Brinck Lena Cool	Johannes	Edward Parkerton, Lisabeth Cool
	Jochem Schoonmaker Rachel van Garden	Lisabeth	Gysbert van Garden, Rachel Decker
	Leonard Cool Sara van Garden	Johannes	Johannes Rosenkrantz, Catharine Rosenkrantz
July 12.	Nicolas Schoonhoven Pieternella Westfael	Benjamin	
	Hendricus Van Weyen Elisabeth van Campen	John	James Handickea, Hanna Handickea, syn Huys vr.
	Jacobus Devoor Eva Dingenman	Abram	Adam Dingenman, Rachel Dingenman
	Antony Maxfield Eva Freeland	Maria	
—— 18.	Hendricus Schoonhoven Johanna Decker	Roedolfus	Roedolfus Schoonhoven, Dorothea Schoonhoven, syn Huys vr.
	William Waert Maria Decker	John	Pieter van Garden, Margriet Decker, syn Huys vr.
	Roelof Brinck Antje Kuyckendal	Isaac	Derrick Kermer, Christina Kermer
	Bernardus Swartwood Margrietje Decker	Maria	

DATE	PARENTS	CHILD	WITNESSES
1741.			
	Boudewyn van der Lip	Dorothea	Rodolfus Schoonhoven, Dorothea Denemarck, syn Huys vr.
	Tenty Engeland		
	Gysbert van Campen	Lucas	
	Sara Decker		
	Johannes Kuyckendal	Johannes	
	Lisabet Brinck		
	Hannes van Garden	Sara	Abraham van Camp, Susanna Du Puy, syn Huys vr.
	Margriet Quick		
	Thomas Brinck	Rachel	
	Antje Kleyn		
—— 23.	Hendrick Kortrecht	Abraham	Samuel Shammers, Sara Kortrecht, syn Huys vr.
	Jannetje Ennist		
1742.			
July 5.	Cornelis Devoor	Lena	Luer Kuyckendal, Lena Consalesduk
	Lena Westfael		
	Hannes Kortrecht	Samuel	Samuel Du Puys, Jenny Medool, syn Huys v.
	Margriet Dennemarken		
	Hendrick van Garden	Catharina	Jacobus Devoor, Eva Dingenman, syn Huys vr.
	Eleonora Decker		
Aug. 1.	Benjamin Smith	Catharina	Adam Dingenman, Sara Buttler
	Catharina Schoonhoven		
Sept. 12.	Jacobus Kuyckendal	Sara	Jan Decker, Dina Kuyckendal, syn H. vr.
	Alida Dingenman		
Sept. 26.	Thomas Quick	Rebecca	Pieter van Aeken, Russje van Aeken, syn Huys vr.
	Rachel Emmans		
" "	Andries Dingenman	Eva	Isaac van Campen, Lena van Campen, syn Huys vr.
	Cornelia Kermer		
1743.			
Oct. 19.	Hendricus Schoonhoven	Jan	Jacobus Devoor, Eva Dingenman, syn Huys vr.
	Johanna Decker		
	Abraham Van Camp, Jr.	Jannetje	Hendrick Kortrecht, Jannetje Ennes, syn Huys vr.
	Catharina Kortrecht		
	Abraham van Tilburgh	Grietje	Johannes Kortrecht, Grietje Dennemark, syn Huys vr.
	Sara Clevensher		

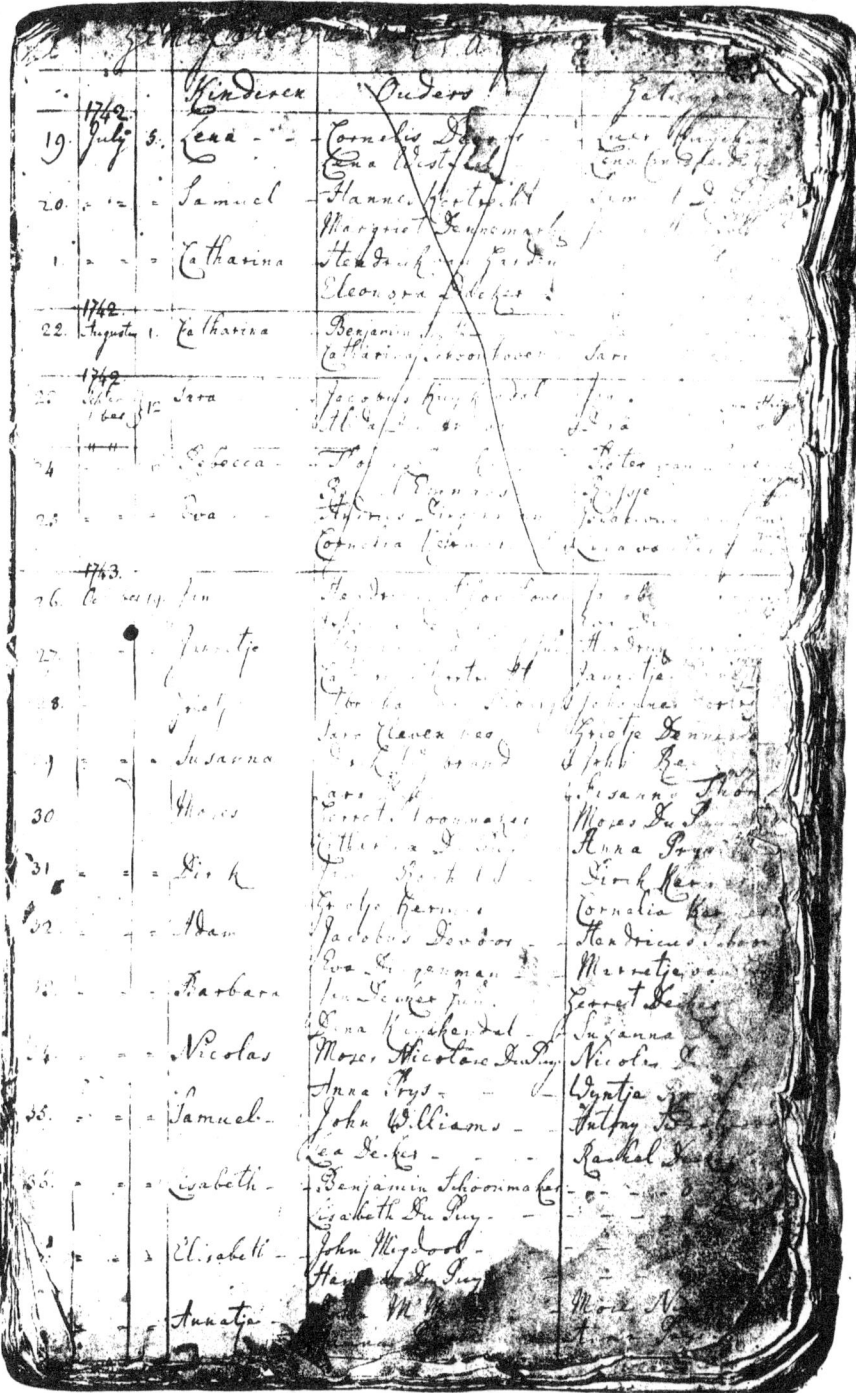

Facsimile Page of Original Church Register of the Walpeck Congregation

DATE	PARENTS	CHILD	WITNESSES
1743.	Dirck Wybrand Sara Deen	Susanna	John Ree, Susanna Thom, syn H. vr.
	Gerret Schoonmaker Catharina Du Puy	Moses	Moses Du Puy, Anna Prys, syn Huys vr.
	James Rochel Grietje Kermer	Dirck	Dirck Kermer, Cornelia Kermer
	Jacobus Devoor Eva Dingenman	Adam	Hendricus Schoonhoven, Marretje van Garden
	Jan Decker, Jr. Dina Kuyckendal	Barbara	Gerret Decker, Susanna Decker
	Moses Nicolase Du Puy Anna Prys	Nicolas	Nicolas Du Puy, Wyntje Rosa
	John Williams Lea Decker	Samuel	Antony Swartwoot, Rachel Decker
	Benjamin Schoonmaker Lisabeth Du Puy	Lisabeth	
	John Migdool Hanna Du Puy	Elisabeth	
	John McMickel Hanna Prys	Annatje	Moses Nicolase Du Puy, Anna Prys
	Christophel Dennemarck Lea Swartwood	Antje	Bernardus Swartwood, Grietje Decker, syn H. vr.
1744. April 24.	Derrick van Vliet Rachel van Keuren	Tjerck van Keuren	Dirck Westbroeck, Jannetje van Keuren, syn Huys vr.
	Hendricus van Weyen Lisabeth van Campen	Lena	Jabob van Campen, Annatje Bevier
	Andries Cool Sara Schooonmaker	Cornelia	Hermanus Cole, Cornelia van Leeuwen
	Charles van Weyen Lisabeth Kermer	Evje	Dirck Kermer, Christina Kermer
	Leonard Cole Sara van Garden	Helena	Gysbert van Garden, Rachel Kortrecht
	Samuel Shammers Sara Kortrecht	Johannes	Johannes Kortrecht, Catharina Kortrecht
	Richard Houwel Anna Daniel	Louwrenia	
	Johannes Brinck Lena Cole	Lisabeth	
	Thomas Brinck Antje Kleyn	Sara	Dirck Van Vliet, Rachel van Keuren, syn H. vr.

DATE	PARENTS	CHILD	WITNESSES
1744.			
—— 25.	Hermanus Rosenkrantz Maria Stout	Alexander	Alexander Rosenkrantz, Maritje Du Puy, syn H. vr.
1745.			
Jan. 13.	Jochem Schoonmaker Rachel van Garden	Lisabeth	Gysbert van Garden, Rachel Kortrecht, syn H. vr.
	Hannes Kortrecht Margriet Dennemerken	Elisa	Hannes Merkel, Tjatje Kortrecht
	Hendrick Kortrecht Jannetje Ennes	Jenneke	Adam Dingenman, Jenneke Bogardes
	Cornelis van Aeken Hester Elie	Jesyntje	Eliphaz van Aeken, Annatje Bevier
	Garret Brinck Maria Ditzoort	Hester	Derrick van Vliet, Rachel van Keuren, syn Huys vr.
	Christoffel Denemerken Lea Swartwood	Claudina Sophia	Joh: Christoffel Denemerken, Christina Lisabetha Bernhardin, syn Huys vr.
	Isack van Campen Lena Rosenkrantz	Maritje	Alexander Rosenkrantz, Maritje Du Puy, syn Huys vr.
	Jacobus Kuyckendal Alida Dingenman	Abram	Abraham van Campen, Susanna Du Puy, syn Huys vr.
Jan. 13.	Antony Swartwood Lena Decker	Neeltje	Willem Decker, Neeltje Roos, syn H. vr.
May 5.	Dirk Van Vliet Rachel van Keuren	Judica	Gerret van Vliet, Judica van Nest, syn H. vr.
	Valentyn Snyder Maria Jory	JohanChristoffel	Johan Christoffel Denemarken, Christina Lisabetha Bernhardin
Aug. 11.	Hendricus Schoonhoven Johanna Decker	Maria	William Waert, Maria Decker, syn H. vr.
	John Houwy Margriet M'Hollen	John	John Keally, Ellonar Mollhallon
Oct. 12.	Abram Hendrickse Decker Lisabeth Cole	Abram	Abram van Campen, Susanna Du Puy, syn Huys vr.
Nov. 18.	Isaac van Kampen Magdalena Rosenkrantz	Madlena	Jan van Kampen, Lisabeth van Kampen

DATE	PARENTS	CHILD	WITNESSES
1745.			
Dec. 15.	Gysbert van Kampen Sara Decker	Sara	Cornelis Kortrecht, Tjatje Kortrecht
	Samuel Schammers Sara Kortrecht	Christina	Gysbert van Garden, Rachel Kortrecht, syn Huys vr.
1746.			
Feb. 2.	Jacobus Devoor Evje Dingenman	Andries	Hendrick Cornelise Kortrecht, Jannetje Ennes, syn Huys vr.
March 2.	Onecht Catharina Decker	Elisabeth	Cornelis van Etten, Heyltje Westbroeck
March 23.	Adam Dingenman Maritje van Garden	Jacob	Hendrick Corn: Kortrecht, Jannetje Ennes, syn Huys vr.
April 27.	Nicolaes Emmens Catharina Rosenkrantz	John	Johannes Rosenkrantz, Susanna Schoonmaker, syn Huys vr.
	Gysbert van Garden, Jr. Rachel Rortrecht	Maria	Alexander van Garden, Maria Cole
	Philip Windemuth Maria Juliana Huber	Johan Christoffel	Johan Christoffel Dennemarken, Christina Elisabetha Bernhardin
	Richard Howel Anna Daniel	Laetitia	Isaac van Kampen, Lena Rosenkrantz, syn Huys vr.
May 24.	Johannes Brink Lena Cole	Helena	Gerret Brinck, Maria Titsoort
	Willem Devoor Catharina Schoonmaker	Rachel	Daniel Devoor, Rachel Devoor
June 22.	Abram van Campen Catharina Kortrecht	Magdalena	Isak Van Campen, Lena Rosenkranz
Aug. —.	Hugh Pugh Lena Brinck	Hugh	Cornelis Brinck, Maria Cole, syn Huys vr.
17.	Thomas Brinck Antje Kleyn	Jenneke	Alexander Thomson, Arriaentje De Long, syn Huys vr.
	Antony Swartwout Lena Decker	Thomas	Thomas Brinck, Margriet Decker
	Jochem Schoonmaker Rachel van Garden	Jacob	Andries Dingenman, Cornelia Kermer, syn Huys vr.
Sept. 14.	Thomas Hisson Catharina Kleyn	John	Thomas Brinck, Antje Kleyn, syn Huys vr.

DATE	PARENTS	CHILD	WITNESSES
1746.			
Oct. 12.	Charles van Weyen Lisabeth Kermer	Joseph	Joseph Sayin, Cathy van Weyen, syn Huys vr.
	Antony Bunschoten Margriet Wells	Antony	Antony van Etten, Jannetje van Etten
Nov. 7.	Cornelis van Aken Hester Relie	Hester	Jacobus Westfael, Sophya van Aken, syn Huys vr.
24.	Susanna Wallen op Belydenis (upon confession)		
1747.			
Jan. 19.	Isak van Kampen Lena Kosenkranz	Catharina	Abram van Kampen, Jr., Catharina Kortrecht
Feb. 1.	Dirck van Vliet Rachel van Keuren	Anna Catharina	Teunis Swart, Rachel van Vliet
	Jacob Swartwout Lydia Decker	Petrus	Cornelis H. Kortrecht, Tjaetje Kortrecht
March 8.	Andries Cole Sara Schoonmaker	Marya	Jan van Garden, Marya Cole
	Hendrick Cornelise Kortrecht Jannetje Ennes	Jacobus	Hendrick Ploegh, Alida Dingenman
	James Russel Grietje Kermer	Isak	Isak Kermer, Lisabeth Kermer
	Gerret Brinck Marya Titsoort	Gerret	Johannes Brinck, Lena Cole, syn Huys vr.
	Hendrick Bosh Marytje Bosh	Angonietje	Lambert Brinck, Angonietje Bosh
April 5.	Christoffel Dennemarke Lea Swartwout	Anna Dorothea	Rodolfus ———, Dorothea Dennemarke
June 14.	Isak Tak Lena Jansen	Sara	Johannes Dupuy, Sara Dupuy
July 12.	Samuel Schammers Sara Kortrecht	Benjamin	Benjamin Westbroeck, Marya Westbroeck
	Jacobus Kuykendal Alida Dingenman	Jacob	Benjamin Kuykendal, Christina Kuykendal
	Onecht Johanna Cole	Nenzi	Benjamin Dupuy, Eyke De Witt, syn Huys vr.
	Johannes Brinck Lena Cole	Johannes	Abram Decker, Lisabeth Cole, syn Huys vr.
	Hendrick H. Kortrecht Jannetje Ennest	Abram	Samuel Schammers, Sara Kortrecht, syn Huys vr.
	Hendrick van Garden Eleonora Decker	Catharina	Jocobus Devoor, Eva Dingenman, syn Huys vr.

DATE	PARENTS	CHILD	WITNESSES
1747.	Andries Dingenman Cornelia Kermer	Eva	Isak van Kampen, Lena van Kampen
Aug. 9.	Andries Cole Sara Schoonmaker	Leendert	Jacobus Cole, Dina Bosch
Oct. 4.	Hendrick Countryman Arriaentje Keyser	Rachel	Dirk van Vliet, Rachel van Keuren, syn Huys vr.
Nov. 1.	Adam Dingenman Maritje van Garden	Hendrick	Dirck van Vliet, Rachel van Keuren, syn Huys vr.
	Bernardus Swartwout Margriet Decker	Maria	Valentyn Snyder, Maria Barbara Jagerin
Dec. 27.	James Henderse Love Marya Cole	Hester	Cornelis van Aken, Hester B.
1748.			
March 13.	Samuel Schammers Sara Kortrecht	Petrus	James van der Merckel, Lea Keyser, syn Huys vr.
	Abram Decker Lisabeth Cole	Benjamin	Benjamin Dupuy, Eyke De Witt, syn Huys vr.
April 3.	Niclaes Emmens Catharina Rosenkranz	Alexander	Herman Rosenkrans, Maritje Dupuy
Aug. 21.	Cornelis van Aken Hester Rellie	Jannetje	Isak van Kampen, Lena Rosenkranz
	Cornelis Hendr: Kortrecht Tjaetje Kortrecht	Hendrick	Hendrick Corn: Kortrecht, Jannetje Ennes, syn Huys vr.
	Andries Dingenman Cornelia Kermer	Cornelia	Jan Kermer, Cornelia Kermer
	Jacobus Cole Dina Cole	Cornelia	Hermannes Cole, Cornelia van Leuven, syn Huys vr.
	Jacobus Devoor Evje Dingenman	Hendrick	Samuel Schammers, Sara Kortrecht, syn Huys vr.
	Willem Devoor Catharina Schoonmaker	Sara	Andries Cole, Sara Schoonmaker, syn Huys vr.
	Cornelis Devoor Lena Westfael	Benjamin	Benjamin Dupuy, Eyke DeWitt, syn Huys vr.
Oct. 2.	Hermanus Rosenkranz Mary Stout	Catharina	Niclas Emmens, Catharina Rosenkranz, syn Huys vr.

DATE	PARENTS	CHILD	WITNESSES
1748.			
	Johannes Kortrecht Margriet Dene- merken	Abram van Kampen	Abram van Kampen, Susanna Dupuy, syn Huys vr.
	Pieter Root Sara van Garden	Lisabeth	Charles van Weyen, Lisabeth Kermer, syn Huys vr.
Oct. 30.	Dirk van Vliet Rachel van Keuren	Tjerk van Keuren	Dirk Westbroeck, Jan- neke van Keuren, syn Huys vr.
	Thomas Hesson Catharina Kleyn	Ann	Dirk Kermer, Jaco- myntje Keyser, syn Huys vr.
Dec. 4.	James van der Merck Lea Keyser	Jeremias	Adam Dingenman, Maritje van Garden
Dec. 24.	Mary Stout Huys Vrouw van Hermannus Rosenkranz op belydenis (upon confession)		
Dec. 25.	Johannes Brinck Lena Cole	Geertje	Daniel Kortrecht, Jenneke Decker
	Thomas Brinck Antje Kleyn	Johannes	Johannes Kleyn, Cath- arina Kleyn
	James Russel Grietje Kermer	James	Alexander Thomson, Jacomyntje Keyser
1749.			
March 5.	Abram van Kam- pen, Jr. Catharina Kortrecht	Daniel	Daniel Kortrecht, Jen- neke Decker
	Isak van Campen Lena Rosenkranz	Alexander	Alexander Rosen- kranz, Maritje Du- puy, syn Huys vr.
April 2.	Jacob Swartwout Lydia Decker	Jenneke	Benjamin Swartwout, Jenneke Decker
	Robert Higgons Hanna Vincent	Henry	Hendrick Kortrecht, Jannetje Kortrecht, syn Huys vr.
	Andries Cole Sara Schoomaker	Elisabeth	Johannes Decker, Hanna van Garden
May 28.	Benjamin Decker Lena Kortrecht	Benjamin	Christiaen Keersbi, Catharina Kortrecht
June 21.	Gysbert van Gar- den, Jr. Rachel Kortrecht	Margareta	Jacobus van Garden, Annatje Kortrecht
	Hendrick Corn: Kortrecht Jannetje Ennes	Cornelia	Alexander Ennes, Femmetje Decker
July 23.	John Williams Lea Decker	Rachel	Hendericus Decker, Jannetje Decker
Aug. 20.	Jochem Schoo- maker Rachel van Garden	Petrus	Jan Kermer, Christina Kermer

DATE	PARENTS	CHILD	WITNESSES
1749.			
Sept. 17.	Christoffel Dennemarken Lea Swartwout	Femmetje	Benjamin Swartwout, Femmetje Decker
	Caspar Schaffer Catharina Bernhardin	Margareta	Jory Windemoet, Margareta Bernhardin, syn Huys vr.
	Gysbert van Kampen Sara Decker	Sara	Isak van Kampen, pen, Magdalena Rosenkranz, syn Huys vr.
Oct. 22.	Abram Kortrecht, Jr. Cornelia van Bunschoten	Elisabeth	Hendricus Decker, Elisabeth van Bunschoten
	Antony Swartwout Lena Decker	Benjamin	Benjamin Swartwout, Cornelia Kermer
	Charles van Way Lisabeth Kermer	Isak Kermer	Isak Kermer, Hannah Kermer
1750.			
Jan. 14.	Niclaes Brinck Catharina Decker	William	Thomas Swartwout, Jenneke Decker
Feb. 11.	Adam Dingenman Maritje van Garden	Adam	Benjamin Kortrecht, Racheltje Schoonhoven
	Samuel Shammers Sara Kortrecht	Joseph	Jan Kermer, Jacobina Bernhardin
	Jan van Garden Lisabeth van der Merckel	Lea	James van der Merckel, Lea Keyser, syn Huys vr.
	Hendrick Bosh Maria Bosh	Catharina	Jacobus Bosh, Christina Bernhardin
April 8.	Niclaes Emmens Catharina Roosenkranz	Isaak	Isaak van Kampen, Lena Roosenkranz, syn Huys vr.
May 6.	Dirk Kermer Jacomyntje Keyser	Evje	Abram Kermer, Sara Schammers, syn Huys vr.
	Edward Johnston Hanna van Garden	William	William van Garden, Cornelia Schoonhoven
	Gerret Brinck Marya Titsoort	Jenneke	Christiaen Kiersbi, Jenneke van Garden
June 10.	Isaak van Kampen Magdalena Rosenkranz	Magdalena	Niclaes Emmens, Catharina Rosenkranz, syn Huys vr.
July 29.	Dirk van Vliet Rachel van Keuren	Jenneke	Johannes Westbroeck, Jr., Maria Westbroeck, syn Huys vr.

DATE	PARENTS	CHILD	WITNESSES
1750.			
Aug. 26.	Isak Tack Lena Jansen	Geertruyd	Evert Bogardus, Geertruyd Croeck, syn Huys vr.
Oct. 7.	Abraham Decker Lisabeth Cole	Cornelia van Leuwen	Hermanus Cole, Cornelia van Leuwen, syn Huys vr.
	Herman Rosenkranz Mary Stout	Anna	Johannes Rosenkranz, Sara Dupuy
	Johannes Dupuy, Jr. Marya van Kampen	Lisabeth	Benjamin Dupuy, Eyke DeWitt, syn Huys vr.
Dec. 9.	Cornelis H. Kortrecht Leentje Rosenkranz	Abraham	Abram van Campen, Jr., Catharina Kortrecht, syn Huys vr.
1751.			
Feb. 3.	Jacob Swartwout Lydia Decker	Jenneke	Johannes Decker, Jenneke Decker
	James Love Marya van Garden	Susanna	Johannes Rosenkranz, Catharina Rosenkranz
March 3.	Jacobus Cole Lena Bosh	Marya	Jacobus Westfael, Jannetje Decker, syn Huys vr.
April 14.	Terrenz Devin Hanna Cole	Niclaes	Niclaes Emmens, Catharina Rosenkranz, syn Huys vr.
May 12.	Valentyn Snyder Maria Barbara Jagerin	Christina Lisabetha	Christoffel Dennemaken, Christina Lisabetha Bernhardin, syn Huys vr.
Nov. 17.	James Russel Grietje Kermer	Mattheus	Edward Johnson, Johanna van Garden, syn Huys vr.
	Edward Johnson Johanna van Garden	Henry	Hendrick van Garden, Eleonora Decker, syn Huys vr.
	Gysbert van Garden Rachel Kortrecht	Hester	Daniel Kortrecht, Hester van Garden
	Antony Swartwout Lena Decker	Jannetje	Gerardus Swartwout, Jannetje Swartwout
Sept. 3.	Johannes Kortrecht Margriet Dennemarken	Elisabeth	Jan van Campen, Catrina van Campen
	Alexander van Garden Annatje Kortrecht	Petrus	Gysbert van Garden, Rachel Kortrecht, syn Huys vr.

DATE	PARENTS	CHILD	WITNESSES
1751.			
Dec. 15.	Samuel Schammers Sara Kortrecht	Cathrina	Niclaes Brinck, Cathrina Decker, syn Huys vr.
	Hendricus Schoonhoven Hanna Decker	Niclaes	Niclaes Schoonhoven, Pieternella Westfael, syn Huys vr.
1752.			
Feb. 2.	Nicolaes Emmens Catharina Rosenkranz	Marya	Jacobus Schoonmaker, Marya Rosenkranz, syn Huys vr.
—— 9.	Abram P. Kortrecht Cornelia Bunschoten	Hendrick	Abram van Campen, Jr., Cathrina Kortrecht, syn Huys vr.
	Jan Kermer Lisabeth van Campen	Abraham	Abraham Kermer, Sara Schammers, syn Huys vr.
March 22.	Jan van Garden Lisabeth Merckel	Hendrick	Edward Johnson, Hanna van Garden, syn Huys vr.
	William Waert Marya Decker	Lisabeth	Hendrick Schoonhoven, Cornelia Schoonhoven
	Christoffel Dennemarken Lea Swartwout	Johan Christoffel	Christoffel Dennemarken, Christina Lis: Bernhardin
May 24.	John Drake Christina Kermer	Evje	Dirk Kermer, Jacomyntje Kepser, syn Huys vr.
May 24.	Jeremias Wright Margriet Mott	James	Cornelis van Aken, Hester Rellie, syn Huys vr.
	" "	Jonathan	Isak van Campen, Magdalena Rosenkranz
	John Drake Christina Kermer	Evje	Dirk Kermer, Jacomyntje Keyser, syn Huys vr.
	George Herrison Elsje McMichel	George	John McMichel, Hanna Prys, syn Huys vr.
July 19.	Adam Dingenman Maritje van Garden	Jacobus	Jacobus van Garden, Maria Elisabeth Contryman
	Jacobus Westfael Jannetje Decker	Levy	Cornelis van Aken, Hester Relie, syn Huys vr.
	Johannes Rosenkranz Grietje DeWitt	John	Jacobus Louw, Lisabeth DeWitt, syn Huys vr.

DATE	PARENTS	CHILD	WITNESSES
1752.			
	Theodorus van Tessel Marytje Boen	Johannes	Jacob Cole, Dina Bosh, syn Huys vr.
Aug. 16.	Niclaes Brinck Catharina Decker	Thomas	Thomas Brinck, Antje Kleyn, syn Huys vr.
	Manuel Consales Jannetje van Etten	Maria	Johannes van Etten, Maria Gunsales, syn Huys vr.
Oct. 29.	Onecht Jenneke Decker	Lisabeth	Dirk van Vliet, Rachel van Keuren, syn Huys vr.
Dec. 10.	Johannes Brinck Lena Cole	Benjamin	Jacob Swartwout, Lydia Decker, syn Huys vr.
1753.			
Feb. 4.	Joh: Mich: Huber Lisabeth Mennes	Johannes	Peter Counterman, Catharina Huber
	Thomas Brinck Antje Kleyn	Thomas	Thomas Swartwout, Jenneke Swartwout
	Gersom Simson Cathrina Brinck	John	John Brinck, Cornelia Brinck
April 1.	Joh: Dan: Becker A: Lisabeth Heckerin	Maria Christina	
—— 29.	Rodolfus Schoonhoven Dorothea Denmarken	Rodolfus	Manuel Gonsales, Jannetje van Etten, syn Huys vr.
	Terrenz Devin Hanna Cole	Leendert	Pieter Root, Sara van Garden, syn Huys vr.
June 3.	John Wordly Beeletje Decker	Isack	Louwrenz Decker, Madlena Stegs
July 1.	Herman Rosenkranz Maria Stout	Joseph	Isack van Campen, Magdalena Rosenkranz, syn Huys vr.
	Abram H. Decker Lisabeth Cole	Hendrick	Andries Cole, Christina Kermer
—— 29.	Adam Dingenman Maritje van Garden	Jacobus	Jacobus Westfael, Jannetje Decker, syn Huys vr.
Aug. 26.	Edward Johnson Johanna van Garden	Ann	Herman Rosenkranz, Mary Stout, syn Huys vr.
Oct. 14.	Daniel Kortrecht Russje van Aken	Hester	Cornelis van Aken, Hester Relje, syn Huys vr.

DATE	PARENTS	CHILD	WITNESSES
1753.			
Oct. 14.	Jacobus van Garden Catharina Kortrecht	Moses	Benjamin Kortrecht, Lisabeth Ennes
	Dirk Keyzer Sara Delang	Abram	Abram van Kampen, Catharina van Kampen
Nov. 11.	Antony Swartwout Lena Decker	Margriet	Bernardus Swartwout, Jr., Margrieta Swartwout
	Jacobus Cole Dina Bos	Leendert	Abram Decker, Lisabeth Cole, syn Huys vr.
Dec. 23.	Dirk van Vliet Rachel van Keuren	Elisabeth	John Broadhead, Ann Nottingham, syn Huys vr.
	Hendrick Bos Marytje Bos	Sara Elisabeth	Dirk Stone, Patience Pots, Nathan McGumly, Sarah Cole, syn Huys vr.
1754.			
Jan. 20.	Alexander van Garden Annatje Kortrecht	Alexander	Isaac van Campen, Madlena Rosenkranz, syn Huys vr.
March 3.	Abram Kortrecht Cornelia Bunschoten	Antoni	Antoni Bunschoten, Margriet Wells, syn Huys vr.
31.	Jacob van Campen Sara Decker	Catharina	Benjamin van Campen, Catharina van Campen
	Jacob Swartwout Lydia Decker	Johannes	Johannes Brink, Lena Cole, syn Huys vr.
April 21.	Niclaes Brink Cathrina Decker	Jacobus	Jacob Swartwout, Lydia Decker, syn Huys vr.
May 19.	James Russel Grietje Kermer	Evje	Jacob van Campen, Sara Decker, syn Huys vr.
	Thomas Hisson Catharina Kleyn	William	Johannes Kleyn, Eva Brink
	Johannes Rosenkranz Grietje DeWitt	Jacob	Isaac van Campen, Magdalena Rosenkranz, syn Huys vr.
	Niclaes Emmens Catharina Rosenkranz	Catharina	
June 9.	(Onecht) Geertje Baen	Catharina	Jacobus Westfael, Cornelia van Leuven

DATE	PARENTS	CHILD	WITNESSES
1754.	Charles Varway Lisabeth Kermer	Hanna	William Smith, Elisabeth Hyndshaw
	Joseph Sawin Catharina Varway	Charity	Aert Varway, Cornelia Kermer, syn Huys vr.
	Johannes Kortrecht Margrieta Dennemark	Christina Elisabetha	Christoffel Dennemark, Christina Elisabetha Bernhardin
	Gysbert van Garden, Jr. Rachel Kortrecht	Eliphas	Eliphaz van Aken, Eleonora Forbis, syn Huys vr.
	Benoni Brown Juno Petty	Ebenezer	Antony van Bunshoten, Margriet Wells, syn Huys vr.
30.	Andries Cole Christina Kermer	Sara	Abram Kermer, Sara Schammers, syn Huys vr.
	Samuel Schammers Sara Kortrecht	Marya	Johannes Dupuy, Marya van Campen, syn Huys vr.
	Jan van Garden Lisabeth van der Merckel	Marya	Benjamin van der Merckel, Lisabeth Kermer
	Manuel Gonsales Jannetje van Etten	Sara	Dirk van Etten, Sara van Etten
	Valentin Vocht Maria Barbara Behm	Andries Madlena	Andries Wagener, Catharina Erwen
	Caspar Sheffer Catharina Bernhard	Maria Susanna	Jan Aersen, Jacobina Bernhardin, syn Huys vr.
Oct. 27.	John Aerson Jacobina Bernhardin	Petrus	Caspar Sheffer, Catharina Bernhardin, syn Huys vr.
	John van Campen Sara Dupuy	Susanna	Abram van Campen, Susanna Dupuy, syn huys vr.
Nov. 17.	Nathan McGomly Sara Cole	Debora	Frederick van der Lip, Lydia Heyns, syn Huys vr.
	Hendricus Schoonhoven Rachel Schoonhoven	Keety	Hendericus Schoonhoven, Cornelia Schoonhoven
	Jan Kermer Lisabeth van Kampen	Sara	Gysbert van Kampen, Sara Decker, syn Huys vr.

DATE	PARENTS	CHILD	WITNESSES
1755.			
Jan. 12.	Joh: Hendrick Hansen Mar: Cathrina Freebes	Cathrina Heylwills	Jacobus Westfalls, Jacomyntje Keyser
Feb. 2.	Aldert Ploegh Cornelia Sluyter	Sara	Jeremias van der Merkel, Lea Keyser, syn Huys vr.
	Daniel Kortrecht Russje van Aken	Jannetje	Hendrick Kortrecht, Jannetje Ennes, syn Huys vr.
	Christoffel Dennemarken Lea Swartwout	Bernardus	Bernardus Swartwout, Lisabeth Brinck
	Jacob van Aken Margriet van Garden	Jacobus	Jacobus van Garden, Lisabeth van Garden
	Johannes Bosch Mary Johnson	Cathrina	Thomas Hisson, Cathrina Kleyn, syn Huys vr.

[The above closes the baptisms in Rev. Mr. Fryenmoet's handwriting. The number of baptisms was 239.]

1756.			
Feb. 23.	John van Campen Sarah Depue	Blandina	Johannes Depue, Eyken DeWitt
	Jacob van Campen Sarah Decker	Jan	Samuel Shammers, Sarah Kortrecht
1757.			
June 17.	Daniel Kortregt Russje van Naaken	Moses	Jacobus van Garden, Catrina, syn Huys vr.
21.	Charles Daily Lena Bush	Willjam	Johannes Bush, Lea Keiser
	Henrik Bush Maria Richardson	Rebekka	

By Van der Linde.

1759.			
	Johannis Van Ette Maria Gonsalies	Johannis	Willm. Smit, Elisabet Henshew
	Samuel Shemmers Sara Kortrecht	Jenneke	Jacob Swartwout, Liedeja Decker
	Jacobus van garde Catriena Kortrecht	Susanna Maraja	Johannes depue, Maria van Kampe, Benjin. van Kampe, Susanna van Kampe
	Benjn. van der Merck Sara Brink	Maria	Petries van garde Geertie brink

DATE	PARENTS	CHILD	WITNESSES
1759.			
	Daniel Kortrecht Rusje Vanake	Levi	Davit Vanake, Madelea Schonemake
	Benjamin Swartwout Corneleja brink	Minne	Minne Visher, Maria brink
	Nicholes Emens Catriena Rosekrans	Eliesabeth	
	Andries Kool Christiena Kermer	Jannetie Lena	Jacobus Kermer, Eliesabet Kermer, Isack van kampe, Lena Rosekrans
	Adam Dingeman Marietie Vangarde	Petries	hendrikus Schoonhover, Gertie Schoonhover
	James Russel Grietie Cermer	Davet	benjn. Schoonhoven, Ludija Cermer
	Jan van Kampe Sara Depue	Susanna	Jacobus van Kampe, Susanna van Kampe

[The above closes the baptisms by Rev. van der Linde.]

1761. BY REV. ROMINE.

April 6.	Nicolaus Brink Hester van Garde	Margrita	Peter van Garden, Maragrita van Garden
	Jacobus van Garden Catrina Cortregt	Abram	billinest Cortregt, Jenneke Cortregt
	Andrew Cool Christina Cermer	Abram	Abram Cermer, Sara Cermer
April 19.	Johannis Rosekrans Maragrita De Witt	Catrina	Jacob Low, Catrina Low
1762.			
Feb. 13.	Jacobus Kermer Catrina Cool	Abram	Aard van Wege, Sarah Kermer, widow
	Isaac van nest Elisabeth van Campen	lea	
	Henderikkus Dekker Annatje Kermer	Henderikkus	
Feb. 14.	Thomas Swartwoudt Elisabeth Ennes	Alexander	
May 2.	Adam Shink Cornelia Brink	Maria	
	Dennis Corsa Rachel Vangarden	Abram	
	William lee Antje Evelandt	Hannis	

DATE	PARENTS	CHILD	WITNESSES
1762.			
	Petrus van Garden Geertje Brink	Jonathan	Stephanus brink, Catrina van Campen
Sept. 22.	Jacob van Aaken Maragrit van garden	Harmanus	Harmanus van Garden, Elsje van Garden
June 13.	gisbert van Campen Titje van Campen	Jan	
	Nicolaas De Pue Elisebeth Schoonmaker	Mosis	
	Elisa Dekker Eva Dingmanse	Andries	Andrew Dingmanse, Lydia Dingmanse
	David van Aaken Magdalena Schoonmaaker	David	
	Cornelius Krom		
Sept. 22.	Andries Dingmanse Cornelia Kermer	Elisabeth	William Smith, Elisa Cath. Smith
Oct. 24.	James Handshaw Maria De Pui	Susanna	
	Harmanus Cool Margriet Swartwout	Mosis	
	Goerge Keeter Antje Bunschooten	Cornelia	Cornelius Benschooten, Gouda vangarden
Dec. 19.	John Tilburg lena ver weye	Abram	Abram tilburg, Sarah tilburg
1763.			
Jan. 16.	Abram Cortregt Rebecca Quick	Annatie	Allexander van garden, Neeltie Quick
	Willem Lee Antie Evelant	leentie	Jan van garden, Elisabeth van De Merken
	Jan Kermer Elisabeth Kermer	Jacob	Jan van tilburg, Lidia Kermer
May 29.	Jacobus vangarden Catrina Cortregt	Elisabeth	
May 30.	Andries Cool Catrina Kermer	Maragriet	
July 31.	Jacobus Bos Eva Brink	Antje	Johannis brink, antje brink
	Elies Dekker Janneke Dekker	Benjamin	Benjamin Dekker, lena Dekker
1764.			
April 15.	Benjamin Cortregt Catrina Hover	Cornelus	Henderick Hover, Cornelia Hover

DATE	PARENTS	CHILD	WITNESSES
1764.			
	Jan van Garden Elisabeth van de Merken	John	
	Adam Schink Cornelia brink	John	
	Cornelius Compen Wyentje De Pui	Elisabeth	
May 13.	Thomas Swartwoud Elisabeth Ennes	Alexander	
June 25.	Gysbert van Garden Rachel Cortregt	Gysbert	Jacob Dekker, Sarah Tilburg
	Isaac Schoonmaker Elisabeth brink	Abram	leendert Cool, Elisabeth Schoonmaaker
	John Cortregt Maria van Vliet	Derik	Derick van Vliet, Rachel van Vliet
	Joseph Hayns, Jr. Heltje Devour	Benjemin	
	Nicolaas Emmens Catrina Roosekrans	lea	
	Benjamin van de merken Sarah brink	Stephanus Brink	
	Petrus van garden Geertje brink	Petrus	
Dec. 3.	Johannis Roosekrans, Esq. Grietje de Witt	Cherk De Witt	
	Harmanus Cool Maragriet Swartwout	Hendrik	
1765. April 18.	john tilburg lena van Campen	Jacob	Isaac van Campen, lena van Campen
	Elias Dekker Janache Dekker	Elisa	Elisa Dekker, Evon Dekker
	Johannis van de merken Janneke Cortregt	Abram	Abram Cortregt, Cornelia Cortregt
	john van Campen Sarah De Pui	Sarah	
	Stephen Stiles Agnietje Kermer	Sarah	Jan Kermer, Sarah Kermer
July 4.	Daniel Cortregt Rusje van aaken	joseph	
	Helmer Schammers Blandina Denemerken	Mosis	Petrus Swartwout, Rachel brink

DATE	PARENTS	CHILD	WITNESSES
1765.			
	Abram Cortregt Rebecca Quick	Rachel	Gysbert van garden, Rachel van garden
Aug. 7.	Sander van garden lydia Kermer	Joseph	
	Ezakiel Dekker Johanna tilburg	Rachel	Cornelius Dekker, Sarah Tilburg
	William van Garden Rachel Cool	lena	Cornelia Cool
1764.			
Oct. 3.	Jacobus van gorden Catrina Cortregt	David	Benjamin De Pui, Catrina van Campen
	Benjamin De Pui Catrina van Campen	——	
1765.			
Nov. 24.	Gerrit Schoonmaker Antje Manknigteside	benjamin	
1766.			
Dec. 26.	Cornelius van Benschoten Heyltje Quick	Heyltje van aaken	Abram P. Cortregt, Rebecca Cortregt
	Andries Cool Chrlstina Kermer	Isaac	
	James Mollen Maria Swartwout	Antje	
Feb. 23.	Eliza Dekker Eva Dingman	Cornelia	Andries Dingman, Cornelia Dingman
April 27.	William Costor Sarah Swartwout	Abraham	
	Jacobus Brink Catharina Hover	Lisabet	Abraham Devins, Lisabeth Hover

[The last three baptisms not by Dom. Romaine.]

By Rev. Thos. Romaine.

1766.			
May 24.	Benjamin van de lea merken Sarah brink		
	Bernardus Swartwoud Elisabeth Brink	Gerardus	
	Mosis Schoonmaker jenneke Van Aaken	David	David van Aaken, lena van Aaken
	Thomas Swartwout Elisabeth Ennes	joseph	

DATE	PARENTS	CHILD	WITNESSES
1766.			
July 6.	Jacobus van de merken Catrina Schoonhoven	Maria	Adolphus Schoonhoven, Maria Schoonhoven
July 27.	benjamin Cortregt Catrina Hover Cobus bos Eva Brink	Anna Rachel	Emmanuel Hover, Hanna Hover benjamin Dekker, Rachel Dekker
Aug. 14.	Jan van gorden Elisabeth van de merken Henry Hover Cornelia Cortregt	Catrina Hendrick	frederick Edwart(?) [Evelant?], Catrina Edwart(?) Manuel Hover, Grietje Ennes
Sept. 7.	Goosen van den Berg Jannetje Hesued(?)	Gysbert	

is ook op voorgande belydenisie gedoopt. [Is also baptised after a previous confession.]

William Costerd(?)

1766.

Sept. 28.	Isaac Schoonmaker Elisabeth Brink	Catrina	
	David van Aaken lena Schoonmaker	Helena	Isaac van Campen, Helena van Campen
	Jacobus Schoonhoven Hendrickje Brink	Peternella	Petrus Schoonhoven, Peternella Schoonhoven
	John Cortregt, Jr. Maritje van vliet	John	
	Johannes Roosekrans, Esq. Grietje DeWitt	Elia	
Oct. 20.	Daniel Marvin Cornelia Schoonhoven	Rachel	
Nov. 9.	Henry Schoonhoven Rebecca Montanje	Redolphus	Redolphus Schoonhoven, Maria Schoonhoven
Nov. 30.	Arie Killman Judic van Vliet William Johnson Elisabeth Root	Elisabeth, b. 4 Nov. Peter	Derik van Vliet, Jr., Catrina van Vliet
1767.			
Jan. 10.	Samuel Hover Sarah Brink	Antje	Johannes Brink, Antje Brink
Feb. 8.	Benjamin Dekker Rachel Brink	lydia	Jacob Swartwout, Lydia Swartwout
Feb. 9.	Isaac van nest Elisabeth van Campen	Catrina	

DATE	PARENTS	CHILD	WITNESSES
1767.	Johannes Cortregt Susanna Kittle	Samuel	Samuel Cortregt, lydia Cortregt
June 5.	Jacob Swartwout lydia Dekker	Abram	
	Daniel Dekker lydia Vredenberg	Jenneke	Jacob Gomaer, Alida Gomaer
July 5.	John Kermer Elisabeth van Campen	Gysbert, b. 4 June	
July 26.	Helmes Chambers blandina Denne- merken	Christoffel b. 11 July	
	Johannis Broer- schen Dekker Maria Tilburg	Mary, b. 23 June	
1768.			
Aug. 6.	George Heeter Elisabeth Ben- schooten	Antony	Antony Benschooten, Jannetje lowe
Nov. 6.	Nicolaas Emmins Catrina Westbroek	Daniel	
Nov. 6.	Alexander van gerden Lydia Kermer	Annatje	Hester van garden
	William Koster Sarah Swartwout	Jacob	
	Johannis Rose- kranz Margrita De Witt	Levy	
Nov. 20.	Eliza Cortregt Alida Dingmanse	Cornelia, b. 20 Oct.	Andries dingmanse, Cornelia dingmanse
	Abram Divoor Elizabeth Hover	Abram	
	Thomas Swart- woud Elisabeth Ennes	Elisabeth, b. 14 Oct.	
	J. Stiles Angenitje Kermer	Catrina	Jan Kermer, Eliza- beth Kermer
1769.			
Jan. 22.	Petrus van de mer- ken Elizabeth Schoon- hoven	John, b. 11 Dec., 1768	John Schoonhoven, Maria Schoonhoven
	Benjamin Dekker Rachel brink	Antje, b. 30 Dec., 1768	
	Jacobus Schoon- hoven Anna Brink	Sarah, b. 5 Oct., 1768	
	Samuel Hover Sarah Brink	John, b. 17 Jan.	

DATE	PARENTS	CHILD	WITNESSES
1769.			
Feb. 5.	Aendries Cool Christina Kermer	Jacob, b. 9 Dec., 1768	
April 27.	Cobus van garden Antje van Etten	Johannis, b. 26 March	Johannis van Etten, Jr., Grietje West- vael
1771.			
May 5.	Aerd verweye Maria Contriene or Contriman (?)	Charles, b. 2 May	
	John verwey Mary beemis	Mery	
	benjamin Dekker Rachel brink	Sarah	
	Peter Vandemer- ken Elisabeth Schoon- hoven	Henderik- kus Schoon- hoven, b. 25 Oct., 1770	Hendrikkus Schoon- hoven, Hanna Schoonhoven

Last of Dom. Romeyn's record

1771.			
July 5.	Terrens Divvins Anna Cole	Rachel	William Van Garden, Rachel Cole, his wife
	Lourence Kinny Maria Cole	Catharina	
July 7.	William Asherly Maragrita Prosser	Rachel	
	Moses Schoon- maker Jannetje Van aaken	Cornelius	
	Alexander Immens Hanny Schoon- maker	Daniel	
	Petrus Swartwout Elisabet Schoon- maker	Isaac	

Following by DR. ROMIEN.

1771.			
Sept. 26.	benjamin Cortregt Catrina Hover	Hendrick, b. 10 May	
	Emanuel Gunsalis Jannetje Van Etten	Samuel, b. 19 June	
	Cobus Schoonhoven Hendrikje brink	benjamin, b. 4 Aug.	benjamin Schoon- hoven, Maragriet Schoonhoven
	Daniel Mervin Cornelia Schoon- hoven	Hendrikkus Schoon- hoven, b. 2 Feb.	John Schoonhoven, Maria Schoonhoven

DATE	PARENTS	CHILD	WITNESSES
1771.	Cobus Vandemerken Catrina Schoonhover	benjamin, b. 21 June	Benjamin Schoonhoven, Maragriet Schoonhoven
	Emanuel van de merken Maria Schoonhoven	Ezechiel, b. 13 Sept.	
	Cobes Cortregt Anna Quick	Sarah, b. 19 May	Eliphas van Aaken, Nelle van Aaken
	Michel Stendly lydia Westbroek	Janneke, b. 26 June	Levi Westbroek, Jenneke Westbroek
	Jacob Dekker Maragrieta tillberg	Maria, b. 3 Aug.	
	Christoffel Cortregt Martha Miller	Christina Elisabeth, b. 20 June	Abram Cortregt, Elisabeth Cortregt
	Ezechiel dekker Anna tillberg	Geestje or Grietje, b. 13 July	
	Jacob Helm Antje van Etten	Elisabeth, b. 28 July	
	Mosis Van Campen Sarah Westval	Cobus, b. 28 Aug.	Jan van Campen, Sarah van Campen

Last of Dom. Romeins

DATE	PARENTS	CHILD	WITNESSES
1771.	Robert Lakkerey Sarah Tak	William, b. 4 Nov. 1770	
	Daniel Depue, Jr. Annatje Westbrook	Elisabeth, b. 25 July, 1771	
	Abraham van Campen Maria Depue	Benjamin, b. 11 Aug.	
	John Van garden Maria Van Kleef	Isack, b. 10 Sept., 1765 Antje, b. 20 Aug., 1768 Albartus, b. 27 Aug., 1770	
Dec. 3.	Abraham Cortregt Neeltje Swartwout	Anthony	
	John Chambers Hannah Hoover	Maria	
1772. April 30.	Daniel van Campen Antje Dekker	Maria	

DATE	PARENTS	CHILD	WITNESSES
1772.			
June 5.	Jacobus Carmer Catharina Kool	Catharina	
	Elias Decker Jenneke Decker	Samuel	Samuel Decker, Jannetje Cortregt
	Henderikus Decker Annatje Kermer	Levi	Johannes Rosekrans, Jr., Margriet Rosekrans, syn vrouw
	Cornelis Van vliere Susanna Snel	Lena	
	William Van Garden Rachel Kool	Benjamin	Benjamin Kool, Sarah Kool, syn vrouw
Aug. 30.	John Emmans Lenah Brink	Nicolas	
	Daniel Kortregt Ruschje Van Naken	Daniel	
	David Van Naken Lenah Schoonmaker	Hester	
	Jeremiah Van de Merk Hester Kortregt	Ruschje	
	Charls Fleming Christina Chambers	Thomas Whiting	
	Patrick Henderson Hester Love	John	
	Petrus Van Nest Catlyntje Davis	James	
	James Bartron Elizabeth Westbroek	Judick Lidia	
	Isaac Cooper Catharina van Kampe	Isaac	Isaac Van Kampe, Lenah Rosekrans
	Daniel Mavin Cornelia Schoonhoven	Catharina	Adolphus Schoonhoven, Catharina Decker
	James Earl Susannah Love	Suffiah	
	Jacob Van Aaken Margarit van Garden	Rachel	
	Necholas Brink Esther van Garden	Cornelia	
	Abraham Devans Elizabeth Haver	Elizabeth	
	James Mullin Maria Swartwoudt	Janneke	
	Mannuel Hover Mary Schoonhoven	Susannah	

DATE	PARENTS	CHILD	WITNESSES
1772. Aug. 30.	Wilhelmus Chambers Cloudina Denmark	Benjamin, b. 3 July	
	Joseph Montanje Sarah Schoonhoven	Abraham, b. 9 May, 1773	
	Elisha Decker Eve Dingman	John, b. 28 Feb.	John Rosakrans, Gretie Dewitt*
	Ezekiel Schoonhoven Hanah Rasor	Marya, b. 20 June	
	Abraham P. Cortright Rebecca Quick	Abraham, b. 9 June	Broer Decker, Martie van Garden*
	Henry Hover Cornelia Cortright	Catharin, b. 11 April	Benjamin Cortright, Catharin Hover*
	Abraham Cortright Neltie Swartwoudt	Jentie Ennes, b. 4 March	
	John van Tilburgh Lena van Wien	Elisabeth	
	Johannes Chram Magdalin Plysser	Necholas	
	Daniel Decker Blandina Vredenburgh	Hannatje	
	Onecht Antje Kinne	Hannatje	Henderikus Decker, Hannatje Kermer
	Benjamin Overfield Maria Gonsalis	Manuel, b. 17 Aug.	Manuel Gonsalis, Jannetje van Etten*
	John van weye Mary Bemis	Jonas	
	Nicholas Depue Catherine Mahon	Elias	Daniel Depue, Jr., Elizabeth Decker*
	Jakobus Bunschoten Elizabeth Kermer	Abraham and Isaak	

By Dr. Jacob R. Hardenberg.

1774. May 22.	Daniel Dupue, Jr. Annatje Westbrook	Lidia	
	Benjamin Kortregt Catrina Hover	Johannes	
	Adam Shick Cornelia Brinck	Benjamin	

---

* Their names appear in the column for the parents.

DATE	PARENTS	CHILD	WITNESSES
1774.			
May 22.	Jeremiah Vandermerck Eshter Kortreght	Leah	Broer Decker, Marritje Vangarden
	Abraham Kermer Ann Immens	Margriet	
	Jacob Decker Margritha van Tilburg	Abraham	
	Eliza Kortregt Alida Dingman	Eva, b. 4 March, 1774	Eliza Decker, Eva Dingman
	John Cortreght, Jr. Marytje van fleet	Rachel	
	Abraham van Campen Maria Depue	Moses	
	Jacobus Swartwout Martha Earl	Mary	
	Timothy Davens Hanna Kool	Mary	
	Jacobus Kortreght Ann Quick	Thomas	
	Jacob van Aken Margrietta Vangarden	Jacob	
	William Kortregt Sarah Hyndshaw	Johannis	

Last of Dr. Hardenbergh's record.

1775.			
June 15.	harmans Coel marrigrit Swartwout	marrigrit	
	Johannis Decker Mari van tilbur	Johannis	
	Lodeweyk hover hester vangarden	Petrus	
	Abraham Divens Elesabet hover	levey	
	Willim Vangarden Rachel Coel	Johanna	
	Elisa Decker Eva Dingman	Antie	Jacob Dingman, Elesabet van Campen
	Andris Dingman Jennike Westbroek	Daniel Westbroek	Johannis Westbrok, Maria Westbroek
	Peetrick hannison hester love	Catrina	
	Johan mebie catrin hanse	Marya	marya Dravese, hendrick hanse

DATE	PARENTS	CHILD	WITNESSES
1775.			
June 15.	Isack Schonmaker Elesabet Brinck	Benjamin	
	Jacobus Cortrecht Abraham Cortrecht Nieltie Swartwout	Annie lena	
	Benyamen Rasor Maria Castnor	Rachel	
	Jacobus Buncehoten Elisabeth Kermer	Jacob	
	hendrick Cortrecht Cornelia Decker	Abraham Decker	Abraham Decker, Maria van garden
	Johan Einans lena Brinck	Johan	
	Niclaes Schoonhoven, Jr. Rachel vanaken	Marrita	
	Noach washbonn Rachel Schonhoven	Elesabeth	hendericus Schouk, Elesebet vandemerk
	Johan Hanon Ellenor Prosser	Johan	
	James Mollen Maria Swartwout	Maria	
	tomas Swartwout Elesabet Ennes	Marie	
	Cristefol Cortrecht Matta Miller	Thomas	
Aug. 31.	David van Aken Lena Schoemaker	Cornelius	
	Cornelius Dekker Geertye Brink	Antye	
	Charles Fleming Christina Shammers	Sarah	
	Jams van Demark Calheen Schonhover	Cathren	
1776.			
Dec. 8.	Daniel Decker Blandina Vredenburg	tomas	
	Niclaes Brinck hester vangarden	David	
	Edward Peiker Matte Gemes	Rebecca	
	Jacobus Swartwout Matte Erel	Benyamen	
	Esegel Schonhoven hanne Rasor	Niclaes	piternel Schonhoven

DATE	PARENTS	CHILD	WITNESSES
1776.			
Dec. 8.	Jacobus miels annatie meselis	jackkemin- tie	
	Elias van de merk Lena Cermer	Johan	
	Welhelmis Cam- mers Cloudina Demerken	Susana	
	Caarls flimmen Cristina Cammers	Cristina Cambers	
	Manuel Cancalis Elesabet Oute	Jannitie	
	Jacob Vanaken Marregrit Vangar- den	Elssie	
	Manuel hover Maria Schonhoven	Sara	
1775.			
Dec. 8.	Benjamin Brinck Sara Cansalis	Jannitie	Manuel Consalis, Jan- nitie van Etten
1777.			
Jan. 15.	Daniel Depue, Jr. Annatje Westbrook	Nicolaas	
June 8.	John Chambers Hannah Hover	Catrien	
	Isaac Shoemaker Elibeth Brink	Johannes	
	John Mebe Catrien Hankes	Johannes	
	Elisha Decker Eva Dingman	James	James Dingman, Maritie Decker
	James Mullen Mary Swartwood	James	
	Jacob van Auken Margriet van gor- den	Elizebeth	
	Daniel van Camp Anne Decker	Jannica	
	Thomas Clark Rachel Cinney	Samuel	
	Peter Swartwood Elizebeth Shoe- maker	Manuel	
	Abraham Corth- reght Natel Swartwood	Cornelia	
	Frederick Warner Christeenne Crinkel	An Catreen	

DATE	PARENTS	CHILD	WITNESSES
1777.			
June 8.	William Brink	Nicolas	
	Sary van tilburg		
	Henry Schonhover	Abraham	
	Rebecca Motani	Garret	
	William Caster	William	
	Sary Swartwood		
	Ruben Cuck	Mary	
	Sary(?) Cole		
	Henrey Corthright	Cornelius	
	Cornelia Decker		
	William Corthright	William	
	Sary Hawndshaw		
	Dolvus Schonhove	Dority	
	Hannah hawndshaw	Williams	
	Stoffel Corthright	Elizebeth	
	Martha Miller		
	Joshep niecles	Benjamin	
	Elizebeth Corthright		
	Rob. Miler	Robert	
	Marget Handshaw		
	James Bortron	James	
	Elizabeth Westbrook		
	Oneght	Lea Kriss	Christian Kriss, Mary Kriss, syn vrouw
	Ann Schoonmaker		
1778.			
Nov. 11.	John Hanan	Richard	
1779.	Ellenor, his wife		
April 2.	Emmanuel Hove	Hannah	
Aug. 18.	William Brink	Cathrena	
	Sarah Vantilbury		
	Thomas Brink	William	
	Mary March		
	Beniaman Kaser	Nancy	
	Mary Chesnor		
	James Swartwood	John	
	Martha(?) Earl		
	Wm. Helmis	Sarah	
	Chaimber		
	Cloudean		
	Beniaman Hyne	Eve	
	Susanah Showas	Adam	
	John Schoonhover	Margit	
	Eleyebeth Courtright		
	Nicholas Schoonhover, Jr.	Hendrickas	
	Rachel Vananker		

DATE	PARENTS	CHILD	WITNESSES
1779.			
Oct. 6.	Jacobus Vandemerk Catrina Schonhoven	Lea	
	Petrus Swartwout Elesabet Schonmaker	Elesabet	
	Lendert Westbrook Marrigrit Brinck	Blandina	
Nov. 18.	hendrick Decker Johanna Bons	Iemimi Abraham Benyamin	
	Daniel Decker Blandina Vredenburg	Arie	
	henry Schonhoven Rebecca Montanye	Redolves	
1780.			
March 19.	Bornodis Denmark Mary Chambers	Cornelea Hover Christofil	
July 2.	Banjamin Corsa Mary Chesnon	Dinis Corsa	
	Henry Cortright Cornilia Decker	Isaac	
	Daniel Decker Blandena Vredenburg	John	
1781.			
Aug. 25.	Beniaman Courtright Caty Hover	Catrina, age 3 yrs., 3 mos.	
	Joseph Moloney Sarah Schoonhover	Mary, b. 24 Jan., 1781	
	James Mullin Mary Swartwood	Thomas, b. 4 July, 1779	
	Samuel Hover Sarah Brink	Henry, b. 17 Oct., 1778	
	James Swartwood Matha Earl	Caty, b. 27 Feb., 1781	
	Peter Taylor Mary Schoonhover	Rachel, b. 4 Oct, 1780	
	Bornodis Dinmark Mary Chaimbers	Leah, Sarah, b. 25 July, 1781	
	Beniaman Brink Sarah Gonsolis	John, b. 25 Nov., 1778	Johannis Brink, Godfather, Elinar Brink, Godmother
	John Mabe Caty Houser	Abraham, b. 14 Nov., 1779	

DATE	PARENTS	CHILD	WITNESSES
1781. Aug. 25.	Manuel Hover Mary Schoonhover	Elizebeth, b. 30 Dec., 1780	
	Abraham Devince Elizebeth Hover	Elizebeth, b. 16 Aug., 1780	
	Elisha Decker Eve Dingman	Hendrickus, b. 16 March, 1779	
	Aaron van gordon Susanah Cockrum	Beniaman, b. 19 Jan., 17—	
		James, b. 25 Aug., 1780	
	Thomas Brink Mary Marsh	Ionathan, b. 31 March, 1781	
	John Dimman Elizebeth Scot	Sarah, b. 4 June, 1781	
	John Emmons Elanah Brink	Sarah, b. 28 April, 1779	
	James Chestnor Susanna Custard	Anne, b. 4 Dec., 1780	
	John Schoonhover Elizebeth Courtright	Mary, b. 1 Aug., 1781	Elisha Courtright, Godfather, Oladan Dingman, Godmother
1783. May 23.	Benjn. Brink Sarah Gunsalis	Manuel, b. 3 Oct., 1781	
	Benjn. Brink Sarah Gunsalis	Samuel, b. 16 March, 1783	
	Abraham P. Cortrecht Rabacka Queck	Resyna, b. 3 May	
	Alexander Vangarden Henne Pomry	Josip, b. 19 Oct., 1782	
	Lodewyk Hover Hester vangarden	Catrina	
	Leendert Divens Elesabet Westvael	Josip	Abraham Westvoel, Maria Martesin
May 25.	Jacobus Dingman Antie Decker	Johannis	
	James Bortrah Elesabet Westbrook	Dirck, b. 3 Jan.	
	James Mollen Mary Swartwout	Benjamin	

DATE	PARENTS	CHILD	WITNESSES
1783.			
May 25.	Samuel Decker	Rosse van-	
	Jannitie Cortrecht	aken	
	Cornelis Decker	Lea	
	Gertie Brinck		
	Johan Emans	Lena, b. 10	
	Lena Brinck	Dec., 1782	
	Elias Decker	Johannis, b.	
	Jennike Decker	22 Feb., 1783	
	Redalves Schon- hoven	Benyamin	
	Hanne Handshaw		
	Gerret van Camp	Johan	
	Elesabet van garden		
	hendrick Stiel	Isack	
	Neele van garden		
	Pieter Corsa	benyamin	
	Pecke Corsa		

[Between these two "onecht" (illegitimate) had been written; it is not plain which entry was meant.]

	lodewyk Worner	henry arins	
	Sara friman		
	Edward Pecker	Angenitje	
	Margrit Jemes	Dilye	
	Henrey Shoemaker	Susannah	
	Blandina van Camp		
1784.			
April 23.	Johannes Craan	Johannes, b.	
	Agnietje Bunschoten	19 Oct., 1783	
	Joseph van Aken	Wilhelmus,	
	Elsje Vredenburgh	b. 17 Feb., 1784	
	Cornelius van Vlieren	Susanna, b. 10 Oct., 1782	
	Susanna Snell		
April 24.	Wilhelmus Sluyter	Elizabeth,	
	Janatje Sluyter	b. 28 Jan., 1784	
	Moses Van Garde	Catharina,	
	Elizabeth van Nette	b. 25 Aug., 1783	
	David van Aken	John Emmons, b. 19 Oct., 1783	
	Catharina Emmens		
	Abraham Westfaal	Jacobus, b.	
	Maria Masterson	14 Nov., 1783	

DATE	PARENTS	CHILD	WITNESSES
1784.			
April 24.	Adolphus Schoonhoven	Nicolaus, b. 2 Oct., 1783	Nic'l Schoonhoven
	Catharina Decker		
	Jacobus Vandermerk	Petrus, b. 4 Oct., 1783	Jacobus V. D. Merk, Elizabeth V. D. Merk
	Margreta Brink		
	Hend'k Decker	Daniel, b. 29 Jan., 1784	
	Margery Westbroek		
	John Schoonhoven	John, b. 18 Oct., 1783	
	Elizabeth Kortreght		
	Isaac Kermer	Jan, b. 4 Sept., 1783	Elizabeth Dingman
	Lea Decker		
	Jonathan Baker	Abraham, b. 9 Feb., 1784	
	Rachel Resep		
	Hendrik Kortreght	Elizabeth, b. 18 Jan., 1784	
	Cornelia Decker		
	Bernardus Deenmark	Jenneke, b. 11 July, 1783	
	Maria Schammers		
April 25.	Salomon Westbroek	Salomon, b. 8 Oct., 1784	Daniel Decker, Blandina Vredenburg
	Jenneke Decker		
	Abraham Broca	Judica, b. 1 April, 1784	
	Ceeletje Westbroek		
	Jacobus Van Nette	Mary, b. 10 March, 1784	Adam Schick
	Maria Schick		
June 6.	Thomas Megeaw	Ellenor,	
	Nelly Prosser	Margeret	
	Jeramia Flemmen	Margeret,	
	Heyltje Muller	Charity, Mary	
	Abraham van Campen	Jacobus	
	Elizabeth Schoonmaker		
Sept. 19.	Daniel Bartron	James Bartron, b. 13 June, 1784	James Bartron, Elisabeth Bertbr——
	Jannetje Daly		
	Gideon Van Ake	Maria, b. 18 Sept.	Vader & Moeder
	Elizabeth Masten		
	Nicklaas Schonhove	Evert, b. 18 Sept., 1784	
	Rachel Vanake		
	Arie Van Garde	Arie, b. 15 Jan., 1783	
	Susanna Van Wye		
	Rudolphus Schonhove	Elizabeth	
	Hanna Handshaw		

DATE	PARENTS	CHILD	WITNESSES
1784.			
Sept. 19.	Isack Van ake Parabel Shyfre(?) Jacob Wolfe	Jacob, b. 10 Aug., 1783 Jannitie	Jacob Margrete } Van Ake
1785. May 8.	Lena Consolis Robert Lockerby Sarah Tack	Robert, b. 29 Oct., 1784	
	Henry Steel Allener V. Gordon	Jacob, b. 13 Feb., 1785	
	John Swartwout Sarah Dacker	Daniel, b. 30 Sept., 1784	
	Gerret Broadhead Efye Decker	Johanna, b. 31 Jan., 1785	Hendricus Decker, Johanna Carmer
	Frederick Warner Christina Conckel	Christina, b. 12 Dec., 1784	John Mushbaugh, Christina Sepile Titer
	Lodewick Warner Sarah Freeman	Catrine, b. 30 Oct., 1784	
	Henry Hanson Geertry Tack	Martha, b. 22 May, 1779	Robert Lockerby
	Casparus V. Aken Annatie V. D. Merken	Jacobus, b. 7 Dec., 1784	Jacobus V. Aken, Jenneka Decker
	Benjamin V. Aken Margriet Chesney	Abraham, b. 10 Dec., 1784	

[The above nine children were all bap. May 8, 1785.]

June 19.	Lodewyck Hover Ester Van Garden	Henderick, b. 17 May, 1785	
Aug. 22.	John Tock Matth Bunnel	Hanna, b. 6 July, 1783	
	Jonas Seely Elizabeth Quick	Cattrina, b. 14 March, 1785	
Oct. 2.	Esegiel Decker Ledea Westbroek	Catrina	
	Abraham Decker Maria Vangarden	Antie	
	Samuel Van Fleren Henne Koeper	Elesabet	
	Pieter Teler Maria Schonhoven	Ridolves, Nellie	
	Johan Crisman Maria Schonhoven	Elesabet	Jan Schonhoven, Elesabet Cortrecht
Nov. 13.	Peter Potman Sarah Caanan	John, b. 27 Sept., 1785	
	Benardus Danmark Maria Shammers	Christina, b. 18 Sept., 1785	

DATE	PARENTS	CHILD	WITNESSES
1785.			
Dec 25.	Peter Corso Lena V. Aken	Hannah, b. 27 Nov.	
	Henry Decker Majory Westbroek	Selitie, b. 27 Oct.	
	John V. Campen Susannah V. Garden	Sarah, b. 12 Sept.	
Dec. 26.	Andris Dingman Cornelia Marven	Ragel, b. 29 Oct.	Maria Marven
	Walter Brown Susanna Kiphart or Dery	Reuben, b. 25 Feb., 1776 Johanna, b. 12 June, 1779 Walter, b. 5 Sept., 1781 Natan, b. 26 March, 1784	
1786.			
March 19.	John Gibson Cattrena Bicker	Mary, b. 9 Oct., 1785	
	Henry Baker Elizabeth Hover	Jonathan, b. 3 Nov., 1785	
	Isaac Van Aken Barbara Shifly	Maragriet, b. 13 Feb., 1786	
March 26.	Moses Depuy Peggy Quick	John, b. 29 Jan., 1782	John Depuy, Elizabeth Decker
April 30.	John Mushpuch Sibble Teter	John, b. 1 April, 1786	
	John Adam Shaver Elizabeth Swartwood	Sary, b. 24 Jan., 1786	Thomas Swartwood, Elizabeth Ennes
	William Brink Mary van Tilburg	John, b. 21 March, 1786	John Decker, Elaneh Emens
	John Schonover Elizebeth Corthreght	Joseph, b. 3 April, 1786	
	James van Demark Margriet Brink	Mary, b. 19 March, 1786	John Van Demark, Mary Van Demark
	Rudulph Schonnover Hannah Haynshaw Jury Decker	Susannah, b. Sept., 1785 Elia, b. 9 Oct., 1785	Johannis Decker
June 11.	John Taylor Elizabeth Swortwood	Samuel, b. 3 Aug., 1783 Jacob, b. 16 Aug., 1785	

DATE	PARENTS	CHILD	WITNESSES
1786.			
June 11.	David Van Auken Catharine Emins	David, b. 6 March, 1786	
	James van Auken Jane Decker	Jacob, b. 1 May, 1786	
	Elias Decker Catharine Lyons	Elisha, b. 28 Aug., 1785	Elisha Decker, Jr., Catharine Decker
	Hendrickus Schoonover, Jr. Jemimy Miller	Henry, b. 14 April, 1786	Henry Schoonover, Rebekah Matanye
	Garret Broadhead Affe Decker	Cornelia, b. 21 May, 1786	
July 23.	Rudolvus Schoonhoven Cattrina Decker	Henry, b. 9 July, 1784	
	Petrus Swartwout Sarah Beakar	Daniel, b. 3 May, 1786	
	Jonathan Baker Rachel Corsan	John, b. 27 April, 1786	
Sept. 10.	John Smith Nancy Baaty	Joseph, b. 24 Feb., 1786	
	Lodewick Warner Sarah Freeman	Jacob, b. 6 July, 1786	
	Aria V. Garden Susanna McCrakken	Susanna, b. 13 Sept., 1785	
Oct. 1.	Waltea Brown Susannah Kithcart	Daniel, b. 14 Sept., 1786	
	Abraham Lane Lana Van Campen	Henderick, b. 18 April, 1783	
	Benajy Monday Cattrina Schoonhoven	Maria, b. 8 Dec., 1765	
1787.			
April 15.	Nicholas Schoonhooven Rachel V. Aken	Joseph, b. 1 Jan., 1787	
	Joannes Cran Anganitie V. Bunschooten	Elizabeth, b. 13 Sept., 1786	
	John Swartwout Sarah Decker	Jacob, b. 13 Feb., 1787	
	Harmanus V. Aken Hannah Wood	Moses, b. 10 March, 1787	
	James Dingman Antie Decker	Daniel V. Campen, b. 24 March, 1787	

DATE	PARENTS	CHILD	WITNESSES
1787.			
June 3.	Robert Lockerby Sarah Tack	Samuel, b. 4 April, 1787	
	Benjamin V. Aken Margaret Chesnon	Benjamin, b. 19 March, 1787	
	Jacobus V. Garden Elizabeth V. Garden	Jenneca, b. 22 Oct., 1786	
	Herry ——, Slave of Joannes Westbrook	Lya, b. 6 Feb., 1783	
	Henry Hage Christina Minor	Cattrina, b. 28 July, 1783	
	John Decker Cattrina Cortrecht	Hannah, b. 3 Dec., 1785 Ezegiel, b. 5 July, 1787	
	Peter Taylor, ongedoopt (unbaptized) Maria Schoonhoven	Daniel, b. 27 May, 1787	
	Jonas Seely Elizabeth Quick	Mary, b. 29 May, 1787	
	Abraham Brokaw Seletie Westbook	Maria, b. 18 Sept.	Joannes Westbrook, Maria Westbrook
	John V. Campen Susanna V. Garden	Jacob, b. ——, 1787	
1788.			
Jan. 27.	Gerret Broadhead Efye Decker	Nicholas, b. 2 Dec., 1787	
	Cornelius Cortright Cattrina Cannady	Mary, b. 29 July, 1787	
	Joseph Swartwout Nelly Schoonhoven	James, b. 23 Nov., 1787	
May 25.	Henry Beaker Elizabeth Hover	Sarah, b. 6 Oct., 1787	
	David Van Aken Cattrina Emmens	Jemima, b. 13 Feb., 1788	
	Ezekiel V. Schoonhoven Hannah Corsan	Ezekiel, b. 11 March, 1788	
	Jonathan Beaker Rachel Corsan	Rachel, b. 30 Jan., 1788	
July 6.	Henry Hagle Christina Minor	Jacob, b. 22 June, 1788	
Aug. 16.	Jacobus Van Denmerken Maragriet Brinck	Johanna, b. 13 July, 1788	Casparus V. Aken, Johanna V. Demerk

DATE	PARENTS	CHILD	WITNESSES
1788.			
Oct. 5.	Thomis Brink Mary Magh	Jams, b. 3 Aug., 1787	
	John Schoonhoven Elezebath Curtregh	Handerecus, b. 15 Aug.	Handerecus Vandemerk, Mary Vandemerk
1789. Jan. 11.	William Brink Sary tilbury	Jini, b. 22 Aug., 1788	
	Barnardus Swartwood*	Catriena, b. 27 Dec., 1788	
	Henry Decker*	Johannis, b. 12 Nov., ——	
April 12.	Jacobus Van Aken Jenneca Decker	Blandina, b. 1 March, 1789	
	Joannes Swartwout Sarah Decker	Annatie, b. 9 March, 1789	
	Frederick Warner Elizabeth Waus	Sarah, b. 15 Feb.	Lodewyk Warner, Sarah Fremen
July 17.	James Swartwood Martha Erel	Martha, b. 30 Oct., 1789	
	Jacob Gornel or Ernel Amy Mulin or Aulin	Jacob, b. 28 March, 1789	
	Joseph Brown Syntha Hilman	Rachel, b. 7 April, 1789	Peter Cregan, Rachall Cregan, Eva Danels
June 29.	Samuel Hover Sarah Brinck	Sarah, b. 4 Aug., 1785	
June 30.	Jacobus V. Bunschoten Elizabeth Carmer	Maria, b. 30 Nov., 1788	Kanelia Van Bunschooten
Aug. 30.	Abraham Van Campen, Jr. Coriany Rosekrans	Magdalena, b. 14 June, 1789	
	Joseph Van Aken Elsche Vredenburgh	Cattrina, b. 2s July, 1789	
	Benjamin Decker Rachel Cortrecht	Elias, b. 11 Aug., 1789	Elias Decker, Jennika Decker
	Nicholas Schoonhoven Rachel Van Aken	Caty, b. 1 July, 1789	Jacobus V. Aken, Cattrina Westbrook
Oct. 11.	Abraham Brokaw Seletie Westbrook	Margery, b. 29 Sept., 1789	

* Possibly two fathers, the mothers' name in both instances having probably been omitted in the original.

DATE	PARENTS	CHILD	WITNESSES
1789.			
Oct. 11.	Benjamin Van Aken Margaret Chesnon	Daniel, b. 21 Aug., 1789	
Nov. 21.	Joseph Swartwout Nelly Schoon- hooven	Thomas, b 29 Aug., 1789	
	Henry Baker Elizabeth Hover	Nancy, b. 17 Aug., 1789	
1790. Jan. 3.	Jacobus Van Gar- den Elizabeth Van Gar- den	A r e, b. 22 Dec., 1788	
Feb. 14.	John Van Camper Susannah Van Gar- den	Maria, b. 26 Dec., 1889	
March 23.	Robert Lockerby Sarah Tack	Benjamin, b. 24 Feb., 1790	
May 9.	Harmanus V. Aken Hannah Wood	Abraham, b. 22 March Sarah, b. 22 March	
	John Semlebarah or Van de Barak Caty Dacker	Cornelius, b. 18 March, 1790	Cornelis Enest, Eliner Dacker
Aug. 8.	Peter Schoon- hooven Neeltie Swartwout	Lena, b. 7 July, 1790	
	Daniel Swartwout Cattrina Van Aken	Lidia, b. 30 March, 1790	
	Joseph Cocks, on whom the child was laid	Cathrina, b. 28 May, 1790	Doloos Schoonhoven, Cathrine Decker
Dec. 6.	Frederick Warner Elisabeth Waus	Adam, b. 22 Oct., 1790	
	Sarah Miner	John, b. 31 Dec., 1789	Henry Hagle, Chris- tina Miner
1791. Jan. 15.	Abraham Van Campen, Jr. Sarah Cape	Moses, b. 31 Oct., 1790	
Jan. 16.	Henry Hagle Christina Miner	Peter, b. 6 Nov., 1790	
Feb. 14.	Gilbert Carmer Margret Decker	John, b. 9 Jan., 1791	
April 17.	Rodolvis Schoon- hoven Hannah Hanshaw	Rodolvis, b. 2 Sept., 1790	
	John Clark Elizabeth Smith	William, b. 1 Oct., 1791	
	Jonathan Beaker Rachel Carson	Mary, b. 19 Jan., 1791	

DATE	PARENTS	CHILD	WITNESSES
1791. April 17.	John Van Arnum, Sarah Depuy	Elizabeth, b. 22 Jan., 1791	
1787. Aug. 13.	Jacob Woolf, Lana Gonsaly	Caty, b. 17 Nov., 1785	
	Benjamin Overfield, Mary Gonsaly	Maria, b. 23 May, 1787 Helena, b. 24 May, 1787	Manuel Gonsaly, Jannitie Van Etten
	Benjamin Empson, Elizabeth Price	Joseph, b. 14 Sept., 1781 Abraham, b. 24 Nov., 1782 Elizabeth, b. 5 June, 1783 Caty, b. 5 June, 1783 William, b. 5 July, 1787	
Aug. 13.	Leonard Devens, Elizabeth Westfal	Hannah, b. 1 June, 1787	
1788. March 27.	Cornelius Van Vliere, Susannah Snel	Daniel, b. 11 June, 1787	
	Isaac Van Aken, Barbara Shaphaly	Elizabeth, b. 13 Feb., 1788	
	Jacob Wolff, Lena Gonsaly	Peter, b. 20 May	
July 7.	Rodolvus Schoonhoven, Hannah Hynshaw	Dorithy, b. 20 May, 1788	
1791. May 29.	Jacobus Swartwout, Martha Erl	Jacobus, b. 16 April, 1791	
	Jacob Snider, Mary Schoonhoven	Joseph Montonye, b. 16 Dec., 1790	
	Joseph Rosekrans, Jemima Emens	David, b. 15 April, 1791	David V. Aken, Caty Emens
	Benjamin Rosekrans, Grietie Schoonhoven	Rachel, b. 17 April, 1791	Nicholas Schoonhoven, Rachel V. Aken
July 31.	Benjamin Epson, Elizabeth Price	Jane, b. 14 June, 1791	

DATE	PARENTS	CHILD	WITNESSES
1791.			
July 31.	Jacobus Van Demerk Margaret Brinck	Sarah, b. 2 Jan., 1791	
Aug. 20.	John Schoonhoven Elizabeth Cortrecht	Elizabeth, b. 3 Aug., 1791	
	Lodewyck Warner Sarah Freeman	Daniel, b. 20 July, 1791	
	Joseph Swartwout Nelly Schoonhoven	Benjamin, b. 31 May, 1791	
Aug. 22.	Thomas Chollins Lea Mollen	Barbary, b. 17 June, 1791	
Dec. 4.	William Brinck Sarah Van Tilbury	Sarah, b. 23 July, 1791	
	Thomas Brinck Sarah Barthron	Jacobus, b. 2 Nov., 1791	
Dec. 16.	Gerrit Van Campen Anny Beaker	Elizabeth, b. 26 Sept., 1791	
1792.			
Jan. 15.	Henderick Decker Majory Westbrook	Andries Dingman, b. 12 Dec., 1791	A. Dingman, J. Dingman
	Jacobus Van Aken Jannica Decker	Daniel, b. 5 Nov., 1791	
Jan. 16.	Benjamin Van Aken Margariet Chesnor	Ann, b. 13 Nov., 1791	
March 5.	John Swartwood Sarah Decker	Esaia, b. 20 Nov., 1791	
	Frederick Waarner Elizabeth Maus	Frederick, b. 8 Feb., 1792	
	Nicholas Schoonhoven Rachel Van Aken	Rachel, b. 3 Dec., 1791	
May 27.	Redolvus Schoonhoven Hanna Hanshaw	Mary, b. 16 April, 1792	
	Samuel Gonsaly Elshe De Witt	Catharine, b. 11 Dec., 1791	
	Henry Van Demerk Daggy Daley	Caty, b. 23 April, 1792	

DATE	PARENTS	CHILD	WITNESSES
1792.			
May 27.	Antony Cortright Lena Emmens	Abram, b. 18 April, 1792	
Aug. 19.	Harmanus Van Aken Hannah Wood	May, b. 15 June, 1792	
Sept. 8.	James Smith, not baptized Lidia Bartron	Rodolvus, b. 25 March, 1792	
Sept. 9.	Benjamin Rose- krans Grietie Schoonhoven	John, b. 19 July, 1792	
Feb. 6.	Alexander Swartwood Caty Schoonmaker	Absalom, b. 28 June, 1791	
Sept. 11.	Benjamin Overfield, not baptized Maragrit Henshaw	Paul, b. 22 May, 1792	
1793.			
Feb. 3.	Abraham Van Campen Rosanny Rosekrans	Margaret, b. 27 Sept., 1792	
1792.			
Dec. 26.	John Van Campen Susannah Van Garden	Susannah, b. 27 April, 1792	
	John Van Arnum Sarah Depuy	Susannah, b. 17 Aug., 1792	
	Gerret Van Campen Hannah Beaker	William, b. 27 Nov., 1792	
1793.			
May 5.	Daniel Barttron Ledia Van Vliet	Elizabeth, b. 24 Aug., 1792	
June 23.	Cornelius Van Horn Catherine Willer	Elizabeth, b. 18 April, 1793	
	Joseph Swartwout Nelly Schoonhoovn	Elias, b. 10 May, 1793	
March 19.	Isaac Van Aken Barbery Shephaly	Rachel, b. 18 Sept., 1792	
	Even Beven Hannah Culver, deceased 4 yrs. ago	Moses, b. 16 Dec., 1788	

DATE	PARENTS	CHILD	WITNESSES
1793.			
March 19.	Even Beven Cattrina Carmer	John, b. 13 Oct., 1792	
June 25.	Abraham Van Campen, Jr. Sarah Cape	Andrew, b. 11 April, 1793	
Aug. 4.	Samuel Consalus Elsy De Wit	Mary, b. 1 July, 1793	
	Daniel Swartwood	David, b. 19	
	Caty Vanaken	Sept., 1793	
	John Schoonhoven Alasabeth Curtright	Abraham, b. 7 Sept., 1793	
	John Depue Hannah Decker	Elesabeth, b. 18 July, 1793	
	Jems Vengarden Elizabath Vengarden	Catey, b. 22 June, 1793	
	Bengamin Emson Elizabath Prize	Roberd, b. 22 May, 1793	
	Peter Cusaw	Jane, b. 3 Sept., 1790	
	Leana Venauken	Isaac, b. 3 July, 1793	
1794.			
Feb. 16.	John Van Demerck Janntie Cortreck	Knelia, b. 17 Dec., 1793	
	Hendericus Van Demerck Elizabeth Wasbon	John, b. 7 Dec., 1793	
1793.			
Sept. 2.	Samuel Van Demerck, deceased	Derck, b. 17 Oct., 1784	
	Jennica Van Vliett	Cherk, b. 16 May, 1788	
Dec. 1.	Abraham Brokaw Seletie Westbrook	Sally, b. 10 Nov., 1793	
1794.			
March 30.	Benjamin Van Aken Margaret Chasnor	Elshe, b. 22 Jan., 1794	
	Henry Decker Marory Westbrook	Blandiena, b. 1 March, 1794	
May 11.	James Swartwout Martha Erl	Ebenezer, b. 10 Jan., 1794	

DATE	PARENTS	CHILD	WITNESSES
1794.			
May 11.	Thomas Brinck Sarah Bertron	Elizabeth, b. 15 April, 1794	
	Isaac Schoonmaker Mary Swartwout	Martha, b. 13 Dec., 1793	
	Elias Van Demerck Lena Carmer	Jeremia, b. 29 Jan., 1794	
July 6.	Harmanus Van Aken Hannah Wood	Philip, b. 6 April, 1794	
	Hendericus Van Demerk Paggy Dayly	Jacobus, b. 12 May, 1791	
	John Swartwout Sarah Decker	Permele Berton, b. 23 April, 1794	
Aug. 17.	James Van Aken Jannetie Decker	John, b. 9 June, 1794	
	Jacob Snider Mary Schonhoven	Rebecca, b. 24 June, 1793	
	Benjamin Over-field, not baptized Margarit Hensaw	Sarah, b. 9 June, 1794	
Oct. 19.	Lodewick Warner Sarah Freman	Maragriet, b. 18 Sept., 1794	
Dec. 21.	Casparus Van Aken Johannah Van Demark	Joseph, b. 8 Oct., 1794	
	Jacobus Van Demerk Margaret Brinck	Benjamin Berton, b. 21 Oct., 1794	Benjamin Barten, Johannah
1795.			
	Samuel Consolis Elcy De Wit	Sarah, b. 23 July, 1795	
	John Depue Hanah Decker	Blandena, b. 14 Aug., 1795	
	Hanery Shoonmaker Blandena Ven Campen	Moses, b. 25 June, 1795	
	Jems Ven gorden ElesaBath Vengorden	Hannah, b. 29 July, 1795	

DATE	PARENTS	CHILD	WITNESSES
1796.			
Jan. 26.	Lewis Fortnor Elizabeth Blair	Margarit Knikendal, b. 2 March, 1795	
May 8.	John Teel Cattherine Van Demerk	Benjamin Van Demerk, b. 7 March, 1796	
July 10.	Hermanus Van Aken Hannah Wood	Genny, b. 5 June, 1796	
	Christian Hydelberk Caty Nince	William, b. 23 June, 1796	
	Alexander Eastlich Betcy Britin	Betcy, b. 30 April, 1796	
	James Smith Ledy Berthron	James, b. 14 May, 1796	
	Casparus Van Aken Johannah Van Demerk	Mary, b. 26 April, 1796	
	Anny Van Garden, not married	Benjamin, b. 8 Jan., 1796	G. V. Bunschoten, Gonda Van Gam
	John Swartwout Sarah Decker	Thomas, b. 21 June, 1796	
	Henry Decker Marjory Westbrook	Abraham, b. 14 June, 1796	
	Benjamin Rosekrans Peggy Schoonhoven	Nicholas, b. 31 Jan., 1796	
1795. June 17.	John Van Demerk Jenny Cortright James Smith Ledy Berthron	Peter, b. 15 June, 1796 David, b. 5 Oct., 1794	
1796.	John Schoonhoven Elizabeth Cortrecht	Rebecca, b. 21 July, 1796	Henry Schoonhoven, Rebecca Montayne
	Daniel Bertran Ledia Van Vliet	David, b. 15 Jan., 1796	
	Benjamin Empson Elizabeth Price	Ann, b. 14 March, 1789 Sarah & Rachel, b. 29 Jan., 1794	

DATE	PARENTS	CHILD	WITNESSES
1794. Oct. —.	Rodolvus Schoonhoven Hannah Hanshaw	Daniel, b. 10 Aug., 1794	
1796. Aug. 21.	Thomas Brinck Sarah Berthron	Thomas, b. 24 July, 1796	
1797. June 25.	Jacobus Van Demerck Margaret Brinck	Nancy, b. 24 Jan.. 1797	
	Benjamin Van Aken Margaret Chesnor	Jacob, b. 15 Sept., 1796	
	Henry Van Demerck Margarit Dayly	Mary, b. 15 Oct., 1796	
July 23.	John Nice Helena Westbrook	William, b. 24 June, 1797	
Aug. 27.	James Westbrook Gertie Brinck	Peter, b. 5 Aug., 1797	
	Samuel Gonsalis Elshe De Witt	Elizabeth, b. 18 July, 1797	
	Jacobus Van Aken Jenneke Decker	Grietie, b. 7 Aug., 1797	
	Jacob Decker Temperance Mash	Ephraim, b. 21 July, 1797	
	Bernardus Swartwout Rymerig Van Etten	Knelia, b. 22 June, 1797	
	David Berthron Ledia Van Vliet	Daniel, b. 6 July, 1797	
	Rodolvus Schoonhoven Hannah Hanshaw	Sarah, b. 22 May, 1797	
	William Schoonhoven Jane Brinck	Benjamin, b. 14 Aug., 1797	
1798. Jan. 7.	Daniel Baker Helena ——	Jane, b. 11 Nov., 1797	
	James Vangardon Elizabeth, his wife	Rebecca, b. 8 Sept., 1797	Testis—Parents
	Abraham Van Campen Sarah, his wife	Sarah, b. 8 Nov., 1797	
	Jonas Smith Ana Maria, his wife	Margaret, b. 29 Jan., 1797	

DATE	PARENTS	CHILD	WITNESSES
1798.			
Jan. 7.	Jonathan Jones Sevila, his wife	Jonathan, b. 28 May, 1797	
	Joshua Westbrook Elisabeth Vanaken	Sarah, b. 9 Sept., 1797	
	Levi Brink Anna Culver	Catherine, b. 14 June, 1797	
March 4.	Henericus Vandemark Eliz ——	Rachel, b. 16 Nov., 1797	Rachel Wasben
	Jacob Smith Susanna ——	Han. George, b. 14 Jan., 1798	George Smith
July 22.	—— Johanna Shonoven	Anna, b. 4 May, 1798	
	Moses Vangorden Elizabeth Van netten	Jeminy, b. 12 May, 1798	
	Levi Rosenkrans Mary Hankinson	William, b. 1 April, 1798	
	Simon Van horn Sarah Dunnum	Simon, b. 8 Jan.. 1796 Caty, b. 28 April, 1798	
	Thomas Brink Sarah Petron	Sarah, b. 10 April, 1798	
1799. April 28.	Herman Van Aken Hannah Wood	Aaron, b. 14 June, 1798	
	Moses Chambers Rhody Riggs	John, b. 17 Dec., 1797	
	Nathaniel Harriot Polly Chambers	Samuel, b. 22 Sept., 1797	
	Derick Brinck Caty Chambers	Matthew, b. 7 March, 1799	
	Benjamin Rosekrans Pegay Schoonhoven	Evert, b. 17 July, 1798	
	James Smith Ledy Berthron	Benjamin, b. 18 June, 1798	
	John Depuy Hannah Decker	Daniel, b. 14 Sept., 1798	
	Jonas Smith Anny Mary ——	John Philip, b. 28 Oct., 1798	Philip Smith, Dorothea, his wife

DATE	PARENTS	CHILD	WITNESSE
1799.			
April 28.	Jonathan Jones Sivilla ——	Nancy, b. 20 April, 1799	
	Wm. Lockerby Anna ——	Mary, b. 2 Aug., 1798	
	Garret Van Camp Anna ——	Mary, b. 27 Sept., 1798	
	James Vandemark, Jr. Margaret ——	Casparus, b. 15 May, 1799	Casparus Vanake and wife
	John Thiel Cathrina ——	Fred'k, b. 5 Aug., 1798	
	John Swartwood Sarah ——	Blandina, b. 30 Sept., 1798	
	John Vandemark Jenny ——	Johanna, b. 3 Oct., 1798	Johanna Vandemark
	Peter Drach Elizabeth ——	Joh. William, b. 4 July, 1798	Peter Oversheimer, Susanna, his wife
	Levi Brink Anna Culver	Thomas, b. 25 Dec., 1799	
1800.			
	James Van Aaken Jane Decker	Hannah, b. 13 July, 1800	
	James Westbrook Geertje Brink	Maria, b. 22 Sept., 1800	
	Aaron Decker Jane Brokaw	Abraham Brokaw, b. 28 Oct., 1800	
	John Vandermerk Jane Cortright	Elizabeth, b. 7 Oct., 1800	
	Thomas Brink Sarah Bertrand	Catharine, b. 17 Feb., 1800	
	John Tiel Catharine Vandermerk	Elizabeth, b. 25 Jan., 1800	
	Henry Vandermerk Elizabeth Wachman	Nicholas, b. 30 Nov., 1799	
	Benjamin Vandermerk Mary Cortright	Jacobus, b. 28 March, 1800	
	John Letts Catharine Van Camp	Moses, b. 31 Jan., 1800	

DATE	PARENTS	CHILD	WITNESSES
1800.	Solomon Hover Peggy Bolton	Benjamin Van Garden. b. 20 April, 1800	
1801.	Henry Decker Magere Wesbroek	Elijah, b. 7 May, 1801	
	Moses Van Gorden Elizabeth Van Natte	Magdalen, b. 24 Sept., 1800	
	Solomon Rosecranse Catharine Van Gorden	John, b. 23 Oct., 1800	
	Henry Washburne Sarah Harris	Noah, b. 16 Nov., 1800	
	John Swartwood Sarah Decker	John, b. 30 April, 1801	
	Gilbert Carmer Margaret Decker	Asa Baldwin, b. 23 Oct., 1800	
	Nicholas Schoonhoven Susannah Lane	Jacob, b. 11 Dec., 1799	
	Abraham Decker Mary ——	Simon Ingles, b. 24 Feb., 1801	
	Evert Hornebeck Jinny Vanake	Leah, b. 8 April, 1800	
	Garret Van Camp Anna Becker	Benjamin, b. 5 July, 1800	
	Simeon Marsh Jenny ——	Margaret, b. 14 Sept., 1800	
	Frederick Warner Elizabeth Wass	John, b. 28 Jan.. 1801	
	John Demmon Elizabeth Scoot	Elijah, b. 24 July, 1797 Jesse, b. 28 July, 1799	
	Jacob Smith Susan Fritche	Frederick, b. 27 Sept., 1800	
	Benjamin Vanaken Margaret Chesner	Hannah, b. 7 March, 1801	
	Isaac Curtwright Susannah Deary	Leah, b. 18 June, 1800	

DATE	PARENTS	CHILD	WITNESSES
1801.	Jonathan Jones Sevilla Teter	Edward, b. 17 Oct., 1800	
	John Van Camp Susannah Van Gorden	Jinny, b. 15 May, 1800	
May 31.	Jacob Cole Phebe Nash	Sarah, b. 16 Sept., 1800	Baptized by Henry Polhemus
May 31.	William Schoonhoven Jane Brink	James, b. 14 Jan., 1799	
Aug. 30.	Levi Decker Marthah Follet	Garret Broadhead, b. 2 Aug., 1801	Garret Broadhead, Affy Decker. Baptized by Rev. Elias van Bunschoten
1802. May 29.	Conrad Klein Margareth ——	Elizabeth, b. 14 May, 1798	John Smith, Margareth, his wife. Baptized by Christian Enderes
	Thomas Decker Susanna ——	Henry Shoemaker, b. 4 Dec., 1801	
	Benjamin Van De Mark Mary ——	Catharine, b. 20 Dec., 1801	
	John Lesch Catharine ——	John Philip, b. 6 March, 1802	
	Philip Smith Dorothea ——	Margareth, b. 27 Feb., 1802	John Smith, Margareth ——
	Michael Smith Sarah ——	John, b. 6 March, 1802	Leonhard Kehrns, Catharine ——
	Abraham Smith Sevele ——	Elisabeth, b. 2 Jan., 1802	Jacob Smith, Margareth Smith
	Andrew Schonauvel Magdalen Schnawbel	Joseph, b. 24 Aug., 1801	
Sept. 30.	Henry Vandemark Elizabeth Wiseborn	James, b. 1 Jan., 1802	
	James Vandemark Margareth Brink	Rachel, b. 31 July, 1801	Rachel Wiseborn and the mother of the child
	Henry Vandemark Margareth Daily	Susanna, b. 16 Nov., 1800	
	Jacob Schmidt Susanna ——	Daniel, b. 21 May, 1802	

DATE	PARENTS	CHILD	WITNESSES
1802.			
Sept. 30.	George Nice Elizabeth Schoonmaker	Daniel, b. 18 Feb., 1802	
	Isaiah Mixter Leah Vandemark	Mary, b. 22 Sept., 1801	
	John Tiehl Catharine Vandemark	James, b. 29 Jan., 1802	
	Elizabeth Decker	Anna, b. 1 March, 1802	Abraham Decker, Mary Van Gorden, the grandparents
	Joshua Westbrook Elizabeth Van Auken	Rachel, b. 20 March, 1802	
	John Dimon Elizabeth Scott	James, b. 28 June, 1801	
	Jacob Cole Phebe March	Abram, b. — Oct., 1802	
	John Peters Elizabeth Smith	Mary, b. 22 Oct., 1802	
1803.			
	Laudewick Smith Mary Binckner	Jacob, b. 2 Jan., 1803	
	Aaron Decker Jane Brokaw	John, b. 8 Jan., 1803	
July 10.	Casparus Van Aken Johannah Van Demerck	David, b. 1 May, 1803	
	John Van Demerck Jane Cortright	Abraham, b. 14 Feb., 1803	
	John Phresuer Lena Bodine	Pheby, b. 18 Sept., 1802	
	Henry Decker Mary Swartwout	Bernardus, b. 9 Jan., 1803	
	Isaac Decker Susannah Cortright	David Van Garden, b. 8 Jan., 1803	David Van Garden, Polly Emmens
	John Frink Rachel Marvin	Henry, b. 27 Jan., 1803	Henry Marvin, Anny Van Horn
	William Schoonhoven Jane Brinck	Rhodolvus, b. 8 Oct., 1801	
	Peter Hover Susannah Cortright	Aariantie Schoonmaker, b. 14 April, 1803	

DATE	PARENTS	CHILD	WITNESSES
1803.			
July 10.	Manuel Brinck Lena Smith	Sarah, b. 6 Dec., 1802	
	Salomon Hover Peggy Cotton	Lodewick, b. 13 July, 1802	
	Gysbert Van Garden Lena Van Garden	Cattrina, b. 6 Nov., 1802	
	John Litch Caty Van Campen	John, b. 22 Nov., 1802	
	Richard French Easter Scrosman	Selitie, b. 16 Aug., 1799 Susy, b. 25 June, 1801	
	John Brinck Betchcy Howel	Benjamin, b. 31 July, 1800 Peter, b. 17 July, 1802	
Oct. 16.	Thomas Decker Susanna Shoemaker	Blandina, b. 5 May, 1803	
	George Nyce Elizabeth Shoemaker	William, b. 22 Aug., 1803	
	Richard French Esther Croswell	Caty, b. 14 Jan., 1803	
1804.			
May 27.	Andries Schnabel Magdalena Caler	Susanna, b. 4 Dec., 1803	George Smith, Susanna Smith
	Henry Washburn Sarah Harris	Nicholas Schoonhoven, b. 17 April, 1803	
	Henry Van Demark Margaret Dayly	Johanna Schoonhoven, b. 26 Aug., 1803	Nicholas Schoonhoven
	Benjamin Van Demark Mary Cortright	William Ennes Cortright, b. 12 Dec., 1803	
	Thomas Brink Sarah Burtron	Daniel, b. 17 Oct., 1802 Henry, b. 8 March, 1804	

DATE	PARENTS	CHILD	WITNESSES
1804. May 27.	John Tiel Caty Van Demark	Rosanna, b. 20 Jan., 1804	
	John Decker Mary Brokaw	Seletje, b. 16 Feb., 1804	
	James Van Aken Janneke Decker	Eliza Johnson, b. 8 March, 1804	
	Leendert Gaeress Catharina Smith	Abraham, b. 1 Oct., 1803 Isaac, b. 1 Oct., 1803	
	Nickolas Schoonhoven Susanna Lane	Ezekiel, b. 22 July, 1801	Ezekiel Schoonhoven
	William Lockerby Ann Chesner	Robert, b. 20 Jan., 1803	
	William Schoonhoven Jane Brink	Levicia, b. 17 April, 1804	
	Isaiah Mixture Lea Van Demark	John, b. 29 July, 1803	

The following children were baptized by CASPAR WACH, Ref. Preacher from the Dutch Valley, Morris Co.

1804. Sept. 4.	Christian Gun Susanna ——	Thomas, b. 2 Jan., 1802 Christian, b. 21 March, 1804	George Smith, Susanna, his wife
	Jonas Smith Anna Maria ——	Barbara, b. 24 Aug., 1803	
	Philip Smith Dorothea ——	Philip, b. 27 April, 1804	
	Jacob Smith Susanna ——	Johannes, b. 10 Aug., 1804	
	Rudolp Kintner Elisabetha ——	Johann Georg, b. 12 Sept., 1803	Georg Michael and wife
	Moses Van Garden Elisabetha ——	Moses, b. 27 Oct., 1803	
	Simeon Van Netten Cornelia ——	Maria, b. 5 March, 1804	
	John Dimon Elisabetha ——	Assa Budd, b. 6 April, 1804	

DATE	PARENTS	CHILD	WITNESSES
1804.			
Sept. 4.	Henry Van de Mark Elisabetha ——	Banadiah, b. 12 June, 1804	
	George Cressman Sarah ——	Daniel, b. 30 June, 1804 John, the same day	
	John Depue Hannah ——	Moses, b. 10 April, 1804	
	Benjamin Van Gorden Elisabetha ——	Henry, b. 7 July, 1803	
	John Van Netten, Jr. Catharina ——	Cornelia, b. 27 July, 1804	
	Lewis Layton Judith ——	Abraham Brokaw, b. 14 May, 1804	
	Benj. Depue Elisabetha ——	Nicolas, b. 29 July, 1804	
	Peter Van est Abigal ——	Rebecca, b. 27 May, 1803	
	Isaac Van est Elizebeth ——	Caty Ann, b.2 7 June, 1803	
	William Smith Susanna ——	John, b. 3 March, 1803 Jacob, b. 20 May, 1804	
Nov. 5.	William Custard Elisabeth Van Camp	Benjamin, b. 3 July, 1803	
	Joshua Smith Elisabetha ——	Benjamin Schoenover, b. 15 Sept., 1804	
1805.			
	John Nice Helena ——	Catharina, b. 2 Jan., 1805	
	Aaron Decker Jane ——	Daniel, b. 31 Jan., 1805	
	Henry Decker Mary ——	John, b. 9 Oct., 1804	
Oct. 13.	James Schoohoven Elizabeth Brooks	William Smith, b. 3 Aug., 1804	
	Richard French Elizabeth V. Vlierden	Marie, b. 18 Jan., 1805	

DATE	PARENTS	CHILD	WITNESSES
1805.			
Oct. 13.	Michael Van Vleet Anna Decker	John, b. 9 Sept., 1805	
1806.			
May 12.	James Van Kampen Sality Decker	Susannah, b. 6 Nov., 1805	Abraham Van Campen. Handwriting of Dom. Van Bunschoten
	Samuel Depuy Eliza Smith	Eleanor Maria, b. 20 May, 1802 Jane, b. 12 Nov., 1803 Samuel, b. 21 Dec., 1805	

The following children were babtized by THOS. POMP, Ref. minister of Eastern Pennsylvania:

1806.

May 15.	Jacob Smith Margareth ——	Philip, b. 6 April, 1806	Philip Smith, Dorothea ——
	Lehnhart Geres Catharine ——	Jonas, b. 12 May, 1806	Jonas Smith, Anna Maria ——
	John Mack Margareth ——	Lena Van Auke, b 14 July, 1805	Diterich Berck, Catharine ——
	Abraham Smith Sibilla ——	Catharine, b. 25 Dec., 1805	Parents
	Benjamin Van de Mark Mary ——	Sarah, b. 4 May, 1806	
	Josua Westbrook Elisabeth ——	Samuel, b. 20 Nov., 1804	
	Jacob Steel Margareth ——	Henry, b. 23 April, 1806	
	Isaac Mixter Lea Van de Mark	Catharine Scoanover, b. 16 Sept., 1805	Mary Pegar
	Benjamin Sheldren Catharine ——	Abraham, b. 9 March, 1804	Mother
Aug. 9.	John Brink Elizabeth ——	Samuel, b. 7 Aug., 1804	
	Robart Howy Charity ——	William, b. 4 Feb., 1806	
	John Teel Catharine ——	Mary Ann, b. 24 May, 1806	

DATE	PARENTS	CHILD	WITNESSES
1806.			
Oct. 19.	Samuel Gunsaules Else ——	Susanna, b. 28 Sept., 1804	
	Henry Decker Mary ——	Catharine, b. 9 July, 1806	
	John Decker Mary ——	Peter, b. 18 Sept., 1806	
1807.			
April 16.	Jacob Smith Susannah ——	Samuel Smith, b. 24 Nov., 1806	
	Derick Brink Catharine ——	James Brink, b. 1 Feb., 1807	
	Christion Smith Mary ——	Elizabeth, b. 24 Sept., 1806	
April 17.	Thomas Brink Sarah ——	Mary, b. 1 Jan., 1806	
	Richard French Elizabeth ——	Sarah, b. 18 Jan., 1807	
	Levi Brink Ann ——	James, b. 13 Oct., 1806	
	Philip Smith Toriteawe (Dorothea) ——	Barbary, b. 7 Oct., 1806	
1808.			
Oct. 16.	Aaron Van Camp Leanah	John, b. 8 Oct., 1807	
1807.			
June 28.	Aaron Decker Jane Brocau	Salita, b. 15 June, 1807	
	Henry Van Demerk Margaret Daley	Benjamin, b. 27 Aug., 1806 Lea, b. 27 Aug., 1806	
	William Custard Elizabeth Van Campen	Susannah, b. 12 Jan., 1805 Sarah, b. 18 Feb., 1807	
Aug. 2.	John Nyce Lanah Westbrook Nathanel Vanaken Nancy Westbrook	George, b. 15 June, 1807 Mahala Mariah, b. 21 Dec., 1806	

DATE	PARENTS	CHILD	WITNESSES
1807.			
Aug. 2.	Henry Marvin Ann Van Horn	Betsseb, b. 19 May, 1807	
July 23.	George Nyce Elizabeth Shewmaker	Jacob, b. 15 July, 1807	Jacob Nyce
	Ioshua Smith Elizabeth Van Auken	Chrysparus Van Naken, b. 21 July, 1807	
	Joshua Westbrook Elisabeth Vannaken	Margret, b. 12 March, 1807	
Aug. 23.	John Depue, Jr. Mary Van gorden	Nicholas, b. 13 April, 1800 Aaron, b. 8 Aug., 1802	
	John Depue Marey Van gorden	Moses, b. 1 Sept., 1804 Elisabeth, b. 28 Nov., 1806	
	Aaron Van Campen Lanah Puder	Elisabeth, b. 14 Jan., 1804 Marey, b. 17 Oct., 1805	
	Benjamin Van Gorden Elisabeth Vandemark	John, b. 10 Dec., 1805	
	Lodovick Smith Mary Kintner	John, b. 6 Oct., 1806	Nathaniel Vanaken & Marey
	Jeames Van Naken Jane Decker	Jeames, b. 29 June, 1807	
	William Lockerby Anna Chestnor	John, b. 5 Sept., 1806	
	Mikel Van Flera Anne Decker	Samuel, b. 9 Aug., 1807	
Oct. 11.	Henry Schoonhover and wife	Abm. Decker	
Sept. 4.	Thomas Decker and wife	Margaret Maria, b. 8 Aug., 1807	
1808.			
	Sallomon Rosecrants and wife	Hannah, b. 2 Jan., 1808	

DATE	PARENTS	CHILD	WITNESSES
1808.			
	Shereman Hide and wife	Susanna, b. 19 April, 1808	
	Jacob Steel and wife	Caty. b. 12 July, 1808	
	Jacob Smith and wife	Catey, b. 8 April, 1808	
	George Cass and wife	Jacob, b. 11 Oct., 1807	
	Isaac Enest and wife	Elijah Clark, b. 28 April, 1808	
	John Brown and wife	Cornelia, b. 27 Sept., 1807	
	Benjamin Vandemark and wife	Anna Mary, b. 24 April, 1808	
1809. May 25.	John Brink and wife Elisabeth	John, b. 26 Sept., 1806 Daniel, b. 23 Nov., 1808	By Rev. Force
	Simeon Swartwood Susanna	Daniel, b. 23 Jan., 1809	
	Jacob I. Vannaken Hannah, his wife	Sollomon, b. 24 Feb., 1809	
	James Schoonover and wife Betsie (Elizabeth Brooks)	Elijah Parmer, b. 18 April, 1809	
	John Decker and wife Mary	Sary, b. 13 April, 1809	
	Henry Decker Mary Swartwood	Anna, b. 12 Sept., 1808	
	Andries Hill Elizabeth Caress	Abraham, b. 23 Dec., 1808	
	Lewis Layton Judith Brokaw	Henry Schoonhoven, b. 22 Jan., 1809	
	Levi Brink Ann Culver	Henry, b. 19 May, 1809	
	Henry Schoonhoven Elizabeth Decker	Mary, b. 15 March, 1809	

DATE	PARENTS	CHILD	WITNESSES
1809.			
	John Buth Jane Utt	Mary Littesua, b. 6 April, 1808	
	Victor Putman Elizibeth Cline	Moria, b. 15 April, 1809	
	Richard French Elizebeth Van vlera	Moses, b. 27 March, 1809	
	William Custard Elizebeth Van camp	William, b. 9 June, 1809	
	Leonard Caress Catherine Smith	Susannah, b. 4 July, 1809	
Oct. 15.	Thomas Decker Susannah Shoemaker	Calvin, b. 14 Sept., 1809	
	James Van Camp and wife Salicha	Abm., b. 19 Oct., 1807	
Dec. 17.	Aaron Decker Jane, his wife	George Washington, b. 22 Oct., 1809	
	James Van Camp and wife Selecha	Mary, b. 23 Aug., 1809	
1810.			
June 3.	John De Puy, Jr. Mary, his wife	Daniel, b. 27 Oct., 1809	
	John Butts and wife Jane	Jacob Butts, b. 12 Oct., 1809	
	Mikle Hellor Elezebeth	Hannah, b. 10 Nov., 1809	
	Joshua Smith Elezebeth	John Anderson, b. 14 Nov., 1809	
	George Cressman Sally	Ira, b. 14 March, 1809	
	Jacob Puss Elezibeth	Peggey, b. 11 Nov., 1809	
	Benjn. Schoonhove Elezebeth	John, b. 4 Sept., 1809	
	James Van Nanker Jane	Sarah, b. 19 July, 1810	
	Aaron Van Camp Lanah	Elijah, b. 14 Oct., 1809	

DATE	PARENTS	CHILD	WITNESSES
1810.			
	Willm. Smith Mary	Margery, b. 8 July, 1810	
	Adam Overpeck Elizebeth	Samuel, b. 25 Jan., 1810	
Sept. 30.	Thomas Brink Sarah	Jenny, b. 24 May, 1810	
1811.			
Dec. 29.	Jane Butts on the profession of her faith		
	John Butts Jane	Fanny, b. 25 Aug.	
	John Decker Mary	Abraham, b. 30 Sept.	
1812.			
March 8.	Solomon West- brook Caty	Margeret, b. 10 Dec., 1811	
	John Van Nanken Rachel	Henry Barn- hart Win- termute, b. 10 Jan., 1812	
	Willm. Smith Mary	Caty, b. 19 March, 1812	
	Joshua Smith Elizebeth	Elijah, b. 31? Feb., 1812	
May 3.	Aaron Decker Jane	Amanda, b. 4 April	
	John Smith Mary	James Barn- hart, b. 2 April	
	Andrew D. Decker Elizebeth	Nancy, b. 29 Jan.	
Oct. 18.	James Brink Catherine	Margeret, b. 13 Sept.	
	John Lits Caty	Jacob, b. 16 Aug., 1806 William, b. 19 April, 1808 Mary Anne, b. 6 Nov., 1810	
1813.			
July 11.	Hontetrick Berg Marjory	David, b. 18 Jan., 1813	
Aug. 8.	John Hellor Blandina	James Van Auken, b. 9 June	
Aug. 8.	Andrew Hill Elizebeth	James, b. 12 Feb.	

DATE	PARENTS	CHILD	WITNESSES
1814.			
May 28.	Andrew D. Decker Elizabeth William Smith Mary	Sarah, b. 25 Feb., 1814 Cecelia, b. 13 March	
Aug. 7.	John Depue, Jr. Mary	Sarah, b. 18 June, 1814	
	John Smith Mary	Parmelia, b. 6 Jan.	
	Andrew Shurrah Elizabeth	William Hankinson, b. 26 Feb.	
	Aaron Decker Jane	Caleb, b. 17 June	
Oct. 2.	Jacob Smith Elizebeth	Susanna Maria, b. 2 April	
1815.			
May 21.	Robert Howy Charity	Abraham, b. 7 Jan., 1815	
July 30.	John Decker Mary	Belinda, b. 9 April	
Nov. 26.	Nathaniel Van Aken Mary	Leah Naamy Jane, b. 27 Oct.	
Nov. 26.	Solomon Westbrook Catharine	Magdalena Wintermute, b. 10 Feb.	
	Andrew Hill Elizabeth	John, b. 26 May	
1816.			
March 17.	John W. Van Auken Rachel	Aram, b. 12 Dec., 1815	
	Philip Smith Doratha	Jane Amanda, b. 22 Nov.	
April 7.	Henry Decker Mary Swartwood	James Washington, b. 26 Oct., 1814	
Nov. 10.	John Depue Mary Van Gorden	Mary, b. 11 Aug., 1816	
Sept. —.	John Garess Susan	Caty, b. 3 July, 1816	
Dec. 8.	Aaron Decker Jane Brokaw	Job, b. 4 Nov.	
1817.			
July 20.	John Decker Mary	Aaron, b. 19 May, 1817	

DATE	PARENTS	CHILD	WITNESSES
1817.			
July 20.	Andrew D. Decker Elizabeth	John Westbroek, b. 11 Oct., 1816	
Aug. 24.	Jacob Smith Elizabeth	Coonrod, b. 12 Aug.	
Sept. 14.	Michael Heller Elizabeth	Jane Belinda, b. 5 Feb., 1817	
	William Bearch Mary	Eliza Jane, b. 21 July	
Oct. 6.	Solomon Westbrook	Susannah Maria, b. 20 July	
	Catharine Stoley Nehemiah Hill Susannah Staly	Margareth Elizabeth, b. 9 June	
May 10.	David Hill Margaret	William Uriah, b. 20 July	

NOTE IN THE ORIGINAL: "Here begins a record of baptisms at first noted on loose bits of paper, and never before entered in the book:

1809.

DATE	PARENTS	CHILD
May 7.	Abraham Smith Sevilla Fruche	Susannah, b. 24 Oct., 1807 Sarah, b. 15 Jan., 1809
May 28.	Daniel W. Dingman Mary Westbrook	Jane, b. 14 March, 1808
	Isaac Carmer, Jr. Hannah Ogden	Sarah, b. 27 Sept., 1808
	Peter Reser Mary Amy	Philip, b. 15 Oct., 1808
	Jacob Smith, Jr. Susannah Fruche	Elias, b. 31 Oct.
June 25.	Lodawick Smith Mary Kentner	Charles, b. 20 Sept., 1808
June 15.	Levy Rosenkrans Mary Hankinson	Cyrus Egbert, b. 12 March, 1809
June 28.	John Dewit Elizabeth Cape	Cornelius, b. 6 Jan., 1807 Catharina, b. 3 April, 1809
July 23.	Gilbert Steel Hannah Decker	Elenor, b. 25 April

DATE	PARENTS	CHILD	WITNESSES
1809.			
Aug. 20.	Cornelius Van Etten Anna Smith	Amos, b. 25 Sept., 1808	
	Daniel Van Etten Caty Decker	Rachel, b. 11 Oct., 1808	
Aug. 13.	Peter Van Neste, Jr. Abigail Layton	Ira Vredenbergh, b. 12 Feb., 1809	
Sept. 10.	John Frazer Lenah Bodine	William, b. 22 Nov.	
	John Lattimore Dorothy Van Etten	Polly, b. 25 July	
Sept. 24.	Benjamin Rosenkrans Margaret Schoonhoven	Sally, b. 4 April, 1808	
Oct. 15.	Simeon Rosenkrans Sarah Shoemaker	John, b. 1 Jan., 1809	
Oct. 29.	John Nyce Lanah Westbrook	Lydia, b. 24 June	
	Isaac Steel Catharine Reser	Margaret, b. 18 Sept., 1809	
Nov. 26.	Abraham Decker Mary Cortright	Elizabeth, b. 30 June	
1810.			
Feb. 4.	Daniel Decker Sarah Shoff	Richard Fulk, b. 3 Sept., 1806 Jane Mapes, b. 15 Nov., 1808	
	John Brown Hannah Broadhead	Jacob Hufty, b. 1 Nov., 1809	
Feb. 4.	Manuel Decker Caty Cortright	Benjamin Cortright, b. 26 May, 1809	
April 1.	Peter Reser Mary Amy	Jacob, b. 5 March, 1810	
April 29.	Solomon Van Etten Caty Rosenkrans	John, b. 19 Jan.	
July 29.	Jacob Reser Rachel	James, b. 31 May	
1811.			
June 2.	Benjamin Depuy Elizabeth	Moses, b. 13 March	
	Frederick Karick Elenor	Jacob, b. 5 July	

DATE	PARENTS	CHILD	WITNESSES
1811.			
	Simeon Swartwood Susannah Schoonoven	Hannah, b. 4 March, 1811	
	Manuel Decker Caty Cortright	Isaac Cortright, b. 12 May, 1810	
	Jacob Westbrook Hannah Van Aken	Mariah, b. 15 May	
Sept. 9.	John J. Rosenkrans Caty Van Campen	Arrietta V. Campen, b. 13 July, 1810	
	Isaac Ennes Hannah	Elenor, b. 16 Feb.	
	Christian Smith Mary	Lusy Ann, b. 7 July	
Oct. 6.	George Coss Elizabeth Smith	Samuel, b. 21 Sept., 1810	
Oct. 28.	Nathan Emery Cornelia Broadhead	Cyrus, b. 4 July, 1810	
	John J. Van Etten Caty	Solomon, b. 13 May	
Feb. 13.	John. W Van Aken Rachel Rosenkrans	Richard Westbrook, b. 18 Oct., 1810	
Feb. 24.	Cornelius Van Etten Anna	Polly, b. 26 Jan., 1811	
June 23.	Joseph Van Gorden Esther Stull	Jane Eveline, b. 9 Feb.	
	John Reser Margaret Ennes	Joseph, b. 23 April	
July 7.	Benjamin Van Gorden Elizabeth Rosenkrans	Jacob Dewit, b. 17 Sept., 1810	
July 28.	Manuel Brink Lanah	Benjamin, b. 7 May, 1805 Joshua, b. 1 March, 1808 Manuel, b. 17 Dec., 1810	
	Robert Howy Charity	Jonathan Van Gorden, b. 16 Aug., 1808	

DATE	PARENTS	CHILD	WITNESSES
1811.	Daniel Brink Jane	Lovisa, b. 3 Aug., 1810	
	Richard Bartron Elizabeth	Daniel, b. 14 March, 1807	
Aug. 18.	Gilbert Steel Hannah	Gilbert, b. 22 July, 1811	
	Ephraim Drake Mary Lattimore	Joshua, b. 24 March	
	James Van Campen Saliche Decker	Elijah, b. 25 Aug.	
	Andrew Hill Elizabeth Gans	William, b. 15 Sept., 1810	
Oct. 30.	Joseph Probasco Margaret	George, b. 14 Dec., 1803	Joh. Loder & wife Anna
Nov. 24.	Jacob J. Van Akin Hannah	Cornelius Brooks, b. 27 Aug., 1811	
	John Heller Blandinah	Daniel, b. 27 Feb., 1811	
May 10.	Lewis Layton Judith Brokaw	Peter Van Neste, b. 1 Dec., 1810	
1812.			
Jan. 14.	Isaac Steel Caty Reser	Caty, b. 29 Dec., 1811	
Jan. 23.	Daniel Van Etten Caty	John, b. 28 April, 1811	
	John Lattimore Dorothy Van Etten	Leah, b. 20 Oct., 1811	
Jan. 29.	Isaac Ennes Hannah	Matilda Jane, b. 3 Jan., 1812	
	Jacob Myres Sarah	Elizabeth, b. 6 March, 1811	
	Asa Rosenkrans Jane Cole	Horris, b. 15 Nov., 1810	
	Simeon Rosenkrans Sarah Shoemaker	Charriek, b. 3 July, 1811	
Feb. 1.	Robert Howy Charity	Daniel Van Gorden, b. 6 Nov., 1811	
April 5.	Rudolph Kintner Elizabeth Wert	Phillip, b. 16 Jan., 1812	
	James Schoonover Elizabeth Brooks	Rachel, b. 14 Jan.	

DATE	PARENTS	CHILD	WITNESSES
1812.			
April 26.	John Westbrook Sarah Broadhead	Margaret, b. 20 Feb., 1812	
	Jacob Hornbeek Leah Van Aken	Priscilla, b. 28 Jan.	
	Peter Reser Mary	William, b. 10 Dec., 1811	
	Johonnas Decker Sarah Atkins	Mercy, b. 5 Oct.	
	Evert Hornbeck Jenny	Jacob, b. 13 April, 1808	
	John Loder Elizabeth Clark	Jepthah, b. 11 Dec., 1811	
	Peter Hover Susannah Courtright	Jane, b. 27 Aug., 1808 Mary, b. 14 Dec., 1810	
June 7.	Jacob Smith, Jr. Susannah Fruche	Elizabeth, b. 10 Jan., 1812	
	Christian Smith Mary	Mary, b. 19 Feb., 1812	
July 5.	Benjamin Rosenkrans Margaret Schoonover	Amanda, b. 4 Feb., 1811	
Oct. 11.	Nathan Emery Cornelia Broadhead	Elenor, b. 28 June, 1812	
Oct. 18.	Jacob Buss Betsey Miller	Polly, b. 1 Sept.	
Dec. 20.	John Brown Hannah Broadhead	Elias, b. 20 March	
	John Van Etten Caty	Sarah, b. 26 Aug.	
	Jacob Westbrook Hannah Van Aken	Solomon, b. 17 Nov.	
	John B. Quick Diana Rosenkrans	Mariah Elizabeth, b. 20 Sept., 1810	
Dec. 25.	John Ennes Mariah Seely	Loiza Seely, b. 18 Sept., 1810 Elizabeth, b. 12 Oct., 1811	
	Abm. Westbrook Anna	Daniel Dingman, b. 17 Feb., 1809 Abraham M., b. 3 April, 1811	Daniel Dingman & wife

DATE	PARENTS	CHILD	WITNESSES
1813.			
Jan. 17.	Henry Decker Mary	Mariah, b. 17 Oct. 1812	
	John Henry Catharine Steel	Isaac, b. 24 Sept., 1812	
Feb. 15.	John Dimon Elilabeth Scot	Hannah, b. 4 Feb., 1808	
Feb. 28.	Daniel Shoemaker Mary	Benjamin, b. 10 Feb., 1812	
	Abijah Mires Elizabeth Dimon	Jonathan, b. 20 July, 1812	
April 11.	Solomon Van Etten Caty Rosenkrans	Daniel, b. 10 Jan., 1813	
	John Van Etten Mariah	Solomon, b. 7 Nov., 1812	
June 13.	Richard Bartron Elizabeth	Sarah Depuy, b. 4 Nov., 1812	
	Simeon Swartwood Susannah Schoonover	Rimerick, b. 25 March	
Dec. 13.	Simeon Rosenkrans Sarah Shoemaker	Samuel Shoemaker, b. 25 July, 1813	
	Asa Rosenkrans Jane Cole	Frazure, b. 28 March, 1813	
Dec. 31.	Isaac Ennes Hannah	Eliza Maria	
1814.			
Jan. 2.	Johonas Decker Sarah Atkins	James Madison, b. 18 July, 1813	
	Solomon Van Aken Margaret	Leah, b. 31 May, 1813	
Feb. 27.	Abraham Decker Mary Cortright	Hannah Anne, b. 22 May, 1812	
May 22.	John Nyce, Esq. Lanah Westbrook	Jacob, b. 2 May, 1813	
June 19.	[A space had been left open in the original for the names of the parents of these two children] James Schoonover Elizabeth	Hannah Maria, b. 3 Aug., 1812 James Martin, b. 12 Feb., 1814 Daniel, Benjamin, twins, b. 23 April, 1814	

DATE	PARENTS	CHILD	WITNESSES
1814.			
July 3.	Rodolvus Smith Sarah Samuel Winans Margaret Depuy	Jacob, b. 17 Aug., 1813 Elizabeth Depue, b. 29 March, 1814	
Sept. 4.	Richard Bartron Elizabeth John Moser Sarah Jacob Rayman Rachel Daniel Brink Jane	James, b. 13 March, 1814 Adam, b. 12 Sept., 1813 George, b. 22 Sept., 1813 Elizabeth, b. 19 Feb., 1814	
Oct. 23.	Cornelius Van Etten Anna Peter Reser Mary Nathan Emery Cornelia Broadhead John Bodine Jane Mapes Jacob Westbrook Hannah Van Aken	Caty Anne, b. 16 Dec., 1813 Peter, b. 9 Nov. Julia Anne, b. 11 Feb., 1814 William, b. 15 June, 1814 Levy, b. 25 Aug.	
Oct. 30.	Michael Heller Elizabeth Depue Simon Heller Sarah Adam Bensley Anna [Parents' names not given in original]	Susannah, b. 3 Sept. Amos, b. 31 Aug. Jacob, b. 30 Sept., 1810 Anna Herrington, b. 15 Jan., 1801 William Hony, b. 15 Feb., 1805	Israel Bensley & wife Caty, guardians
Nov. 20.	Thomas Blake Susannah	Priscilda, b. 19 Aug., 1814	
Dec. 25.	Jacob J. Van Aken Hannah	Mary Anne, b. 12 Nov.	
1815.			
Feb. 12.	Gilbert Steel Hannah	Belinda Hornbeek, b. 12 Feb., 1814	

DATE	PARENTS	CHILD	WITNESSES
1815.			
Feb. 12.	Isaac Steel Caty	Isaac, b. 29 Oct.	
Feb. 19.	Elizabeth, wife of John Dewit, on her own profession John Dewit Andrew Elizabeth Cupes, b. 15 Aug., 1814		
March 1.	Henry Dewit Rachel	Lovina, b. 18 Jan., 1808 Sally, b. 26 Dec., 1811	
	John Henry Catharine Steel	William, b. 24 Sept., 1814	
	[Parents' names not given in original]	Jacobus Cortright, b. 27 Aug., 1814	Peter Hover & wife Susannah, guardians
		Elizabeth Van Gorden, b. 2 July, 1815	
March 12.	John Howy & wife Mary	Mariah, b. 15 Oct., 1815	Catharine Howy, guardian
March 22.	William I. Cortright Christian (?) Mires	John Drake, b. 12 Jan., 1811 Sally, b. 1 Feb., 1815	
April 9.	John H. Dewit Cornelia Winecoop	Peter, b. 1 March, 1815	
June 11.	John Van Etten Mariah Rosenkrans	Anthony, b, 22 Sept., 1814	
Sept. 3.	John Howy Mary	Peter, b. 7 Jan., 1815	Peter & Susannah Van Demark, guardians
	Henry Peters Sarah Gunsaly	Elizabeth, b. 19 Sept., 1814	
	James Place Susannah Depue	Benjamin, b. 24 Nov., 1814	
Oct. 29.	Jacob Buss Elizabeth Miller	George, b. 3 Oct., 1815	
1816.			
Jan. 14.	Jacob Smith, Jr. Susannah	Susannah, b. 8 April, 1815	
Feb. 4.	Nathan Emery Cornelia Broadhead	Cornelia, b. 16 Dec.	

DATE	PARENTS	CHILD	WITNESSES
1816.			
	Cornelius Cortright Hannah Steel	Sarah, b. 28 Dec.	
	Henry Steel, Jr. Susannah Livengood	Mariah, b. 19 Oct.	
March 3.	Frederick Karick Elenor	Mariah, b. 5 Nov., 1815	
	Simeon Swartwood Susannah Schoonover	Cornelia, b. 31 July, 1815	
March 10.	John Westbrook Sarah Broadhead	Jacob, b. 28 Nov., 1815	
	Peter Birk Caty Man	Elizabeth	
May 5.	Daniel Ennes Susan Reser	Jacob, b. 23 Nov., 1815	
	John Reser Peggy Ennes	Anthony, b. 7 April, 1816	
	Peter Reser Mary Amy	Henry, b. 18 Nov., 1815	
May 12.	Andrew Van Campen Anne Michaels	Mary, b. 15 Oct., 1815	
	Rodolvus Smith Sarah Akle	Susannah, b. 3 Sept., 1815	
	Benjamin Depue Elizabeth Buzzard	Benjamin, b. 18 Dec., 1815	
May 20.	George Van Neste Hannah Emery	Isaac Hankinson, b. 4 Feb., 1814 Jacob Ross, b. 4 April, 1816	
June 9.	Simeon Rosenkrans Sarah Shoemaker	Margaret Dewit, b. 18 Aug., 1815	
June 30.	John Brown Hannah Broadhead	Nicholas Broadhead, b. 10 July, 1814	
	John Quick Susannah Loder	Hiram, b. 17 March, 1816	
	Cherick Van Gorden Sally Loder	Polly Reser, b. 10 May, 1815	
	Thomas Lake Susannah Hover	George Nyce, b. 18 April, 1816	

DATE	PARENTS	CHILD	WITNESSES
1816.			
Sept. 8.	Adam Bensley Anne Emson	Catharine, b. 26 Nov., 1814	
	Adam Overpeck Elizabeth Man William Overfield Sarah Coolbaugh	Israel, b. 10 May, 1816 Sarah Anne, b. 1 April, 1816 Susannah, b. 1 Jan., 1812 Elizabeth, b. 10 Nov., 1813	
Oct. 20.	John Shoemaker Mary Gunsaly	Samuel, b. 3 July, 1814 Blandina, b. 30 July, 1816	
	John Swartwood Mary Miller John Mosier Sarah Overfield Jonas Hanners Barbary Mann	Jacob, b. 4 Aug., 1816 Dan, b. 20 Oct., 1815 John, b. 2 Nov., 1813 Sally Anne, b. 29 Feb., 1816	
May 17.	James Schoenover Betsey Brooks	Mary, b. 14 Sept., 1816	
Dec. 1.	Johanes Decker Sarah Adkins	Ruth Mariah, b. 13 Sept., 1816	
Dec. 28.	James Van Campen Ceselia Decker John Bodine Jane Mapes	Moses, b. 24 Oct., 1816 Abraham Van Campen, b. 6 May, 1816	

NOTE IN THE ORIGINAL: "Here follows a record of some omissions:"

1815.			
April 25.	Frederick Warner Mary Ganis	Eliza Ann, b. 20 Jan., 1815	
1814.			
Oct. 1.	Isaac P. Van Gorden Jane Frazer	John Wilson, b. 21 Nov., 1813	
1812.			
Dec. 25.	Evan Bevans Catharine Carmer	Jacob Bevans, b. 26 Oct., 1812	

DATE	PARENTS	CHILD	WITNESSES
1812.	Isaac Carmer Hannah Ogden	Luther, b. 8 Dec., 1810	
1803. Oct. 3.	Levy Decker Mattha Follet	John Brown, b. 11 June, 1803	
	Daniel Cortright Elizabeth Swartwood	Thomas, b. 1 Sept., 1802	
	Jacob Decker Temperance Mash	Moses, b. 10 Sept.	
	Isaac Cortright Susannah Dayly	Abraham Peter, b. 21 Sept., 1801	
	Samuel Decker Rebeca Custerd	Catharina Mapes, b. 22 July, 1802	
1805. Oct. 14.	John Dewitt Elizabeth Cape	Susannah, b. 29 Aug., 1804	
		Sarah, b. 8 May, 1805	
	Abram Van Camp Sarah Cape	John, b. 19 April, 1805	
1807. June 21.	Peter Man Hannah Hany	Susannah, b. 22 Oct., 1806	
	Solomon Rosenkrans Catharine Van Gorden	James, b. 6 Oct., 1805	
	Gilbert Steel Hannah Decker	Sarah, b. 10 Feb., 1807	
	Peter Hover Susannah Cortright	Elizabeth Nice, b. 25 June, 1806	
1808. Dec. 25.	John Westbrook Sarah Broadhead	Hannah, b. 30 Sept., 1808	
1809. Feb. 12.	Daniel Shoemaker Mary Taylor	Susannah, b. 12 April, 1808	
1813. July 24.	George Emery Elizabeth Keen	John Keen, b. 6 June, 1810	
		Hannah, b. 9 April, 1812	
	Abraham Keen Sarah Emery	Mary, b. 25 Jan., 1812	

Regular Record Recommences Here.

DATE	PARENTS	CHILD	WITNESSES
1817.			
Jan. 25.	[Names of parents left open in original]	Solomon Kittle, b. 22 May, 1815	Honteter Berk, Marjory Kittle, guardians
May 31.	Peter Hetsel Elizabeth Gunn	Jacob, b. 29 Nov., 1815	
Aug. 3.	Jacob Westbrook Hannah Van Aken	John, b. 11 May, 1817	
	Frederic Vadakin Susanna Stetler	Ira, b. 27 Feb., 1817	The mother
Aug. 10.	Rodolvus Smith Sarah Aken	Mary, b. 25 March, 1817	
	William Clark Sarah Schoonover	Elizabeth Smith, b. 16 Nov., 1816	
Aug. 17.	Isaac Carmer Hannah Ogden	Susannah, b. 23 June, 1817	
Aug. 31.	Cornelius Van Etten Anna Smith	Robert Keneday, b. 6 May, 1816	
	Daniel Van Etten Caty Decker	Oliver Perry, b. 29 Nov., 1816	
Sept. 10.	James Wallace	Margaret Matilda, b. 24 June, 1811 William Alexander, b. 10 Nov., 1813 Francis Barton, b. 28 Dec., 1815	
Oct. 30.	John Merring Maryanne Coss	Jacob, b. 13 Feb., 1817	
Dec. 7.	Gilbert Steel Hannah	Leah, b. 4 Sept., 1816	
	Isaac Steel Caty Reser	Elizabeth, b. 1 Sept., 1817	
	John Henry Catharine Steel	Mary, b. 14 June, 1817	
Dec. 28.	Peter Reser Mary Amy	Sarah, b. 10 March, 1817	
	Solomon Westbrook, Jr. Hannah Coolbaugh	Margaret, b. 16 Nov., 1817	
1818.			
Jan. 1.	John W. Van Auken Rachel Rosenkrans	Ensly Roy, b. 14 Dec.,	

DATE	PARENTS	CHILD	WITNESSES
1818.			
Feb. 1.	Solomon Van Etten Catharine Rosenkrans	Dorathy, b. 17 Aug., 1817	
	James Van Gorden Sarah Rosenkrans	Solomon Rosenkrans, b. 8 Dec., 1817	
April 26.	Robert Howy Charaty	James Nyce, b. 2 Oct., 1817	
	Benjamin Stetler Hannah	Hannah, b. 15 March, 1818	
May 24.	Jacob Steel Margaret Berk	John, b. 6 June, 1817	
May 31.	Benjamin Depue Elizabeth Blizzard	James Van Campen, b. 22 Oct., 1817	
July 5.	John G. Hantze Fina Hagerty	John Gottlob, b. 19 Jan., 1818	
	Isaac P. Van Gorden Jane Frazure	Solomon Hornbeek, b. 29 Jan.	
	George W. Nyce Elizabetn Shoemaker	Hannah, b. 25 May	
	John Van Etten Mariah Rosenkrans	Mariah, b. 24 Oct., 1816	
	Jacob Reser Rachel Van Gorden	Elizabeth, b. 15 Dec., 1817	
July 12.	Jacob Buss Elizabeth Miller	John, b. 21 March, 1818	
	James Schoonoven Elizabeth Brooks	James, b. 4 July	
June 14.	John Brown Hannah Broadhead	David Decker, b. 19 Feb., 1818	
	Even Bevans Catharine Carmer	Sydney, b. 10 Sept., 1808 John, b. 11 Oct., 1815	
July 15.	Levy Middaugh Margaret Van Auken	Elizabeth, b. 8 May, 1818	
July 19.	John McCane Lucretia Peach	Sally Anne, b. 12 April, 1812	

DATE	PARENTS	CHILD	WITNESSES
1818.			
Aug. 9.	Nathan Emery Cornelia Broadhead	Oliver Perry, b. 6 April, 1818	
	Daniel Ennes Susanna Reser	Catharine, b. 10 June, 1818	
July 19.	John McCane Lucretia Peach	Sharlotte, b. 10 Sept., 1813	
Aug. 23.	Simeon Swartwood Susanna Schoonoven	Susannah, b. 23 March, 1818	
Sept. 13.	Jacob Kettle Mary	Mary Halbert, b. 12 May, 1816	
Sept. 6.	Andrew Van Campen Anna Michael	John Michael, b. 2 Jan., 1818	
	John Garis Susannah Lance	Peter, b. 18 Jan., 1818	
Sept. 20.	John Lattimore Dorothy Van Etten	Solomon Van Etten, 4 July	
Sept. 20.	Cornelius Van Etten Mariah Smith	Hilay, b. 18 Dec., 1817	
1817.			
Oct. 7.	Daniel Shoemaker Mary Taylor Simeon Rosenkrans Sarah Shoemaker	Moses, b. 30 April, 1817 JuliaMariah, b. 16 Sept., 1817	
1818.			
Oct. 18.	[Parents' name not given in original]	Daniel Shoemaker, b. 15 Jan., 1818	Fanny Hetzel for dau. Mary's child
Nov. 17.	John I. Rosenkrans Catharina Van Camp	Cornelia Winecoop, b. 3 Aug., 1818	
1817.			
Nov. 22.	Andrew Hill Elizabeth Garis	Sarah, b. 15 Oct., 1817	
Nov. 29.	William H. Nice Margaret Westbrook	John, b. 10 Aug., 1818	Presented by John and Lenah Nyce
	John T. Quick Mariah Middaugh	Elsey Jane, b. 15 Dec., 1817	

DATE	PARENTS	CHILD	WITNESSES
1817.			
Dec. 15.	Chrisse Bull Catharine Rosenkrans	Hannah Rogers, b. 1 Nov., 1810 Elizabeth Maria, b. 10 June, 1813 Rosenkrans Chrisse, b. 11 June, 1816	
Dec. 27.	Aaron Decker Jane Brokaw	Paul, b. 16 Nov., 1818	
	John Decker, Jr. Margariet Van Auken	Mary, b. 9 Jan., 1818	
1819.			
Jan. 5.	John Resen Peggy Ennes	Elizabeth, b. 31 Oct., 1818	
Jan. 5.	John Van Gelder Phebe Coles	John Jinkins, b, 22 March, 1816 Henry Owins, b. 1 Aug., 1818	
Jan. 31.	Cornelius Van Etten Anna Smith	Margaret, b. 19 Oct., 1818	
	Cornelius Courtright Hannah Steel	Nelly, b. 12 April, 1818	
	Elisha Mapes Elizabeth Reser	Catharine, b. 9 Sept., 1818	
Feb. 14.	John Swartwout Mary Miller	Margaret, b. 7 Sept., 1818	
Feb. 21.	James Van Campen Cecillia Decker	Henry, b. 9 Dec.	
June 27.	Henry Steel, Jr. Susannah Livengood	Elenor, Eveline, twins, b. 25 April, 1819	
	Abraham Steel Eve Livingood	Nicholas Livingood, b. 7 April	
June 22.	John Van Etten Mariah Rosenkrans	Lanah, b. 27 Nov., 1818	
July 11.	Elyah Depuy Jane Depuy	Susan, b. 20 Dec.	

DATE	PARENTS	CHILD	WITNESSES
1819.			
Sept. 5.	John Eylenberg Mary Roberts	George, b. 12 Oct.	
Sept. 12.	William Berk Mary Imson	Cyrus, b. 30 June, 1819	
Sept. 28.	Gilbert Steel Hannah Decker	Catharine, b. 16 Jan., 1819	
	Henry Dewit Rachel Steel	Mariah, b. 25 Feb., 1819	
Oct. 17.	Isaac Steel Catharina Reser	Elenor, b. 8 July	
1820.			
Jan. 23.	Abm. Coolbaugh Margaret Dingman	Susannah, b. 19 May, 1819	Presented by Susannah Coolbaugh
Jan. 30.	Jacob Smith, Jr. Susannah Fruche	Sarah, b. 17 May, 1819	JamesForee,
	George Coss Elizabeth Smith	b. 13 Jan., 1819	
Feb. 13.	Jacob Westbrook Hannah Van Auken	Hannah Jane, b. 30 Dec., 1819	
April 9.	Nathan Emery Cornelia Broadhead	Phebe Jane, b. 10 Feb., 1820	
	Nicholas Broadhead Margaret Owens	Effe, b. 24 Dec., 1819	
	Johonas Decker Sarah Atkins	Amos Atkins, b. 12 Sept., 1818	
	John Henry, Jr. Catharine Steel	John, b. 25 Jan., 1820	
	Jacob Steel Margaret Berk	Sarah, b. 14 Oct., 1819	
	John Westbrook Sarah Broadhead	Richd. Broadhead, b. 8 Feb., 1820	
April 30.	John W. Van Auken Rachel Rosenkrans	Lydia Mariah, b. 4 Dec., 1819	
	John Decker Mary Brokaw	Jane, b. 13 Dec., 1819	
May 11.	Daniel Warner Elizabeth Ayres	Lewis, b. 4 Sept.	
June 11.	Soloman Van Etten Catharine Rosenkrans	Hulda, b. 13 Oct.	
July 2.	Andrew D. Decker Elizabeth Overpeck	Cecilia, b. 15 April, 1819	

DATE	PARENTS	CHILD	WITNESSES
1819.			
Aug. 15.	Abraham Decker Catharine Smith	Mary, b. 19 April, 1819	
1820.			
Aug. —.	Isaac P. Vangorden Jane Frazer	Hannah Jane, b. 20 Nov., 1819	
Sept. 17.	Daniel Van Etten Caty Decker	Cornelia, b. 24 Aug.	
Oct. 1.	Cornelius Court- right Hannah Steel	Mariah, b. 3 Aug., 1820	
Oct. 8.	Solomon Rosen- krans Catharine Van Gor- den	Esther, b. — Feb., 1818	
	James Van Gorden Sarah Rosenkrans John Van Gorden Mary	Elsey, b. 4 Nov., 1819 John Van Gordon, b. 23 July, 1818	Their child by adoption
Oct. 9.	Daniel Seaman Susannah Kneicht	Ira Kintner, b. 29 July, 1817 Isaac Nelson, b. 1 July, 1820	
Nov. 26.	Solomon West- brook, Jr. Hannah Coolbaugh Wm. H. Nyce Margaret West- brook	John Cool- baugh, b. 24 May, 1820 Solomon Westbrook, b. 28 Sept., 1820	
	Frederic McCarty Rachel Cole	Gideon, b. 27 Jan., 1817 Nelson, b. 4 July, 1819	
1815.			
Aug. 26.		Philip, b. 8 May, 1815	
1821.			
Jan. 6.	James McCarty Jane Van Auken	Philip, b. 26 April, 1818 John, b. 28 May, 1819	
Jan. 21.	Eleasor Mapes Elizabeth Reaser	Mary, b. 8 July, 1820	

DATE	PARENTS	CHILD	WITNESSES
1821.			
May 27.	Rodolves Smith Sarah Akle	Hannah, b. 4 Nov., 1820	
June 12.	Jacob Miller Catharine Gunsaules	Samuel Gunsaules, b. 8 May, 1812	
June 17.	Abraham Steel Effy Livengood	Solomon, b. 23 Feb., 1821	
July 8.	John Bedell on his own confession		
July 15.	Martin W. Dingman Bellinda Hornbeck	Priscilla Mariah, b. 17 Oct., 1820	
Aug. 12.	John Nyce, Jr. Mariah Van Campen	Elenor, b. 1 Jan., 1821	John Nyce, Lenah Westbrook
	Jacob Reser Rachel Van Gorden	Jemimah, b. 15 March	
	John Resen Margaret Ennes	Sarah, b. 18 July	
Aug. 19.	Thomas Decker Susannah Shoemaker	Sarah Anne, b. 7 Nov., 1812	
	Samuel Shoemaker Margaret Chambers	Mary Anne, b. 19 July, 1820	
	Leavitt B. Bristol Seleche Decker	John Decker, b. 22 June, 1821	
	Jacob J. Van Auken Hannah Brooks	Jane, b. 20 April	
	John Decker, Jr. Margaret Van Auken	Bellinda, b. 3 Feb., 1820	
	Aaron Decker Jane Brokaw	James Force, b. 20 June, 1821	
Sept. 9.	John Van Etten, Jr. Catharine Ennes	Mary Margaret, b. 17 Oct., 1820	
Oct. 14.	Andrew Van Campen Anna Michael	Sarah, b. 30 July, 1820	
	Moses Shoemaker Sarah Van Campen	Henry, b. 5 April, 1821	
Oct. 14.	Andrew Sharrer Elizabeth Smith	Susannah Smith, b. 4 Aug.	
Dec. 2.	Nicholas Broadhead Margaret Owens	Joannah, b. 28 Nov.	Effy Broadhead

DATE	PARENTS	CHILD	WITNESSES
1821.			
Dec. 9.	Abraham Decker Catharine Smith	James Van Campen, b. 10 Sept.	
	John Depue, Jr. Mary Van Gorden	Caty Anne, b. 6 Oct.	
	William Overfield Sarah Coolbaugh	Washington, b. 12 Aug., 1818 Sarah Van Campen, b. 17 March, 1820	
Dec. 7.	John Coolbaugh Mary Ilenberger	Andrew Jackson, b. 24 May, 1821	
1822.			
Jan. 6.	Moses W. Coolbaugh Mary Nice	William Findley, b. 1 July, 1821	
	John Eylenbergh Mary Roberts	Elizabeth Jane, b. 15 April	
	John Shoemaker Mary Gunsaules	Catharine, b. 18 July, 1818 Sarah, b. 18 Jan., 1821	
	Henry Decker Mary Swartwood	Wilson Monroe, b. 15 July, 1819 Hannah Mifflin, b. 8 Sept., 1821	
	James Schoonover Elizabeth Brooks	Rodolvus, b. 29 Oct., 1821	
Feb. 3.	John Jinnings Sarah Overpeek	Mehaly Maria Van Auken, b. 19 July, 1821	
	George Overpeck Merey Chitister	Susannah Van Campen, b. 21 June, 1821	
March 31.	John W. Van Auken Rachel Rosenkrans	Hanna Jane, b. 8 June, 1821	
April 1.	John Brown Hannah Broadhead	Henry Marvin, b. 9 Feb., 1820	
April 21.	James McCarty, Jr. Jane Van Auken	Jacob Van Auken, b. 22 May, 1815	

DATE	PARENTS	CHILD	WITNESSES
1822.	Aaron Van Auken Mary McCarty	Jane Elizabeth, b. 24 Dec., 1821	
1821. April 28.	Adam Overpeek Elizabeth Mann	Philip, b. 20 Sept.	
1822. April 28.	Joseph Van Auken Catharine Miller	Margaret, b. 12 Nov., 1821	
May 12.	John Van Etten Jr., Mariah Rosenkrans Jacob Warner Elizabeth Van Horn	David, b. 20 Nov,, 1820 Catharine, b. 21 March, 1821	
May 26.	Jacobus Van Auken Hannah Rummerfield	Elizabeth, b. 7 June, 1821	
June 23.	Daniel Schoonover Cornelia Swartwood Manuel Gunsaules Susannah Depue George Peters Margaret Miller Henry Peters Sarah Gunsaulis	Bernardus Swartwood, b. 1 Oct., 1821 Samuel, b. 9 Nov., 1821 Henry, b. 16 Jan., 1821 Else, b. 26 Jan., 1817 Delinda, b. 16 April, 1819 Charles Ridgeway, b. 12 Feb., 1822	
July 21.	John Decker Mary Brokaw Elijah Depuy Jane Depue	Daniel, b. 25 April, 1822 Benjamin, b. 6 Sept., 1821	
Aug. 11.	Thomas P. Gustin Susannah More	Anthony, b. — Oct., 1814	
Oct. 13.	Samuel Shoemaker Margaret Chambers Jacob Miller Catharine Gunsaules	Henry, b. 21 Jan., 1822 Philip, b. 3 June, 1822	
Oct. 27.	Solomon Westbrook, Jr. Hannah Coolbaugh	Hiram, b. 26 July	
Nov. 3.	John Van Gorden Mary James Van Gorden Sarah Rosenkrans	Mariah, b. 4 Sept., 1822 Amanda, b. 9 Feb., 1822	

82

DATE	PARENTS	CHILD	WITNESSES
1822.			
	Peter Berk Catharine Man	Peter, b. 25 May, 1818 Cornelia Van Etten, b. 20 Feb., 1821	
	George G. Golden Mary Magdalen Berk	Bethuel, b. 11 May, 1818 Isaiah, b. 12 May, 1819 Elisha, b. 28 May, 1820	
	John Henry, Jr. Catharine Steel	Simeon, b. 5 April, 1822	
Dec. 8.	Melcher Depue Eliza Gunsaules	Ensy, b. 19 Aug., 1822	
Dec. 21.	James Van Campen Cecillia Decker	Elizabeth, b. 12 May	
Dec. 22.	George Peters Margaret Miller	John, b. 18 Aug.	
	James Smith, deceased Lydia	Simon, b. 31 July, 1814 Jonah, b. 24 Dec., 1816	
Dec. 28.	Nathan Emery Cornelia Broadhead	James Hamilton, b. 10 May, 1822	
	Daniel Ennes Susannah Reser	Elizabeth, b. 28 July, 1821	
Dec. 28.	Johannes Decker Sarah Atkins	Simeon, b. 3 Nov., 1820	
Dec. 29.	Martin W. Dingman Bellinda Hornbeek	Solomon Hornbeck, b. 19 Sept.	
	John Van Gelder Phebe Coles	Cornelius Timpson, b. 8 April, 1820 George, b. 20 Aug., 1822	
1823.			
Feb. 23.	George G. Golden Mary Magdalen Berk	William Nyce, b. 7 Jan., 1823	
May 4.	Event Rosenkrans Mary Smith	Benjamin, b. 31 Dec., 1822	
May 18.	Jacob Westbrook Hannah Van Auken	Laffaryne, b. 15 Feb., 1823	
May 25.	Solomon Westbroek Elizabeth Seafos	John, b. 14 March	
	John Decker, Jr. Margaret Van Auken	Jane, b. 28 Oct., 1822	

DATE	PARENTS	CHILD	WITNESSES
1823.			
	Andrew D. Decker	Elijah, b. 11	
	Elizabeth Overpeck	Dec.	
June 22.	George Overpeck	Elizabeth, b.	
	Massa Chidister	8 May, 1823	
July 6.	Michael Heller	Sarah, b. 5	
	Elizabeth Depue	Oct., 1819	
		Mary Elizabeth, b. 23 Feb., 1822	
	Simeon Swartwood	Charles Ridge-	
	Susannah Schoonover	way, Clarissa, twins, b. 13 Sept., 1822	
July 13.	Cornelius Courtright	Amanda, b. 25 Oct., 1822	
	Hannah Steel		
	Cornelius Van Etten	Amanda, b. 27 May, 1822	
	Anna Smith		
July 27.	Jacob Smith, Jr.	Mary, b. 3	Christian Smith &
	Susannah Fruchey	Feb., 1823	wife Mary Kithaline
Aug. 3.	Moses Coolbaugh	James, b. 29	
	Mary Nyce	Nov.	
Aug. 17.	Leavitt B. Bristol	Mariah, b. 30	
	Seleche Decker	May	
Sept. 1.	Jacob Warner	Lewis, b. 22	
	Elizabeth Van Horn	March	
Sept. 7.	Jacob Steel	Simon, b. 12	
	Margaret Berk	May, 1822	
Aug. 26.	John Van Auken	Persilly Margaret, b. 18 July, 1823	
	Rachel Rosenkrans		
Sept. 12.	Anthony Reser	Isaac, b. 26	
	Jemimah Decker	Nov.. 1819	
		Daniel, b. 2 June, 1822	
Nov. 30.	John Lattimore	John Craig, b.	
	Dorathy Van Etten	15 July, 1823	
	John Van Etten, Jr.	Simeon, b. 20	
	Mariah Rosenkrans	March, 1823	
	Solomon Van Etten	Manuel, b. 11	
	Catharine Rosenkrans	Jan., 1822	
	Daniel Van Etten	Cornelius, b.	
	Catharine Decker	22 July, 1823	
	William Berk	Elemanda, b.	
	Mary Imson	9 Nov.	
Dec. 28.	John J. Linderman	Hannah, b.	
	Rachel Broadhead	11 Oct., 1823	

DATE	PARENTS	CHILD	WITNESSES
1823.			
Dec. 29.	Hontiter Berk Marjory Kettle	William Smith, b. 30 Sept.	
	John Eylenberger Mary Roberts	James Nyce, b. 13 Aug.	
1824.			
Jan. 4.	Benjamin, aged 22 yrs., aged 19 yrs., Elizabeth, aged 17 yrs., Van Gorden James Van Gorden Elizabeth Van Gorden	James, Richard, b. Aug., 1808 Anne, b. Nov., 1810 Samuel, b. Nov., 1812	Baptised on their own profession of faith
Jan. 14.	Richard Bartron Sarah Overpeck	Elizabeth, b. 11 Aug., 1816	Benjamin Imson, Elizabeth Imson, guardians
	Nathaniel Eldrige Dianna Van Gorden	Hannah Nyce, b. 12 Aug., 1821	
1811.			
May —.	John Van Gorden Mary	Lucinda, b. 15 Dec., 1810	
1824.			
Feb. 2.	George Coss Elizabeth Smith	Catharine, b. 11 July, 1823	
Feb. 16.	Jacob J. Van Auken Hannah Brooks	Sarah, b. 21 Aug., 1823	
March 21.	Gilbert Steel Hannah Decker	Hannah Jane, b. 28 Sept., 1823	
May 2.	John V. Coolbaugh Mary Eylenberge William Overfield Sarah Coolbaugh	Abraham, b. 8 Oct. Amiel, b. 19 Jan., 1824	
May 9.	Daniel Warner Elizabeth Ayres	Hannah, b. 24 Aug., 1823	
June 13.	John Westbrook Sarah Broadhead	Jane, b. 22 March, 1824	
June 27.	Rodolvus Smith Sarah Eakle George Peters Margaret Miller Jacobus Van Auken Hannah Rummerfield Abraham Decker Catharine Smith	Julianna, b. 26 Oct., 1823 Daniel, b. 27 Nov., 1823 Sarah, b. 25 Oct. Jason, b. 19 March, 1824	

DATE	PARENTS	CHILD	WITNESSES
1824.			
	John Jinnings Sarah Overpeck	Hannah, b. 1 April, 1824	
July 25.	Joseph Van Auken Catharine Miller	Calvin, b. 4 Nov., 1823	
	Adam Overpeck Elizabeth Mann	Caty Mariah, b. 9 March, 1824	
	Aaron Decker Jane Brokaw	Hiram, b. 25 Dec., 1823	
Sept. 5.	Isaac Steel Leah Decker	Catharine Reser, b. 4 May, 1824	
Oct. 3.	Garret Broadhead, Jr. Cornelia Dingman	Abraham Coolbaugh, b. 6 Aug.	
	Jacob Reser Rachel Van Gorden	Jacob, b. 5 Aug., 1824	
	Michael Shoff Catharine Livingood	John Nicholas, b. 20 May	
Oct. 17.	George Fishler Johanna Van Scoda	Susannah, b. 27 Jan., 1821 John Van Scoda, b. 25 Oct., 1822 Nathaniel, b. 31 Aug., 1824	
	Henry W. Clifford Hannah Schoonover	Mary Green, b. 1 Oct., 1822	
Dec. 6.	Ezekiel Schoonover Barbara Gariss	Leonard, b. 14 Sept., 1810 Hannah Sch., b. 14 Aug., 1815 Ira, b. 10 Oct., 1819	
	William Custard Elizabeth Van Camp	John Van Camp, b. 17 Nov., 1813 Elizabeth, b. 9 July, 1820 Mason, b. 22 Jan., 1824, Cyrus, b. 23 Jan., 1824, twins	
Nov. 14.	Jacob Shutz Susannah Easterline	Caty Anne, b. 1 Sept., 1824	George Shafer, Caty Hempt

DATE	PARENTS	CHILD	WITNESSES
1825.			
Jan. 9.	Moses Van Campen Elizabeth Overfield	Emely, b. 22 Jan., 1813 Susan, b. 17 June, 1815 Sarah Mariah, b. 8 June, 1817 William, b. 14 March, 1819 Jacob S. Thompson, b. 18 Nov., 1823	
1823. Sept. —.	Andrew Van Campen Anna Michael	Moses, b. 12 July, 1823	
1825. Jan. 23.	John Reser Margaret Ennes	Catharine, b. 20 Aug., 1824	
	Simon I. Decker Lanah Mack	Abraham, b. 8 Oct., 1824	
	Elisha Mapes Elizabeth Reser	Philip, b. 12 Sept., 1824	
July 10.	Nathan Emery Cornelia Broadhead	Susan, b. 19 Aug., 1824	
July 24.	Abraham B. Decker Sally Bevans	Jane, b. 18 Feb., 1825	Aaron Decker & wife Jane Brokaw
June 26.	Moses Litts Catharine Seaphos	Mary Anne, b. 16 July, 1823	
	George Wintamute, Jr. Magdalen Staley	David Hunt, b. 31 May, 1824	
Aug. 31.	Solomon Westbrook Hannah Coolbaugh	La Fayette, b. 15 Dec., 1824	
	Henry Decker Mary Swartwood	William Wayne, b. 19 May, 1825	
	Henry Peters Sarah Gunsaules	Mariah Louiza, b. 16 Dec., 1824	
Sept. 4.	Martin W. Dingman Bellinda Hornbeck	Margaret Jane, b. 15 Sept., 1824	
Sept. 18.	George Crouse Margaret Titman	George Wintamute, b. 23 Oct., 1823	

DATE	PARENTS	CHILD	WITNESSES
1825.			
	John Van Auken Anna Depue	Elijah, b. 27 April, 1825	
Oct. 2.	Cornelius Court- right Hannah Steel	Daniel, b. 28 July, 1825	
	James Van Gorden Sarah Rosenkrans	Drusilla, b. 18 July, 1824	
	Gilbert Hover Margaret Blake	Susan, b. 22 July, 1819 John Linder- m a n , b. 6 Feb. 1824	
Oct. 16.	Andrew Van Cam- pen Anna Michael	Abraham, b. 26 July, 1825	
	Samuel Shoemaker Margaret Chambers	Moses Cham- bers, b. 10 June	
	Moses Depue Anna Miller	Daniel, b. 28 March	
	Benjamin Van Gor- den Jane Courtright	Elizabeth, b. 24 March	
Oct. 30.	Frederic McCarty Rachel Cole	Daniel, b. 19 April, 1824	
	Aaron Van Auken Mary McCarty	Joseph M c - Carty, b. 1 Oct., 1823	
	Philip McCarty, Jr. Rachel Van Etten	Cornelius Van Etten, b. 12 July, 1825	
Dec. 25.	Philip Reser Polly Loder	Philip, b. 9 Nov.	John Reser & wife Margaret Ennes
1826.			
April 16.	Abraham Westfall Mary Van Etten	Sarah Jane, b. 15 Jan., 1826	
May 14.	John Rosenkrans Elizabeth Jane	Susannah, b. 11 May, 1825	
	John Henry Catharina Steel	David, b. 12 June, 1825	
May 28.	Abraham Decker Catharine Smith	Caroline, b. 1 March, 1826	
	George Maring Anna Margaret Swartswelder	Margaret, b. 6 March, 1825	
	Andrew D. Decker Elizabeth Overpeek	Reggy Mariah, b. 18 May	

DATE	PARENTS	CHILD	WITNESSES
1826.			
June 11.	Sarah Decker wife of Joseph Hang Andrew Dingman, Jr. Caroline Sayre Soforyne Westbrook Susannah Van Campen	Daniel, b. 12 April, 1826 Mary, b. 13 Jan., 1826 Margaret, b. 9 April	
1819. Aug. 22.	Jacob Warner Elizabeth Van Horn	Henry Arns, b. 24 April, 1819	
1826. July 23.	Jonas Hanna Barbara Man	Mary, b. 13 Jan., 1823 Philip, b. 24 Oct., 1825	
	Simon Heller Sarah Carpenter	Elenor, b. 15 Sept., 1823	
	Samuel Gunsaules Hannah Depue	Samuel, b. 12 Oct., 1823 Sarah, b. 10 Feb., 1826	
	William Overfield Sarah Coolbaugh	Joseph Ritner, b. 19 May, 1826	
	Simeon Swartwood Susannah Schoonover	Andrew Jackson, Oliver Perry, twins, b. 2 March 1826	
	Benjamin Smith, decd. Susannah Quick	Lydia, b. 18 Aug., 1820 James, b. 4 March, 1822 Benjamin, b. 8 Aug., 1824	
	Daniel Schoonover Cornelia Swartwood	Benjamin Franklin, b. 16 Nov., 1825	
	George Peters Margaret Miller	Sarah Anne, b. 10 Jan., 1826	
Aug. 5.	Simon I. Decker Lenah Mack	Isaac Steel, b. 9 March, 1826	
Aug. 20.	Joseph Van Auken Catharine Miller	Elizabeth, b. 12 Nov., 1825	
	Benjamin Hanna Hannah Tack	Mary, b. 19 Jan.	

DATE	PARENTS	CHILD	WITNESSES
1826.			
Sept. 3.	Simeon Rosenkrans Mariah Van Etten	Deborah Ann, b. 13 Oct., 1825	
Sept. 17.	Elijah Depue Jane	Sarah Overfield, b. 2 May, 1826	
Oct. 1.	John Decker, Jr. Polly Heator	Molly, b. 20 Nov., 1825	Child brought for baptism by Mariah Decker
	John Van Etten, Jr. Catharine Ennes	John, b. 9 June, 1826	Brought by his mother
Oct. 15.	Jacob Miller Catharine Gunsaules	Manuel, b. 16 Sept., 1824	
	Jacobus Van Auken Hannah Rummerfield	Chrispaurus, b. 18 Sept., 1825	
Nov. 5.	Evert Rosenkrans Mary Smith	Peggy Mariah, b. 4 Sept., 1826	
Nov. 7.	Nathaniel Eldredge Dianna Van Gorden	Sarah Elizabeth, b. 4 June, 1825	
Nov. 12.	James Van Campen Cecilia Decker	Bellinda, b. 17 Oct.	
Dec. 3.	John Bedell Sally Ann Elyea	Jane, b. 15 Jan., 1826	
Dec. 11.	John Swartwood Mariah Miller	Rimareth, b. 11 Dec., 1822 Barnardus, b. 16 Nov., 1824	
1827.			
Feb. 4.	Jacob Westbrook Hannah Van Auken	Hymen, b. 14 Nov., 1826	
	Melcher Depue Eliza Gunsaules	Sarah, b. 27 June, 1824 Samuel, b. 17 Dec., 1826	
	James Place Susanna Depue	Susannah, b. 7 Nov., 1826	Presented by Elizabeth, wife of Benjamin Depue
	John Meser Sarah Overfield	James Gunsaules, b. 2 May	
Feb. 11.	John Rosenkrans Elizabeth Jayne	Hannah, b. 2 Jan., 1826	
	Jacob Steel Margaret Berk	Jacob, b. 1 Nov., 1825	
	Peter Walter Lenah Van gorden	Moses, b. 21 Jan., 1825	
	James Van Gorden Sarah Rosenkrans	Moses, b. 17 Nov., 1826	
	Isaac Steel Leah Decker	Child's name not given	

DATE	PARENTS	CHILD	WITNESSES
1827.			
April 7.	Jacob Shuttz Susannah Easterline Moses Shoemaker Sarah Van Campen	Sarah, b. 14 March Abraham Van Campen, b. 11 Dec., 1826	
March 14.	John Shoemaker Mary Gunsaules	John Van Campen, b. 24 July, 1825	
	Daniel Laban Susannah Ase	Philip Garis, b. 18 Dec., 1826	
March 18.	Samuel Van Syckel Charity Merit	John Merit, b. 2 Nov., 1821 Letitia Merrit, b. 22 Jan., 1827	
April 1.	John Jinnings, Jr. Sarah Overpeck	Daniel, b. 19 Feb., 1827	
June 17.	Solomon Van Etten Catharine Rosenkrans	Hannah, b. 26 March, 1826	
June 24.	Solomon Westbrook Hannah Coolbaugh Samuel Gunsaules Hannah Depue	Moses W. Coolbaugh, b. 4 Feb., 1827 William Overfield, b. 25 March	
July 1.	Hugh Lattimore, an adult, bapt.		
	John D. Kerrick Peggy Mariah Decker	Child's name not given	
July 15.	Abm. Decker Sarah Bevans Daniel Decker, Jr. Marinda Doty Elisha Mapes Elizabeth Resen	Catharine, b. 10 Aug., 1826 Elijah, b. 22 Jan., 1825 George, b. 25 Nov., 1826	
July 24.	Isaac P. Van Gorden Jane Frazer Peter Reser Mary Amy	Isaac, b. 11 Sept., 1826 Barbary, b. 17 July, 1819 Margaret, b. 22 April, 1821 Daniel, b. 11 May, 1823	
	Nathan Emery Cornelia Broadhead	Hannah Eliza, b. 15 June, 1826	
Sept. 16.	Jonas Hanna Barbary Man	William, b. 24 May, 1827	

DATE	PARENTS	CHILD	WITNESSES
1827.			
	Moses Depue	Nathan, b. 10	
	Anna Miller	May, 1827	
Aug. 3.	Hugh Lattimore	Joseph Curtright, b. 21 Jan., 1816 William, b. 16 March, 1818 Charles, b. 30 March, 1820 Hannah Mariah, b. 12 May, 1822 GeorgeWashington, b. 11 May, 1827	
Aug. 19.	Martin W. Dingman Belinda Hornbeck John Henry Catharine Steel Peter Walter Lenah Van Gorden	Lea Elizabeth, b. 15 May, 1827 Thomas, b. 1 Aug. Elenor Elizabeth, b. 11 May, 1827	
Aug. 26.	John Swartwood Mariah Miller Solomon Westbrook Elizabeth Seafos	Philip, b. 12 Jan., 1827 Child's name not given	
1830.			
Jan. 1.	Moses Shoemaker Sarah Van Campen	John, b. 11 July, 1829	
Jan. 2.	Nicholas Depue Caty Yotter	Moses, b. 16 Oct., 1828	
Jan. 3.	Abraham B. Decker Sarah Bevans	Sarah Eveline, b. 10 Dec., 1828	
1831.			
Jan. 9.	James Van Campen Sarah Pifer Moses Depue Ann Miller	Andries, b. 25 July, 1830 Margaret, b. 25 July, 1829	
May 16.	George Coss Rachel Kittel Thomas Dixon Susannah Snabel	Daniel, b. 28 March, 1830 Mary Ann, b. 2 Aug., 1829	
Dec. 2.	William Smith Elizabeth	Susannah, b. 7 Nov., 1830	
1828.			
June 14.	John W. Van Auken Rachel Rosenkrans	Eveson Wheat, b. 22 Aug., 1828	

DATE	PARENTS	CHILD	WITNESSES
1829.			
	Daniel Smith Barbary	JonasSamuel, b. 29 Feb., 1829	
Dec. 29.	—— Honterberg Marjory	Jacob, b. 20 Oct., 1829	
	Samuel Mood Sarah	Samuel West- brook, b. 25 Aug., 1829	
	Daniel Decker, Jr. Marinda	Levi Van Et- ten, b. 2 Oct., 1829	
1830.			
Feb. 28.	Andrew Dingman Caroline	Evi Sayre, b. 21 Aug., 1829 Susan Eliza- beth, b. 8 Aug., 1827	
	Wm. T. Wilson Hannah	John West- brook, b. 9 Aug., 1829	
	John J. Linderman	Garret Brod- head, b. 13 Oct., 1829	
June 20.	John Eylenberg Mary	Hannah Nyce, Wil- liam Nyce, twins, b. 30 March, 1830	
	Daniel Nyce Balinda	Sara Eliza- beth, b. 22 Feb., 1830	

MARRIAGES.

1741.
July 26. Christophel Dennemarck, y. m., b. at Rosendal, and Lea Swartwood, y. d., b. at Pipeck; both lived at Smithfield

Sept. 7. Adrian Quick, y. m., b. at Minnissinck, and Rachel Dingeman, y. d., b. at Kinderhoock; both live here

Oct. 20. Isaac Van Camp, lived at Smithsfield, Bucks Co., and Lena Rosenkrantz, lived at Walpeck.

1742.
Aug. 11. John Williams, y. m., b. at Briston, Old England, lived at Fishkill, Dutchess Co., and Lea Decker, y. d., b. at Esopus, lived in Bucks Co.

1744.
Sept. 22. Johannes Volckertse, y. m., b. at New York, lived at Smithsfield, and Mally Dodesinck, y. d., b. and lived at Lisabethstown.

1745.
Nov. 17. Adam Dingman, y. m., b. at Horly, and Maritje Van Garden, y. d., b. at Shippekonck; both live here.
April 3. Christiaen Kiersbi, y. m., b. in Germany, and Lisabeth Van Campen, wid. of Hendricus Van Weyen, both live here.
June 8. Jacob Swartwout, y. m., b. at Pynpeck, and Lydia Decker, y. d., b. at Menissinck; both lived at Smithsfield.

1746.
Sept. 10. Johannes Merckel, y. m., b. at Kingston, lived at Smithsfield, and Anna Elizabetha Schnauben, y. d., b. at Punstadt, Germany, lived at Palingskill.
Nov. 7. Andries Reifsmyder, j. m., b. in Hochduytslant, lived at Smithfield, Bucks Co., and Susanna Waller, j. d., b. in New England; m. by J. C. Freyenmuth.

1749.
Feb. 5. Niclaes Brink, j. m., b. at Walpeck, and Catharina Decker, j. d., b. at Rochester, lived at Palingskill.
May 16. Jan Van Garden, j. m., b. at Rochester, and Lisabeth Van der Merkel, j. d., b. at Rochester; both lived at Walpeck.
June 26. Edward Johnston, j. m., b. in England, and Johanna Van Garden, j. d., b. at Metshepeconk; both lived at Walpeck.

1750.
April 8. Cornelis H. Kortrecht, wid. of Tjatje Kortrecht, lived at Walpeck, and Helena Rosekrantz, j. d., b. at Metshepeconk, lived at Smithfield Township.
April 25. Terrenz Devin, wid. of Maritje Kuykendal, lived at Walpach, and Hanna Cole, b. at Rochester, lived at Walpach.
April 23. Juriaen Tappan, wid. of Maria Kortrecht, lived at Kingston, and Susanna Thomas, wid. of John Ray, lived at Smithfield.
May 6. Alexander Van Garden, j. m., b. at Shippeconck, and Annatje Kortrecht, j. d., b. at Rochester; both lived at Smithfield.
Aug. 13. Christiaen Keesbrei, wid. of Elisabeth Van Campen, lived in Bucks Co., and Janneke Van Garden, j. d., b. at Shippeconk, lived at Pachoquarry; m. by J. C. Freyenmuth, aged 29.
Nov. 11. Hendricus Decker, j. m., b. at Menisink, and Annatje Kermer, j. d., b. at Walpach; both lived at Walpeck.

1751.
Feb. 26. Jacobus Westfael, wid. of Sophia Van Aken, and Jannetjen Decker, j. d., b. at Upper Smithfield; both lived at Upper Smithfield.
Feb. 18. Eliphay Van Aken, j. m., b. at Esopus, and Elenor Forbus, j. d., b. at Jerlant, lived at Upper Smithfield.

1752.
March 1. Daniel Kortrecht, Jr., b. at Mormel, and Russie Van Aken, j. d., b. at Upper Smithfield; both lived at Upper Smithfield.

Aert Van Weyen, wid. of Temperenz Gladden, lived at Walpeck, and Cornelia Kermer, j. d., b. at Nameneck.

Johannes Decker, j. m., b. at Minnisink, lived at Upper Smithfield, and Mary Van Tilburgh, j. d., b. at Burlington, Conn., lived at Walpeck.

Jacob Van Campen, wid. of Rachel Decker, lived at Walpeck, and Sara Decker, j. d., b. at Warrit.

June 19. Johannes Bash, j. m., b. at Walpeck, lived at Walpeck, and Mary Johnson, j. d., b. at Philadelphia.

June 28. Hendericus Scoonhoven, j. m., b. at Walpeck, and Rachel Schoonhoven, j. d., b. at Neder Smithsfield, lived at Walpeck.

1752.
Aug. 19. Louwrenz Decker, j. m., b. and lived on the Drowned Lands, and Lena Decker, j. d., b. and lived at Upper Smithfield.

1753.
April 15. Jacobus Van Garden, j. m., b. at Minnisinck, and Catharine Kortrecht, wid. of Abram Van Campen, both live at Upper Smithfield.

Nov. 5. Andries Cole, wid. of Sara Schoonmaker, lived at Walpeck, and Christina Kermer, j. d., b. at Kingston.

Nov. 17. Jan Van Campen and Sara Dupuy, by licence from his Excellency, Gov. Belcher.

Dec. 24. Bernardus Swartwout, j. m., b. at Machackimach, lived at Upper Smithfield, and Lisabeth Brinck, j. d., b. and lived at Walpack.

Dec. 26. Pieter Conterman, j. m., b. in Hooghduytschlant, lived at Palmyskill, and Catharina Hover, j. d., b. in Hooghduytschlant, lived at Walpeck.

1754.
March 31. Benjamin Swartwout, j. m., b. at Pinpeck, lived at Upper Smithfield, and Cornelia Brinck, j. d., b. at Shippekonk.

June 4. Thomas Swartwoud, b. at Pinpeck, lived at Upper Smithfield, and Elisabeth Ennes, b. at Mormel.

1755.
Jan. 12. Benjamin Dupuy, j. m., b. at Rochester, and Cathrina Van Campen, j. d., b. at Peckoqually; both lived at Peckoqually.

1768. Here end marriages by Rev. Mr. Fryenmoet.

Aug. 8. William Cortregt, son of Hendrick Cortregt, and Sarah Handshaw, daughter of James Handshaw; m. by Thomas Romien.

1869.
May 6. Abram Middag and Susanna Lester.
May 19. Johannes D. Westbrook and Maria Brink.
These in writing of Dom. Romien.

Minisink Machackemeck Church Records

MACHACKEMECK BURYING GROUND, PORT JERVIS, N. Y.

RECORDS OF BAPTISMS OF THE REFORMED CHURCH AT MACHACKEMECK (DEERPARK).

BAPTISMS.

DATE	PARENTS	CHILD	WITNESSES
1716.	By D°. Petrus Vas		
Aug. 19.	Stephanus Ditsoort Sara Hoornbeeck	Jacobus	Willem Provoost, Eva Swartwout
	Jacob Kuyckendal Sara Westfael	Jacobus	Abel Westfael, Annatjen Hoornbeeck
	Joost Hoornbeeck Eegje Van Vliet	Judic	Jan Decker, Femmetje Decker
	Jacobus Koddebeck Margriet Provoost	Abraham	Juriaen Westfael, Maritje Koddebeek
1717.			
June 5.	Jacob Decker Anna Kortrecht	Lea	Jacobus Swartwoud, Jr., Femmetje Decker
	Teunis Quick Claertje de Hooges	Benjamin	Jacob Westfael, Margriet De Duytser
	Cornelis Kuykendael Maritje Westfael	Johannes	Abel Westfael, Antje Bogaert
1718.			
Jan. 29.	Thomas Quick Grietje Decker	Margrita	Gerrit Decker, Geertje Decker
	Jan Middagh Geertje Klearwater	Abraham	Hendrick Van Garden, Malletje Middagh
	onecht Cathrina Hoksen	Elizabeth	Jacobus Swartwoudt, Reymerig Quick
	Juriaen Westfael Maritje Koddebeck	Benjamin	Hendrick Decker, Jesyntje Swartwout
1719.			
Jan. 28.	Jacob Westfael Margriet de Duyser	Maria	Nicael Westfael, Margriet de Duyser
	Abel Westfael Antje Bogaert	Sara	Stephanus Ditsoort, Sara Hoornbeeck

DATE	PARENTS	CHILD	WITNESSES
1719.			
Jan. 28.	Mattheus Kuykendael Jannetje Westfael	Petrus	Petrus Kuykendal, Reymerig Quick
	Jacob Kuykendal Sara Westfael	Dina	Saloman Dayis, Reymerig Quick
	Johannes Quick Bregje Middagh	Geertje	Jan Decker, Antje Quick
1737.	(Probably by Dom. G. W. Mancius)		
Aug. 23.	Jacob dekker, Jun. Rachel Hoorenbeek	Lydia	jurge Westphal, blandina De Wit
	Gerret brink Sara ditsoort	Geertje	john De Wit, Lena van Gorden
	Dyrk Wessebroek Jenneke van Keuren	Johannes	johannes Wessebrock, Antje Rosa
	Henrick dekker Annaatje ditsoort	Elias	Harme van Garde, Elsje Koetebek
Aug. 24.	Pieter Kuikendal Femmetje Dekker	Jacob	johannes Dekker, lisabeth de Wit
	Jacobus Rosekrans Sara Dekker	Daniel	thomas Dekker, jenneke Van Nieuwegan
1738.			
May 30.	Cornelis Wessebrock Antje Rosa	Petrus	Johannes Wessebrock, Antje Rosa
	Sammuel Schamers Sara Kortrecht	Lisabeth	Cornelis Kortrecht, Christina Rosekrans
	Arie van Fredenburg Sara Rosekrans	Blandina	Jurge Westval, Blandina De Wit
	Dirk quik Apolonie van Gorde	Jenneke	Gysbert van Gorde, Maria Cool
	Abraham Kermer Sara Schammers	Lydia	Jacob van Nette, Antje Wessebrock
	Willem Kortrecht Margriet Jansen	Elias	Johannes Westval, Mareitje Koettebek
	Henrick Haldrin Annatje Dekker	Lea	Broer Dekker, Antje van Nette
	Hue pue Lena Brink	Margriet	Jacobus Ditsoort, Abigail Bel
May 31.	Salomon Davids, Jun. Lea Dekker	Beletje	Salomon Davids, Beletje Quik

DATE	PARENTS	CHILD	WITNESSES
1738.			
May 31.	Henrick Henrickse Kortrecht Margriet Dekker	Lea	Johannes Dekker, Lisabeth De Wit
	Henrich Kuikendal Lisabeth Cool	Catryntje	David Cool, Leonora Westval
	Gysbert Bogard Catharina dekker	Ezechiel	Henrick Dekker, Anna Ditsoort
	petrus Dekker MagdalenaOsterhout	Catharina	Salomon Dekker, Femmetje Dekker
	Jacob Middag Sara Kuikendal	Ephraim	Adrian Quik, Lisaabeth Westval
Oct. 31.	Abraham Van Aaken Jannetje De Wit	Lydia	Petrus Dekker, Lena Oosterhout
	David Cool Lenora Westval	Catryntje	Henrick Kuikendal, Lisabeth Cool
	Cornelis Krom Rebecca Schoonhoven	Lydia	Henrick Krom, Lydia Krom
	Thomas Schoonhoven Maria Westval	Cornelis	Cornelis Krom, Rebecca Schoonhoven
	Johannis Wessebrock Magdalena Wessebrock	Anthonie	Anthonie Wessebrock, Aeltje Van Oetten
	Willem Kottebek Jacomyntje Elting	Abraham	Abraham Kottebek, Noemi Kottebek
Nov. 1.	Jan Van Oetten Marretje Westval	Helena	Benjamin Westval, Lena van Oetten
	Johannes van Garden Margriet Quik	Elisabeth	Willem Ennes, Lisabeth Quik
	Lambertus Brink Rachel van Gorden	Jenneke	Isaac van Aaken, Rachel De Wit
	Arie Kortrecht Lisabeth Cool	Lydia	Cornelis Brink, Maria Cool
	Gysbert van Garden Maria Cool	Jenneke	Cornelis Cool, Sara Westval
	Johannes Kortrecht Margriet Dennemarke	John	Johannes Westval, Apolonie Kortrecht

DATE	PARENTS	CHILD	WITNESSES
1738.			
Nov. 1.	Cornelis van Aaken Hester Relje	Gideon	Jan van Oetten, Marretje Westval
	Cornelis Brink Maria Cool	Maria	Gysbert van Garden, Maria Cool
	Johannes Brink Lena Cool	Maria	
1739.			
May 29.	Aard Middag Ariaantje van Oetten	Jannetje	Jacobus Koettebek, Jannetje Wessebroek
	Matheus Brink Abigail Bel	Petrus	Andries Dekker, Divertje Maul
	Anthonie Benschoten Margriet Wels	Antje	Henrick Janse Kortrecht, Gerretje Benschoten
	Andries Cool Sara Schoonmaker	Catharina	Henrik Dekker, Catharina Schoonmaker
	Lieur Kuikendal Lena Consales Duk	Joseph	Joseph Consales, Sara Consales
	Broer Dekker Antje van Oetten	Elisa	Abraham Kermer, Sara Schammers
	Henrich Van Garden Lenora Dekker	Lena	Willem Cool, Mareitje Koettebek
	Cornelis Devoor Lena Westval	David	David Devoor, Eiisabeth Kermer
May 29.	Johannes Hoogteeling Marretje Horenbeek	Petrus	Johannes van Garden, Margriet Quik
	Jochem Schoonmaker Rachel van Gorden	Isaac	Bastian Kortrecht, Rachel Dekker
	Jacob van Oetten Antje Wessebroek	Dirk	Dirk Wessebroek, Jenneke van Keuren
	Lenert Cool Junior Sarah van Gorden	Rachel	Harme Rosekrans, Arriaantje Osterhout
	Alexander van de Winkel Antje Rosekrans	Antje	Johannes Wessebroeck, Antje Rosa
	Isaac van Aaken Rachel de Wit	Joseph	Cornelis Wessebroek, Antje Rosa
	Johannes Westval Apolonia Kortrecht	Jurian	Jurian Tappen, Maria Kortrecht

DATE	PARENTS	CHILD	WITNESSES
1739.			
May 29.	Evert Horenbek Lena Koettebek	Benjamin	Benjamin Koettebek, Naomi Koettebek
	Andries Dekker Divertje Maul	Sara	Stephanus Ditsoort, Sara Horenbeek
	Willem van Gorden Antje Fredenburg	Gonda	Harme van Gorden, Elsje Koettebek
	Willem Ditsoort Sara Dekker	Bernhardus	Bernhardus Swartwoud, Margriet Dekker
	Abel Westval Antje Bogard	Lydia	Jurye Westval, Blandina De Wit
	Gerret Brink Maria Ditsoort	Maria	Lambertus Brink, Rachel van Garden
	Philip Teeler Maria Bosch	Samson	
May 30.	Gerardus van Niuwegen Jannetje de Wit	Tjaadje	Pieter Gemaar, Tjaadje de Wit
	Barent Mollin Glaasje Andriesse	Margriet	Thomas Dekker, Jannetje van Niuwegen
	in onegt Catharina Clark	Mardochia	Willem Koettebek, Jacomyntje Elting
	Therrens Dieven Marretje Kuikendal	Jacobus	Jacobus Swartwoud, Antje Gemaar
Oct. 30.	Jacob Bogard Nelletje Kuikendal	Jeseintje	Jan Vliet, Jeseintje Swartwoud
	Jan Vliet Jeseintje Swartwoud	Jacobus	Jacobus Swartwoud, Antje Gemaer
	Henrick Kuikendel Elizabeth Cool	Femmetje	Pieter Kuikendel, Femmetje Dekker
	Pieter Kuikendal Femmetje Dekker	Jacob	Johannis Deker, Elizabeth De Wit
Oct. 31.	Dirk Wessebroek Jenneke van Keuren	Tjerk van Keuren	Josaphat Du Bois, Tjaadje van Keuren
	Samuel Schammers Sara Kortregt	Wilhelmus	Henrich Kortregt, Jr., Jannetje Ennes
	William Waard Mareitje Dekker	Hermanus Dekker	Hermanus Dekker, Christina Keiser
	Pieter van Garden Margriet Dekker	Hester	Cornelis van Aaken, Hester Relje
	Gysbert van Kampen Sara Dekker	Martinus	Willem van Garden, Helena van Aaken

DATE	PARENTS	CHILD	WITNESSES
1739.			
Oct. 31.	Johannes Cool Pieternella van Aaken	Catharina	Josias Cool, Lena van Aaken
	Willem Kortregt Margriet Janse	Willem	Laurent Kortregt, Sara Teneik
	Willem Cool Mareitje Koettebek	Petrus	Henrich Kortregt, Gerretje Benschoten
	Henrick Cornelis Kortregt Jannetje Ennest	William Ennest	William Ennest, Lisabeth Quik
	Benjamin Dekker Helena Kortregt	Daniel	Salomon Dekker, Lena van Oetten
	Harme van Garde Elsje Koettebek	Benjamin	Harme Rosekrans, Ariaantje Osterhout
	Moses Joons	Hanna	Matheus Brink, Abigail Bel
1740.			
June 17.	Thomas Dekker Janneke van Niuwegen	Joris	Joris Davids, Naomi Koettebeck
	Johannes Kortregt Margriet Dennemark	Christoffel	Johan Christoffel Dennemarken, Christina Elizabeth Bernhardin
	Abraham Louw Dina Koettebeck	Jannetje	Harme van Garden, Elsje Koettebeck
	David Cool Eleonora Westval	Josias	Josias Cool, Mareitje Kemmel
	Bastian Kortregt Rachel Dekker	Rachel	Henrich Henrichse Kortregt, Margriet Dekker
	Jacobus Rosekrans Sara Dekker	Geertje	Simon Westval, Geertje Westval
	Johannes van Garden Margriet Quik	Jacobus	Jacobus Quik, Jannetje Wessebroek
	Cornelis Cool Sara Westval	Johannes	Johannes Westval, Sara Cool
	Hue Pue Dina Brink	Pieter	Thomas Schoonhoven, Maria Westval
	Abraham Kermer Sara Schammers	Jacobus	Broer Dekker, Annetje van Oetten
	Jacob Dekker Jun Rachel Horenbeek	Cornelis	Abel Westval, Antje Bogard
	Petrus Dekker Magdalena Osterhout	Josias	Thomas Dekker, Janneke Van Ninwegen

DATE	PARENTS	CHILD	WITNESSES
1740			
June 17.	Pieter Gemaar Tjaadje Dewit	Jacob de Wit	Gerardus van Ninwegen, Jannetie Dewit
	Bernhardus Swartwoud Margriet Dekker	Lisabeth	Arie Kortregt, Lisabeth Cool
	Arie Kortregt Lizabeth Cool	Elisabeth	Samuel Swartwoud, Lisabeth Gemaar
	Lambertus Brink Rachel van Garden	Arie	Arie Fredenburg, Sara Rosekrans
	Jan van Oetten Marrietje Westval	Jacob	Jacob van Oetten, Antje Wessebroek
June 18.	Salomo Davids Junior Lea Dekker	Daniel	Daniel Kuikendal, Lizabeth van Aaken
	Jacobus Dekker Neeltje Ditsoort	Leaatje	Salomo Davids Jun., Lea Dekker
	Johannes Dekker Lena Quik	Wilhelmus	William Ditsoort, Sara Dekker
Sept. 19.	Andries Dingemans Cornelia Kermer	Cornelia	Charles Van Weyen, Elizabeth Kermer
	Johannes Westbroek, Junior Magdalena Westbroek	Johannes	Hannes Westbroek, Antje Rosa
	Jan Bomen Anna Middag	Margarit	Terrins Devin, Marytje Kuykendal
	Andries Dekker Divertje Moul	Andreas	Jan Waert, Geertje Westfael
	Hendrick Hendrickson Kortrecht Margriet Dekker	Lidia	Abraham Kortrecht, Margriet Kuykendal

Aenteekeninge der gedoopte Kinderen in de gemeyntje van Menissing door den dienst van Joh: Casparus Freyenmuth, Predikant aldaer beginnende synen dienst met den 7th dag Juny., 1741.

Translation:

Record of the baptized children in the congregation of Menissing through the ministration of JOH: CASPARUS FREYENMUTH, preacher there, commencing his ministry on the 7th day of June, 1741.

1741.
Maendt dag

June 7.	Cornelis Brinck Maria Cool	Hermanus	Andreas Cool, Lisabeth Cool
	Mattheus Brinck Ebbegken Bel	Jan	William Kortregt, Margrit Janson
	Gisbert Van Garden Maria Cool	Catharina	William Decker, Neelgje Roos

DATE	PARENTS	CHILD	WITNESSES
1741.			
June 7.	Anthony Van Benschoten Margrita Wels	Cornelis	Cornelis Elmendorf, Engelje Heerenmans
	William Enness Lizabeth Quick	Cornelia	Lammert Brinck, Cornelia Viervan
	Derrick Quick Plone van Garden	Rachel	Lambart Brinck, Rachel van Garden
	Hannes Nethier Gertje Decker	Margaritje	Nicolas Best, Margareth Best
	William Ditschious Sara Decker	Sara	Salomon Decker, Neelgje Decker
June 28.	Johannes Westfael Apollonia Kortregt	Johannes	Gisbert Roos, Geertje Westfael
Sept. 6.	Johannes Hooghdeylen Maritje Hoornbeek	Jonathan	Sebastian Kortrecht, Racheltje Decker
Oct. 9.	Johannes Kool Pieternella van Aeken	Abraham	Abraham van Aeken, Lisabeth van Aeken
Nov. 11.	William Kortrecht Margriet Janson	Josias	Cornelis Cool Kortrecht, Margriet Westfael
Nov. 24.	Jacob Bogart Pieternella Keukendal	Sara	Johannes Westfael, Lea Westfael
	Abraham Middagh Lea van Aeken	Samuel	Benjamin Westfael, Johanna van Aeken
1742?			
Feb. 7.	Herman van Garden Elsje Cuttenbeck	Daniel	Isaeck van Aeken, Rachel De Wit
	Benjamin Westfael Annatje van Aeken	Maria	William Cool, Maria Cuttenbeck
March 21.	Broer Decker Antje van Netten	Elias	Hannes Westbroeck, Antje Rosa
	Lambart Brinck Rachel van Garden	Daniel	Hannes Westbroeck, Antje Rosa
May 16.	Benjamin Decker Lena Kortrecht	Lena	Cornelis Kortrecht, Cathrina Rosenkrantz
	Aert Middagh Ariantje van Etten	Martinus	Benjamin Westbroeck, Maria Westbroeck
July 25.	Jan van Etten Maritje Westfael	Daniel	Daniel Westfael, Margarita Westfael

DATE	PARENTS	CHILD	WITNESSES
1742?			
July 25.	Jacob Decker, Rachel Hoornbeck	Cathrina	Daniel Westfael, Margarita Westfael
Oct. 17.	Abraham Kermer Sarah Schammers	Angontje	Samuel Schammers, Sara Kortrecht
1743.			
May 3.	Jurk Wessebroek Jenneke Van Keuren	Lisabeth	Jacob van Oetten, Antje Wessebroek
	Antonie Benschoten Margriet Wels	Jenneke	Turk Wessebroek, Jenneke van Keuren
	Gerret Brink Maria Ditsoort	Lydia	
	Peter Gemaar Tjaadje De Wit	Ezechiel	Antonie Wessebroek, Aaltje Van Oetten
	Thomas Schoonhoven Maria Westval	Sara	Joel Quik, Sara Westval
	Johannes Dekker Lena Quick	Debora	Johannes Kuikendal, Debora Schoonhoven
	Arie Kortregt Lisabeth Cool	Catharina	Benjamin Wessebroek, Catharina Dekker
	William Ennes Elisabeth Quik	Benjamin	Benjamin Quik, Heilje Wessebroek
	Willem Van Garden Antje Fredenburg	Arie	Gysbert Van Garden, Maria Cool, his wife
	Gysbert van Garden Maria Cool	Lena	Salomon Wels, Lena Dekker
	Jacobus Quik Maria Wessebrock	Thomas	Thomas Quik, Margriet Dekker
	Andries Dekker Divertje Maul	Divertje	Willem Kortregt, Margriet Janse
	Henrich Kortregt Margriet Dekker	Daniel	Jacobus Dekker, Neeltje Ditsoort
	Henrick Halring Annaatje Dekker	Laurenz	Laurentz Dekker, Rachel Dekker
	Abraham van Kampen Susanna Depue	Moses	Moses Depue, Marretje Depue
	Cornelis van Aaken Hester Denis	Jannetje	Jacob van Oetten and wife, Antje Wessebroek

Baptized by Dº. G. W. Manzius.

DATE	PARENTS	CHILD	WITNESSES
1743.			
Oct. 17.	Evert Hoornbeeck Lena Cuttenbeck	Lydia	Abraham Kuttenbeck, Lydia Westfael
	Hugh Pugh Lena Brinck	Isaac	Isaac van Aaken, Rachel Dewit
	Cornelis Krom Rebecca Schoonhoven	Annatje	[Jaems or] Joris Davis, Debora Schoonhoven
	Johannes Hooghteeling Maretje Hoorrenbeeck	Maria	Cornelis Krom, RebeccaSchoonhoven
	Terrins Devin Maritje Kuykendal	Antje	Hester Swartwout, Gerardus ——
	Daniel? Cortreght?	[Page torn.]	
	Gerardus van Nimwegen Jannetje De Wit	Cornelis?	William Kuttenbeck, Jacomyntje Elting
Oct. 18.	Dirk Quik Apolonie Van Garden	Benjamin	Benjamin Quik, Lena Quik
	Benjamin Westval Annaatje Van Aaken	Cornelis	Cornelis van Aaken, Sara van Aaken
	Johannes Cool Pieternella van Aaken	Josephat	Josephat dubois, Tjaadje van Keuren
April 23.	Joh: Casp: Freyenmuth Lena van Etten	Dorothea	Jan Van Etten, Maritje Westfael his wife
	Cornelius Westbroeck Antje Rosa	——	Derrick Westbroeck, Jannetje van Keuren his wife
	Jan Van Etten Maritje Westfael	Cathrina	Cornelis van Etten, Cathrina Westbroeck
	William Waert Maritje Decker	Benjamin	Jan van Etten, Maritje Westfael, his wife
April 26.	Julick Borck Maria Bowman	John	John Bouman, Abigail Bel
	John Bouman Hannah Middagh	Hanna	Julick Borgh, Abigail Bel

("door my onwettigh V. D. M." *i. e.*, by me unlawfully, minister of the Word. The following baptisms to Oct. 3, 1742, are crossed by pencil marks. The baptisms are called "unlawful" probably from difficulties about authority from Coetus.)

| April 14. | Thomas Schoonhoven
Maria Westfael | Debora | Cornelis Westfael, Catharina Cole |

DATE	PARENTS	CHILD	WITNESSES
1743.			
April 14.	Abraham Wildfield Maria Welsch	Thomas	Thomas Decker, Jannetje van Nimwegen
	Gerardus van Nimwegen Jannetje De Witt	Jacob	Samuel Swartwood, Lisabeth Gemar
April 14.	Casparus Kimber Femmetje Williamse	Petrus	Jacob Westfael, Margariet de Dutscher
	Cornelis Krom Rebecca Schoonhoven	Maria	Jorian Westfael, Lisabeth Westfael
	Jan Van vliet Jesyntje Swartwood	Maria	Jacob Westbroek, Maria Westbroek
	Josias Cole Maria Kimber	Wilhelmus	William Cole, Maria Cuttebeck
	torn	torn	Abraham Kortrecht, —— ka Kuikendal
Aug. 23.	Evert Hoornbeeck Lena Cuttebeck	Maria	Ludwig Hoornbeeck, Maria Hoornbeeck
Oct. 25.	Abraham van Aeken Jannetje De Witt	Blandina	Jory Westfael, Blandina De Wit
	Jacobus Decker Neeltje Ditsoort	Jonathan	William Ditsoort, Sara Decker
	Aaron Vredenburgh Sara Rosenkranz	Lydia	Mattheus Vredenburgh, Lydia Westfael
1742.			
Jan. 17.	Willem Cuttebeck Jacomyntje Etten	Benjamin	Evert Hoornbeeck, Lena Cuttebeck,
	David Cool Leonora Westfael	Margrietje	Cornelis Westfael, Lizabeth Westfael
March 7.	Hendrick Kuykendal Elisabeth Cole	Hendricus	Daniel Kuyckendal, Catharina Cole
	Thomas Decker Jannetje van Nimwegen	Petrus	Pieter Kuyckendal, Femmetje Decker
	Jacobus Rosenkranz Sara Decker	Salomon	Salomon Decker, Catharina van Aeken
Oct. 3.	Mattheus Brinck Abigail Bell	Jacobus	
1744.	BAPTIZED BY Dº. G. W. MANZIUS.		
April 23.	Johannes Westfael Apollonia Kortrecht	Lisabeth	Johannes Decker, Lisabeth De Witt

DATE	PARENTS	CHILD	WITNESSES
1744.			
April 23.	Simon Westfael Jannetje Westbroek	Jury	Jury Westfael, Blandina De Witt
	Salomon Davis, Jun Lea Decker	Joel	Joel Quick, Lisabeth van vliet
	Abraham Van Aeken Jannetje De Witt	Sara	Arie Vredenburgh, Sara Rosenkranz
	Jacobus Kuttebeck Neeltje Decker	Jacobus	Abraham Louw, Dina Kuttebeck
	Jan van vliet Jesyntje Swartwood	Catharina	Philip Swartwood, Elizabeth Swartwood
	Willem Kortrecht Margriet Jansen	Daniel	Daniel Westfael, Lisabeth Mey

"Door my J. C. Fryenmuth V D M beginnende Synen wittigen dienst."

By me J. C. Fryenmuth, minister of the word of God beginning his lawful service.

Dec. 23.	Jacobus Rosenkranz Sara Decker	Johannes	Hendrick Decker, Annatje Decker
	Josias Cole Maria Kemmel	Femmetje	William Cool, Jun., Catharina Cole
	Abram Middagh Lena van Aeken	Daniel	Cornelius van Aeken, Sarah Westbroek
	Hendrick Kuykendal Lisabeth Cole	Willem	Willem Cole, Maria Kuttebeck
	Thomas Decker Jannetje van Nimwegen	Alida	Hannes Decker, Lisabeth De Witt
	Joris Davis Debora Schoonhoven	Samuel	Samuel van vliet, Lizabeth van vliet
	Johannes Westbroeck Magdalena Westbroeck	Antje	Benjamin Westbroeck, Helltje Westbroeck
	Jacob Bogaert Nelly Kuykendal	Lizabeth	Johannes Kuykendal, Lisabeth Decker
	Andries Decker Dievertje Maul	Christoffel Maul	Johannes Maul, Lisabeth Maul
1745. Jan. 6.	Broer Decker Antje van Etten	Cornelis	Cornelis Westbroeck, Antje Rosa, his wife
	Jacobus Quick Maria Westbroeck	Johannes	Johannes Westbroeck, Antje Rosa, his wife

DATE	PARENTS	CHILD	WITNESSES
1745.			
Jan. 6.	Mattheus Brinck Abigail Bell	Samuel	Johannes Casparus, Freyenmuth, V.D. M., Magdalena van Etten, his wife
	Bastiaen Kortrecht Rachel Decker	Sara	Abraham van Aeken, Jr., Sara van Aeken
	Hannes Bogaert Sara Hooghteeling	Hannatje	Cornelis Westfael, Hannatje Westfael
	Cornelis Brinck Maria Cole	Lenart Cole	Aert Middagh, Ariaentje van Etten, his wife
Jan. 20.	David Cole Leonora Westfael	Sara	William Cole, Jr., Sara Cole
	Petrus Decker Lena Oosterhout	Annatje	Daniel Kuyckendal, Annatje Decker
	Willem Kuttebeck Jacomynte Elten [Eltinge]	Roelof Elten	Gerardus van Nimwegen, Jannetje De Witt, his wife
Feb. 3.	Benjamin Decker Lena Kortrecht	Samuel	William Ennes, Elisabeth Quick, his wife
	Antony Bunschoten Margriet Wells	Jesyntje	Pieter Van Aeken, Russie Dami, his wife
March 24.	Hendrick Hendrickse Kortrecht Margriet Decker	Moses	Bastian Kortrecht, Rachel Decker, his wife
	Gysbert van Garden, Jun Rachel Kortrecht	Petrus	Alexander van Garden, Tjaetje Kortrecht
April 21.	Herman Rosenkranz Arriaentje Oosterhout	Jacobus Rosenkranz	Jacobus Rosenkranz, Sarah Decker, his wife
May 19.	Arie Kortrecht Lisabeth Cole	Samuel	Johannes Westfael, Apollonia Kortrecht
June 16.	Salomon Davis, Jun Lea Decker	Jonas	Joel Quick, Lena Rosenkranz
	Abram Wildfield Mary Wells	Neeltje	Pieter Kuykendal, Femmetje Decker
June 30.	Arie Vredenburgh Sara Rosenkranz	Catharina	Dirk Rosenkranz, Catharina Rosenkranz
July 14.	Pieter Gemar Tjaatje De Witt	Maria	Samuel Swartwout, Lisabeth Gemaer, his wife

DATE	PARENTS	CHILD	WITNESSES
1745.			
Aug. 4.	Benjamin Westfael Annatje van Aken	Sara	Hannes van Aken, Jenneke van Aken
Oct. 6.	Simon Westfael Jannetje Westbroeck	Aeltje	Antony Westbroeck, Aeltje van Etten, his wife
Oct. 27.	Thomas Schoonhoven Maria Westfael	Jacob	Jacob Westfael, Lisabeth Westfael
Nov. 10.	Johannes Kuyckendal Lisabeth Decker	Catharina	Bastiaen Kortrecht, Rachel Decker, his wife
	Willem Kortrecht Margriet Jansen	Susannetje	James McCartery, Lisabeth Mey
Nov. 24.	John Williams Lea Decker	Johannes	Broer Decker, Anneke van Etten, his wife
Dec. 8.	Dirk Westbrock Jenneke van Keuren	Lydia	Cornelis Westbroeck, Antje Rosa, his wife
	William Ennes Elizabeth Quick	Daniel	Hendrick Cornelise Kortrecht, Jannetje Ennes, his wife
Dec. 22.	Jacobus Decker Neeltje Ditsoort	Joel	Jacobus Koddebeck, Neeltje Decker, his wife
1746.			
Jan. 1.	Aert Middagh Arriaentje van Etten	Gideon	Salomon Westbroeck, Lena Westbroeck
Jan. 12.	Evert Hoornbeeck Lena Cuddebeck	Elisabeth	Johannes Decker, Elisabeth De Witt, his wife
	Evert Hoornbeeck Lena Cuddebeck	Lena	William Cole, Maritje Cuddebeck, his wife
	Jacob Middagh Sara Kuykendal	Elisabeth	Jacobus Middagh, Elizabeth Consales Duke
Feb. 9.	Salomon Decker Lena Quick	Salomon	Salomon Kuyckendal, Femmetje Decker
	Jan Van Etten Maritje Westfaal	Maria	Antony Van Etten, Maria Westbroeck
Feb. 26.	Cornelis Westbroeck Antje Rosa	Samuel	Jan Van Etten, Maritje Westfael, his wife
April 20.	Andries Dingenman Cornelia Kermer	Alida	William Ennes, Alida Dingenman

DATE	PARENTS	CHILD	WITNESSES
1746.			
May 4.	Cornelis Krom Rebecca Schoonhoven	Elisabeth	Jacob Westfael, Elisabeth Westfael
	Willem Titsoort Sara Decker	Jacobus	Jacobus Rosenkranz, Sarah Decker, his wife
May 18.	Dirk Quick Aplony van Garden	Abram	Abram Isakse van Aken, Sara van Aken
June 15.	Abram Louw Dina Kuddebeck	Sara	Willem Kuddebeck, Jacomyntje Elten, his wife
June 29.	Jacobus Kuddebeck Neeltje Decker	Hendricus	Jabobus Decker, Neeltje Titsoort, his wife
July 13.	Joh: Casparus Fryenmuth Magdalena van Etten	Antje	Jacob van Etten and wife, Antje Westbroeck
	Willem Waert Maria Decker	Rachel	Abraham Kermer and wife, Sara Schammers
July 27.	Johannes Cole Pieternella van Aken	Sara	Jacobus Rosenkranz, Sara Decker, his wife
Aug. 10.	Jacob Westbroek Lydia Westfael	Blandina	Antony Westbroek, Aeltje van Etten, his wife
Sept. 7.	Benjamin Westbroeck Catharina Westbroeck	Antje	Johannes Westbroeck, Antje Rosa
	James McCarty Lisabeth Mey	Willem	Willem Kortrecht, Margriet Jansen
	John Prys Lucretia Ramsey	Apollonia	Johannes Westfael, Apollonia Kortrecht, his wife
Sept. 11.	Johan Jory Windemuth Johanna Margreta Elisabetha Bernhardin	Maria Margreta Maria Juliana	Johannes Snauber and wife, Anna Elisabetha Windemoedin. Jory Philip Windenmuth. Maria Juliana Huber, his wife
Sept. 21.	David Cole Elleonora Westfael	Jacob	Jacob Westfael, Sara Westfael
Oct. 5.	Gysbert Van Garden Maria Cole	Petrus	Arie Kortrecht, Lisabeth Cole, his wife

DATE	PARENTS	CHILD	WITNESSES
1746.			
Oct. 19.	Jacob Bogaert Nelli Kuykendal	Jacob	Cornelis Westfael, Lisabeth Westfael
	Bastiaen Kortrecht Rachel Decker	Jonas	Joris Davis, Debora Schoonhoven, his wife
Nov. 16.	Johannes Westbroeck, Jun Lena Westbroeck	Johannes	Johannes Westbroeck, Antje Rosa, his wife
Nov. 30.	Cornelis van Etten Heyltje Westbroeck	Antje	Jacob van Etten, Antje Westbroeck, his wife
	Abram van Tilburgh Sara Clavonsher	Sara	Abram Kermer, Sara Schammers, his wife
1747.			
Jan. 11.	Andries De Witt Brechje Nottingham	Henry	Egbert Dewitt and wife, Mally Nottingham
Feb. 1.	Andries Decker Dievertje Maul	Elisabeth	Johannes Corn. Westbroeck, Elisabeth Swartwout
Feb. 22.	Jacobus Quick Marya Westbroeck	Petrus	Herman Rosenkranz, Arriaentje Oosterhout, his wife
	Arie Kortrecht Lisabeth Cole	Lydia	Gysbert van Garden, Marya Cole, his wife
	John Boman Hanna Middagh	John	Abram Middagh, Lena van Aken, his wife
March 15.	Gerardus Van Nimwegen Jannetje de Witt	Annatje. Elisabeth.	Abram Kuddebeck, Annatje Decker. Samuel van Vliet, Lisabeth van Vliet
March 9.	Caspar Sheefer, Catharina Bernhardin	Valentyn	Valentyn Vocht, Barbara Behmin
March 29.	Benjamin Westfael Annatje Van Aken	Jury	Abram Van Aken, Margriet Westfael, his wife
	Johannes van Garden Margriet Quick	Samuel	Arie Kortrecht, Lisabeth Cole, his wife
	Johannes Decker Lena Quick	Johannes Van Aken	Johannes van Aken, Margriet Rosenkranz
April 12.	Hendrick H. Kortrecht Margriet Decker	Femmetje	Salomon Kuykendal, Elisabeth Kuykendal

DATE	PARENTS	CHILD	WITNESSES
1747.			
April 19.	Broer Decker Annatje Van Etten	Jacob	Andries Decker, Dievertje Moul, his wife
	Cornelis Brinck Maria Cole	Johannes	Johannes Westbroeck, senior, Antje Rosa, his wife
May 10.	Abram Middagh Lena van Aken	Salomon	Salomon Kuykendal, Margriet Rosenkranz
	Abram van Aken Jannetje De Witt	Lydia	Jacobus Rosenkranz, Lydia Westfael
June 21.	Thomas Schoonhoven Marya Westfael	Debora	Cornelis Westfael, Catharina Cole
	Gerardus Van Nimwegen Jannetje De Witt	Jacob	Samuel Swartwout, Lisabeth Gemar, his wife
	Cornelis Krom Rebecca Schoonhoven	Maria	Johannes Krom, Anna Cock, his wife
	Jan van Vliet Jesyntje Swartwout	Marya	Jacob Westbroeck, Marya Westbroeck
	Josias Cole Marya Kimbel	Wilhelmus	William Cole, Marya Cuddebeck, his wife
	Terrenz Devin Marya Kuykendal	Abraham	Cornelis Kuykendal, Maritje Westfael, his wife
	Johannes Cole Pieternella Van Aken	Abraham	Abraham Van Aken, Lisabeth Van Aken
	Jacob Bogaert Pieternella Kuykendal	Sara	Cornelis Westfael, Lisabeth Kuykendal
	Abraham Middagh Lena Van Aken	Samuel	Benjamin Westfael, Anna van Aken, his wife
	Willem Cuddebeck Jacomyntje Etten	Benjamin	Evert Hoornbeck, and wife, Lena Cuddebeck
	David Cole Leonora Westfael	Margrietje	Cornelis Westfael, Lisabeth Westfael
	Benjamin Westfael Anna van Aken	Marya	William Cole, Marya Cuddebeck, his wife
	Hendrick Kuykendal Elisabeth Cole	Hendricus	Daniel Kuykendal, Catharina Cole

DATE	PARENTS	CHILD	WITNESSES
1747.			
June 21.	Thomas Decker Jannetje Van Nimwegen	Petrus	Pieter Kuykendal, Femmetje Decker
	Jacobus Rosenkranz Sara Decker	Salomon	Salomon Decker, Catharina van Aken
	Salomon Davis Lea Decker	Catharina	Abraham van Aken, Jun, Catharina van Aken
June 21.	Bastiaen Kortrecht Rachel Decker	Catharina	Johannes Westfael, Apollonia Kortrecht, his wife
	Petrus Decker Leentje Oosterhout	Helena	Abram Wildfield, Jun., Helena Rosenkranz
	Abram Louw Dina Kuddebeck	Noemi	Abram Kuddebeck, Noemi Kuddebeck
	Johannes Westbroeck, Jr. Magdalena Westbroeck	Alida	Jacob Westbroeck, Jannetje Westbroeck
July 5.	Hendrick Decker Annatje Titsoort	Benjamin	Joel Quick, Femmetje Decker
	Cornelis Brinck Marya Cole	Hermannus	Andries Cole, Lisabeth Cole
	Mattheus Brinck Abigail Bel	Jan	Willem Kortrecht, Margriet Jansen, his wife
	Gysbert Van Garden Marya Cole	Catharina	Willem Decker, Neeltje Rosa, his wife
	Willem Ditsoort Sara Decker	Sara	Salomon Decker, Neeltje Decker
	Johannes Westfael Apollonia Kortrecht	Johannes	Jan van Etten, Maritje Westfael, his wife
	Johannes Hooghteeling Maritje Hoornbeeck	Jonathan	Bastian Kortrecht, Racheltje Decker, his wife
	Willem Kortrecht Margriet Jansen	Josias	Cornelis Kortrecht, Margriet Westfael
	Jacobus Decker Neeltje Ditsoort	Jonathan	Willem Ditsoort, Sarah Decker, his wife
	Aaron Vredenburgh Sara Rosenkranz	Lydia	Mattheus Vredenburg, Lydia Westfael

DATE	PARENTS	CHILD	WITNESSES
1747.			
July 5.	Herman Van Garden Elsje Kuddebeck	Daniel	Isak Van Aken, Rachel De Witt, his wife
	Broer Decker Antje Van Etten	Elias	Johannes Westbroeck, Antje Rosa, his wife
	Aert Middagh Arriaentje Van Etten	Martynus	Benjamin Westbroeck, Marya Westbroeck
	Jan Van Etten Maritje Westfael	Daniel	Daniel Westfael, Margareta Westfael
	Mattheus Brinck Abigail Bel	Jacobus	Thomas Quick, Marya de Witt, his wife
	Abraham Kermer Sarah Schammers	Angonietje	Samuel Schammers, Sara Kortrecht, his wife
	Johannes Van Garden Margriet Quick	Sara	Benjamin Quick, Jenneke Van Garden
Aug. 2.	Abram Van Aken, Jun Margriet Westfael	Catharina	Benjamin Westbroek, Catharina Westbroeck, his wife
Sept. 13.	Johannes Dirkse Westbroeck Sara Tack	Jenneke	Thomas Decker, Annatje Decker
	Joris Davis Debora Schoonhoven	Engeltje	Salomon Kuykendal, Margriet Rosenkranz
Oct. 11.	Salomon Decker Lena Quick	Lydia	Juriaen Westfael, Lydia Westfael
	Thomas Decker Jenneke van Nimwegen	Hendrick	Hendrick J. Kortrecht, Gerretje van Benschoten, his wife
Oct. 13.	Hendrick Kuykendal Lisabeth Cole	Jacob	Salomon Kuykendal, Lisabeth Kuykendal
	Leendert Titsoort Geeshi Ritt	Sara	Willem Titsoort, Neeltje Titsoort
Oct. 25.	Jury Philip Windemoet Maria Juliana Huber	Johannes	Johannes Merckel, Anna Elizabetha Snauber
1748.			
Jan. 3.	Thomas Schoonhoven Marya Westfael	Weyntje	Joris Davis, Debora Schoonhoven, his wife

DATE	PARENTS	CHILD	WITNESSES
1748.			
Jan. 3.	Matheus Brinck, Abigail Bel	Lisabeth	Petrus Brinck, Hannah Johns
Jan. 24.	Symon Westfael, Jannetje Westbroeck	Jury	Daniel Westfael, Lydia Westfael
March 6.	Jan Van Etten, Maritje Westfael	Margarita	Jacobus Rosenkranz, Marya Cuddebeck
March 20.	Salomon Davis, Lea Decker	Elisabeth	Samuel van Vliet, Elisabeth van Vliet
April 10.	James McCarty, Lisabeth Mey	Maria	Joseph Westbroeck, Maria Westbroeck
May 15.	Dirk Rosenkranz, Catharina van Aken	Jannetje	Jacobus van Aken, Jannetje De Witt
July 17.	Joh: Casparus Fryenmoet, Magdalena Van Etten	Heyltje	Cornelis Van Etten, Heyltje Westbroeck, his wife
	Herman Rosenkranz, Arriaentje Oosterhout	Benjamin	Arie Vredenburgh, Sara Rosenkranz, his wife
	William Ennes, Elisabeth Quick	Margriet	Margriet Decker
	Willem Kortrecht, Margriet Jansen	Gerretje	Hendrick J. Kortrecht, Gerretje van Bunschoten, his wife
Aug. 17.	Cornelis Ab. Westfael, Lisabeth Westfael	Annatje	Cornelis Westfael, Annatje Westfael
Sept. 19.	Josias Cole, Marya Kimmel	Petrus	Joris Kimmel, Lisabeth Kimmel
	Jacobus Oosterhout, Annatje Terwillige	Lena	Johannes van Aken, Lena Rosenkranz
	(onecht) Geertje Kortrecht	Sylvester Symon	David Cole and wife, Eleonora Westfael
Oct. 9.	Abram Louw, Dina Kuddebeck	Margriet	Jan Van Vliet, Jesyntje Swartwout, his wife
Nov. 27.	Cornelis Cole, Claesje Jongbloet	Jacob	Jacob Van Etten, and wife, Antje Westbroeck
1749.			
Jan. 8.	John Prys, Lucretia Ramsey	Elizabeth	Benjamin Dupuy, Elizabeth Swartwout, his wife

DATE	PARENTS	CHILD	WITNESSES
1749.			
Jan. 29.	Gysbert van Garden Marya Cole	Abram	Johannes Westfael, Apollonia Kortrecht, his wife
	Dirk Quick Apollonia Van Garden	Catharina	Thomas Quick, Catharina Quick
	Daniel Westfael Marya Westbroeck	Abram	Abram Chambers, Lena Westbroeck
	Benjamin Westfael Annatje van Aken	Margriet	Benjamin Quick, Hannah Joons, his wife
Feb. 12.	Symon Westfael Jannetje Westbroek	Simeon	Jacobus van Aken, Jannetje De Witt
Feb. 26.	Benjamin Westbroeck Catharina Westbroek	Johannes	Johannes Westbroeck, Maria Westbroeck, his wife
	Salomon Westbroek Hester Bevier	Louis	Antony Westbroeck, Aeltje van Etten, his wife
	Antony V. Bunschoten Margriet Wells	Maria	Johannes Westbroek, Maria Westbroeck, his wife
March 12.	Johannes Westbroeck, Jr Magdalena Westbroeck	Samuel	Jacobus Swartwout, Antje Westbroeck, broeck, his wife
March 24.	Jan Alderse Rosa Catharina van Etten	Marya	Isak Rosa, Marya Rosa
	Johannes Westfael Aplony Kortrecht	Hendrick and Samuel	Hendrick J. Kortreckt, Gerretje Van Bunschoten, his wife, Arie Kortrecht, Lisabeth Cole, his wife
	Johannes van Garden Margriet Quick	Cornelis	Cornelis Quick, Margriet De Witt
March 26.	William Waert Marya Decker	Maria	Johannes Westbroek, Jun, Maria Westbroeck, his wife
	Bastaien Kortrecht Rachel Decker	Jacob	Jacob Westbroeck, Lydia Westfael, his wife

DATE	PARENTS	CHILD	WITNESSES
1749.			
April 9.	onecht Rebecca Krom	Gonda	Jacobus Rosenkranz, Eleonora Westfael
May 7.	Andries Decker Dievertje Maul	Casparus Fryen- moet. Johannes. Petrus	J. C. Fryenmout, Magdalena Van Etten, his wife Johannes Decker, and wife, Lisabeth De Witt, Pieter Gemaer and wife, Tjaetje de Witt
	Abraham Van Aken, Jun Catharina Rosen- kranz	Maria	Cornelis van Aaken, Sara Westbroeck
May 21.	Jacob Bogaert Nelli Kuykendal	Margriet	Johannes van Gar- den and wife, Margriet Quick
June 18.	Abram van Aken Hoornbeek Catharina Ter- wilgen	Margrietje	Jacob van Aken, Sara van Aeken
Aug. 12.	Aert Middagh Ariaentje Van Etten	Rachel	Dirk Ketel, Rachel Van Etten, his wife
Sept. 10.	Arie Kortrecht Lisabeth Cole	Samuel	Johannes Westfael, Apollonia Kort- recht, his wife
Sept. 27.	Hendrick Kuyken- dal Lisabeth Cole	Benjamin	Willem Cole, Sara Cole
	Johannes Cole Pieternella Van Aaken	Johannes	Johannes Van Aaken, Jenneke Van Aaken
	Joris Davis Debora Schoon- hoven	Jenneke	Thomas Decker, Jenneke Van Nim- wegen, his wife
	Petrus Decker Magdalena Oos- terhout	Samuel	Gerardus Swartwout, Hester Swartwout
Oct. 29.	David Cole Eleonora West- fael	Benjamin	Jan van Vliet, Jes- yntje Swartwout, his wife
	Benjamin Dupuy Lisabeth Swart- wout	Samuel	Samuel Swartwout, and wife, Lisabeth Gemaer
Nov. 26.	Petrus Quick Johanna Consales	Benjamin	Daniel Consales, Maria Consales
	Hendrick H. Kort- recht Margriet Decker	Sara	Willem Cole, Sara Cole

DATE	PARENTS	CHILD	WITNESSES
1749.			
Nov. 26.	Abram Middagh, Lena Van Aken	Dorothea	Mattheus Terwilligen, Jenneke van Aken
Dec. 10.	Abraham Schuymer, Lena Westbroeck	Jsaak	Antony Westbroeck, Aeltje van Etten, his wife
	Benjamin Quick, Hanna Joons	Mattheus	Mattheus Brinck, Abigail Bell
1750.			
Jan. 21.	Daniel Kuykendal, Lisabeth Van Aken	Petrus	Pieter Kuykendal, Femmetje Decker, his wife
March 4.	Cornelis Cole, Claesje Jongbloet	Cornelis Westbroeck	Cornelis Westbroeck, Antje Rosa, his wife
	Salomon Decker, Lena Quick	Maria	Evert Roos Westbroeck, Maria De Witt
March 18.	Thomas Schoonhoven, Marya Westfael	Benjamin	Benjamin van Vliet, Lisabeth van Vliet
April 15.	Salomon Davis, Lea Decker	Petrus	Petrus Kuykendal, Catharina Decker
	Dirk Rosenkranz, Catharina Van Aken	Herman	Herman Rosenkranz, Arriaentje Oosterhout, his wife
	onecht Catharina Hoogh-teeling	Jacob & Sara	Jan Van Vliet, Jesyntje Swartwout, his wife, Thomas Decker and wife, Jenneke Van Nimwegen
April 29.	Joseph Westbroeck, Lisabeth Kuyckendal	Annatje	Pieter Kuyckendal, Femmetje Decker, his wife
	Joseph Wallen, Neeltje Decker	Lisabeth	Abram Van Aken, Jr., Catharina Rosenkranz, his wife
May 1.	David Devoor, Gerretje Hydt	Johannes & Cornelis	Cornelis Devoor and wife, Lena Westfael, Wilhelmus Devoor and wife, Catharina Schoonmaker
	Willem Devoor, Catharina Schoonmaker	Alida	Jacobus Devoor, Evje Dingenman, his wife
	Mattheus Devoor, Neeltje Schermerhoorn	Mattheus	Cornelis Devoor and wife, Lena Westfael

DATE	PARENTS	CHILD	WITNESSES
1750.			
May 1.	Daniel Devoor Lydia Westfael	Elisabeth	Johannes Dupuy, Rachel Devoor, his wife
	Daniel Devoor, Jun. Mally Leed	Lisabeth	Paul Dewitt, Catharine Dupuy, his wife
	Pieter Dewitt Marytje Roos	Jacob	Martinus Dewitt, Saertje Joons
	Lucas Schermerhoorn Sara Tyse	Lucas	Jacobus Devoor, Evje Dingenman, his wife
	John Schendeler Margriet Robert	Antje	Isaak Slover, Lisabeth Robert
May 13.	Mattheus Brinck Abigail Bell	Geertje	Mattheus Brinck, Lisabeth Brinck
May 27.	Jan van Etten Maritje Westfael	Samuel	Johannes Westfael, and wife, Apollonia Kortrecht
June 24.	Dirk Kittel Rachel Van Etten	Johanna	Johannes van Etten, and wife, Maria Consales
	James McCarty Lisabeth Meyer	John	Jan Rosa and wife, Catharina van Etten
July 2.	Martinus Dewitt Saertje Joons	Maria	Pieter Dewitt, Marytje Roos, his wife
July 8.	Andries Reifsnyder Susanna Wallon	Jacobus	Andries Decker, and wife, Dievertje Maul
Aug. 5.	Jacobus Oosterhout Annatje Terwilge	Jacobus	Arie Vredenburgh, Sara Rosenkranz, his wife
	Cornelis Westfael Lisabeth Westfael	Margriet	David Cole, Eleonora Westfael, his wife
	Joris Kimbel Sara Westfael	Petrus	Casparus Kimbel, Lena Kimbel
Aug. 19.	Cornelis Westbroeck Antje Rosa	Lydia	Joseph Westbroeck, and wife, Lisabeth Kuykendal
	Jury Philip Windemoet Maria Juliana Huberin	Abraham	Abraham Westbroeck, Jr, Sara Westbroeck
Sept. 23.	Jacobus van Sickel Sara van Aken	Johannes Casparus	J. C. Fryenmoet, Magdalena van Etten his wife
Nov. 4.	Salomon Westbroeck Hester Bevier	Moses	Daniel Westfael, Maria Westbroeck

DATE	PARENTS	CHILD	WITNESSES
1750.			
Nov. 7.	Vincent Robert Annatje Van Etten	Antje	Petrus van Etten, Lisabeth Robert
	John Right Alida Dingenman	John	William Right, Evje Dingenman
	Isaac Slover Elisabeth Robert	Abraham	Vincent Robert, Annatje van Etten, his wife
	Jacobus Devoor Evje Dingenman	John	Willem Devoor, Catharina Schoonmaker, his wife
	Michiel Palmetier Lydia Kuykendal	Margarita	Johannes Kuykendal, Clara Quick
	Jacob Roef Catharina Mykreed	Hans Michel	Hans Adam Adam, Catharina Mykreed
Nov. 18.	Pieter Gemaer Tjaati De Witt	Elisabeth	Benjamin Dupuy and wife, Elisa-Swartwout
	Philip Swartwout Antje Wynkoop	Jacobus	Jacobus Swartwout and wife, Antje Westbroeck
	Benjamin Westbr. Vernooy Lydia Westfael	Elisabeth	Benjamin Thomson, Elisabeth Westfael, his wife
Dec. 2.	Daniel Westfael Maria Westbroeck	Antony	Antony Westbroeck, Aeltje van Etten, his wife
Dec. 16.	John Prys Lucretia Ramsey	Johannes	Johannes Westbroeck, Lena Westbroeck, his wife
Dec. 30.	J. C. Fryenmoet Magdalena van Etten	Maria	Johannes van Etten, Maria Consales, his wife
	Jan A. Rosa Catharina Van Etten	Rebecca	Antony Westbroeck, Aeltje van Etten, his wife
1751.			
Jan. 20.	Cornelis van Etten Heyltje Westbroeck	Johannes	Johannes van Etten, Maria Consales, his wife
Feb. 10.	Manuel Consales Jannetje Van Etten	Elisabeth	Daniel Consales, Elisabeth Van Vliet

DATE	PARENTS	CHILD	WITNESSES
1751.			
Feb. 24.	Abram Shymer Lena Westbroeck	Marie	Daniel Westfael and wife, Marie Westbroeck
	Jacobus Quick Jenneke van Aken	Cornelis	Cornelis Quick, Catharina Quick
	Benjamin Westfael Annatje van Aken	Jacobus	Johannes Westfael and wife, Aplony Kortrecht
	onecht Hanna Middagh	Benjamin	Jan. A. Rosa, Antje Rosa
March 24.	Johannes Westbroeck Magdalena Westbroeck	Elisabeth	Cornelis Westbroeck, Jun., Elisabeth Kittel, his wife
	Abram Hooghteeling Hoornbeeck	Jannetje	Symon Westfael and wife, Jennetje Westbroeck
	Cathrina Terwilge Evert Hoornbeeck Lena Kuddebek	Evert	Jsack van Aken, Rachel De Witt, his wife
April 5.	Thomas Morfi Mary Lundy	John	Jan Van Etten and wife, Maritje Westfael
	Andries Cole Sara Schomaker	Andries	Herman Rosenkranz, Mary Stout, his wife
	John Wordly Beletje Decker	Cornelis	Jacobus Westfael, Jannetje Decker, his wife
May 7.	Isack Schoonhoven Catharina Van Vlieren	Debora	Hieronymus Van Vlieren, Sara Devoor
	Paul De Witt Catharina Dupuy	Sara	Johannes Dupuy, Rachel Devoor, his wife
	Johannes Kuykendal Clara Quick	Jacobus	John Bight, Alida Dingenman, his wife
	John Hoeper Maria Bishoff	Joseph	Martin Feber, Anna Maria Conterman, his wife
May 19.	Symon Westfael Jannetje Westbroeck	Jan De Witt	Johannes Westbroeck and wife, Magdalena Westbroeck

DATE	PARENTS	CHILD	WITNESSES
1751.			
May 19.	Johannes van Garden Margriet Quick	Petrus	Petrus Kortrecht, Lisabeth Brinck
Aug. 14.	Johannes Kuykendal Lisabeth Decker	Jacob	Mattheus Terwilge, Sara Terwilge
	Petrus Quick Johanna Consales	Philippus	Philippus Swartwout, Antje Wynkoop, his wife
Sept. 8.	Antony Van Etten Annatje Decker	Thomas	Thomas Decker, Jenneke Van Nimwegen, his wife
	Jacob Westbroeck Lydia Westfael	Johannes	Johannes Westbroeck and wife, Magdalena Westbroeck
	John Chandlar Margriet Robert	Hester	Abram Codebek and wife, Hester Swartwout
Oct. 6.	Johannes Westfael Apollonia Kortrecht	Joseph	Abram Van Aken, Jr., Elisabeth van Bunschoten
	Johannes van Etten Maria Consales	Magdalena	J. C. Fryenmoet, Magdalena Van Etten, his wife
Aug. 18.	Christiaen Kiersbi Antje Vredenburgh	Josua	Willem Van Garden, Jenneken van Garden, his wife
	William Ennes Elisabeth Quick	Joseph	Joseph Westbroeck, Elisabeth Kuykendal, his wife
	Thomas Heely Elisabeth Fishcharrelt	John	Mattheus Brinck, Elizabeth Brinck
Sept. 31.	Daniel Devoor Lydia Westfael	Brechie	Thomas Quick, Brechie Middagh, his wife
	Mattheus Devoor Neeltje Schermerhoorn	David	David Devoor, Gerretje Hydt
Sept. 21.	Michiel Henneshit Lisabeth Schermerhoorn	Sara	Lucas Schermerhoorn, Sara Tyse
	Hendrick Kuykendal Elisabeth Cole	Annatje	Johannes Westbroeck, Sara Tack, his wife

DATE	PARENTS	CHILD	WITNESSES
1751.			
Nov. 12.	Andries Decker Dievertje Maul	Jacob	Jacob Van Aken, Margriet van Garden
	Aert Varway Cornelia Kermer	Hendricus	Jan Kermer, Lisabeth Kermer
Nov. 20.	Jsak Middagh Femmetje Decker	Jsak	Petrus Kuykendal, Jenneke Terwilge
Nov. 18.	David Cole Eleonora Westfael	Samuel	Samuel Van Vliet, Johanna Westfael
Dec. 29.	Benjamin Westbroeck Cathrina Westbroeck	Wilhelmus	Cornelis Westbroeck, Antje Roos, his wife
	Salomon Westbroeck Hester Bevier	Aeltje	Jesse Bevier, Marytje Bevier
	Jan van Sickelen Margriet De Witt	Reynier	Reynier Van Sickelen and wife, Hanna van Leuven
	Thomas Neffi Rebecca Schoonhoven	Rebecca	Willem Cole, Johanna Westfael
1752.			
Jan. 19.	Daniel Consales Lisabeth Van Vliet	Manuel	Manuel Consales, Rymerick Quick, his wife
Feb. 2.	Abram Codebek Hester Swartwout	Jacobus	Jacobus Swartwout, Antje Westbroeck, his wife
	Salomon Decker Lena Quick	Jacobus	Jacobus Quick, Jenneke Van Aken, his wife
	Hendrick Kortrecht Margriet Decker	Jenneke	Thomas Decker, Jenneke Van Nimwegen, his wife
Feb. 16.	Jacobus Rosenkranz Catharina Cole	Alida	Josias Cole, Marytje Kimbell, his wife
	Benjamin Dupuy Lisabeth Swartwout	Moses	Moses Dupuy, Maria his wife
	Johannes Decker Lena Quick	Jacobus	Jacobus Middagh, Sara Decker
	Joris Davis Debora Schoonhoven	Annatje	Antony van Etten and wife, Annatje Decker
Feb. 23.	Johannes Decker Mary Tilburgh	Antje	Broer Decker, Antje Rosa

DATE	PARENTS	CHILD	WITNESSES
1752.			
Feb. 23.	Abram Symers Lena Westbroeck	Jacob	Jacob Westbroeck, Lydia Westfael, his wife
March 27.	Mattheus Brinck Abigail Bell	Mary	Benjamin Quick and wife, Hannah Joons.
March 29.	James McCarty Lisabeth Meyer	Lisabeth	William Ennes, Lisabeth Quick, his wife
March 30.	Daniel Westfael Maria Westbroeck	Margriet	Jan Van Etten, Maritje Westfael, his wife
April 5.	Salomon Davis Lea Decker	Salomon	Jacobus Swartwout, Antje Westbroeck, his wife
	Johannes Cole Nelli Van Aken	Willem	Willem Cole, Tjaetje Cole
	Thomas Schoohoven Marya Westfael	David	David Cole, Eleonora Westfael, his wife
May 31.	Abram Westbroeck Maria Helm	Michel	Michel Helm, Johanna Louw, his wife
June 24.	Daniel Kuykendal Lisabeth van Aken	Samuel	Cornelis van Aken and wife, Sara Westbroeck
	Philip Swartwout Antje Wynkoop	Cornelis	Jacobus Wynkoop, Jenneke Bogardus
	Jacobus Middagh Sara Decker	Blandina	Benjamin van vliet, Blandina Rosenkranz
	Joel Quick Christina Middagh	Joris	Joris Davis and wife, Debora Schoonhoven
	Bastiaen Kortrecht Rachel Decker	Elisabeth	Petrus Westfael, Lisabeth Kortrecht
Aug. 9.	Thomas Doff Mary Kane	Elisabeth	Johannes Westfael, Apollonia Kortrecht, his wife
Oct. 1.	Jan A. Rosa Catharina Van Etten	Isaak	Jsaak van Aken, Rachel De Witt, his wife
	Gysbert van Garden Maria Cole	Johannes	Johannes Kortrecht, Catharina Middagh
	Andries Dingenman Cornelia Kermer	Andries	Abram Kermer, Sara Schammers, his wife
Oct. 22.	Jacob Bogaert Nellie Kuyckendal	Benjamin	Benjamin Van Vliet, Debora Van Vliet

DATE	PARENTS	CHILD	WITNESSES
1752.			
Oct. 22.	Abram van Aken Catharina Rosenkranz	Lydia	Herman Rosenkranz, Ariaentje Oosterhout, his wife
Nov. 5.	Jan van Etten Maritje Westfael	Margrieta	Johannes van Etten, Maria Gonsales, his wife
	Thomas Morphy Mary Lundy	Mary	Hendrick Kortrecht, Margriet Jansen
	Joseph Westbroeck Lisabeth Kuykendal	Dirk	Dirk Westbroeck, Jenneke van Keuren, his wife
Dec. 31.	Abram Dirkse Westbroeck Blandina Rosenkranz	Jenneke	Dirk Westbroeck, Jenneke Van Keuren, his wife
	Benjamin Quick Johanna Joons	Anna	Cornelis Brinck, Jun., Anna Quick
1753.			
Jan. 14.	Jacob van Aken Margriet van Garden	Abraham	Isaak van Aken, Rachel De Witt, his wife
	Anthony van Etten Annatje Decker	Antje	Jacob van Etten and wife, Antje Westbroeck
	Jan Van Sickelen Grietje De Witt	Cornelis	Cornelis De Witt, Sara Hoornbeek, his wife
	Andries Reifsnyder Susanna Wallen	Maria	Maria Hoornbeeck
Jan. 28.	Johannes Corn Westbroeck Maria Westbroeck	Jenneke	Dirk Westbroeck, Jenneke Van Keuren, his wife
	Jacobus Quick Jenneke Van Aken	Jacobus	Jacobus van Aken, Sara Van Aken
Feb. 25.	Evert Rosa Westbroeck Marya Kortrecht	Arie	Petrus Kortrecht, Lisabeth Cole
	Benjamin Westr. Vernooy Lydia Westfael	Petrus	Petrus Westfael, Sara van Aken
March 25.	Cornelis Quick Marya Westfael	Lea	Johannes Westfael, Apollonia Kortrecht, his wife
March 11.	John Prys Lucretia Remsen	Philip	Philip Swartwout, Antje Wynkoop, his wife
	John Chandler Margriet Roberts	Antje	Jacobus Swartwout, Antje Westbroeck, his wife

DATE	PARENTS	CHILD	WITNESSES
1753.			
March 11.	Cornelis Westfael Lisabeth Westfael	Jacob	Jacob Westfael, Margriet Westfael
	Joris Kimber Sara Westfael	Sara	Jacob Westfael, Johanna Westfael
	Dirk Rosenkranz Cathrina Van Aken	Arriaentje	Petrus Rosenkranz, Arriaantje Rosenkranz
April 8.	Samuel Fench Lena Rosenkranz	Jacobus	Jacobus Rosenkranz, Catharina Cole, his wife
April 20.	Hendricus Decker Hanna Kermer	Cornelia	Andries Dingenman, Cornelia Kermer, his wife
	Christiaen Keersbi Jenneke van Garden	Heyltje	Jacobus Westbroeck, Heyltje van Garden
April 23.	onecht Elisabeth Van Namen	Sara	Broer Decker, Sara Schammers
June 17.	Johannes Westbroeck Magdalena Westbroeck	Sara	Salomon Kuyckendal and wife, Sara Cole
July 8.	Symon Westfael Jannetje Westbroeck	Wilhelmus	Arie Vredengurgh, Sara Rosenkranz, his wife
Aug. 19.	onecht Hester Meckentesh	Jacobus	Dirk Westbroeck and wife, Jenneke van Keuren
	Jury Philip Windemoet Juliana Huber	Petrus	Petrus Kortrecht, Maria van Garden
Aug. 5.	Samuel van vliet Tjatje Cole	Jacobus	Jan van vliet, Jesyntje Swartwout, his wife
Oct. 7.	Benjamin Westfael Annatje van aken	Cornelis Van Aken	Cornelis van Aken, Sara Westbroeck, his wife
	Jury Philip Windemoet Juliana Huber	Petrus	Petrus Kortrecht, Maria van Garden
Oct. 21.	Petrus Kuyckendal Catharina Kittel	Salomon	Salomon Kuyckendal, Sara Cole, his wife
	Thomas Neffi Rebecca Krom	Helena	Symon Westfael, Jannetje Westbroeck, his wife
Nov. 11.	Abram Shuymers Lena Westbroeck	Hester	Salomon Westbroeck, Hester Bevier, his wife

DATE	PARENTS	CHILD	WITNESSES
1753.			
Dec. 9.	Joseph Westbroeck Lisabeth Kuykendal	Levi	Dirk Westbroeck, Jenneke van Keuren, his wife
Nov. 25.	Abram Codebek Hester Swartwout	Petrus	Gerardus Swartwout, Maria Oosterhout, his wife
	Johannes Cole Pieternella van Aken	Maria	Jacobus van aken, Maria Cole
Dec. 16.	Daniel Gonsales Elisabeth van vliet	Benjamin	Benjamin van vliet, Debora van vliet
1754.			
Jan. 27.	Benjamin Dupuy Lisabeth Swartwout	Margrietje	Jacob Hoornbeeck and wife, Elisabeth Dupuy
Feb. 3.	J. C. Fryenmoet Magdalena van Etten	Heyltje	Cornelis van Etten, Heyltje Westbroeck, his wife
Feb. 17.	Jacobus Middagh Sara Decker	Jacob	Jacob Middagh, Sara Kuyckendal, his wife
	Daniel van Aken Lea Kittel	Lydia	Abram van Aken, Janetje de Witt, his wife
	James Wales Lisabeth Kimmer	Femmetje	Casparus Kimmer, Lena Kimmer
Feb. 24.	Mattheus Brinck Abigail Bell	Hester	Salomon Westbroeck, Hester Bevier, his wife
March 17.	onecht Grietje Wildfield	Sophia	Jacob Westfael, Lisabeth Westfael
March 24.	Abram Westbroeck Maria Helm	Martinus	Joseph Westbroek and wife, Lisabeth Kuyckendal
	William Ennes Lisabeth Quick	John	John Van Etten, Maritje Westfael, his wife
April 7.	Abram Middagh Lena van Aken	Moses	Hendrick H. Kortrecht, Margriet Decker, his wife
	Jacobus Gonsales Sara Westbroeck	Manuel	Samuel Gonsales, Rymerich Quick
April 28.	Antony van Etten Annatje Decker	Jenneke	Thomas Decker, Jenneke van Nimwegen, his wife
April 14.	Salomon Decker Lena Quick	Grietje	John Van Sickelen, Grietje De Witt, his wife

DATE	PARENTS	CHILD	WITNESSES
1754.			
April 14.	Jacob De Witt Jannetje van Sickelen	Jacob	Cornelis De Witt, Sara Hoornbeck, his wife
	Francis M'Gee Catharina Quick	Mary	Mattheus Brinck, Ann Quick
May 12.	Jacob Westbrock Lydia Westfael	Saffrein	Petrus Kortrecht, Maria Westfael, his wife
	Cornelis Middagh Lisabeth Bunschoten	Hendrik Kortrecht	Hendrich Kortrecht, Gerretje Bunschoten
	Jan A. Rosa Cathrina Van Etten	Jacob	Jacob van Etten, Antje Westbroeck, his wife
	Benjamin Westbroeck Cathrina Westbroek	Maria	Abram Westbroeck, Maria Helm, his wife
June 2.	Johannes van Etten Maria Gonsales	Manuel	Manuel Gonsales, Jannetje van Etten, his wife
June 22.	Cornelis van Etten Heyltje Westbroeck	Gideon	Gideon Westbroeck, Sara van Etten
	Cornelis Westbroeck, Jr. Lisabeth Kittel	Rachel	Richard Kittel, Rachel van Etten, his wife
July 13.	Salomon Westbroeck Hester Bevier	Moses	Benjamin Westbroeck, Cathrina Westbroeck, his wife
May 23.	Johannes Kuykendal Lisabeth Decker	Lisabeth	Jacobus Middagh, Elizabeth Kortrecht
	Joel Quick Christina Middagh	Maria	Elisa Middagh, Maria Cole
June 23.	James M'Carty Elisabeth Mey	Philip	Philip Windemoet, Maria Juliana Huber, his wife
	Cornelis Cole Claesje Jongbloet	Heyltje	Cornelis van Etten, Heyltje Westbroeck, his wife
June 16.	Philip Swartwout Antje Wynhoop	Annatje	Abram Kodebek and wife, Hester Swartwout
	Thomas Schoonhohoven Marya Westfael	Samuel	Benjamin Thomson, Lisabeth Westfael, his wife

DATE	PARENTS	CHILD	WITNESSES
1754.			
July 5.	Joris Davis Debora Schoonhoven	Maria	Josias Cole, Maria Kimber, his wife
July 7.	Cornelis Westfael Grietje Decker	Dievertje	Andries Decker, Dievertje Maul, his wife
Oct. 10.	Daniel Westfael Maria Westbroeck	Aeltje	Antony Westbroeck, Aeltje van Etten, his wife
Oct. 20.	Bastiaen Kortrecht Rachel Decker	Salomon	Salomon Kortrecht, Lea Kortrecht
Nov. 3.	Daniel Kuychendal Lisabeth van Aken	Maria	Abram Van Aken, Jr., and wife, Catharina Rosenkranz
	Johannes van Aken Marya van Garden	Lisabeth	Daniel Kuykendal, Lisabeth van aken, his wife
	James Risla Catharina Hooghteiling	Margriet	Jacob Westfael, Maritje Hooghteeling
Dec. 15.	Johannes Decker Mary van Tilburgh	Abraham	Abraham van Tilburgh, Sara Clevins, his wife
	Cornelis Quick Marya Westfael	Samuel	Daniel Westfael, Alida Middagh
	Johannes van Garden Margriet Quick	Margriet	Johannes Westfael, Margriet Jansen
	Abram Shymers Lena Westbroeck	Hester	Salomon Westbroeck, Hester Bevier, his wife
Aug. 18.	Abram Westbroeck Blandina Rosenkranz	Dirk	Hendrick Kortrecht, Grietje Decker, his wife
	Jeremias Kittel Lea Davis	Rachel	Richard Kittel, Rachel van Etten, his wife
	Daniel Devoor Lydia Westfael	Engeltje	Cornelis Devoor, Lena Westfael, his wife
Dec. 29.	John Chandlar Margriet Robert	Samuel	Pieter Kuykendal, Femmetje Decker, his wife
1755.			
Jan. 26.	Abram Kittel Christina Westfael	Apollonia	Johannes Westfael, Gerritje Bunschoten
	Thomas Wells Lisabeth Dewitt	Rebecca	Abram J. van aken, Marya Dewitt

DATE	PARENTS	CHILD	WITNESSES
1755.			
Feb. 9.	Mattheus Ter Wilgen, Jr. Lisabeth Ratier	Blandina	Wilhelmus Vredenburgh, Blandina Vredenburgh
	Hendrick Kuykendal Lisabeth Cole	Josias	Joseph Westbroeck, Marya Kimber
Feb. 16.	Joris Kimber Sara Westfael	Margriet	Philip Decker, Margriet Westfael
March 2.	Juriaen Westfael Cathrina Terwilgen	Petrus	Petrus Westfael, Ariaentje Rosenkranz, his wife
March 9.	Thomas Duff Mary Keen	William	William Ennes, Lisabeth Quick, his wife
March 23.	John Williams Lea Decker	Ezechiel	Ezechiel Decker, Johanna van Tilburgh, his wife
	Ezechiel Decker Johanna van Tilburgh	Lea	John Williams, Lea Decker, his wife
	Thomas Murphy Mary Lundy	Timothy	
April 20.	Cornelis Brink Lisabeth van Garden	Petrus	Petrus Brink, Lisabeth Brink
	Johannes C. Westbroeck Maria Westbroeck	Jenneke	Dirk Westbroeck, Jenneke van Keuren, his wife
July 7.	Petrus Kortrecht Marya Westfael	Lydia	Jacob Westbroeck, Lydia Westfael, his wife
Oct. 19.	Abram Westbroeck Maria Helm	Johanna	Jacob Helm, Annatje Westbroeck
1756.			
Feb. 13.	Symon Westfael Jannetje Westbroeck	Aeltje	Dirk Rosenkranz, Cathrina van aken, his wife
	Andries Reifsnyder Susanna Wallen	Joseph	Philip Decker, Sara Decker
	Johannes van Aken Marya van Garden	Femmetje	Cornelis van aken and wife, Sara Westbroeck
	Cornelis Westfael Grietje Decker	Margrietje	Jacob Westfael, Margrietje Cole
	Antony van Etten Annatje Decker	Margrieta	Johannes Decker, Jun., Margrieta Gemaer, his wife
	Jacob van Aken Margriet van Garden	Benjamin	Petrus Westfael, Arriaentje Rosenkranz

132

DATE	PARENTS	CHILD	WITNESSES
1756.			
Feb. 15.	Alexander Ivory Jenneke Decker	Jacobus	Jacobus Westfael, Jannetje Decker, his wife
	Salomon Westbroeck Hester Bevier	William	Aert Middagh, Arriaentje van Etten
April 11.	Johannes Westbroeck Lena Westbroeck	Joel	Antony van Etten, Annatje Decker, his wife
	Dirk Rosenkranz Cathrina van Aken	Lydia	Daniel van Aken, Lea Kittel, his wife
	Johannes Cole Pieternella van Aken	Willem	Willem Cole, Sara van Aken
	Andres Grub Cathrina Romvelden	Sara	Jacob Vigli, Rymerick Decker
April 14.	Mattheus Brink Abigail Bell	Gerret	John Michel Henry, Grietje Quick
	Aert van Weyen Cornelia Kermer	Hendricus	James Mollin, Lisabeth Kermer
	Johannes van Etten Maria Gonsales	Rymerich	Samuel Gonsales, Rymerick Gonsales
	Benjamin Westfael Annatje van Aken	Lisabeth	Jacobus Van Aken, Sara van Aken
July 4.	Salomon Decker Lena Quick	Joseph	Cornelis Quick illegible
	Abram Westbroeck Blandina Rosenkranz	Jacobus	Westbroeck illegible
	Gideon Westbroeck Jannetje M. (rest illegible)	Josephet	Abraham Westbroeck (illegible)
Aug. 22.	Jeremias Kittel Lea Davis	Salomon	Jacobus Davis, Lea Decker
	Johannes Shaubas Catharina Smidt	Susanna	John Kortrecht, Margriet Johnson

Here end the baptisms in handwriting of Rev. J. C. Fryenmoet.

1756.			
Nov. 26.	Abraham Symor Lena Westbroek	Mari	Daniel Westval, Mari Westbroeck
	Jacobus Middag Sarah Decker	Catrina	Harme Rosekrans, Catrina van Aake
	Philip Windemoet Mari Hoever	Elizabeth	Johannis Westvael, Elizabeth Windemoet

DATE	PARENTS	CHILD	WITNESSES
1756.			
Nov. 26.	Andries Dekker Divertje Moul	Philippus	Benjamin Vanoy, Lidia Westvael
1757. June 19.	In handwriting of Rev. J. H. Goetschius.		
	Hans C. Westbroek Maria dirkse Westbroek	Seletje and Meseri	The parents
	Benjamin Westbrock Catrina Westbrock	Lidia	Anatje Westbroeck, Petrus, broeder and suster (brother and sister
	Alexander Tvori Janatje Dekker	Wilhelmus	Willem Dekker and syn vrow (and his wife) Nieltje
	Cornelius Quick Maria Westphaal	Lea	Bastian Kortregt and wife, Ragel
	James Everigame Anna Quick	James	Thomas Quick, Margreth, Suster and Broeder (brother and sister)
	Petrus Brinck Alida Middag	Cornelius	Cornelis Brinck, Jun, Elisabeth, his wife
	William Ennes Elisabeth Quick	Cornelius	Cornelius Quik and his wife Maria
	Cornelius Westbroeck Elisabeth Kittel	Susanna	Susanna Kittel, Anthoni Westbroek
	Benjamin Vernoi Lidia Westphaal	Joseph	Joseph Westbroek and his wife Debora
	Hester Mekkentash	Heiltje	Cornelius van Netten, Heiltje Westbroek, his wife
June 24.	Joel Quick Christina Middag	Jacob	Ephraim Middag, Margret Mollen
	Petrus Kuykendal Catrina Kittel	Lisabeth	Cornelius Westbrock, Jr., Lisabeth Quik, his wife
	Petrus Rosenkrans Maria Brinck	Lidia	Jan Lady, Ariantje Rosenkrans
June 25.	Abraham Van Aaken, Jun. Catrina Rosenkrans	Sara	Salomon Kuikendaal, Sara Kool, his wife
	Jacobus Quick Janetje van Aaken	Tomas	Abraham Middag and his wife, Lena Van Aaken
	Abraham Middag Lena van Aaken	Emanuel	William Clinton, Sara van Aaken, his wife

DATE	PARENTS	CHILD	WITNESSES
1757.			
June 26.	Jan Davis Willemtje Lineden	Jan and Jany	Thomas Schoonhoven, Maria, his wife, Daniel Rosenkrans, Debora Schoohaven

The following are in handwriting of Domine G. W. Mancius.

DATE	PARENTS	CHILD	WITNESSES
1758.			
Feb. 11.	Abraham Kittel Christina Westval	Jacob	Jacob Helm, Lena van Etten his wife
	Cornelis Brink, Jun. Elisabeth van Garden	Johannes	Johannes Westval, Margriet Quik
	Mattheus Brink, Jun. Sara Terwilge	Margrietje	Jan Kortregt, Grietje Quik
	Evert Rosa Westbroek Maria Kortregt	Jacobus	Cornelis Westbroek, Antje Rosa, his wife
	Benjamin Quik Johanna Johnst	Benjamin	Petrus Brink, Jannetje Middag
Feb. 12.	Isaac van Aaken Margriet Horenbeek	Joseph	Jacob van Aaken and wife, Margriet van Garden
	Willem Vredenburgh van Garden Jenneke Terwilge	Jacobus	Jacobus Osterhout, Annaatje Terwilge, his wife
	Johannes Dekker Debora van Vliet	Levi	Antonie van Etten and wife, Annaatje Dekker
	Jacobus Westval Jannetje Dekker	Joseph	Joseph Westbroek, Debora Krom
	John Breslar Elisabeth Kermer	John	Bastian Kortregt, Rachel Dekker
	Johannes Van Aaken Maria van Garden	Johannes	Gysbert van Garden, Maria Cool, his wife
	Antonie van Etten Annaatje Dekker	Levi	Johannes Dekker and wife, Debora van Vliet
Feb. 13.	Jan Middag Elisabeth Kortregt	Margrietje	Cornelis Cool, Grietje Cool
	Daniel Dekker Blandina Vredenburgh	Sara	Arie Vredenburgh, Sara Rosenkrans
	Salomon Kortregt Cornelia Cool	Catryntje	Salomon Kuikendal, Sara Cool, his wife

DATE	PARENTS	CHILD	WITNESSES
1758. Feb. 13.	Jurian Westval Catharina Terwilge	Joseph	Benjamin Vernoi Westbroek, Lydia Westval, his wife
	Daniel van Aaken Lea Kittel	Catharina	Petrus Kuikendal, Catharina Kittel, his wife
	Robert Sinor Lea Middag	Sara	Antonie Westbroek, Lea Kortregt
	James Rusle Catharina Hoogteeling	Annaatje	George Moor, Seitje Terwilge
	James Ransen Lydia Krom	Ruth	William Krom, Debora Davids
	Jacob Neerbas Anna Maria Rakien	Willem	Daniel van Aaken, Lea Kittel, his wife
1759. Jan. 27.	Daniel Kuykendal Elizabeth Van Ake	Catryntie	Martynes Kuykendal, Catryntie Kool
	Jacob Van Ake Margariet van Garde	Caspares	Cobus van Sickele, Sarah van Ake
	Johannes Leydi Aryantie Rosekrans	Jacobus	Jacobus van Ake, Catrina van Aeke
	Kornelius van Ette Huyltie Westbroek	Magdalena	Johannes Westbroek, Magdalena Westbroek
	Eliza Middag Marytie Kimber	Tunis	Elias Middach, Elizabeth Buntschote
	Bryan Hammen Blandientie van Ake	John	Abraham Van Ake, Jannetie De Wit
	Benjamin Van Vliedt Johanna Westfael	Samuel	Johannes Deckker, Debora van Vliedt
	Cornelius Westfael Elizabeth Westfael	Cornelius	Cornelius Schoonhove, Grietie Deckker
Jan. 27.	John Davis Willempi Snedeker	Petrus	Petrus Middag, Leonora Westfael
	Wilhel⁵ Vreden- Elizabeth van Garde	Elsie	Harme van Garde, Elsie Kuddebeck
	Johannes Westfael Maregriet Quick	David	Jacob Westfael, Leonora Westfael

DATE	PARENTS	CHILD	WITNESSES
1759.			
Jan. 27.	Syme Westfael Jannetie Westbroek	Salomon	Salomon Kuykendal, Sarah Kool
Jan. 28.	Jacob Figeli Belitie Davids	Syme	Syme Westfael, Jannetje Westbroek
	J. H. Deckker Grietje Gamaer	Tomas	Jan Vliedt, Janneke Van Innewege
	Jan van Vliet Lea Deckker	Esyntie	Johannes Deckker, Grietje Gemaer
	Tomas Quick Hannah Middach	Eliza	Eliza Middach, Mareytie Kember
	Alida Westbroek	Heyltie	Cornelius van Ette, Heyltje Westbrock
	Rabecka Schoonhove	Jan vyert	Tonie van Ette, Annatie Deckker
	Abraham Westbroek Blandina Rosekrans	Leonard	Leonard Wintermoet, Jannetie Middach
	Joseph Westbroek Debora Krom	Elizabeth	J. Dirikse Westbroek, Elizabeth Westbroek
	Cornelius Westbroek Elizabeth Citel	Cornelia	Jan Citel, Sarah Cortrecht
	Bn Weltvael Anatje Van Acce	Rusje	Dirrik van Ette, Rusje Westvael
	Tomas Morphe Mary Londi	Mare	Daniel Westvael, Elizabeth Brink
	Jerimia Cittel Lea Davids	Cornelius	Antone Westbroek, Elizabeth Cittle
	Phillip Wintemuth Maria Hoeverin	Elizabeth	James Meguarde, Elisabeth Majerin
	Abraham Seymor Lena Westbroek	Elizabeth	William Ennest, Elizabeth Quick
	Petrus Kotregt Maria Westvael	Janncke	Johannes Cortregt, Jenneke van Garde
	Hendrik Cortregt Catrina Middag	Maria De Wit	John Cortregt, Gerretje Bonschote
	James Mollen Maria Swartwout	Heyltje	Cornelius Cool, Klasje Jonkbloet
	Mateus Brink Abigail Bell	Elisabeth	Adam Cheat, Maria Dewit
	Jacob Swartwout Lidea Dekker	Catrina	Nicolaes Brink, Catrina Germer

The following are in the handwriting of Rev. I. C. Fryenmoet.

1759.			
Aug. 19.	Antony Westbroeck Susanna Kittel	Maria	Daniel Westfael, Maria Westbroeck, his wife

DATE	PARENTS	CHILD	WITNESSES
1759.			
Aug. 19.	Jacobus Quick Jenneke Van Aken	Lisabeth	Cornelis Van Etten, Heyltje Westbroeck, his wife
	Dirk Van Etten Russie Westfael	Sara	Jacob Van Etten, Sara Van Etten
	William Ennes Lisabeth Quick	Alexander	Johannes van Etten, Maria Gonsales, his wife
	Salomon Decker Lena Quick	Thomas	Thomas Wells, Lisabeth De Witt, his wife
	Petrus Brink Alida Middag	Aert	Petrus Brink, Jun., Jannetje Middagh
	Petrus Rosenkranz Marya Brink	Herman	Herman Rosenkranz, Arriaentje Oosterhout
	Jacobus van Aken, Jun. Lisabeth Bunschoten	Levi	Cornelis Van Aken, Sara Westbroeck, his wife
	Antony van Etten Annatje Decker	Alida	Tjerk Van Keuren Westbrock, Alida Decker
	Thomas Wells Lisabeth De Witt	Annatje	Elias Kortrecht, Anna De Witt
	onecht Jenneke Quick	Lydia	Johannes Westfael Sara Decker
Aug. 26.	Joel Quick Christina Middag	Beletje	Jacob Viegli, Beletje Davis, his wife
	Thomas Schoonhoven Marya Westfael	Joris	Jacobus Davis, Debora Schoonhoven
	Joris Kimber Sara Westfael	Petrus	Josias Cole, Margriet Mollen, his wife
	onecht Maria Cole	Lisabeth	Salomon Kuykendal, Sara Cole, his wife
	Robert Simour Lea Middagh	Jacomyntje	Willem Kodebek, Jacomyntje Elten, his wife
	Clea Farletier Margriet Titsoort	Moses	Abram Kortrecht, Margriet Kuykendal, his wife
	Mattheus Terwilligen Lisabeth Latier	John	Juriaen Westfael, Cathrina Terwilligen, his wife
	Andries Kroeg Cathrina Romfeld	Lisabeth	John Leydy, Arriaentje Rosenkranz, his wife

DATE	PARENTS	CHILD	WITNESSES
1759.			
Aug. 26.	Abraham Middagh Lena van Aken	Souverign	Abram Van Aken, Jun., Cathrina Rosenkranz, his wife
	Petrus Kuykendal Cathrina Kittel	Christyntje	Pieter Kuykendal, Femmetje Decker, his wife
	Philip Swartwout Antje Wynkoop	Gerardus	Johannes Oosterhout, Jannetje Swartwout, his wife
	Hugh Shellet Anna Quick	Grietje	Andries Decker, Saertje Decker

Baptized by the Rev. I. H. Goetschius.

Nov. 21.	Johanes Westbroek Magdalen Westbroek	Gideon	Daniel van Vliet, and his wife Sara
	Daniel van Aaken Lea Kettel	Eliza	Jeams Klerk, Sara van Aaken
	Abraham Kudebek Hester Gemaa	Willem	Willem Kudebek and his wife Jakemyntje
Nov. 22.	Martinus Kuykendaal Catryntje Kool	Hermanus	Hermanus Van Inwegen, Grietje, his wife
	Jan Middag Lisabeth Kortregt	Seeletje	Hans Dekker, Jun., and his wife Grietje
	Jacob De Witt Lea Kortregt	Heiltje	Johanes De Witt, Hyltje De Witt
	Salomon Cortregt Cornelia Kool	Hendrick	Hendrik Kortregt, and his wife Margrita
	Josias Kool Margret Mollen	David	Jan Devis and wife, Leanora Westfael
1760. April 20.	Benjamin Westbroek Catrina Westbroek	Cornelius or Cornelia	
	Abram Westbroek Blandina Rosekrans	Cobus	
	Benjamin Van Noj Lydia Westvael	Usselje	Evert Roosa Westbroek, Maria Westbroek
	Petrus Cortregt Maria Westvaal	Arie	
	Johannes van Aaken Maria van Gorde	Usseltje	Gysbert van Gorden, Catrina van Gorden

DATE	PARENTS	CHILD	WITNESSES
1760.			
April 20.	Wilhelmus Vredenburg Elisabeth Van Gorden	Arie	Arie Vredenburg, Sara Vredenburg
	Johannis Schouwers Catrina Smith	Maria	James McKater, Maria McKater
	William Nylen Sara Van Aak	Elisabeth	Cornelius van Aaken, Sara van Aaken
	Jacob Helm Helena Van Etten	Maria	Jacob Van Etten, Maria Helm
	Cornelius Brink Elisabeth van Garde	Maragrita	Juri aen Westvaal, Maragrita Quik
	Abram Westvaal Elisabeth Titsoort onecht Jenneke van Garden	Maria Johannes Cortregt	Andries Dekker Maragritie Dekker William Ennes, Elisabeth Ennes
April 22.	Daniel Devoor Lydia Westvaal	Abram and Isaac	Cornelius Schoonhoven, Lena Schoonhoven, David Devoor, Eva Davids
	Jurian Westvaal Catrina Terwyligen	Sara	Benjamin Tam son, Elisabeth Tamson
	William Vredenburg Van Gorden Janneke Ter Wyligen	Sytje	Mathew Ter Wyligen, Sytje Ter Wyligen
	Abram van Aaken Catrina Roosenkrans	Cornelius	Juriaan Westvaal, Catrina Westvaal
	Abram Coddebak Hester Swartwout	Abram	Abram Coddebak, Jun., Hester Gemaar
	Jsaac Schoonhoven	Ezechiel	Walter van Tuil, Maria van Vliet
	Elisa Middag Maria Timber	Casparus	Petrus Kuykendal, Catrina Kuykendal
	Hendrick Kuikendal Elisabeth Cool	Tatji	Martinus Kuikendal, Catrina Kuikendal
June 29.	John Cral Antje Dekker	Samuel	Cobus van Vliet, Catrina van Vliet
	Stephanus Dekker Annatje Kuikendal	Neeltje	Henderikkus Kuikendal, Lea Dekker

DATE	PARENTS	CHILD	WITNESSES
1760.			
June 29.	Martinus Dekker Janneke Westbroek	Petrus	Abram Cool, Catrina Cool
	Derick Wintviel Elisabeth Kortregt	Emmanuel	Corneles Cool, Maria Cool
	Harmanus Van Nimwegen Gritje Cool	Gerardus	Gerardus Van Nimwegen, Gritje van Nimwegen
	onegt Lydia Krom	Benoni	Abram Van Aaken, Leonora Westvaal
July 6.	James Clark Sarah Van Aaken	Elisabeth	Daniel Van Aaken, Lea van Aaken
	Joseph Westbroek Debora Krom	Derik	Abram Westbroek, Blandina Westbroek
Nov. 9.	Joel Quik Christina Middag	Antje	Daniel Kortregt, Antje Westbroek
	Cornelius Schoonhoven Lena Devoir	Thomas	Thomas Schoonhoven, Maria Schoonhoven
	Johannis Lydi Ariantje Rosekrans	Henderikkus	Harmen Rosekrans, Ariaentje Rosekrans
	Simon Westvaal Janetje Westbroek	Blandina	Peter Kuikendal, Catrina Kuikendal
	Matheus Terwilligen Elisabeth Rattier	Isaac	Isaac Middag, Femetje Middag
	Cornelius Cool Maria Dekker	Lena	Petrus Dekker, Lena Dekker
Dec. 21.	Abram Shymer Lena Westbroek	Maragrit	John Cortregt, Maragrit Johnson
	Hendrik Cortregt Catrina Middag	Hendrick Johnson	Elias Cortregt, Gerritje van Benschouten
	Mateues Brenck Sara Terwielger	Yuerrean	Yuerrean Westvael, Griette Quick
1761. Jan. 3.	Christian Chress Maria Dey	John	
Jan. 18.	Johannes van Etten Maria Consalus	Jacobus	Jacob Helm, Lena Helm
March 8.	Johannis Westvaal Maragrita Quik	Benjamin	Benjamin Quick, Hannah Quik
	Petrus Brink Alida Middag	Petrus	John Brink, Elisabeth Westvaal
	Evert Roos Westbroek Maria Cortregt	Antje	Benjamin Westbroek, Catrina Westbroek

DATE	PARENTS	CHILD	WITNESSES
1761.			
March 20.	Abram Kettel Christina Westvaal	Richard	Richard Kettel, Rachel Kettel
	Daniel Cortregt Russe van Aaken	Gideon	John Cortregt, Lydia Cermer
	Jacob Vigely Oseltje Davids	Zacharias	Jacob Westbroek, Lydi Westbroek
May 3.	Cherk Van Cuiren Westbroek Maria Helm	Abram	
June 14.	Antony Van Ette Annatie Dekker	Hendricus	Salomon Kuikendal, Sarah Kuikendal
	Johannes Dekker, Jr. Grietie Gomaar	Theatie	Peter Gomaar, Maria Gomaar
	Cobus Van Aken, Jun. Elisabeth Bunschoten	Gerritje	Cobus Bunschoten, Gerritie Cotregt, widow
July 26.	Peter Brink Catrina Davids	Jacobus	Jacobus Brink, Catrina Cortregt
	Thomas Welsch Elisabeth De Witt	Jacobus	Cornelius De Witt, Sarah Dekker
Aug. 2.	Daniel Dekker Blandina Vredenburg	Hendrik	Harmanus Van Nimwegen, Maragrietie van Nimwegen
Sept. 13.	Salomon Dekker Lena Quik	Jacob	Jacob Westbroek, Lydia Westbroek
Sept. 20.	Johannis van Aken Maria van Garden	Wilhelmus	Harmanus Brink, Lena Brink
Oct. 17.	Derick van Etten Russia Westvaal	Joseph	Johannis Westbroek, Lydia Westbroek
	Jacob Helm Helena van Etten	Samuel	Jan van Etten, Maragret van Etten
Oct. 18.	Petrus Westbroek Lydia Vredenburg	Cornelius	Cornelius Westbroek, Lea Westbroek
Nov. 10.	Jeremie Kettle Maria Davids	Daniel	Daniel Van Aaken, Lea Van Aaken
	Daniel Westvaal Maria Westbrock	Hannatje	Benjamin Westvaal, Hannatje Westvaal
	Jacobus Westvaal Jannetje Dekker	Elisabeth	Jacobus Kermer, Elisabeth Kermer
	Jacob De Witt Jannetje Van Sikkelen	Rynier	
Dec. 27.	Philip Windemout Maria Hoogeling	Benjamin	

DATE	PARENTS	CHILD	WITNESSES
1762.			
Feb. 21.	Gisbert van Garden, Jun. Annatje Westbroek	Samuel	Samuel Westbrock, Lea Westbrock
March 21.	Abram Westbroek Blandina Rosekrans	Sara	
April 9.	Benjamin Westbroek Catrina Westbroek	Abram	
	Cornelius Van Etten Heyltje Westbroek	Magdalena	Johannis Casparus, Fryenmoet, Magdelena Frynmoet
May	onegt Rebbecka Schoonhooven	Christoffel	Abraham Van Aaken, Catrina Kuykendal
June 9.	Daniel Devoir Lidja Westvael	Helena	
	Johannis De Pui Rachel Devoir	Susanna	Do. Thomas Romein, Susanna Romein
	Josias Cool Maragriet Mullen	Hejltje	Joris Cimmer, Sarah Cimmer
	Thomas Schoonhove Maria Westfael	Josias	Josias Cool, Maragriet Cool
	onegt Sarah Schoonhove	Joseph and Benjamin	Jacobus Rosekrans, Elisabeth Westfael, Cornelius Devoir, Leonora Westfael
	Petrus Middag Debora Schoonhoove	Jacobus	Ephraim Middag, Sarah Middag
July 18.	Andries Crub Catrina Rumvelt	Petrus	Petrus Lot, Sarah Lot
	Hendrick Johnson Elisabeth Coon or Boom	Lea	Abram Johnson, Lea Johnson
July 27.	Benjamin van Noj Lydia Westvaal	Sarah	
	Ezechiel Dekker Johanna Tillburg	John	John Tillburg, Lena Tillburg
Oct. 16.	onegt Elisabeth Westvaal	Johannis	Johannis Westvaal, Maragriet Westvaal
Nov. 26.	Cherk van keuren Westbroek Maria Helm	Janneke	
	Abram Van Aaken, Jun. Maria Dewitt	Rachel	Abram Van Campen, Rachel van Campen

DATE	PARENTS	CHILD	WITNESSES
1762.			
Dec. 12.	Johannis Lyde Ariaantje Roosekrans	Maragriet	Isaac Van Aaken, Maragriet van Aaken
	Christophel Catting- ton Maria Oosterhout	Joseph	
1763.			
Jan. 1.	Edmond Panborn Maria Oostrander	William	
	Benjamin De Pui —— Swartwoudt	John	John De Pui, Lena De Pui
Jan. 2.	Petrus Rosekrans Maria Brink	Cornelius	Cornelius Dekker, Catrina van Aaken
Jan. 9.	Jacobus Westvaal Jannetje Dekker	Abram and Sarah	Abram Chambers, Lena Chambers, Daniel Westvaal, Maria Westvaal
Jan. 23.	Petrus Cool Jannitie Keter	Gideon Westbroeck	Daniel Westvael, Maria Westfael
Feb. 6.	Johannis van Etten Maria Gonsalis	Elisabeth	Peter Helm, Elisabeth Helm
	John Van Sikelen Grietie Dewit	Abram	Abram Van Aeken, Maria Van Aeken
	Hugh Shirrid Anna Quik	Lena	Samuel Westbroek, Grietje Ennes
	Hannis Van de Merken Janneke Cortregt	Jannetje	Hendrik Cortregt, Jannetje Cortregt
	Jeremias Kettel Lea Davids	Abram and Joseph	Abram Chambers, Lena Chambers, Joseph Westbroek, Debora Westbroek
	David or Daniel Cortregt Rusja van Aaken	David	Andries Dingman, Cornelia Dingman
	William Krom Catrina van Garden	Cornelius	Joseph Westbroek, Debora Westbroek
Feb. 23.	Peter van Nest	Isaac	Isaac van Nest
Feb. 28.	Stephanus Dekker Femetje Kuikendal	Jacobus	William Kuikendal, Hanna Forbis
	John Croel Antje Croel	Lea	Jacob Dekker, Lea Lea Dekker
	Brient Hamel Blandina Van Aaken	Daniel	

DATE	PARENTS	CHILD	WITNESSES
1763.			
March 20.	Cornelius Cool Maria Dekker	Martinus	Martinus Dekker, Jonecke Dekker
	Philip Swartwoud Antje Wynkoop	Cornelius Wynkoop	Cornelius Cool, Maria Cool
March 27.	Abram Kittel Christina Westvaal	Mosis	Adam Beemer, Catrina Cortregt
April 3.	Johannis Van Garden Cornelia Cool	David or Daniel	David or Daniel Westvaal, Maria Westvaal
	Johannis Cortregt Susanna Kittel	Gisbert	Gisbert van Garden, Jr., Annatje van Garden
May 1.	Hendrick Williamse Cortregt Catrina Middag	William	William Cortregt, Maragriet Cortregt
May 8.	Matheus Ter Willigen Elisabeth Ratier	Maria	Jacobus Divans, Maria Divans
	Jacob Turner Elsje Meclean	Elisabeth	Benjamin De Pui, Elisabeth De Pui
	Harmanus Van Nimwegen Maragriet Cool	Caletta	John Davids, Leonora Davids
	Abram Cuddebek Hester Gemaar	Jacob	Jacob Gomaar, Alida Gomaar
May 9.	Benjamin Thomson Elisabeth Westvaal	Catrina	Jacobus Rosekrans, Catrina Rosekrans
	Benjamin Forguson Mary Buk or Cuk	Benjamin	Thomas or Hanna Forguson
May 22.	Jacob Feydlie Belletje Davids	Adam	Adam Beemer, Engeltje Davids
June 12.	Stephanus Tietsoort Catrina Kuikendal	Sara	Salomon Kuikendal, Sara Kuikendal
	Josias Dekker Sarah Tietsoort	Boudewyn	Hendrikkus Dekker, Femmetje Cole or Foly
	Jacobus Quik Janneke van Aaken	Greetje	Johannes Westvaal, Maragriet Westvaal
July 5.	Benjamin Westvaal Annatje van Aaken	Daniel	Daniel Westvaal, Maria Westvaal
	Derik Wintviel Elisabeth Cortregt	Joseph	John Wood, Catrina Cortregt
	Petrus Brink Alida Middag	Hendrik	Hendrik Cortregt, Catrina Cortregt

DATE	PARENTS	CHILD	WITNESSES
1763.			
July 5.	Joseph Westbroek Debora Krom	Maria	
July 17.	Petrus Wesbroek Lydia Vredenburg	Sarah	Arie Vredenburg, Sarah Vredenburg
Aug. 1 or 10.	Henderikus De Pui Sarah Middag	Sarah	Jurian Westvaal, Margrita Westvaal
	Jacob De Witt Janetje Van Sikkelen	Maria	
Aug. 26.	Martinus Middag Elisabeth Kettle	Ariantje	Aard Middag, Ariantje Middag
June 24.	Peter Dekker Catrina Cool	Sarah	Josephus Cool, Sarah Cool
Sept. 4.	Joel Quick Christina Middag	Sarah	Jacob Middag, Elizabeth Middag
	Antony Van Etten Annatje Dekker	Blandina	David Dekker, Blandina Dekker
	Cleophas Latier Maragretje Titsoort	Barnardus	William Titsoort, Sarah Cool
Sept. 18	Dirck Van Etten Russie Westvaal	Petrus	Petrus Westvaal, Antje Van Etten
	Thomas Romein Susanna Van Campen	Nicolaas	
Oct. 30.	Daniel Cool Lydia Krom	William	William Krom, Maria Van Garden
	Jacob Nerapas Anna Maria Roaki or Rohbek?	Elisabeth	Frederick Rys (Prys or Kyer or Ryer), Francasje Prys
Nov. 13.	Leendert Wintemaut Phebe Comstok, (unbap.)	Philip	Philip Wintemaut, Maria Wintemaut
Nov. 28.	George Moore? Lena Roosekrans	Elisabeth	Cornelis Westvaal, Elisabeth Westvaal
Dec. 11.	Jacob Helm Helena Van Etten	Celette	Teunis? Van ——, Lyda Van Etten [Names faded]
Dec. 12.	——nes Rendle Sarah Van Gorden	Antje	
Dec. 17.	Maritje Wintviel, (Windfield), (widow)	John or Josua	Antony Van —— and wife
	Daniel Van Aaken Lea Kittel	Nathaneel	Daniel Middag, Catrina Van Aaken

DATE	PARENTS	CHILD	WITNESSES
1764.			
Jan. 8.	Daniel Kuikendal Elisabeth Van Aaken	Femetje	Johannis Van Aaken, Maria Van Aaken
	Antony Westbroek Sarah Dekker	Johannis	Johannis Westbroek, Magdalene Westbroek
	Henderikkus Johnson Elisabeth Boom?	Hendrik	Hendrick Cortregt, Debora Schoonhooven
	Jacob De Witt Lea Cortregt	Bodwyn	Derck Wintviel, Elisabeth Wintviel
	Joris or Jan Middag	Femetje	Daniel Cortregt, Sarah Middag
Jan. 28.	Johannis Dekker, Jr. Maragietje Gomar	Janche	Jacob Gomar, Alida Gomar
Feb. 12.	Abram Westbroek Blandina Roosekrans	Grietje	John Cortregt, Maragriet Cortregt, widow
Feb. 26.	Adam Dingman Maratje Van Garden	Eva	
March 1.	Jacobus Kermer Catrina Cool	Sarah	Andries Cool
March 25.	Abram Cool Annatje Dekker	Elisabeth	Johannis Cool, Maria Cool
	Abram Westbroek Agnietje Herlokker	Hendrik, 2 yrs. old, Yanneke	Derick Westbroek, Maria WestBroek, Martinus Dekker, Janche Dekker
	William Kuikendal Lea Dekker	Hendrick	Hendrik Kuikendal, Elisabeth Kuikendal
	Hendrikkus Kuikendal Sarah Dekker	Cornelia	Salomon Cortregt, Cornelia Cortregt
	Peter Beemer Elisabeth Hanneschat	Catrina	
	Charles Baseter Janneke Westbroek	Elizabeth	Johannis Westbroek, Sarah Westbroek
	Henry Beemer Sarah Hof	John, in his 3d yr., & Thomas	
	Johannis Beemer Ann Elisabeth	Elisabeth	Mathys Strouds or Strouder, Elisabeth Van Glien

DATE	PARENTS	CHILD	WITNESSES
1764.			
March 26.	Stephen Haccate (or Maccarte) Nancy Gibbons	Stephen, 6 yrs. old, Huwe, 4 yrs. old, Maragriet, 1 yr. old.	
	Huwe Haccate (or Maccate) Mary McCann	James, 3 yrs. old	
	Hendrick Johnson Jeruche Hunt (or Kint)	Geertje	
April 8.	Symon Westvaal Jannetje Westbroek	Ruben	Jacobus Van Vliet, Sarah Cool

The Manuscript from 1760 to 1771 is so poor that in many instances the copying is mere guesswork.

April 8.	Jacob Gomaar Alida Dekker	Petrus	Peter Gomaar, Elisabeth Gomaar
	Petrus Kuikendal Catrina Kettle	Martinus	Daniel Roosekrans, Catrina Roosekrans
	Frederick Sheyger or Keyser Feronica Hekke	Petrus	Frederick Staats, Sebella Staats
	Isaac Van Aaken Maragriet Hoornbeek	Jacobus	Jacobus Hoornbeek, Lydia Hoornbeek
	Benjamin Van Vliet Grietje Dekker	Annatje	Cornelis Westvaal, Elisabeth Westvaal
April 22.	Abram Glimps Janche Quick	Abram	Johannis Westvaal, Maragret Quick
	Petrus Brink Catrina Davids	Mosis	John Brink, Janche Van Garden
	Sarah Westvaal	Rosyna (oneght)	Benjamin Westvaal, Annatje Westvaal
	Jacobus Devour Maria Gomaer	Tjaatje	Johannes Dekker, Jr., Gritje Dekker
	Jacobus Davids Elisabeth Keeter	Jenneke	Jacob Van Nimwegen, Jenneke Davids
	Jacobus Roosekrans Catrina Cool	Salomon	Solomon Cortregt, Cornelia Cortregt
July 13.	Johannis Van Aaken		
July 20.	Petrus Cortregt Maria Westvaal	Symon	

DATE	PARENTS	CHILD	WITNESSES
1764.			
Nov. 25.	Wilhelmus Cool Lea Westbroek	Jeseos or Jacob	Lisa Dekker, Maria Dekker
	Wilhelmus Vredenburg Elisabeth Van Gorden	Catrina	Benjamin Rosekrans, Catrina Vredenburg
Dec. 2.	Gysbert Gysbertse Van Gorden Annatje Westbrock	Helmus	
	Jacobus Van Gorden Antje Van Etten	Heyltje	Cornelius Van Etten, Heyltje Van Etten
Dec. 16.	Jury Wintermoet, Jr. Catrina Cortregt	Elisabeth	Stoffel Wintermout, Elisabeth Cortregt, widow.
	Abram Kettle Cristina Westvaal	Jan, b. Nov. 28	Daniel Van Etten, Catrina Roos
Dec. 30.	Abram J. or Y. Van Aaken Maria Dewitt	Sarah	Cornelius De Witt, Sarah De Witt
1765.			
Jan. 6.	Cornelius Quick Maria Westvaal	Jurian	Jurian Westvaal, Maragriet Westvaal
	John Lydye Ariantje Rosekrans	Jacob	Jacob Van Etten, Jannetje Van Etten
April 27.	Daniel Van Etten Lydia Westbroek	Ferdenandus	Joseph Westbroek, Debora Westbroek
	Cherk Van Kuiren Westbroek Maria Helm	Maria	
	Petrus Hoogteeling Maria Westvaal	Leenty	Benjamin Hornbak, Lena Hornbak
April 14.	Petrus Rosekrans Maria Brink	Joseph	Joseph Hornbeek, Lydia Hornbeek
	Henry Bennet Sarah Dekker	Cobus	Cobus Hornbeek, Maria Hornbeek
	Brient Hommel Blandina Van Aaken	Abram	Abram Van Aaken, Jannetje van Aaken
	Cristoffel Cottenton Maria Oosterhout	John	
	Martinus Dekker Janneke Westbroek	Johannis	Johannis Westbroek, Sarah Westbroek

DATE	PARENTS	CHILD	WITNESSES
1765.			
April 14.	Matheus Terwilliger / Elisabeth Ratier	Jacobus	Jacobus Oosterhout, Annatje Oosterhout

[The foregoing six entries of April 14, are later on repeated in the original.]

1766. [Sic.: Probably error for 1765.]

DATE	PARENTS	CHILD	WITNESSES
May 28.	Jan Middag / Elisabeth Cortregt	Benjamin	Benjamin Quick, Catrina Quick
	Jacob De Witt / Lea Cortregt	Mary	Jonathan Middag, Maria De Witt
	Antony Westbroek / Sarah Dekker	Alexander	
May 29.	Johannis Beemer / Elisabeth Nagtigaal	Sarah	Johannis Westbroek, Sarah Westbroek
	William Kuikendal / Lea Dekker	Joseph	
	Henderikus Kuikendal / Sarah Dekker	Mosis or Moris	
	Hendrick Beemer / Lena Blenkenberg	Sarah	Johannis peckor Pach, Sarah Howel
	Leendert Wintermout / Phebe Comstock	Elisabeth	Johannis Beemer, Elisabeth Beemer
	Charles Basetis or Baxter / Janche Westbroek	Maria	Jacob Dekker, Maria Westbroek
	Peter Bemer / Elisabeth Hennischeth	Peter	Derick Westbrock, Maria Westbrock
1765.			
Oct. 28.	Abram Westbroek / Agnietje Horbeker	Sarah	Johannis Westbroek, Sarah Westbroek
	Alexander McClean / Lois Headly	John, Robert	
	Jacob Figly or Figby / Beeletje Davids	Eva	Jacob Kuikendal, Sarah Cortregt
	Cleophas Latier / Margaret Titsoort	Wilhelmus	Stephanus Titsoort, Catrine Titsoort
May 19.	Martinus Middag / Elisabeth Kettle	Jannetje	Johannis Westbroek, Jannetje Middag
June 9.	Jeremias Kettle / Lea Davids	Petrus	Gysbert Van Gorden, Maria Van Gorden

DATE	PARENTS	CHILD	WITNESSES
1765.			
June 9.	Petrus Cool Jannetje Keter	Simion	
Aug. 18.	Petrus Brink Alida Middag	Rachel	Gideon Middag, Rachel Middag
	Petrus Westbroek Lydia Vredenburg	Blandina	Daniel Ennis, Catrina Vredenburg
Nov. 11.	Antony Van Etten Annatje Dekker	Maria	Johannis Van Etten, Maria Van Etten
	Jurian Westvaal Grietje Quick	Hendrik Cortregt	Josias Cortregt, Gerritje Cortregt, widow
Nov. 17.	Cobus Van Aaken Elisabeth Benschoten	Johannis	Johannes Van Aaken, Maria Van Aaken
	Daniel Van Aaken Lea Kittle	Absolom	
Dec. 1.	Hendrik Cortregt Catrina Middag	Janitje	John Cortregt, Jannitje Cortregt
	Jacob Dekker Grietje Tilburg	Magdalena	Broer Dekker, Catrina Roosa
Dec. 27.	Abram Westbroek Blandina Rosekrans	Casia	
1766.			
March 22.	Derik Van Etten Russie Westvaal	Sarah	Johannis B. Westbroek, Maria M. Carty
	Harmanus Brink Lena Van Garden	Petrus Van Garden	Gysbert Van Garden Jr., Annatje Van Garden

The following two entries are in different handwriting from those preceding and following them.

1767.			
Nov. 16.	John Van Tillburgh Helena Van Weyen	Hendrikus, b. Oct. 29, 1767.	
	Martinus Middag Elizabeth Kettle	Elpina	
1765.			
Dec. 8.	Petrus Kuikendal Catrina Kettle	Lea	Daniel Van Aaken, Lea Van Aaken
	Elisa Middag Maritje Kimber	Helena	Casparus Kimber, Helena Kimber
	Jacob Nerepas Anna Maria	Benjamin	
1766.			
Feb. 19.	Symion Westvaal Sarah Cool	Symon	Symon Westvaal, Jannetje Westvaal

DATE	PARENTS	CHILD	WITNESSES
1766.			
March 29.	James Clark Sarah Van Aaken John Bill Mary Owens	Catrina no child given	Abram Van Aaken, Catrina Van Aaken Isaac (or Simon) Van Thuil, Catrina Van Thuil
1768.			
Feb. 13.	Derick Westviel or Wintviel Elisabeth Cortregt William Crom Maria Cool Abram Kuddebek Hester Gomaer	Femmetje b. Aug. 16, 1767 Sarah, b. Jan. 12 Jacobus, b. Jan. 4	 Soloman Kuikendal, Sarah Kuikendal Daniel Van Vliet, Sarah Van Vliet
1766.			
July 22.	Jacobus Davids Elisabeth Keter Daniel Cool Lydia Krom	Ann Cornelius	Thomas Kyte, Lea Kyte Ephraim Middag, Annatje Middag
Dec. 12.	Jacob R. Dewitt Janneke De Pui	Mosis John Bodly	Mosis a son, Benjamin De Pui
1767.			
Jan. 18.	Johannis Van Aaken Maria Van Garden	Jacobus	Jacobus Van Aaken, Elisabeth Van Aaken
Feb. 7.	Wilhelmus Cool Lea Westbroek	Cornelius Westbroek	Cornelius Westbroek, Sarah Kuikendal
Feb. 15.	Samuel Westbroek Catrina Fredenburg	Jacobus, b. Jan. 6	Johannis B. Westbroek, Antje Westbroek
March 29.	Jacob Westbroek Lydia Westviel Jacob De Witt [This is the way it appears in the original. He may have been a witness.]	Maria	
April 13.	Daniel Ennes Lydia Hornbek Helmus Vredenburg Elisabeth Van Garden Joel Quick Christina Middag Abram Sluiter Annatje Westvaal	Cobus Benjamin Salomon Geertje	Cobus Hornbek, Grietje Hornbek Benjamin Van Garden, Catrina Van Aaken Jacob Cool, Janneke Davids Silvester Cortregt, Maragriet Westvaal

DATE	PARENTS	CHILD	WITNESSES
1768.			
Jan. 23.	Samuel Gonsalis Elisabeth Van Vliet	Benjamin, b. Dec. 24	Benjamin Kuddebek, Catrina Cuddebek
Jan. 31.	Aard Van Dyke Catrina Schenk	Aard, b. May 25	
	Joseph Van Aaken Elisabeth Westvaal	Abram, b. Jan. 18	Abram Van Aaken, Maria Van Aaken
June 12.	Elias Cortregt Phebe Comstock	Anne, b. Feb. 12	
July 3.	Abram Kittle Christina Wesfal	Engeltie	Johannes Wesbrook, Engeltie Wesbrook
Aug. 1.	Jacob Helm Lena Van Etten	Catrina, b. July 1, 1768	

Names of children baptized across the mountain. (Overbergsche gedoopte Kinderen.)

1766.			
Nov. 22.	Daniel Kuikendal Elisabeth Van Aaken	Elisabeth	Hendrik Kuikendal, Elisabeth Kuikendal
Nov. 25.	Daniel Rosekrans Catrina Cool	Jacobus	Johannis Rosekrans, Alida Rosekrans
	John Williams Wyntje Van Winkelen	Cate	Peter Middag, Debora Middag
Nov. 26.	Josias Dekker Sarah Titsoort	Leentje	Samuel Dekker, Leentje Dekker, wife of Petrus Dekker
	Elk McQueen Ann Forva (or Corva)	Mary	
1768.			
May 28.	Hendrikkus De Pui Sarah Middag	Henry	
	Leendert Brink Rachel Cortregt	Femetje	Derik Wintfiel, Elisabeth Wintfiel
1767.			
May 28.	William McClean Sarah Van Aaken	Catrine	Daniel Kuikendal, Elizabeth Kuikendal
	William Howel Maritje Davids or Daniels	Petrus	Petrus Beemer, Elisabeth Beemer
	Abram Joh. Westbroek Angenetje Horlikke or Horbekker	Maria	Thys Straudes, Maria Westbroek

DATE	PARENTS	CHILD	WITNESSES
1767.			
May 28.	Frederik Hayn or Hoyn Catrina Dekker	Frederik	
1768.			
Sept. 18.	Johannis Beemer Elisabeth Nagtigaal	William, 9 weeks old next Tuesday	William Beemer
	Henry Brown Sarah Hof	Henry, b. June 12-67	
	John Lambert (or Havelent?) Sarah Stout	Elisabeth	Nicalaas van Teesselen, Elisabeth Ryker
	Elisabeth Strader	John, b. July 16, 1766	William Strader, Catrina Strader
	James Clark Sarah Van Aaken	Jacobus, b. Sept. 8	
Sept. 25.	Samuel Mattoks Maria Schouwers	Catrina, b. Aug. 14	Jacob Everit, Hanna Everit
Oct. 16.	Antony Van Etten Anna Decker	Tomas	Ezechiel Gemaer, Naomie Low
Oct. 23.	Jacob Van Etten Jannetie Low	Diana, b. Sept. 30	Daniel Van Gorden, Naomie Low

Children bapt. by me in this Congregation of Namanach & Machagkemch, since the year 1767.

1767.			
June 21.	Cornelis Cool Maria Dekker	Catrina	Salomon Dekker, Jr., Jannetje Roosekrans
	Johannes Turner Antje Devour	Esaias	
	Salomon Dekker Lena Quick	Petrus	Petrus Quick, Annatje De Witt
	Lydia Dekker onegt	Catrina	Abram Van Aaken, Esq., Catrina Van Aaken
Nov. 20.	Jurian Wintermout Catrina Cortregt	Mary, b. Nov. 2	Johannis Wintermout, Mary Wintermout
June 28.	Gysbert Van Gorden, Jr. Annitje Westbroek	Antje, b. May 22	Cornelis Westbroek, Antje B. Westbroek
	Cherk Van Keuren Westbroeck Maria Helm	Sarah	
July 12.	Harmanus Van Nimwegen Grietje Cool	Annetje, b. June 20	Jacob Van Nimwegen, Antje Van Nimwegen

DATE 1767.	PARENTS	CHILD	WITNESSES
July 12.	Matheus Terwilligen, Elisabeth Latier	Cleophas	Abram C. Van Aaken, Maria Van Aaken
	Josias Cool, Maragriet Mullen	Petrus, b. May 7	John Davids, Jr., Antje Van Etten
	John Wittiker, Eva Davids	Richard, b. Feb. 10	Harmanus Van Nimwegen, Grietje Van Nimwegen
July 26.	Thomas Kyte, Lea Keeter	Elisabeth Hoornbeek, b. July 2	Jacob Hoornbeek, Elisabeth Hoornbeek
	Elias Dekker, Janeche Dekker	Catrina	Johannis Van Etten, Maria Van Etten
Aug. 2.	John Waaker, Sarah Middag	Petrus, b. March 9	Petrus Middag, Deborah Middag
	Benjamin Schippard, Mary Nerapos	Lydia, b. May 27	Jacobus Quick, Lydia Van Aaken
	Benjamin De Pui, Elisabeth Swartwout	Elisabeth, b. July 8	Jacob R. Dewitt, Jenneke Dewitt
Aug. 23.	Abram Wintviel, Sarah Dekker	Abram, b. May 28	
	Cornelis Schoonhoven, Lena Devoir	Elisabeth, b. July 13	Benjamin Devoir, Hanna Rogers
	Jonathan Koole, Elisabeth North	Beulah, b. June 13, 1766	
Aug. 30.	Petrus Cool, Yannetje Keeter	William	
	John Lydie, Arriantje Roosekrans	Benjamin, b. June 30	Benjamin Roosekrans, Ann De Witt
Sept. 12.	Cleophas Latier, Maragriet Titsoort	Petrus	Abram C. Van Aaken, Catrina Van Aaken
	Jacobus Roosekrans, Jr. Jannitje Keeter	Engeltje, b. Sept. 2	Josephus Cool, Femitje Cool
	Elisa Middag, Maritje Cimber	Cornelius, b. July 18	Cornelus Cool, Maria Cool
	Jacobus Devour, Maria Gomaer	Elias, b. July 19	Elias Gomaer, Annatje Van Nimwegen
Dec. 7.	Abram Cortregt, Rebecca Quik	Ysaac	
Dec. 13.	Daniel Van Aaken, Lea Kettle	Yannetje, Rachel, b. Oct. 31	Derik Kettle, Rachel Kettle, Abram Van Aaken, Jannitje Van Aaken

DATE	PARENTS	CHILD	WITNESSES
1767.			
Dec. 13.	Cobus C. Van Aaken Elisabeth Benschoten	Johannes	Johannis Van Aaken, Maria Van Aaken
1768.			
Sept. 29.	John Kanneda Maritje Van Vliet	Jacobus, b. Sept. 5	Jacobus Van Vliet, Antje Swartwout
	Johannis Dekker, Jr. Sarah Hornbeek	Benjamin, b. Aug. 26	
	Johannis Dekker Debora Van Vliet	Magerie, b. Aug. 31	
	Benjamin Kuddebak Catrina Van Vliet	Jeryna or Jesyus, b. Aug. 31	
Nov. 6.	Daniel Van Vliet Sarah Kuddebek	Abram, b. Oct. 15	Abram Kuddebek, Jr., Hester Kuddebek
	Peter Dekker Catrine Dekker	Jeneke, b. Sept. 8	Benjamin Schoonmaker, Jinneke Schoonmaker
	Henry Bross Mary Cole	Abram, b. Feb. 29	Abram Cole, Mary Cole
Dec. 25.	Johannis J. Westbrock Engeltje Davids	Benjamin, b. Nov. 12	
1769.			
Feb. 5.	Daniel Ennis Lena Hornbeek	Elisabeth	
Feb. 18.	Cornelis Westvaal Elisabeth Westvaal	Zacharias, b. Jan. 8	Samuel Kool, Divertje Westvaal
	Peter Lot Sarah Sanders	Grietje, b. Nov. 29	Benjamin Van Garden, Grietje Low
March 12.	Jacob Gomaar Alida Dekker	Annatje, b. Feb. 12	Antony Van Etten, Annatje Van Etten
March 19.	Benjamin Waerd Barbara Sheffard	Johannis, b. Feb. 4	

PAULINGS KILL.

March 3.	William Beer Mary Lowrie	Peter, b. Oct. 15, 1768	
	Benjamin Kuikendal Anne Jones	Daniel, b. Dec. 17, 1768	
	William Goodwin Ruth Gibs	Sellie, b. Nov. 10, 1768	

DATE	PARENTS	CHILD	WITNESSES
1769.			
March 3.	Nicholas Elbertson Jupe Atos or Ater	Engeltje, b. Nov. 16, 1768 [After this name there appears some writing which seems to indicate that the woman was a widow, but the writing is so poor as to be undecipherable.]	
May 12.	Antony Westbroek Sarah Dekker	Elisabeth, b. Oct. 16, 1768	
	Cobus Van Winkelen	Aron, b. April 10	
	Duly Thomas Nehemiah Petteson Eusebia Gillet	Hester, b. Sept. 9, 1768	
	Jacob Cuddebek Maria Westbroek	Heyltje, b. Feb. 20	
May 29.	Josias Dekker Sarah Titsoort	Symon, b. Oct. 20, 1768	
June 27.	Alexander McGuym Anna Cova or Fero	Alexander, b. May 7, 1769	
	Abram Cool Annatje Dekker	Petrus, b. Sept. 5, 1768	
	Stephen Hacate Agnes Geavins	Eleonora, b. May 1, 1765 George, b. Aug. 4, 1767	
	Jacob Steel (Stol or Slot) Sarah Pepinger	Jacob, b. Dec. 7, 1768	
	William Howel Maritje Davids	Femitje, b. Feb. 9, 1769	
	Henry Beemer Sarah Hof	Petience, b. Feb. 16	
	Hendrik Barret or Bayert	Neeltje, b. May 12, 1768	
1769.	Elisabeth Range		
March 27.	James Patrik Elizabeth Prys	Maria, b. Dec. 8, 1767	Joseph Drake, Maria Horenbeek
May 31.	Charles Besetis Antje Westbroek	John, b. Feb. 5, 1769	Johannnis Westbrock, Sarah Westbrock

DATE	PARENTS	CHILD	WITNESSES
1769.			
May 31.	Hendrikkus Kuikendal Sarah Dekker	Jonathan, b. Dec. 20	Stephanus Titsoort, Catrina Titsoort
	Stephanus Dekker Femmetje Kuikendal	Elisabeth, b. Nov. 19	Hendrik Kuikendal, Elisabeth Kuikendal
	Stephanus Titsoort Catrina Kuikendal	Femitje, b. May 7	Hendrickus Kuikendal, Sarah Kuikendal
	William Kuikendal Lea Dekker	Emanuel, b. March 19	
	Peter Beemer Elisabeth Hennishot	Rebekka, b. May 1	
	William Jones Hanna Jones	William, b. Jan. 28	
	Benjamin Quick Hannah Jones	Maria, b. Jan. 7, 1760 David, b. Oct. 6 1762	
1768.			
June 26.	Teunis Quick Elisabeth Warner	Maragriet, b. Oct 11, 1767	Hendrik Avarts, Maragriet Avarts (or Avants or Vernits)
1769.			
Sept. 8.	Abram Sluiter Antje Westvaal	Elizabeth, b. July 19	Cornelis Westvaal, Elisabeth Westvaal
	Jacob Dewit Jannetje Van Sikkelen	Andrus, b. Aug. 27	
	James Rutson or Ratran Elizabeth Westbroek	Blandina, b. June 27	
	Abram Westbrock Blandina Roosekrans	Therk, b. Aug. 19, 1768	
Sept. 17.	John Stuart Ann Stuart	John, b. June 15	
	Benjamin Quik Catrina Cortregt	Rachel Corregt, b. July 29	
	Johannis B. Westbroek Lydia Hornbek	Catrina, b. July 15	Nicolaas & Catrina Ennes
1770.			
Jan. 14.	Benjamin Ennes Lena Van Etten	Elisabeth, b. Nov. 17, 1769	William Ennes, Elisabeth Ennes

DATE	PARENTS	CHILD	WITNESSES
1770.			
Feb. 9.	Gerty Brink onegt	Jacob Kuikendal, b. Dec. 3, 1769	Johannis Westvael, Maragriet Westviel
April 1.	Joel Quick Catrina Middag	Divertje, b. Dec. 17	Cobus Van Vliet, Divertje Westvaal
	Cobus Davids Elisabeth ——	Solomon, b. Feb. 25, 1770	Petrus Davids, Elisabeth Westbroek
Nov. 9.	Abram Van Aaken Maria De Witt	Rachel, b. Nov. 9, 1762	Abram Van Campen, Rachel Van Campen
	Abram Van Aaken Maria De Witt	Sarah, b. Dec. 2, 1764	Cornelis De Witt, Sarah De Witt
1770.			
July 29.	Petrus Cortregt Maria Westvaal	Sophryn, b. June 7	
	Samuel Williamse Lydia Cortregt	John, b. July 13	Johannes Williamse, Rachel Williamse
Sept. 12.	Jacobus Roosekrans Jannetje Keeter	Levi, b. April 8 or 3	Levi Westbrock, Susanna Keeter
	Abram Westval Antje Westbrock	Maria, b. Aug. 9	Daniel Westvaal, Maria Westvaal
Oct. 29.	Henry Schoenhoven Rebecca Mattanje	Joseph Mattanje b. Oct. 6	Joseph Mattanje, Maria Mattanje
	George Heeter or Keeter Antje Bunschoten	Maria, b. Oct. 5 or 8	
Nov. 4.	Samuel Middag Maragriet Westvaal	Lena, b. Oct. 20	
	Cobus Roosenkrans Maria Hornbeek	Helena, b. Oct. 11	Evert Horenbeek, Lena Horenbeek
	Benjamin Corua (or Corsen) Jannetje Hornbeek	Petrus, b. Oct. 20	Petrus Vernoy,? Antje Swartwout?
Nov. 14.	Jonathan Hoogteeling Dorethea Middag	Johannis, b. Nov. 1	Benjamin Vernoy, Maritje Hoogteeling
Nov. 25.	Mosis Cortregt Antje Van Etten	Annatje, b. Oct. 14	
Nov. 30.	Daniel Cortregt Antje Westbroek	Gedion, b. Oct. 21	Gideon Westbroek, Elisabeth Westbroek
1771.			
April 25.	Jesaias Cortregt Cornelia Cool	William Johnson b. March 25	Cornelius Van Garden, Maragriet Cotregt

DATE	PARENTS	CHILD	WITNESSES
1771.			
May 11.	Benjamin Wood Barbara Shiffer	Lisa Maragariet, b. Nov. 16, 1770	Hannes Shiffer, Lisa Maragriet
Sept. 22.	Samuel Westbrock Catrina Vredenburg	Daniel, b. Aug. 20	Daniel Dekker, Blandina Dekker
	William Johnson Maritje Dingeman	Johannis Batton or Baltus, b. June 17	Baltus Nerepas, Catrina Nerepas
	Petrus Westbroek Lydia Vredenburg	Benjamin, b. July 5	Helmus Westbrock, Maragritje Westvaal
	Eldert Oosterhout Maria Kettle	Rachel, b. May 13	Cornelis Van Garden, Rachel Westbrock
	Nathaniel Wasburg Christina Scheever	Patience, b. Oct. 12, 1768	
	Elias Cortregt Debora Comstok	Maragriet, b. March 18, 1770	
	Johannis B. Westbrock Lydia Hoornbeek	Lena, b. Aug. 18	Daniel Ennes, Leentje Ennes

The following entry is in English and in a different handwriting:
William Phenix, born on Sunday March 3, 1765 about 6 o'clock in the afternoon.
John Phenix, born on Wednesday, 6th of April 1768, at 11 o'clock at night. Parents, Andrew Phenix, (born at Minisink.) Effy Lane. Baptized by the Rev. Thos. Romeyn.

Dec. 1.	Daniel Van Aaken Lea Kittle	Joshuah	Anthony Van Etten, Annatje Dekker
Dec. 2.	Hendrick Cortregt Catharina Middag	Hendrick Jansen	Hendrik Westphaal, Susanna Cortregt
	Andrew Phoenix Efje Lane	Hendrick	
	Jeremiah Kittle Lea Davis	Catharina	Petrus Kuykendal Jr., Elisabeth, his daughter
1772. April 28.	Thomas Kyte Leah Keater	Johannes Hardenbergh, b. Jan. 29	Johannes I. or G. Hardenbergh, Cornelia Du Bois
	Jacob De Witt Gomaar Alida Dekker	Elisabeth, b. Dec. 25, 1771	Petrus Gomaar, Grietje Van Etten
	Elias Gomaar Margrietje Depuy	Tiatje, b. Feb. 19, 1772	Jacobus Devins, Maria Gomaar

DATE	PARENTS	CHILD	WITNESSES
1772.			
April 28.	Abram C. Van aken Catharina Rosenkrants	Abraham, b. April 11, 1772	
	Johannis Dekker, Jr. Sarah Hoornbeek	Jenneke, b. April 8, 1772	Helmus Westvaal, Jenneke Van Etten
April 29.	Johannes Van Etten Maria Gonsalis	Catharina	Hendrick W. Kortreght, Catharina Middag
	Jacobus Hoorbeek Margriet Ennes	Elisabeth Ennes	William Ennes, Catharina Ennes
	Benjamin Ennes Magdalena Van Etten	Alexander	Johannes Van Etten, Maria Gonsalis
	Jacob Van Etten Jannetje Louw	Margaret, b. Feb. 18, 1772	Martinus Westbrook, Margaret Louw
	Enos Randall Rebecca Kerker	Lenah. b. Feb. 13, 1772	
	Cornelius Brink Elizabeth Van Garden	Samuel, b. May 7, 1772	
	Abraham Quick Elizabete Kortright	Joseph	Joseph Van Auken, Elizabeth Westvall
	Christopher Decker Maria McCharty	Andries	William M. Charty, Elizabeth M. Charty
	Johannis Jorner Antje Devous	David	
	Petrus Lott Sarah Saunders	Petrus	Petrus Vernon, Rachel Van Auken
	Abram Westbrook Blandina Rosenkrans	Femmetje	
June 7.	Samuel Williams Lidia Kortregt	Samuel	
Aug. 27.	Moses Kortregt Antje Van Nette	Levi	Salomon Middag, Margaritje Van Nette
	Jacob Schoonhoven Appolony Prys	Elizabeth	John Prys, Lyntje Van Vliet
	Jacob Dewitt Leah Kortregt	Samuel	
Aug. 28.	Petrus Kortregt Maria Westfaal	Antje	
	Joseph Van Nake Elizabeth Westfaal	Isaac	

DATE	PARENTS	CHILD	WITNESSES
1772.			
Aug. 28.	Jacobus Brink Ariaantje Rosekrans	Lidia	
	Petrus Hoogteling Maria Westfaal	Abraham	Jacobus Westfaal, Lidia Kortregt
1773.			
Feb. 9.	Petrus Rosenkrants Maria Brink	Catherina	Abram C. Van Aaken, Catharina Rosenkrantz
	Wilhelmus Kool Leah Westbroek	Maria, b. Oct. 16, 1772	
	Harmanus Kool Margriet Swartwout	Sarah	
	William Custard Sarah Swartwout	Mary	
	Joel Dekker Jenneke Kortreght	Moses	Jan Middag, Elizabeth Kortregt
	Johannes Westbroek, Jr. Engeltje Davis	Heyltje	
	Jacobus Swartwout Jenneke Davis	Antje	Philip Swartwout, Debora Schoonhoven
	Divertje Westvaal oneght	Cornelius	Jacob and Leonora Westvaal
	Benjamin De Puy Elizabeth Swartwout	Jacobus	
	Jacob Kortreght Fametje Deenmerk	Elizabeth	Jonas Kortregt, Elizabeth Davis
	Jonas Kortregt Elizabeth Davis	Jacob	Jacob Kortregt, Femetje Deenmerk
	Leonard Brink Rachel Kortregt	Jonas	
	John Wallace Grietje Van Nimwegen	Isayas	Gradus Van Nimwegen, Catharina Van Vliet
	Johannes Quick Catharina Van Aaken	Sarah	
	Ephraim Middag Annatje Krom	Ephraim	Annatje Davis
	John McCartey Susanna Keater	Necholaas	

DATE	PARENTS	CHILD	WITNESSES
1773.			
Feb. 10.	Gysbert Van Garden Jr. Annatje Westbroek	Catharina	
	Daniel Dekker Rachel Williamson	Lena	Benjamin Dekker
	Lodewyk Hover Hesther Van Garden	Salomon	
	Alexendar Van Garden Lidia Karmer	Elia	
	Benjamin Rosenkrants Mary McGee	Francis	Francis McGee, Catharina Quick
	Jurry Wintermout CatharinaCortregt	Lidia	Samuel Williamson, Lidia Kortregt
	Jonathan Hoogtelink Dorothea Middagh	Lena	Daniel Ennes, Lena Hoornbeek
	Aart Van Dyk CatharinaSchenck	Catharina	
	Hendrik Westvaal Susanna Kortregt	William	
	Johannes Rosenkrants Jr. Maria Rosa	Catharina	William Ennes, Catharina Van Etten
	Johannes B. Westbroek Lidia Hoornbeek	Maria	Helmus Westbroek, Maria Westbroek
	Cornelius De Witt, Jr. Lidia Brink	Lodewyk Hoorbeek	AbrahamVan Aaken Jr., Maria De Witt
	Joseph Ennes Margriet Van Etten	Elizabeth	
	Jan Van Garden Elizabeth Van De Merken	Elias	Elias Van De Merken, Jenny Chesly
	Cornelius Dekker Geertje Brink	Maria	
	Isaac Schoonmaker Elizabeth Brink	Jacob	
	Gideon Middag Gerretje Kortregt	Rachel	Cornelius Van Garden, RachelMiddag
	Jacobus Van Garden Leah Van Garden	Seletje	

DATE	PARENTS	CHILD	WITNESSES
1773.			
June 17.	Cornelius Cuykendal Cristena Wornes	Samuel, b. April 2, 1772	Samuel Cuykendal, Mary Wornes
June 20.	Jacobus Keter Anna De Wit	Maria, b. March 10	Cornelius De witt, Liedia De wit

Baptized by Dom. Joh. Casparus Fryenmoet preacher at Kinderhook.

DATE	PARENTS	CHILD	WITNESSES
Oct. 17.	Jacobus Van Garden Antje Van Etten	Gideon	Gideon Van Etten, Rymerich Van Etten
	Jacobus Westfall Jannetje Decker	Elisa	Elisa Decker, Eva Dingeman, his wife
	Cornelis Van Garden Lydia Kortrecht	Souvregn	Petrus Kortrecht, Maria Westfael, his wife
	Abram Laen Lena Van Campen	Cathrina	Jacobus Van Garden, Cathrina Kortrecht, his wife
	Daniel Ennes Lena Hoornbeeck	Maria	
	Abraham Westfael Antje Westbroeck	Daniel	Daniel Westfael, Maria Westbroeck, his wife
	Samuel Westfael Margaret Lichert	Lisabeth, Apollonia	Johan Jurry Lichert, Elisabeth Wagenaer, his wife, Jacob and Apollonia Kittel
	Samuel Van Garden Jenneke Swartwout	Abraham	Abraham Chambers, Lena Westbroeck, his wife
	Wilhelmus Vredenburgh Elisabeth Van Garden	Josua	
	Angonitje Kermer oneght	Marritje	Cornelis Westbroeck, Sara Kermer. his wife
	Christina Everit onecht	Maria	Hendrik Kortrecht, Maria Westbroeck
	John Kortrecht Jannetje Middagh	Margriet	Hendrick W. Kortrecht, Margriet Jansen, widow of Wm. Kortrecht
	Daniel Van Garden Johanna Westbroeck	Maria	
	Bastean Meir Elisabeth Laen	Petrus Wilhelmus	Peter Lote, Sara Lote

DATE	PARENTS	CHILD	WITNESSES
1773.			
Oct. 17.	Isaac Van Aken Maragret Hornbeck	Seletie	
	Elias Cortrecht Debera Comstock	Febe	
	Samuel Metticks Mary Shauers	Samuel	Samuel Kittel, Rachel Westbroeck
1774.			
May 23.	Benjamin Ennes Magdalena Van Netten	Johannes	Johannes Van Netten, Mare Counsoles
	Daniel Decker Ragel Helms	Benjamen	Benjamen Decker
Nov. 16.	Samuel Kittle Russia Westfael	Catharina, b. Nov. 5, 1774	Samuel Quick, Johanna Kittle
	Jacobus Davis Elizabeth Keator	Polly	
	Daniel Cortregt Russie Van Aaken	Daniel	
	Petrus Cortregt Maria Westfael	Jannetje	
	Elias Dekker Jennetje Dekker	Manuel	Manuel Van Etten, Rymerig Van Etten
	Jacob Helm Helena Van Etten	Rymerig	Manuel Van Etten, Rymerig Van Etten
	Martinus Westbroek Grietje Low	Maria	
	Cornelius Brink, Jr. Elizabeth Van Garden	Cornelius	Cornelius Van Garden, Lidia Kortrecht
	Abram Kittle Christina Westfaal	Jurrian	Jurrian Westfaal, Margariet Quick
	Jacob Chambers Phebe Wallon	Neeltje	
	Jerremy Kittle Leah Davies	Elizabeth	Jerremy Van Aaken, Rachel Westbrock
	Matheus Brink Sarah Terwilligen	Samuel	Samuel Van Garden, Margariet Westfael
	John McCartey Susanna Keater	Elizabeth	
	James Wells, Jr. Jenneke Westbroek	Abraham	

DATE	PARENTS	CHILD	WITNESSES
1774.			
Nov. 16.	Jacobus Van Garden	Elizabeth	Wilhelmus Vredenburgh, Elizabeth Van Garden
1775.	Lea Van Garden		
June 14.	Gideyoen Meddag Gerte Choertrecht	Chatrein	Hendrick W. Choertrect, Chatreina Middag
	Samwel Decker Jantet Choertrecht	Lena	
	Hendrick Westfael Susanna Chaortrecht	Danel	
	Jacobus Kermer Catharina Cool	Elizabeth	
	Aldert Ploeg Cornelia Sluyter	Abraham	
	James Shirly Ann Quick	Catharina	Benjamin Rosenkrants, Mary McGee
	Sammuel Williams Lidia Kortreght	Jacobus	Jacobus Westbroek, Antje Westbroek
	Samuel Van Garden Jenneke Swartwout	Lidia	
	Dyrck Wintfield Elizabeth Kortregt	Peggy	
	Samuel Westbroek Catharina Vredenburg	Josua, b. March 23	
	Jacob Eberth Hanna Longerfeld	Marshal	
	Samuel Crosman Christina Eberth	Jacob	Jacob Eberth, Hanna Longerfeld
	Petrus Hoogteeling Maria Westvaal	Wilhelmus	
	Jonathan Hoogteling Dorothea Middag	Antje, b. Dec. 25 1774	
	Elias Kortreght Debora Comstock	Josias	Josias Kortregt, Cornelia Kool
	Daniel Van Garden Johanna Westbrock	Elsje	Evert Hoornbeek, Elsje Vredenburgh
	Cornelius Van Vlieren Susanna Snell	Jeronimus	Elias Van der Merken, Lena Kermer
	Nathaniel Washburn Christina Shafer	Anna Barbar	

DATE	PARENTS	CHILD	WITNESSES
1775.			
June 14.	John Steward Ann Beamer	Nicholas	
	Jacob Kortregt Femmetje Deenmarken	Jacob	
	John Cortrecht Jannyte Meddagh	Are	
Sept. 1.	Johannes I. Westbroeck Hester Schembers	Jacob	Jaen Westbroek, Leida Westvael
	Josep Lenes Margriet Vanett	Wilhelmus	
	Jackobeus Molnier Ragel Middaeg	Naomey	
	Edtwort Breffoert Roedy Comstock	Rebecca	
Sept. 27.	Josep Van Aken Elisabet Westfael	Aploney	
	Samuel Metex Mary Schoenwars	Migel	Jackobus Westfael, Johaenna Chettel
1776.			
Nov. 25.	Petris Roskrans Maria Brink	Abraham	
	Jarmiah Van Naken Ragel Westbrook	Cornelis	Martines Midag, Elisabeth Kettel
	Josias Cortreght Cornelia Kole	Blandina	
	Cornelis Van Garden Lidea Cortreght	Albert	Albert Van Garden
	Samuel Qick Yennek Cortreght	Marey	Cornelis Van Garden
	Johannis Rosecrans Maria Rosa	Jan	
	Abraham Westvale Antie or Lintie Westbrock	Catrena	
	Jacobes Brink Arejate Rosecrans	Dereck	Dereck Welbingt or Bulbungh (illegible), Jannete Rosecrans
	Cornelis Westvale Catrena Nerepas	Jacob	Jacob Nerepas, Maria ——
	Jacob Cheiners Lidia Westvale	Hester	
	Jonnethan Clark Altie Westvale	Daved	
	Danel Decker Ragel Willims	Leja	Samuel Willims, Ledeja ——

DATE	PARENTS	CHILD	WITNESSES
1776. Nov. 25.	Samuel Cortreght Gretie Westvale	"Elsabth"	Elsabeth Kole, Are Westbrook
	Jacob Chimers Febe Wallin	Lena	
	Cornelis Brink Sara Westvale	Jure	Jure Westval, Hannah Westval
	Jacobes Van Garden Antje Van Netten	Sara	
	Danel Ennes Elena Hornbeek	Lidea	Johannes Westbrook, Ledia Hornbeek
	Danel Middag Maria Bunschoten	Levi	
	Benjaman Ennes Magdalen Van Netten	Maria	Manel Van Netten, Maria Helm
	Johannes Van Netten Maria ——	Semijon	Semyon Westvale, Sarte Cole
	Abraham Kettle Cristena Westvale	Maria	
	Jacob Kettle Mareja Hendrik	Janneke	
	Phenes Wells Plonea Kettle	Betick	
	"Noah" or Nathaniel Wasborn Cristina Shever	Marcia	
	Abraham Kermer Anne Emens	Elesabeth	
	Samuel Westval Maregrita Liker	Catrina	
	Peter Brinck Catrina David	Salmon	Samuel Brink, Ragel Kettle
	Jones Cortreght Lesabeth Davids	Petres	
	Andres Dingman Jannke Westbrook	Cornelia	Andres Dingman, Catrena Cole
	Isack Van Naken Mareyte Hornbeek	Seletta	
	Benjamin Hornbeek Rebecka Wells	Sara	Joseph Van Nak, Sara Wells
	James Mollener Ragel Medag	John	
	Rusce Westvale ——	James Ma Carte	Hendreck W. Kortright, Hanna Westval

DATE	PARENTS	CHILD	WITNESSES
1776.			
Nov. 25.	Leendert Col Jen Brenck	Marey	
	Edtward Breffert Rody Comstac	Mary	
Dec. 25.	Daniel Van Aken Lea Kittel	Lea	
1777.			
June 1.	Benjamin Course J a n n e t j e Van Nake	Maria	Joseph Dreck, Gretje Van Nake
	Jacobus Quick Hannah Peltin	Polly	Molly Every
	Simion Westvaal Sara Coole	Jurry	
	Cornelius Schoonhove Lena Devoor	Benjamin	Daniel Rozekrans, Catrinty Coole
	Samuel Westbroek Maria Van Nake	Benjamin	Cornelius Van Nake Sartye Van Nake
	Thomas Kyte Leah Keator	J a c o b H o o r n- beeck, b. Nov. 1 6, 1775.	J a c o b Hoornbeck, Elisabeth Depuy
	Daniel Rozekrans Catryntye Coole	Jacob	Jacob Coole, Lidea Van Nake
	Josias Coole Margrita Mollin	Samuel	Samuel Coole, Janny Davis
	Johannis D e c k ker Jr. Sara Hoornbeek	Janneke	Janneke Van Inwege
	Hendrick Decker Gertje Brynck	Garretye	E v e r t Hoornbeek, Gerretye Van Nake
	Cornelius Van Imwege Leentje W e s t broek	Gradus	Harmus V a n Imwege, Grietye Cool
	Nehemyah Petterson Esaba Jillet	Esaba	
	Joseph Deckker Aeltye Westvael	Nancy	
	Jonathan Paers Blandina Terwilliger	Sara	John Wallis, Gretje Van Imwege
	Elias Gomaer Grietye Depuy	Samuel	Samuel Depuy, Antye Swarthout
	Clefus Littier Margriet Tithoor (Titsoort)	Josias	

DATE	PARENTS	CHILD	WITNESSES
1777.			
June 1.	Benjamin Van Garde Elisabeth Van Noy	Joseph	
	Moses Depuy Sara Low	Abraham	Ezegeel Gomaer, Noemmy Low
	Daniel Van Garde Johanna Westbroeck	Lena	Cornelius Van Imwege, Lena Westbroeck
May	Lendert Brenk Ragel Kortrect	Cathrynte	
July 9.	Samuel Decker Jannete Cortreght	Catrena	
	Jacobes Kermer Catrina Cole	Andres	
	Cornelis De Wit Lideia Brenck	Jacob	Rener De Wit, Ragel Van Naken
	Samuel Crosman Cristion Everit	Febe	Bastian Miers, Lisabeth Langevelt
	Nathannel Warsbon (Washburn) Cristina Shaver	Abeneser	
	Elias Cortreght Debora Comstock	Elias	
	Johannes Hendreks Lidia Kelder	Joseph	Joseph Van Naken, Elisabeth Westvale
	Christophel M. Decker Mariea McKarter	Jacobus	James McCarty, Lisabeth Barraber My (perhaps wife of) Pellip Westervelt

(This Pellip Westervelt or Westerm had been inserted afterward. These and many following baptisms were entered by a very illiterate person.)

Aug. 24.	Jeur (Jurry) Wintermoet Catrina Cortrecht	Greitet	Margriet Week
	Samuel Westbrook Catrina Vredenburgh	Wilhelmus b. Aug. 9	Wilhelmus Westbrook, Marya Cortreght
	Martines Westbrook Maregreta Low	Abraham	
	Johannes Cortreght Susanna Kittle	Susanna	
1778.			
Jan. 24.	Cornelis Van Garden Ledea Cortreght	Maragreta	Aron Cortreght, Maregreta Brinck

DATE	PARENTS	CHILD	WITNESSES
1778.			
Jan. 24.	Johannes Ja. Westbrook Hester Shimer	Abraham	Abraham Shimer, Lana Westbrook
	John McCarty Susanna Keter	Willim	
	Cornelis Brenck Sara Westvale	Russe	Jacobus Westvale, Russe Westvale
	Joseph Ennes Maregreta Van Netten	John	
June 23.	Jacob Helm Lena Van netten	Hester	
	Isack Van naken Grete Horenbeck	Gretie	
1769.			
March 19.	Thomas Kyte Leah Keater	Anna	Samuel Depuy, Antje Swartwout
1780.			
Oct. 29.	Haremanus Van Imwegen Maregreetje Coll	Janetje	
	Daniel McSweeny Greetje Terwilleger	Timothy	
	Sam'l Depuy Antje Swartwoud	Elisabeth	Benj. Depuy, Elisabeth Swartwout
	Elias Gumaer Greetje Depuy	Elias	
	Benj. Cuddeback Catharin Vanfleet	Benjamin	
	John Brooks Rachel Blizard	Gorge	Thos. White, Elisabeth Park
	Moses Depuy Jr. Sarah Low	Martynes	
	John De witt Westfael Maria Davis	Samuel	
	Wilhelmus Westfal Margret Hayns	Cathrina	
	Benj. Westfael Seletta Middag	Solomon	
	Benj. Gunsalis Alida Van Etten	Elizabeth	Henricus Van Etten, Elizabeth Decker
	Jacobus Quick Johanna Peltin	Thomas	

DATE	PARENTS	CHILD	WITNESSES
1780. Oct. 29.	Sylvester Cortreght Anatje Davis	Janneke	
	Johannis Westbrook, Jr. Angeltje Davis	Maria	
	Joseph Shawars Elisabeth Cortreght	Jacobus	Jacobus Rosekranse, Maria Hornbeck
	Asa Otley Sara Westbrook	Samuel	
	Francis Little Lena Nefe	William	Abraham Westfael, Blandina Van Etten
	Levi Van Etten Jannetje Westbrook	Jacob	Jacob Westbrook, Lydia Westfael
	Anthony Van Etten Annatje Decker	Anthony	Francis Little, Lena Nefe
	Jacobus Van fleet Maregreet Palmetier	Esyntje	
	Moses Cortreght Antje Van Etten	Safferyn	
	Daniel Van fleet, Jr. Martha Brown	William	Solomon Cuykendal, Sarah Cool
	Elias Middagh, Jun. Sara Van Aken	Elisabeth	
	Johannis Brink Blandina Westfaal	Jannatje	Simon Westfael, Jannetje Westbrook
	Daniel Van Aken Leah Kettle	Jeremiah	
	Solomon Middagh Elisabeth Westfael	Solomon	
	Samuel Middagh Maregreet Westfael	Dorothy	Jonathan Hogdeling, Dorothy Middagh
	Benjn. Hoornbeck Rebecka Wells	Joseph	Joseph Hoornbeck, Maregreet Hoornbeck
	Jacob Shymer Lydia Rosekrance	Hester	
	Johannis Quick Cathrina Van Aken	Marya	
	Petrus Quick Hanna De Witt	Johannis	
	Benjn. Van Garden Elizabeth Varnoje	Lydia	Benjn. Varnoje, Lydia Westfael

DATE	PARENTS	CHILD	WITNESSES
1780.			
Oct. 29.	Hendrick Decker Greetje Brynoek	Phebe	Petrus Varnoje, Sartje Varnoje
	Jonathan Hogdeling Dorothy Middagh	Saferyn, Petrus	Saferyn Middag
	Jacobus Decker Osseltje Van Aken	Helemus	John Van Aken, Jr., Elisabeth Van Aken
	Mary Bennett	Sarah Van Etten	Henery Bennett, Sarah Decker
	Hendrick C. Middagh Janetje Van Aken	Cathrina, Garetje	Helmus Van Aken, Cathrina Van Aken, Jacobus Van fleet, Janetje Van Aken
	Hendrick Bennet Susanna Bennet	Maria, Cornelia	Henery Bennet, Sarah Decker, Cornelius Cole, Maria Decker
	Sarah Hoghdeling	Joseph Brass	Benj. Hornbeck, Sarah Wells
	Christopher Decker Mary McCarty	Polly	
	James Williams Anna Barbara Squerrel	Greetje	
Nov. 1.	Hendrick W. Cortreght Cathrina Middagh	Cathrina	
	Petrus Westbrook Lydia Vredenburgh	Lydia, b. Aug. 28, d. Dec. 31, 1780. [It is uncertain whether this note refers to Cathrina or Lydia.]	
	Thomas Kyte Leah Keator	Rachel, b. Aug. 31, 1778	John Hasbrouck, Mary Hasbrouck
	Johannis J. Westbroek Hester Shymer	Abraham	Abraham Shymer, Lena Westbrook
	Jacob Eberth Hannah Langevelt	George	
	Jacobus Van Garden Antje Van Etten	Mary	Benjn. Rosekrance, Mary McGee
	Abraham Westfael Antje Westbrook	Benjamin	
	Jonathan Clark Altje Westfael	Abraham, Isaac	Abraham Westfael, Antje Westbrook

DATE	PARENTS	CHILD	WITNESSES
1780.			
Nov. 1.	Samuel Cortreght Margret Westfael	Lydia	Daniel Westfael, Annatje Westfael
	Johannes Cortreght Susanna Kittle	Johannes	
	Saml. Kittle Rusie Westfael	Jacob	
	Jacobus Rosekrance Jannetje Keator	John	
	Solomon Lane Lena Westbrook	Bethia	
	Johannes Rosekrance Maria Rosa	Abraham	
	James Wells Jannetje Westbrook	Sarah, Isaac	
	Cornelius Brink Sarah Westfael	Benjamin	Benjn. Westfael, Seletta Middagh
	Samuel Williams Lydia Cortreght	Margeree	
1784.			
July 9.	Jarnton Cleck (Jonathan Clark) Aeltey Westfael	Jacoeb	
1782.			
Aug. 18.	Haremanus Van Inwegen Margaret ——	Jacob	
	Abraham Westfael Blandina Van Etten	Joseph	Isaac Van Tuyl, Cathrina Terwilliger
	Daniel Van Aken Leah Kettle	Margery	
	Aldert Osterhout Marya Kettle	Nathan	Nathan Van Aken, Tryntje Wood
	Hagge Skinner Elisabeth Westbrook	Hagge, Magdelana	
	Daniel Van Fleet, Jr. Martha Brown	Rebeca	
	Daniel Myers Cathrina Van Aken	Daniel Van Aken	Daniel Van Aken, Leah Kettle
	Jacob Van Etten Sarah Decker	John	

DATE	PARENTS	CHILD	WITNESSES
1782.			
Aug. 18.	Elias Gumaer Margaret Depuy	Elisabeth	Benjn. Depuy, Elisabeth Swartwoud
	Garret Brink Cathrina Cortreght	Samuel	
	John Myres Anne Kettle	Mary	
	Benjn. Gunsalis Alida Van Etten	Anthony	Johns Decker, major, Annatje Decker
	Sylvester Cortreght Annatje Davis	Wilhelmus	
	John Brooks Rachel Blysard	Sarah	
	Jacobus Decker Usseltie Van Aken	Sarah	Simeon Westfael, Sarah Cole
	Hendrick Cor. Middagh Fametje Van Aken	Wilhelmus	
	Cornelius Van Inwegen Lena Westbrook	John	
	Uriah Masterson Hyltje De Witt	Leah	
	Jacobus Swartwoud Janneke Hoornbeck	Philipus	
	Elias Middagh Sarah Van Aken	Cathrina	Cornelius Van Aken, Cathrina Van Aken
	John Evens Ann Birney	Elisabeth, John	
	Levy Van Etten Janetje Westbrook	Solomon	Solomon Westbrook, Mary Westbrook
	Jacob Wilson Margaret Van Etten	Thomas	Jacob Gumaer, Alida Decker
	Johans Decker, major Sarah Hoornbeek	Mary	Moses De Witt, Mary Van Etten
1781 (sic).			
Sept. 6.	Johannes Westbrook Angeltje Davis	Benjamin	
	Jacob Dewitt Gumaer Alida Decker	Teatje	Peter Cuddeback, Esther Cuddeback
	Wilhelmus Westfael Margaret Hayns	Altye	

DATE	PARENTS	CHILD	WITNESSES
1781.			
Sept. 6.	Petrus Cuddeback Margaret De Witt	Moses	Moses De Witt, Janneke De Witt
	Jacobus Cuddeback Syntye Van Vliet	Geradus Swartwoud	John [s] Osterhoudt, Jannetje Swartwoudt
	Hendricus Van Etten Elizabeth Decker	Jesaias	Jesaiah Decker, Maria Van Etten
	Daniel Cortreght Antje Westbrook	Janneke	
	Daniel McSweeny Margaret Terwilliger	John	
	Jacob Shymer Lydia Rosekrance	Cathrina	
	James Ralls Peggy Gieter	Elisabeth	Jonas Cortreght, Elisabeth Davis
	Jacobus Quick Hannah Pelten	Samuel	Johannis Van Aken, Elizabeth Van Aken
	Christopher Decker Mary McCarty	Maria	
	Bastian Myres Elisabeth Longevelt	Elisabeth	Nicholas Christopher, Elisabeth De Camp
Nov. 25.	Petrus Varnoye Hannah Conclin	Elisabeth	Nicholas Conklin, Elisabeth Van Ditmars
	Elias Conklin Seletta Helm	Helena	Jacob Helm, Helena Van Etten
	Jacob Shymer Phebe Wallen	Mary, b. 28 Aug.	
	Benj. Van Garden Elizabeth Varnoje	Jacobus, b. July 25	
	Adam Dennis Mary Helm	John, b. 7 April	
	Wm. Halbert Mary Showers	Joseph, b. Dec. 30, 1780	Joseph Showers, Elisabeth Cortreght
	Jacobus Rosekrance Mary Hoornbeck	Blandina	Abm. Westfael, Blandina Van Etten
Aug. 31.	Jacob Dewit Lea Cortreght	Sapherin (Severyn), b. Feb. 3, 1781	
	Cornelers Schoonhover Helena Devor	Jacob, b. Jan. 19, 1780	

DATE	PARENTS	CHILD	WITNESSES
1781.			
Aug. 31.	Josias Decker Sara Teckworth	Maregreta, b. Nov. 4, 1780	
	Jacob Cortreght Femete Demarken	Ante, b. Oct. 2, 1781	
	Jacobus Teehore (Titsoort) Elesabeth Medag	Joel, b. Aug. 23, 1781	
	Solomon Cortreght Anna Ayrs	Sarah, b. Nov. 1, 1779	
	Derick Quick Jenneke Bunschoten	Saperine, b. March 5, 1781	
	Gerit Brink —— Cortreght	Solomon, b. July 5, 1780	
	Elias Decker Helena Depu	Hendrick, b. April 22, 1781	
	Hendric Brass Sarah Kool	Maria, b. Sept. 3, 1777	
	Jonathan Middagh Sarah Cortreght	Bostean or Roslean, b. Jan. 18, 1781	

These children were bap. by me Aug. 31, 1781—David Marenus.

	Jacobus Hornbeck Greetje Ennes	Lena, b. Dec. 23, 1780	
	Benjn. Hoornbeck Rebekah Wells	Jacobus. b. Feb. 23, 1780	Jacos Hoornbeck, Greetje Ennes
	Anthony Bunschoten Margret Decker	Lena, b. Feb. 23, 1779	Solomon Decker, Lena Quick
	Sam'l Morrow Lydia Decker	Lydia, b. July 8, 1781	
	John Steward Ann Rymer	Ann, b. April 25, 1780	
Nov. 27.	Francis Little Helena Neffe	Jannekie	
	Asa Otley Sarah Westbrook	Antie	

DATE	PARENTS	CHILD	WITNESSES
1781.			
Nov. 27.	Wm. Rose Mary Dewitt	William	
	Wm. Cuddeback Seletta Van Inwegen	Samuel	Thos. White, Elisabeth White
	Daniel Myers Cathrina Van Aken	—	
1782.			
Aug. 16.	Jacob Rosa Mary Rosa	Elisabeth	
	Solomon Lane Magdalena Westbrook	Elisabeth	Gideon Van Etten, Cornelia Westbrook
	Benjamin Hayns Susanna Shawer	Joh[s] Shawer	
	Hendrick Decker Geretie Brink	Moses	
	John Redford Teatje Van Garden	John	
	Wm. Neerpass Anna Hyse	Jacob	
	John Cortreght Janetje Middagh	Nicholas	
	Wm. McCarty Sarah Swartwoud	James	
	John McCarty Susanna Keator	John	
	Wm. Conklin Elisabeth Brink	Nicholas, Esther	Nicholas Conklin, Mary Conklin
	John Conklin Oseltje Varnoje	Jannetje	Joseph Varnoje, Jannetje Varnoje
	Arie Westbrook Maria Dor Cortreght	Jacobus	Evert Rosa Westbrook, Mary Cortreght
	Johan[s] Rosekrance Mary Rosa	Isaac	
	John Van Sickelen Rebekah Masterson	John	
	Hendrick Jas. Upinhuysen Anatje Reysly (Rigley?)	Elisabeth	Johannis Neerpas, Elisabeth Neerpas
	Abm. Quick Elisabeth Cortreght	Simeon	
	Benj'n Fisher Mary Bartran	Jacobus	

DATE	PARENTS	CHILD	WITNESSES
1782.			
Aug. 16.	Johannes Van Etten, Jr. Cornelia Decker	Johannes	Johannes Van Etten, Rachel Williams
	Joseph Van Aken Elisabeth Westfael	Sarah	Jacobus Van Sickkle, Sarah Van Aken
1783.			
June 22.	Sam'l Depuy Antie Swartwoud	Samuel Swartwoud	
	Arie Vrelingbergh Jane Van Aken	Caty Vrelingbergh	Benj'n Vrelingbergh, Caty Vrelingbergh
	Jacob Cole Lydia Van Aken	Jacob	
	Wm. Cuykendal Leah Decker	Jonathan	
	Josephas Cole Famatie Cole	Petrus	
	Evert Hoornbeeck Esther Cuddeback	Abraham	Abram Cuddeback, Esther Gamaer
	Cornelius Myers Catelyntje Cuykendael	Christopher	
	Joseph Wyndfield Cathrina Quick	Abraham	
	Moses Cortreght Antje Van Etten	Maria	Petrus Schoonmaker, Maria Van Etten
	Jacob Schoonhoven Apolonia Price	Levi	
	Salomon Cuykendael Marie Westbrook	Cathrina	
	Jacobus Cuykendael Gertruy Van Vliet	Jacobus	
	Jacobus Van Vliet Maregreet Palmetier	Michael	
	John Kenedy Marya Van Vliet	Thomas	Wm. Cuddeback, Esyntje Cuddeback
	Henricus Van Etten Elisabeth Decker	Annatje	Annatje Van Etten
	Joseph Schoonhoven Tryntje Wood	Rachel	Josias Cole, Rachel Wood
	Jacob Shymer Lydia Rosekrance	Derick	
	Sarah Hooghteling	Gertruy	

DATE	PARENTS	CHILD	WITNESSES
1783. June 22.	Isaac Opdegraf — Cathrina Van Aken	Sarah, Abraham Maregretie	
1785. May 5.	Peter Van Etten Maregrietie Brink	Derick	
	John Quick Maregreet Van Aken	Joseph	Joseph Van Aken, Elizabeth Westfael
	Wm. Cole Sarah Wells	Jesse	
	Cornelius Westbrook Mary Westbrook	Blandina	Lydia Vrelinbergh
	Jacob Helm Lena Van Etten	Jacob	
	Wm. Neerpass Anna Hyse	Caty	Benj'n Neerpass, Caty Vrelingbergh
	Hendrick Brass Sarah Cole	Henericus	
	Joseph Thomson Charity Brink	Margaret	
	James Westfael Caty Quick	Peter	Peter Hoogteling, Marya Westfael
	Simon Cortreght Cathrina Ennes	Maria, b. Nov. 10, 1784	Petrus Cortreght, Maria Westfael
1784.[?] Aug. —.	Thomas Kyte Leah Keator	Thomas, b. Aug. 25, 1781	
	Josias Kortreght Cornelia Roos or Kool	Elisabeth, b. Aug. 9, 1779	
	Hendricus Brink Helena Van Garden	Moses, b. May 14, 1780	Moses Van Kampen, Sarah Oberfield
	Benjn Wood Lydia Rosekrance	Helena, b. Dec. 7, 1780	Har Rosekrace, Cathrina Wood
	Jacobus Brink Anantie Rosekrance	Abigail, b. Jan. 7, 1779 Mary, b. June 18, 1781	John Smith, Abigail Bell Benj. Rosekrance, Mary McGee
	Peter Brink Cathrina Davis	Jacob, b. Oct. 17, 1779 Cathrina, b. April 2, 1781	Johannis Rosekrance, Marya Roosa

DATE	PARENTS	CHILD	WITNESSES
1784. Aug. —.	Cornelius Westfael Cathrina Neerpass	Jacob, b. Jan. 28, 1779	Jacob Neerpass, Christina ——
	Benjn Fisher Mary Bartron	Johannis, b. Jan. 28, 1779	Johannis D. Westbrook, Marya Brink
	John McCarty Susanna Keator	Josephat, b. April 22, 1780	
	Marya Brink	Ephraim, b. June 18, 1779	Josias Kortreght, Cornelia Cole
	James Mullener Rachel Middagh	Joseph, Ruben	
	Gideon Middagh Garetie Cortreght	William Cortreght, b. Oct. 10, 1779	
	Christina Eberth	Cathrina, b. May 16, 1781	Hendrick W. Cortreght, Cathrina Middag
	Samuel Westbrook Cathrina Vrelingbergh	Petrus, b. Jan. 4, 1781	
1781. April 18.	Cornelius De Witt Antje Westbrook	Maria	
Aug. 19.	Johannes Van Etten Rachel Williams	Daniel	
	Benjamin Ennes Helena Van Etten	Benjamin	
1781. March 13.	Rynier De Witt Sarah Quick	Famatie, b. March 15, 1781	
	Leonard Cole Janekie Brink	Margret, b. Aug. 17, 1781	
	Israel Wells Rachel Van Aken	Abraham, b. Feb. 11, 1781	
	Levy Van Aken Marya De witt	Elisabeth, b. April 17, 1781	Jacobus Van Aken, Elisabeth Bunschoten
1784. April 20.	Johannis Brink Blandina Westfael	Ruben Westfael	
	Sylvester Cortreght Annatie Davis	Deborah	
	Wilhelmus Westfael Margaret Hayns	Lydia	

DATE	PARENTS	CHILD	WITNESSES
1784.	Jacobus Quick Hannah Pelton	Cornelius	
	Jacob Gumaer Alida Decker	Jacob	
	Daniel Cortreght Antje Westbrook	Solomon	
	Ezekiel Gumaer Naomi Low	Abraham	
	Abraham Westfael Blandina Van Etten	Annatje	Annatie Van Etten
	William Cuddeback Seletta Van in Wegen	Abraham	Abraham Cuddeback, Esther Gumaer
Above baptized 20 April, 1784, by Dom. Soloman Freligh.			
June 8.	Samuel Caski Sarah Decker	Martin	Martin Decker, Mary Van Etten
	Isaac Opdegraf	Jacob	
	Wilhelmus Tichort Maregreet Middagh	Stephanus	
	Anthony Bunschoten Maregreet Decker	Cornelius	Cornelius Middagh, Lena Middagh
	Francis Little Lena Neffe	Caty	
	Jacob Wilson Margaret Van Etten	Mierom	
	Elias Middagh Sarah Van Aken	Abraham Van Aken	
June 13.	Benjamin Cole Sarah Kimber	Samuel, Margaret, Sarah	
	Samuel Kimber Maria Bennet	Sarah	
	Samuel Van fleet Janetie Clark	Annatie	Cornelius Van fleet, Annatie Van fleet
Sept. 26.	Solomon Kuykendal Maria Westbrook	Famety, b. Aug. 13	
	Jacobus Rosekrance Maria Hoornbeck	Ariantie, b. Aug. 13	
	Petrus Gomaer Anntje Van in Wegen	Elisabeth, b. Aug. 5	Corn⁸ Waller, Janetie Waller
	Cornelius Van in Wegen Lena Westbrook	Jacob, b. Aug. 4	Jacob Van in Wegen, Annatie Van in Wegen

DATE	PARENTS	CHILD	WITNESSES
1784.			
Sept. 26.	Jacob Schoonhoven Apolonia Price	Jannekie, b. Sept. 21	Jocobus Swartwoud, Jannekie Swartwoud
	Daniel Myers Cathrina Van Aken	Jacob, b. March 26, 1784	
	Lodewyck Van de Marck Garetie Van Aken	Elizabeth, b. July 25, 1784	Jacobus Van Aken, Elizabeth Bunschoten
	Harme Rosekrance Elisabeth Van Aken	Jesaias, b. May 6, 1784	
	Absalom Van Aken Magdalena Van Aken	Margaret, b. July 22, 1784	Isaac Van Aken, Margaret Hoornbeek
	Daniel McSweeny Greetie Terwilliger	Rachel, b. 24 May, 1783	
	John English Lydia Westbrook	Levy, b. Aug. 23, 1784	
1785.			
May 1.	Haremanus Van in Wegen Margrita Cool	Josias, b. Jan. 6, 1785	
	Samuel Depuy Antie Swartwoud	Antie, b. March 11, 1785	
	Abraham Cuddeback Janneke Dewitt	Hesther, b. Dec. 26, 1784	Abm. Cuddeback, Hester Swartwoud
	Henericus Van Etten Elisabeth Decker	Deborah, b. March 26, 1785	Johannes Decker, Deborah Van fleet
	Cornelius Van Aken Hester Depuy	Helena, b. Jan. 22, 1785	Benj. Depuy, Helena Depuy
	Jacobus Van fleet Maregreet Palmatier	Elisabeth, b. March 20, 1785	
	Samuel Kasky Sarah Decker	Mary, b. March 13, 1785	
	Evert Hoornbeck Hesther Cuddeback	Joseph, b. Feb. 16, 1785	
	Walter Simon Phene Lane	Jacob, b. April 27, 1785	Jacob Hoornbeck, Lydia Hoornbeck
	Samuel Morrow Lydia Decker	David, b. Jan. 2, 1781	

DATE	PARENTS	CHILD	WITNESSES
1785.			
May 1.	Wilhelmus Westbrook Alchie Westbrook	Joseph Jobs, b. May 30, 1785	
	William Crafford Cathrina Smith	Moses, b. Jan. 23, 1785	
	John Van Etten Margaret Berklow	Henery, b. Dec. 30, 1783	
	Rynier Dewitt Sarah Quick	Maria, b. May 7, 1784	
	Joseph V. Noy Mary Conklin	Benjamin, b. Dec. 29, 1784	Benjamin V. Noy, Lydia Westfael
	Elias Cortreght Deborah Comstack	William, b. May 15, 1784	
Aug. 27.	Elias Conklin Seletta Helm	Elisabeth	
	Daniel Ennis Magdalana Hoornbeck	Phebe, b. Aug. 4, 1785	
	Jacob Shymer Phebe Wallen	Susanna, b. June 21, 1785	
	Aaron Westbrook Marya Dewitt Cortreght	Emy, b. June 15, 1785	Roger Clark, Emy Skinner
	Cornelius Kettle Cornelia Westbrook	Rachel, b. July 14, 1785	Manuel Windfield, Rachel Kettle
	Peter Brink, Jun. Anna Grootvelt	Cornelius, b. June 25, 1785	Cornelius Brink, Sarah Hoghteling
	Israel Wells Rachel Van Aken	James, b. Aug. 6, 1785	
Sept. 18.	Samuel Morrow Lydia Decker	Solomon	
	David Westfaal Fametie Middagh	Grietie	Cleophas Latier, Greetie Tiechean [Tietshoort]
	Johannes Westfael Rachel Brink	Petrus Brink	Petrus Brink, Rushie Westfael
	Peter Van Etten Margaret Brink	Samuel	Lydia Rosakrance
	Arie Vrelingbergh Sarah Van Aken	Maria	Abm. Van Aken, Martin Dewitt

DATE	PARENTS	CHILD	WITNESSES
1785.			
Sept. 18.	Jeremiah Vandemark Esther Cortreght	Cathrina, b. Sept. 10, 1785	
	Aaron Cortreght Heylte Van Garden	Dorothy, b. Oct. 1 [sic.]	
1786.			
March 5.	Josias Cortreght Knelia Cole	Gideon, b. Feb. 5, 1786	
	Abraham Westfaal Antie Westbroek	Salomon, b. Jan. 23, 1786	
	Salomon Westbroeck Maragriet Dewitt	Jacob, b. Jan. 30, 1786	Ledia Westfael
March 8.	Levi Van Aken Maria De Witt	Hannah, b. Jan. 28, 1786	
	Elisa Decker Eva Dingman	Cattrina, b. April 5, 1782	
	Jacob Aptsepack Elizabeth Maticks	John, b. Nov. 13, 1785	
	Henry Horton Margaret Kimber	Bethiah, b. May 30, —— Sarah, b. March 10, ——	
	Petrus Van Noey Hannah Conkling	Elias, b. Nov. 23, 1785	
Jan. 22.	Jeptha Kelleam Mary Lot	Peter, b. Oct. 8, 1785	
	Samuel Hellem Annatie Westfal	Peter, b. Sept. 17, 1784	
	John McCarty Susannah Cator	Abraham, b. Nov. 26, 1785	
	Hendrick Openhouise Annatie Risly	Jacob, b. Dec. 1, 1785	
	Ezechiel Lane Jannetie Middag	Majory, b. Nov. 22, 1785	
	James Bunnel Elizabeth Shimer	Lena, b. Nov. 4, 1785	

DATE	PARENTS	CHILD	WITNESSES
1786.			
June 2.	Cornelius De witt Antie Westbroeck	Hester, b. Sept. 26, 1785	
	David Shoemaker Mary Tayler	Thomas, b. May 18, 1785	
	Antony Van Bunschooten Maragriet Decker	Maria, b. Sept. 10, 1785	
	Philip Traver Maria Shoemaker	Annatie, b. Dec. 22, 1785	
June 8.	Samuel Kettle Rushe Westfaal	Blandina, b. May 12, 1786	
	Abraham Carmer Sarah Allvord	Jacobus, b. b. April 26, 1786	
	Cornelius Brinck Sarah Hoogteling	Petrus, b. May 27, 1786	Petrus Brinck, Rushe Westfaal
	Joseph Ennes Margriet Van Etten	Joseph, b. ——, 1786	
July 9.	Abraham Westfaal Maria Masterson	Maria, b. June 1, 1786	
July 30.	Andries Decker Elizabeth Engler	Knelia, b. Oct. 20, 1785	Joannes Van Etten, Knelia Decker
	Ashkenas Shappee Mary Cooly	Jene, b. Sept. 15, 1780 Kezia, b. Nov. 15, 1782 Robert, b. Dec. 19, 1785	
Nov. 5.	William Crofford Cathrina Smith	Mary, b. April 15, 1786	
	Anthony Van Aken Rebecca Wells	Lodewyck, b. Oct. 11, 1786	Lode. Van Demark, Gerritie V. Aken
Dec. 31.	Saferyn Westbroek Blandina Westbroek	Jenneca, b. Nov. 8, 1786	

DATE	PARENTS	CHILD	WITNESSES
1786.			
Dec. 31.	James Rider Cattrina Showers	Cattrina, b. Oct. 4, 1786	
	Daniel Van Garden Johanna Westbroet	Martynus, b. Nov. 5, 1786	Martynus Desbri, Maragret Lowis [or Louw]
	Jacobus Westbroeck Geertie Brinck	Samuel, b. Dec. 10, 1786	
	Jonathan Clark Altie Westfal	Elisah, b. March 28, 1786	
	Leuwis Mead Levina Mead	Christian, b. Sept. 15, 1784	
Dec. 22.	Nelly Desha	Heyltie, b. Nov. 17, 1786	Morgan Desha, Heyltie Van Garden
	Salomon Lane Magdalena Westbroek	Melesen, b. Oct. 26, 1785	
	William Van Garden Lena Sherred	Samuel, b. b. Aug.—, 1785	
	Joseph Walles Elisabeth Wever	Sarah, b. Oct. 16. 1786	
	Aaron Van Campen Cathrina More	Elisabeth, b. July 11, 1786	
	William Aray Mary Painter	Isaac, b. Aug. 30, 1784	
	Andrew Cuikendal Margaret Tomson	Elisabeth, b. Jan. 8, 1785 Sarah, b. Nov. 3, 1786	
	Michael Seely Elshe Van Campen	Susannah, b. Feb. 23, 1784	
	Daniel Smook Francke Fortner	Sarah, b. July 25, 1784 John, b. Sept. 5, 1785	

DATE	PARENTS	CHILD	WITNESSES
1786.			
Dec. 22.	Adam Aray Caty Johnson	Jonathan, b. Sept. 25, 1776 Isaac, b. Feb. 3, 1779 David, b. April 1, 1782 Elisabeth, b. Feb. 25, 1784 Lydia, b. March 8, 1786	
1787.			
Feb. 11.	William Desha Elizabeth Wintermoet	Caty, b. Dec. 16, 1786	
	Daniel Van Garden Grietie Middag	Charity, b. Jan. 2, 1787	
	Samuel Middag Maragriet Westfal	Samuel, b. Aug. 20, 1786	
April 1.	Johannes J. Westbroek Hester Shymer	Hester, b. March 1, 1787	
	Art Brinck Lena Hoogteling	Caty, b. Sept. 3, 1768	Petrus Hogteling
April 22.	Welhelmus Westbrook Altie Westbrook	Hester, b. March 16, 1787	
	Jacobus Westfal Cattrina Quik	Hester, b. April 4, 1787	
	Daniel Westfal Maria Westbrook	Cherk, b. March 15, 1787	
	Walter Semon Fanny Lane	Solomon, b. Jan. 15, 1787	Solomon Lane, Lena Westbrook
	Aaron Cortrecht Heyltie Van Garden	Jacobus, b. March 28, 1787	Jacobus Van Garden, Antie Van Etten
	Israel Wells Rachel Van Aken	Jesse, b. March 26, 1787	

DATE	PARENTS	CHILD	WITNESSES
1787.			
April 22.	Jacob Dewitt Maria Decker	Jacob, b. Nov. 1, 1786	
	Benjamin Fisher Maria Barthran	Simeon, b. March 11, 1787	
June 7.	Cornelius Cettel Cornelia Westbrook	Chelly, b. Feb. 8, 1787	
June 11.	George Boman Elshe Metler	Eva, b. March 6, 1787	
	Antony Van Etten Magdalena Van Etten	Maria, b. July 9, 1787	
	William Cole Sarah Wells	Rebecca, b. June 21, 1787	"At" —— Van Aken, Reb. Wells
	William Van Garden Lena Sherred	Salomon, b. July 15	
	James Brinck Martha Arnot	Fanny, b. May 1, 1787	
	William Rouly Jane Daly	Samuel, b. May, 16, 1787	
Oct. 28.	Abraham Carmer Sarah Allward	Jemime, b. Sept. 27, 1787	
	William Crafford Cattrina Smith	Elizabeth, b. Aug. 3, 1787	
	Lodewyck Van Demerk Gerretje Van Aken	Jacobus, b. Sept. 29, 1787	Jacobus Van Aken, Elizabeth Van Bunschooten
	Jacob Shimer Pheby Wallon	Abraham, b. Aug. 4, 1787	Abraham Shimer, Lena Westbrook
	Samuel Helm Hannah Westfal	Jacob, b. Aug. 27, 1787	
	John Van Sickle Jane Rosakrans	Jacobus, b. Sept. 21, 1787	
	Jonathan Van Garden Lidia Van Sikle	Petrus, b. Aug. 19, 1787	

DATE	PARENTS	CHILD	WITNESSES
1788.			
April 27.	Solomon Lane Lantie Westbrook	Fanny, b. Nov. 17, 1787	
	Peter Van Noey Hannah Conkling	Ledia, b. Feb. 23, 1788	
June 1.	Rynier De Witt Sarah Quick	Maragriet, b. March 8, 1788	
May 29.	Jacobus Westbrook Geertie Brinck	Cattrina, b. May 9, 1788	
June 1.	Leonard Cole Jenneca Brinck	Joseph, b. March 10, 1788	
	William Cole Sarah Fuller	Andris, b. April 18, 1788	
	David Mooren Tabitha Boorten	William, b. Nov. 8, 1785	
	Antony Van Bunschooten Maragriet Decker	Thomas, b. Jan. 29	
June 22.	James Bolett Elizabeth Chimer	Cattrina, b. Oct. 28, 1787	
	John Lonsbery Mary Carr	John, b. April 22, 1784	
	William Cortrecht Elizabeth Brinck	Hester, b. b. March 1, 1788	
	Samuel Helm Polly Tiff	Bethcy, b. May 30, 1788	
July 13.	Ary Westbrook Mary Cortright	Alexander, b. April 16, 1787	
	Moses Brinck Anny Cortrecht	Joseph, b. Feb. 2, 1788	
	Robert Carman Sarah Tifft	Joseph, b. May 27, 1787 Deborah, b. Aug. 21, 1779 Roberd, b. May 4, 1781	

DATE	PARENTS	CHILD	WITNESSES
1788.			
July 13.	Robert Carman Sarah Tifft	Patty, b. Feb. 22, 1783 Sarah, b. Oct. 22, 1784 Susannah, b. July 6, 1786 Charlothy, b. Feb. 27, 1788	
	Jepthah Killam Mary Lott	John, b. Nov. 25, 1787	
Aug. 24.	Jacobus Brinck Arriantie Rose- krans	Mattheus, b. June 28, 1788	
	Joseph Kettle Sarah Van Etten	Maria, b. June 17, 1788	
	Soveryn Westbrook Blandina West- brook	Jacob, b. Aug. 3. 1788	Lidea Westfael
Oct. 12.	Abraham Westfal Antie Westbrook	Lidia, b. Sept. 18, 1788	
	Joseph Ennes Maragriet Van Etten	Daniel, b. Sept. 21, 1788	
Oct. 26.	Robard Faulkner Ariaantie Schoon- maker	Cornelius Schoon- maker, b. March 23, 1786 Abraham, b. Feb. 4, 1788	
	Jefred Root Rachel Peer	Catherine, b. Feb. 22, 1788	
	Nicholas Van Loon Experience Parks	Hannah, b. Sept. 22, 1787	
	Barnardus Deen- merk Mary Chambers	Lea, b. Sept. 14, 1788	
	Wilhelmus Cham- bers Clouwdiana Sophia Deenmerk	Lea, b. July 1, 1786	

DATE	PARENTS	CHILD	WITNESSES
1788.			
Oct. 26.	James Erl Susanna Love	Samuel, b. Oct. 11, 1784 Mathew, b. May 11, 1786	
	Samuel Penet Anny Van Garden	Benjamin, b. March 3, 1788	
Oct. 27.	Ezechiel Williams Lidia Westbrook	Lea, b. May 20, 1788	
	Peter Dingman Creshe Stofflebeen	Eva, b. June 2, 1787	
	John Taylor Elizabeth Swartwout	Lidia, b. June 4, 1788	
	Thomas Drake Agnas Fourman	Ruth, b. Nov. 12, 1786 George, b. Oct. 17, 1788	
	Peter Swartwout Sarah Baker	Mary, b. June 20, 1788	
Oct. 28.	Joannes Rosekrans Maria Rosa	Rebecca, b. Jan. 28, 1785 Jacob, b. July 10, 1786 Joannes, b. April 29, 1788	
	Simeon Miller Elizabeth Peer	James, b. Sept. 3, 1788	
Oct. 25.	Elias Decker Caty Lions	Clara, b. Oct. 12, 1787	
	Andrew Decker Elizabeth Inglet	Eva, b. March 2, 1788	
	Elisha Decker Rachel Dyckman	Maria, b. Aug. 22, 1788	
Oct. 29.	Daniel Middag Maria Van Bunschoten	—	

DATE	PARENTS	CHILD	WITNESSES
1788.			
Oct. 29.	Philip Jacson Sarah McDool	Anny, b. Nov. 4, 1788	
Oct. 30.	William Richerd Rachel Devenport	Nathaniel, b. Sept. 20, 1788	
	Nathan Dreaper Hannah Cortright	Saly, b. May 27, 1788	Wyomy [place of baptism]
Nov. 9.	Jacob Plouegh Lidia Cortright	Jenny, b. April 9, 1788	
	Abraham Westfaal Maria Masterson	Elizabeth, b. Oct. 8, 1788	
	Jonathan Hoghtel-ing Dortea Middag	Grietie, b. June 15, 1788 Simeon, b. June 10, 1786	
Dec. 28.	Thomas Van Etten Elizabeth Ennes	Daniel, b. Nov. 8, 1788	
Nov. 15.	Cornelious De Witt, Jr. Antie Westbroock	Elizabeth, b. Sept. 6, 1788	
1789.			
Feb. 8.	Salomon Westbrook Maragriet De Witt	Joannes, b. Jan. 9, 1789	
	Willaim Cortreght Cattrina Helm	Samuel, b. Jan. 2, 1789	
March 29.	Aaron Cortright Hyltie Van Garden	Petrus, b. Jan. 9, 1789	
March 31.	Johannes Van Etten Rachel Williams	Solomon, b. Feb. 12, 1789	
	Jacobus Van Etten Maria Schick	Josua, b. Feb. 21, 1789	
April 18.	Samuel Kittle Rushe Westfal	Simeon, b. March 18, 1789	
June 6.	Jacobus Van Garden Antie Van Etten	Jacobus, b. April 29, 1789	

DATE	PARENTS	CHILD	WITNESSES
1788.			
Oct. 26	James Erl Susanna Love	Samuel, b. Oct. 11, 1784 Mathew, b. May, 11 1786	
	Samuel Penet Anny Van Garden	Benjamin, b. March 3, 1788	
Oct. 27.	Ezechiel Williams Lidia Westbrook	Lea, b. May 20, 1788	
	Peter Dingman Cresshe Stofflebeen	Eva, b. June 2, 1787	
	John Taylor Elizabeth Swartwout	Lidia, b. June 4, 1788	
	Thomas Drake Agnes Fourman	Ruth, b. Nov. 12, 1786 George, b. Oct. 17, 1788	
	Peter Swartwout Sarah Baker	Mary, b. June 20, 1788	
Oct. 28.	Joannes Rosekrans Maria Rosa	Rebecca, b. Jan. 28, 1785 Jacob, b. July 10, 1786 Joannes, b. April 29, 1788	
	Semeon Meller Elizabeth Peer	James, b. Sept. 3, 1788	
Oct. 25.	Elias Decker Caty Lions	Clara, b. Oct. 12, 1787	
	Andrew Decker Elizabeth Inglet	Eva, b. March 2, 1788	
	Elisha Decker Rachel Dyckman	Maria, b. Aug. 22, 1788	

DATE	PARENTS	CHILD	WITNESSES
1788.			
Oct. 29.	Daniel Middag Maria Van Bunschoten	No child given	
	Philip Jackson Sarah McDool	Anny, b. Nov. 4, 1788	
Oct. 30.	William Rechard Rachel Devenport	Nathaniel, b. Sept. 20, 1788	
	Nathan Dreaper Hannah Cortright	Saly, b. May 27, 1788	Wyomy [place of baptism]
Nov. 9.	Jacob Plough Lidia Cortright	Jenny, b. April 9, 1788	
	Abraham Westfal Maria Masterson	Elizabeth, b. Oct, 8, 1788	
	Jonathan Hoghtaling Dortea Middag	Grietie, b. June 15, 1788	
		Simeon, b. June 10, 1786	
Dec. 28.	Thomas Van Etten Elizabeth Ennes	Daniel, b. Nov. 8, 1788	
Nov. 15.	Cornelius DeWitt, Jr. Antie Westbrook	Elizabeth, b. Sept. 6, 1788	
1789.			
Feb. 8.	Salomon Westbrook Maragreit De Witt	Joannes, b. Jan. 9, 1789	
	William Cortreght Cattrina Helm	Samuel, b. Jan. 2, 1789	
March 29.	Aaron Cortreght Hyltie Van Garden	Petrus, b. Jan. 9, 1789	
March 31.	Johannes Van Etten Rachel Williams	Solomon, b. Feb. 12, 1789	
	Jacobus Van Etten Maria Schick	Joshua, b. Feb. 21, 1789	

DATE	PARENTS	CHILD	WITNESSES
1789.			
April 18.	Samuel Kettle Russie Westfal	Simeon, b. March 18, 1789	
June 6.	Jacobus Van Garden Antie Van Etten	Jacobus, b. April 29, 1789	
June 7.	Jacob Schimer Phiby Wallon	Elizabeth, b. April 3, 1789	
June 11.	Daniel Westfal Maria Westbroock	Benjamin, b. May 25, 1789	
July 26.	Jacobus Westfal Cattrina Quick	Jennika, b. June 23, 1789	
June 28.	John Leutie Elizabeth Fansworth	Josiah, b. Sept. 14, 1781 William, b. Feb. 4, 1785 Rossanah, b. May 20, 1785 Elizabeth, b. May 24, 1789	Wyomy [place of baptism]
June 30.	Ebenezer Earl Susannah Ray	Roberd, b. Dec. 4, 1789	
July 1.	James Earl Susanna Love	Ebenezer, b. May 28, 1789	
	Benjamin Cursan Mary Chesnor	Elizabeth, b. June 5, 1782 Benjamin, b. March 25, 1785 Mary, b. Feb. 20, 1789	
	Moses Chamber Susanna Young	Peter, b. March 10, 1789	

DATE	PARENTS	CHILD	WITNESSES
1789.			
July 1.	Stephen Arnold Lois Darbishire	Lois, b. Dec. 11, 1783 Persela, b. June 25, 1786 Delilah, b. March 28, 1788	
July 3.	Perregrin Jones Mary Van Garden	Mary, b. June 17, 1789 Isaac, b. Sept. 11, 1779	Abraham Westbrook Blandina Rosekrans
	Cornelius Cortright Caty Cannaday [Kennedy]	Benjamin, b. March 19, 1789	
July 6.	Thomas Reed Jenny Hover	Catterine, b. March 17, 1787 Benjamin, b. Feb. 15, 1789	
	Nathan Draper Hannah Cortright	John, b. May 14, 1789	
July 7.	John King, Jr., Mary Walker	John, b. Aug. 5, 1786 Jacob Walker, b. Sept. 17, 1788	John King Margaret Miller
	Samuel Finch Mary King	David, b. June 27, 1788	
July 8.	Philip Jackson Sarah McDool	Asa, b. Jan. 8, 1789	
	David Shaunts Doritia Shoonmaker	Elizabeth, b. April 25, 1788	Wyomy
April 18.	Benjamin Fisher Maria Bartron	Samuel, b. April 4, 1789	
	Helmus Westbrook Altie Westbrook	Cathrina, b. June 11, 1789	

DATE	PARENTS	CHILD	WITNESSES
1789.			
April 18.	Cornelius D. (or P.) Westbrook Maria Westbrook	Blandina b. Dec. 31, 1784	Ledia Westfaal
May 24.	Daniel Van Garden, Jr. Margaret Middag	Joannes, b. April 20, 1789	
	William Van Garden Helen Sherred	Anny, b. April 18, 1789	
Dec.	Gideon Cole Maria Van Etten	Jannitie, b. Dec. 1, 1789	
1790.			
April 25.	Abraham Westbrook Jannetie Van Aken	Maria, b. Feb. 13, 1790	
1795.			
Aug. 17.	Peter Kittle Nelly Shimer	Jacob, b. Aug. 2, 1794	
	Samuel Brinck Cattrina Kettle	Susannah, b. Feb. 24, 1795	
	Johannes Kortright Susanna Kettle	Elizabeth, b. March 29, 1772	
	Abraham Cuddeback Hester Gornor	Cornelius, b. Jan. 2, 1772	
	Elias Middagh Maria Decker	Maria, b. Jan. 29, 1772	
	Jacobus Quick Janake Van Anken	Leenah, b. Feb. 8, 1772	
	Johannes Decker Debora Van Vliet	Celletie, b. Jan. 8, 1772	
1789.			
Aug. 15.	James Brinck Martha Ernet	Hannah, b. July 7, 1789	
Aug. 17.	Jonathan Clark Altie Westfal	Jonathan, b. March 8, 1789	
Sept. 20.	Samuel Quick Maria Helm	Caty, b. Aug. 14, 1789	

DATE	PARENTS	CHILD	WITNESSES
1789.			
Sept. 20.	George Lane Blandina Middag	James, b. Sept. 30, 1787	James Bennet Catrine Middag
Aug. 19.	John Brink, Jr. Lena Cole	William, b. April 11, 1789	
Nov. 29.	Isias Cortreght Knelia Cole	Andriss, b. Nov. 8, 1789	
Dec. 7.	Hendrick Optehoms Hennah Rysly	Jacobus, b. Oct. 8, 1789	
Dec. 20.	Peter Quick Hannah Dewitt	Jannitie, b. Nov. 15, 1789	
	Jeremia Rosekrans Sarah Stricklin	Jannitie, b. Oct. 8, 1789	
	James Wells Catrine Van Aken	John, b. Feb. 5, 1788	
		Polly, b. Aug. 28, 1789	
	John Van Sikel Jannitie Rosekrans	Maria, b. Nov. 3, 1789	
Dec. 21.	Gideon Cole Maria Van Etten	Jannitie, b. Dec. 1, 1789	
	Elisha Van Aken Cattrina Cole	Elisah, b. Jan. 16, 1789	
1789. March 8.	Antony Van Aken Rebecka Wells	Elizabeth, b. Feb. 5, 1789	
	Jonathan Van Garden Lidia Van Sikel	Grietie, b. Feb. 21, 1789	
	Abraham Carmen Sarah Allward	Daniel, b. Sept. 3, 1789	
1790. April 4.	William Crofford Catterine Smith	William, b. Oct. 22, 1789	
May 15.	Jepthah Killan Mary Lott	Pheby, b. March 23, 1790	

DATE	PARENTS	CHILD	WITNESSES
1790.			
May 15.	William Cole Sarah Wells	Thomas, b. April 5, 1790	
June 5.	Aaron Vredenburgh Sarah Van Aken	Elizabeth, b. May 3, 1790	Helmus Vredenburgh, Elizabeth Van Garden
	Jaspar Taylor Cattrine Edmond	Samuel, b. April 28, 1786 James, b. Aug. 30, 1788	
July 25.	Samuel Cortrecht Gretie Westfal	Reuben, b. April 23, 1890	
	Hendrick Westfal Maragriet Brinck	Jurean, b. June 26, 1790	
	Jacobus Enness Hannah Dewitt	Bethey, b. June 14, 1790	
Aug. 15.	Boudewyn Brinck Rachel Van Aken	Samuel, b. March 2, 1789	"Geswœre Vader" [Sworn father] Johannes Westfal, sponsor
	Samuel Helm Annatie Westfal	Abraham, b. July 2, 1790	
Sept. 5.	Jacobus Westbrook Geertie Brinck	Elizabeth, b. Aug. 5, 1790	
	Peter Van Noye Hannah Conkling	Mary, b. Aug. 27, 1790	Joseph Van Noye, Mary Conkling
	Robert Carman Sarah Tefft	John White, b. Feb. 8, 1790	
Sept. 25.	William Simon Fanny Lane	Lea, b. Oct. 17, 1789	
	Samuel Westfal Anny Lane	Bethiah, b. Aug. 21, 1790	
	Jonathan Hogaling Dorothea Middag	Ephraim, b. Aug. 25, 1790	
	Maria Cortrecht	Debora, b. Sept. 4, 1790	

DATE	PARENTS	CHILD	WITNESSES
1790.			
Sept. 25.	John Quick Grietie Van Aken	Maria, b. Aug. 28, 1790	
	John Van Garden Rachel Brinck	Abraham, b. April 22, 1790	
	Henry Devenport Kesia Westbrook	Jacobus, b. Sept. 26, 1790	
Nov. 1.	Cornelius Cortrecht Cattrina Caneda	Caty, b. Oct. 11, 1790	
		John, b. Oct. 12, 1790	
	James Brinck Ariaantie Rosekrans	Ester, b. Sept. 14, 1790	
	Adriaan Line Elizabeth Cortreght	Conrad, b. July 26, 1789	
1791. June 15.	Coenrad Line Alida Look	Maritie, b. Sept. 19, 1789	
	Elias Decker Caty Line	Coenrad, b. Nov. 13, 1789	
	John Fairchild Mary Fredericks	Mary, b. April 1, 1790	
	Andrew Decker Elisabeth Engelar	John, b. May 23, 1789	
June 27.	Frederick Onson Elizabeth Walker	Elizabeth, b. Feb. 20, 1790	
	Leonard Westbrook Margaret Brinck	Chark, b. June 22, 1789	
June 29.	Joseph Dewey Susannah Begly	Rhody, b. Nov. 20, 1771 Susannah, b. June 18, 1780 Sarah, b. June 9, 1786 Pheby, b. Aug. 12, 1788	

DATE	PARENTS	CHILD	WITNESSES
1791.			
July 4.	John Windle Mary Fish	James, b. May 3, 1790	
	Edward Edgerton Prudence Delay	James, b. July 28, 1789	(Was baptized and received as church member July 4, 1790
	Richard Westbrook Anny Hover	Sarah, b. Oct. 28, 1789	
	William Howke Peggy Westbrook	Blandina, b. Feb. 11, 1790	
	John Ryan Sarah Walker	John, b. Dec. 3, 1786 Sarah, b. June 10, 1790	
July 7.	Abraham Van Gargen Elizabeth Love	Isaac, b. Aug. 28, 1789	Bapt. at Wyomy
Jan. 1.	Daniel Westfal Maria Westbrook	Abraham Westbrook, b. Dec. 8, 1790	
1789. May 24.	Jacob Miers Sarah Cortrecht	Josias, b. March 24, 1789	
	Soveryn Westbrook Blandina Westbrook	Lidia, b. Dec. 5, 1790	Lidia Westbrook, sponsor.
	Benjamin Westbrook Lena Ennes	Lidia, b. Dec. 22, 1790	Lidia Vredenburgh, sponsor.
1791. May 15.	Abraham Westfal, Jr. Maria Masterson	Jannitie, b. March 14, 1791	
June 5.	William Cortrecht Elizabeth Brink	Cattrina, b. March 5, 1791	
	William Cortrecht, Jr. Cattrina Helm	Hester, b. Oct. 19, 1790	
	Stephen Manrow Pheby Cortright	William, b. May 13, 1791	

DATE	PARENTS	CHILD	WITNESSES
1791.			
June 5.	Samuel Helm Polly Tiff	Daniel, b. July 2, 1790	
	Jacob Shimer Pheby Wallon	Jacob, b. April 9, 1791	Jacob Shimer, Lidea Van Aken
	Peter Brink Lidia Brink	Nelly, b. April 26, 1791	Henry Brink, Nelly Krandal
July 17.	Joseph Ennes Maragreit Van Etten	Cattrine, b. May 27, 1791	
	Benjamin Fisher Maria Bartron	Elia, b. June 13, 1791	
Aug. 7.	William Crawford Cattrina Smith	John and Amy, b. May 18, 1791	
Sept. 18.	Cornelius P. Westbrook Maria Westbrook	Lidia, b. Aug. 4, 1791	Lidia Westfal
	Cornelius Little Knelia Westbrook	Salomon, b. Feb. 9, 1791	
Oct. 23.	Daniel Van Garden, Jr. Margaret Middag	Knelia, b. Aug. 18, 1791	
	William Van Garden Helena Sherred	Catrina, b. Aug. 28, 1791	
	Abraham Westfal Antie Westbrook	Allie, b. Sept. 13, 1791	
Nov. 20.	Nathaniel Meed Mary Buril	Daniel Burril, b. Aug. 11, 1791	
1792.			
Jan. 22.	Jasper Taylor Catterina Edmond	Jane, b. June 19, 1791	
	Jacob Swartwout Cattrina Van Etten	Joannes, b. Jan. 22, 1792	Joannes Van Etten Rachel Williams
Feb. 15.	Abraham Decker Elizabeth Ennes	Magdalena, b. Jan. 16, 1792	

DATE	PARENTS	CHILD	WITNESSES
1792.			
Feb. 15.	Jacobus Westfal Cattarina Quick	Hannah, b. Feb. 2, 1792	
April 13.	Gideon Van Etten Blandina Barthron	Joannes, b. April 1, 1792	Joannes Van Etten, Mary McGee
	Peter Brinck Busche Westfal	Polly, b. Nov. 2, 1791	
	Jacobus Ennes Hannah Dewitt	Jennica, b. May 12, 1792	
Aug. 26.	Samuel Westfal Anny Lane	Jacobus, b. March 31, 1792	
	Derick Sutfin Cattrina Van Dyke	Gysbert, b. May 30, 1792	
Sept. 16.	Mattheus Kittle Elizabeth Gieter	John Kittle, b. May 25, 1792	(Charged with being father of gelege vader.) George Gieter, Antie Van Bunschoten, sponsors.
Oct. 28.	Petrus Kittle Neeltie Chimer	Pheby, b. Sept. 15, 1792	
	Jepthah Killam Mary Lott	George, b. July 21, 1792	
1789.			
May 24.	Daniel Ennes Helena Hoornbeck	Sarah	
	Cornelius Kettle Cornelia Westbrook	Margery	
1792.			
Dec. 9.	Souweruyn Westbrook Blandina Westbrook	Peter, b. Oct. 26, 1792	
1793.			
March 24.	Tobyas Horenbeck Cathrina Van Denmark	Elizabeth, b. Feb. 26, 1793	
	Reremiah Rosekrans Sarah Stricklen	Jeremiah, b. Jan. 1, 1792	(Not. bap.)

DATE	PARENTS	CHILD	WITNESSES
1793.			
March 24.	John Van Sikele Jannitie Rosekrans	Andrew, b. June 19, 1791	
April 21.	Daniel Westfal, Jr. Maria Westbrook	Sarah, b. March 11, 1793	
	Jacobus Brinck Arianje Rosekrans	Janitie, b. Feb. 7, 1793	
	Abraham Carmer Sarah Carter	Peter	
June 10.	Hendrick Jatus? Optenhousen Annatie Risly	Cattrina, b. May 27, 1792	
May 12.	Jacob Shimer Pheby Wallon	Isaac, b. March 15, 1793	
	Salomon Westbrook Maragriet Dewitt	Salomon, b. April 5, 1793	
Jan. 26.	Ryneer Dewitt Sarah Quick	Jacobus, b. March 18, 1792	
	Andrew Dewitt Maria Middag	Moses, b. Sept. 20, 1792	
June 9.	John Quick Grietie Van Aken	Rachel, b. April 12, 1792	Isaac I. Van Aken, Rachel Van Aken
June 30.	Benjamin Bush Hannah Winne	Mary, b. March 6, 1793	
	Jaspar Taylor Catharine Edmond	Jerred, b. April 2, 1793	
Aug. 9.	Benjamin Westbrook Lena Ennes	Elizabeth, b. June 20, 1793	
Sept. 8.	Gideon Van Etten Blandina Berthron	Anthony, b. Aug. 15, 1792	Mag. Van Etten, Ant. Van Etten
Oct. 23.	John Sickle Jannetie Rosekrans	Grietie, b. April 19, 1793 Elizabeth, b. April 19, 1793	

DATE	PARENTS	CHILD	WITNESSES
1793.			
Oct. 23.	Philip Mullen Elizabeth Decker	Maria, b. Oct. 16, 1793	
	William Edwards Caty Wells	Sally, b. April 19, 1793	
Nov. 17.	Aare Vredenburgh Sarah Van Aken	Benjamin, b. Oct. 25, 1793	
	William Cole Sarah Wells	Nelly, b. July 31, 1793	
	Jonatan Hogteling Doritia Middag	Doritea, b. March 27, 1793	
	Stephen Parrish Lena Hogteling	Zebelon, b. June 25, 1793	
	Benjamin Dupuy Osie Styvers	Hannah, b. Oct. 26, 1791	
Dec. 25.	Henry Westfal Margaret Brinck	Joshuah, b. Nov. 6, 1793	
	George Quick Lena Quick	Jane, b. Sept. 11, 1790	
		Henry, b. Sept. 1, 1793	
Aug. 28.	Abraham Westfal Maria Masterson	Simion, b. Aug. 2, 1793	
1794.			
March 22.	Luther Foster Ruth Hedger	Silas Howell, b. July 28, 1793	
April 27.	Peter Brinck Lidya Brinck	Harmanus, b. Aug. 19, 1793	Harmanus Brinck, Lena Brinck
	Samuel Hinkly not bap. Jane Waldrum	Lena, b. April 3, 1793	Lena Brinck
	Peter W. Brinck Ann De Grootvelt	Elizabeth, b. June 18, 1792	
May 18.	Cornelius P. Westbrook Maria Westbrook	Petrus, b. May 2, 1794	

DATE	PARENTS	CHILD	WITNESSES
1794. Aug. 3.	Daniel Cortright Elizabeth Swartwout	Mary, b. July 13, 1794	
	Rynier Van Sickle Margaret Moore	Rynier, b. Sept. 18, 1787 Lucy, b. Aug. 20, 1789 Janny, b. Nov. 13, 1792 Ledy, b. March 20, 1794	
Aug. 4.	Samuel C. Seely Patience Marrell	Maria, Cornelia, twins, b. Feb. 15, 1791 Sharlott, b. Oct. 28, 1792 Hariott, b. March 16, 1794	
April 1.	Derick Suttin Catherine Van Dyck	Jacob, b. Feb. 19, 1794	
June 12.	Evert Horenbeck Jannetie Van Aken	Greitie, b. April 12, 1794	
Sept. 14.	Benjamin Bush Hannah Winne	Anny, b. May 6, 1794	
	William Cortright Cattrena Helm	Joannes, b. Oct. 8, 1793	
Oct. 9.	Daniel McKenzee Elizabeth McIntosh	Mary, b. Aug. 15, 1794	
Nov. 16.	Abraham Everit Deborah Cortright	Aaron Westbrook, b. Sept. 22, 1794	
	Abraham Westbrook Jannetie Van Aken	Cattrina, b. Oct. 13, 1794	

DATE	PARENTS	CHILD	WITNESSES
1794. Dec. 28.	Rynier De Witt Sarah Quick	Anny, b. July 25, 1794	
	Jonathan Van Garden Lidia Van Sickle	Geertie, b. Aug. 4, 1794	
1795. Jan. 9.	Benjamin Depuy Osie Styvers	Hannah, b. July 17, 1791 Sarah, b. Dec. 20, 1794	
	Henry (member) (Blacks) Dina (no member)	Steven, b. 1785 Moses, b. Jan. 8, 1791 Hannah, b. June 3, 1793	
Jan. 20.	Jacobus Westfal Cattrine Quick	Elizabeth, b. Nov. 19, 1794	
	George Quick Liza (Lena) Quick	Simon, b. Nov. 15, 1794	
March 25.	Francis Rosekrans Ruth Drake (not bap.)	Caty, b. Jan. 20, 1795	
	Soveryn Westbrook Blandina Westbrook	Joseph, b. Jan. 18, 1795	
May 3.	Anthony Van Etten "Magdenina" Van Etten	Cornelius, b. April 1, 1795	
March 25.	Daniel Westfal Maria Westbrook	Janneca, b. Feb. 4, 1795	
May 9.	Edward Wood Cathrena Brinck	Emanuel, b. Jan. 16, 1795	Emanuel Brinck, Elizabeth Rosekrans.
1794. June	John Van Orman Sarah Dupuy	Osee, b. May 12, 1794	
1795. March 1.	Thomas Van Etten Ellzabeth Ennes	Saly, b. July 1, 1794	

DATE	PARENTS	CHILD	WITNESSES
1795.			
June 13.	Jacob Shimer Pheby Wallen	Ledy, b. Feb. 28, 1795	Jacob Shimer, Jr., Ledy Rosekrans
	James Bunnel Elizabeth Shimar	Pheby, b. Dec. 25, 1794	
May 25.	Philip Mullen Elizabeth Decker	Hannah, b. Sept. 18, 1794	
June 28 & 29.	Gideon Cole Maria Van Etten	Joannes Van Etten, Rachel, twins, b. May 29, 1795	Joannes Van Etten Rachel Williams
July 4.	Cornelius Kittle Cornelia Westbrook	Lea, b. May 27, 1794	
	Gideon Van Etten Blandina Barthron	James, b. June 19, 1794	James Barthron, Elizabeth Westbrook
	Jacob Myers Sarah Cortright	Roxeny, b. Nov. 4, 1794	
July 26.	John Van Sikele Jannitie Rosekrans	Sarah, b. March 31, 1795	
	Jeremiah Rosekrans Sarah Strickling	Suse, b. May 31, 1795	
	Esrael Wells Jeny Lott	Nathan, b. March 4, 1795	
	Ira Fuller Hannah Swartwout	Denis, b. Feb. 12, 1795	
	William Dutcher Sarah Fuller	Scinthy, b. March 13, 1795	
	William Edwards Pheby Wells	Mahely, b. Feb. 2, 1795	
Aug. 16.	Daniel Cortrecht Plony Westval	"July," b. July 23, 1795	
	Jacobus Ennes Hennah Dewitt	Moses, b. July 18, 1795	

DATE	PARENTS	CHILD	WITNESSES
1795.			
Aug. 16.	John Nyce Lina Westbrook	John Westbrook, b. July 6, 1795	
Sept. 27.	Benjamin Westbrook Lena Ennes	Sarah, b. Aug. 15	
Nov. 8.	Jacobus Brinck Arriantie Rosekrans	Susannah, b. Feb. 16, 1795	
1796. April 3.	Derick Sutfin Cathrine Van Dyke	John Powelson, b. March 15, 1796	
May 15.	John H. B. Ryt Lea Ven Demark	Thomas, b. March 23, 1796	Thomas Ryt Lea Catee
	Henry Westes Dina Westes Ethiopians	Lize, b. Oct. 30, 1796	
Aug. 3.	Peter V. Brinck Ledia Brinck	John, b. Feb. 2, 1796	John Brinck Elener Cole
July 17.	Hendrick Westfal Greitee Brinck	Abby, b. May 8, 1796	
Aug. 7.	Evan Bevans Caty Parmer	Bethey, b. March 31, 1795	
1795. Feb. 23.	Abraham Carmer Sarah Alward	Daniel, b. Sept. 3, 1788	
	Abraham Carmer Sarah Carter	Nichols, b. June 9, 1794	
1796. Aug. 7.		Catharine, b. Feb. 19, 1796	
	Frederick Wydelig Maria Herchsel	George, b. Dec. 11, 1785 Eva, b. March 8, 1789 Hester, b. Dec. 27, 1795	

DATE	PARENTS	CHILD	WITNESSES
1796.			
April 24.	Cornelius Dewitt Antie Westbrook	Cornelius, b. March 29, 1796	
	Jonathan Van Garden Lidia Van Sickle	Pheby, b. Feb. 24, 1796	
Oct. 2.	Peter Brinck, Jr. Jacamyntie McCary	Dennis, b. Aug. 1, 1796	
1797.			
Feb.	Gideon Van Etten Blandina Barthron	Antie, b. Jan. 7, 1797	
April	Jacob Swartwout Catrina Van Etten	Elizabeth, b. March, 1797	
May 14.	Gideon Van Gordon Elizabeth Ennes	Jacobus, b. June 20, 1796	
	Alexander Ennis Janetie Dewitt	Maria, b. Jan. 17, 1797	
May 18.	George Quick Lena Quick	Caty, b. Feb. 15, 1797	
June 4.	John H. B. Ryt Lea Van Demerck	Rachel, b. May 14, 1797	
	Jacob Westbrook Jenny Decker	Maria, b. April 17, 1797	
	Thomas Van Etten Elizabeth Ennes	William, b. May 10, 1797	
Sept. 3.	Daniel Cortright Plony Westfall	Janntie, b. Aug. 7, 1797	Cornelius B. Westbrook Jannetie Westfall
	Wilhelmus Ennes Mary Ennes	Lena, b. Aug. 3, 1797	
	Jacob Myers Sarah Cortright	William Johnson, b. July 24, 1797	William Johnson Cortright Blandina Cortright
Sept. 7.	Tobias Hoornbeek Cattrina Van de Merck	Lourance, b. Sept. 24, 1795	
	John Van Sikel Jannitie Rosekrans	Jenneke, b. March 15, 1797	

DATE	PARENTS	CHILD	WITNESSES
1797.			
Sept. 7.	Hendrick Cortrecht Cattrina Van Garden	William, b. Aug. 1, 1797	
	James Van Aken Ann Wells	Henry, b. Oct. 5, 1796	
	Baptized by Johannes Duryee, V. D. M.		
Oct. 29.	Benjamin Westbrook Lenah Ennes	Petrus, b. Sept. 30, 1797	
	Daniel Westfall Mariah Westbrook	Cornelius, b. Oct. 7, 1797	
1798. June 13.	Edward Wood Caty Brinck	Lany, b. May 16, 1798	Har. Brinck, Lente Van Garden
	John Low Rushe Van Demerck	Elisabeth, b. Feb. 2, 1798	
	Jacob Probasco Sarah Van Woert	Abraham, b. March 28, 1798	
	John William Elizabeth Cortright	Lidia, b. Nov. 28, 1797	
	Josephat Westbrook Elizabeth Cortright	Dedion, b. Nov. —, 1797	
	Simeon Cole Gretie Van Aken	Peter, b. Dec. 17, 1797	
	Samuel Boyd, sworn father Elizabeth Hogteling	Benne Boyd, b, June 16, 1798	
June 24.	Derick Sutphen Caty Van Dyke	Richard, b. June 30, 1798	
	John Van Orman Sarah Depui	Johannes Depui, b. March 29, 1798	
	Baptized by Rev. E. Van Bunschoten		
	James Brinck Arriantje Rooscrans	Andrew Dingeman, b. April 30, 1798	

DATE	PARENTS	CHILD	WITNESSES
1798.			
June 24.	Abraham Westbrook Jannetje Van Aaken	Sarah, b. June 14, 1798	Aaron Vredenburg Sarah Van Aaken
	Isaac Evert Mary Davies	John Davies, b. March 23, 1798	Jane Davies
	Christopher Longstreet (Mother not baptized)	Andrew, b. June 8.	
	Abraham Kermer Sarah Carter	Silas, b. Oct. 18, 1797	

Baptized by Rev. I. M. Horlingen

DATE	PARENTS	CHILD	WITNESSES
Oct. 21.	Benjamin Fisher Maria Bartron	Elizabeth, b. Aug. 6, 1798	
	Aaron French Mary Myers	Elizabeth, b. July 1, 1798	
	Adam Myers Navmi Mulliner	Roger, b. Nov. 2, 1797 Rebeckah, b. Nov. 22, 1795	
	Bastian Myers Sarah Van Gorden	Johannes, b. July 23, 1798	John Van Gorden, Mary Van Gorden
	Elias Patterson Rusha Brinck	Sarah Patterson, b. Sept. 27, 1798	
	Benjamin Vredenburgh Mary Case	Elizabeth, b. Oct. 9, 1798	
1800.			
March 9.	Even Beven Caty Carmer	Nicholas, b. Aug. 23, 1798	
	Abraham Carmer Sarah Carter	Elijah, b. Sept. 8, 1799	
	George Quick Lena Quick	James, b. Feb. 4, 1799	

DATE	PARENTS	CHILD	WITNESSES
1800.			
March 9.	Abraham Hogtelin Lena Wood	Peter, b. Nov. 16, 1799	
	Thomas Decker Jane Case	Caty, b. Feb. 6, 1800	
	Simeon Van Etten Kornelia Dingeman	Daniel Dingman, b. Jan. 12, 1800	
	Levi Decker Martha Follet	Hendericus, b. Nov. 8, 1799	
	Jacob Decker Temperance Marsh	Margaret Westbrook, b. Dec. 5, 1799	
	Anthony Van Etten Magdalina Van Etten	Simeon, b. Dec. 10, 1799	
	Derick Sutfin Catherine Van Dyke	Nicholas Arrosmith, b. Jan. 22, 1800	
Aug. 24.	Abraham Westbrook Ann Buckley	Mariah, b. Jan. 19	
	Bastian Myers, Jr. Sarah Van Garden	Elizabeth, b. Aug. 2, 1800	
	Evan Bevans Catharine Carmer	James Carmer, b. June 3, 1800	
	David Barthron Mary Van Etten	Hyltie, b. Oct. 28, 1799	
	Isaac Everit Mary Davis	Betsy, b. Feb. 10, 1800	
	Abraham Depuy Sarah McCaby	Benjamin, b. March 12, 1800	
	John Low Rushe Van Demerck	Jeremia Van Demerck, b. Sept. 11, 1799	

DATE	PARENTS	CHILD	WITNESSES
1800.			
Aug. 24.	Jacob Myers Sarah Cortright	Mahala, b. April 24, 1800	
	William I. Cortright Christena Myers	Hannah, b. July 17, 1799	
	Aaron French Mary Myers	Christena, b. March 17, 1800	
	Jacob Crasman Esther Begel	Mary, b. Sept. 2, 1799	
	Sovereiyn Hoornbeck Annatie Decker	Blandina, b. Aug. 5, 1800	
	Peter Brinck Jackmyntie McCaby	John McCaby, b. Jan. 21, 1800	
	Stephen Doolittle, absconded Elizabeth Brinck	Peter, b. April 7, 1799	Peter Brinck, Jackemyntie McCaby
	Peter Quick Hannah Dewitt	Roger Clark, b. Nov. 23, 1799	
	Peter Welfelt, absconded Jenneke Barthron	Adam, b. Aug. 4, 1799	Benjamin Fisher, Maria Barthron
	John Van Arnom Sarah Depuy	Benjamin, b. June 1, 1800	
	Jacob Chimer Pheby Wallon	Margaret, b. June 29, 1800	Abraham Skirmer, Margaret Van Ellen
	James Bunel Elizabeth Shimer	Jacob, b. Aug. 18, 1799	Jacob Shimer, Pheby Wallon
Sept. 8.	Jacob Probasco Sarah Woeltman	Mary, b. June 6, 1800	
	Isaac Decker Rosanna Cortright	Elinor, b. Aug. 13, 1800	
	Gidean Vannalten Blandina Patson	Jacob, b. Sept. 20, 1800	
	Daniel Cortright Plony Westfal	Samuel, b. Oct. 5, 1800	Samuel Cortreght, Grietyie Westfaal

DATE	PARENTS	CHILD	WITNESSES
1801. March 29.	Daniel Westfal Mary McCavy	Abraham, b. Nov. 27, 1800	
	Harry Westpertus Dina Westpertus (probably blacks)	William, b. Dec. 3, 1799 Diana, b. Feb. 10, 1801	
	Daniel Van Etten Catherine Decker	Dorothy, b. Sept. 18, 1800	
	Daniel W. Dingman Maria Westbrook	Martinus Westbrook, b. March 18, 1801	
	George Brink Dorcas Doolittle	Jose, b. Jan. 13, 1799 Sarah, b. Sept. 18, 1800 Clara, b. Nov. 9, 1795	
	William Johnston Cortright Christian Meyers Andrew Decker Mary Dewitt	Maria, b. May 9, 1801 Christopher, b. Oct. 31, 1800	
	Peter Rubart Mary Van Garden	John, b. Feb. 18, 1801	
	John H. Kite Leah Van Der Merk	Maria Dingman, b. Dec. 2, 1800	Daniel W. Dingman Maria Westbrook
	Abraham Westbrook Jane Van Aken Jacob Westbrook Jenny Decker	Solomon, b. Dec. 28, 1800 Sally, b. March 21, 1801	Wilhelmus Westbrook, Aaltje Westbrook
	Thomas Van Etten Elizabeth Ennes	Hannah, b. March 4, 1801	

DATE	PARENTS	CHILD	WITNESSES
1801.			
Aug. 23.	Abraham Westbrook Anna Buckly	Marten, b. —— 19, 1801	
	Peter Bras Susannah Wood, deceased	Sarah, b. June 18, 1797	
	Soverine Westbrook Blandina Westbrook	Margaret, b. March 28, 1801.	
	John Williams Elizabeth Cortreght	Grietie, b. Feb. 6, 1800	
	Peter V. Brinck Lidia Brinck	Areantie, b. Oct. 26, 1800	James Brinck, Areantie Rosekrans
	William Hoogtaling Susannah Cortright	Cornelius Brinck, b. July 4, 1801	
	James Fisher Charity Tilman	Mary, b. May 2, 1801	
	Christopher Longstreet Elizabeth Fountain	Christopher, b. June 1, 1801	
	Benjamin Brinck Phanny Mulford	George Brinck, b. Feb. 8, 1801	
	James Williams Rhody Heds	Sarah, b. March 11, 1800 Lydia, b. Feb. 22, 1801	
1802. Oct. 2.	Henry Westfall Margaret Brinck	John, b. Oct. 3, 1800	
	Robert Killgore Rachel Kyte	Polly Melford, b. Nov. 29, 1801	
	Abraham Hoogteelen Lena Wood	Ledy, b. Feb. 16, 1802	
	Benjamin Westbrook Lena Ennes	Lena, b. Sept. 2, 1801	

DATE	PARENTS	CHILD	WITNESSES
1802.			
Oct. 2.	Jacob Probasco Sarah Woertman	Petrus Van Nest b. April 26	
	Simeon Van Etten Kornelia Dingman	Jenneca, b. Dec. 17, 1801	
Oct. 3.	Isaac Everet Mary Davis	George Baxter, b. June 14, 1802	
	Aaron Thomas Elizabeth Davis	Mary, b. March 10, 1796	Isaac Everet, Mary Davis
	Francis McCoemac Elizabeth Van Noey	Sary, b. July 6, 1802	
	William Ennes Sary Brison	Joseph, b. June 2, 1802	
	Gideon Cole Maria Van Etten	Dorethy, b. June 4, 1802	
	John C. Low Reese Van Demerk	Caty, b. April 6, 1802	
	Marshal Everet Cary Van Garden	Moses, b. July 9, 1802	
	John Van Etten Caty Kuikendal	Maria, b. June 8, 1802	
Nov. 9.	Nicholas McCarty Lena Decker	Lea, b. Jan. 20, 1800	
	Gideon Van Ette Blandina Betran	Majore, b. July 4, 1802	Johanes Van Ette, Mary Magee
	James Fisher Charity Tilman	Permelia, b. Sept. 12, 1802	
Feb. 2.	Abraham Depuy Sarah McKaby	Jonetie, b. April 21, 1801 Isaac, b. Oct. 23, 1802	

DATE	PARENTS	CHILD	WITNESSES
1803.			
Feb. 2.	Thomas Van Etten Elizabeth Ennes	Phebe, b. Jan. 11, 1803	
	Wm. Hoogtaling Susannah Cort- right	John Cort- right	
April 21.	Daniel Westfall Mary Westbrook	Janey, b. Jan. 11, 1803	
	Jacob Kettle Mary Jamison	Samuel, b. Sept. 19, 1802	
	Herme Rosekrans Elizabeth Van Auken	Petrus, b. Oct. 14, 1798	
	Jacob Myers Sarah Cortright	Belinda, b. Sept. 24, 1802	
	Peter Rubart Mary Van Gor- don	Margaret, b. Oct. —, 1803(?)	
	Aaron French Mary Myers	Ester, b. Feb. 9, 1802	
	Phillip Decker Magdalen Horn- beck	Cobus, b. Dec. 30, 1802	
	Bastian Myers Sary Van Gorden	Cobus, b. June 30, 1802	
	Soverine Hornbeck Hannah Decker	Joseph, b. Dec. 5, 1802	
	Aaron Freden- burgh Sarah Van Naken	Jane, b. Dec. 29, 1802	
	Joseph Hornbeck Margaret Van Naken	Sarah, b. May 28, 1802	
	Daniel Westfall Mary McKady	Matthew, b. Dec. 4, 1802	
	John Kinte (Kyte?) Leah Van De- mark	Jeremiah, b. March 17, 1803	
	Daniel "Fanstah" (Van Etten) Catherine Decker	Samuel	

DATE	PARENTS	CHILD	WITNESSES
1803. April 21.	Henry (nothing else)	Henry Clinton, b. May 19, 1803	
Sept. 12.	John Fisher Mary Dewitt	Sarah, b. July 9, 1803	
	Cornelius Van Etten Anne Smith	Rachel, b. Aug. 4, 1803	
Oct. 2.	Peter Cortright Catherine Cebler	Jacob Evrit, b. Aug. 16, 1802	
1805. Aug. 1.	Gideon Cole Mary Van Etten	John, b. June 4, 1805	
1807. Oct. 14.	Abraham M. Westbrook Anne Buckley	Hugh, b. March 26, 1804 Ruben Buckley, b. March 26, 1805 Eliza Hagerty, b. Aug. 29, 1806	
	Jocob Westbrook Jenny Decker	Abraham, b. Aug. 6, 1805 Solomon, b. Sept. 1, 1807	
	Abraham I. Westbrook Phebe Ennis	John, b. July 21, 1807	
	Josaphat Westbrook Elizabeth Cortright	Jannetye, b. Aug. 25, 1799 Susannah, b. Nov. 24, 1802	
	Henry Cortright Catharine Van Garden	Susannah, b. March 25, 1799	

DATE	PARENTS	CHILD	WITNESSES
1807.			
Oct. 14.	Peter Kittle Elenor Shymir	Jeremiah, b. Feb. 3, 1799	
	Samuel Cortright Margrietje Westval	Petrus, b. June 28, 1798	
	Jacob Westbrook Jane Decker	Esther, b. Jan. 13, 1798	
	Gideon Van Etten Blandina Bertron	Maria, b. Nov. 16, 1798	
	Evert Hornbeck Jannetje Van Auken	Daniel, b. May 3, 1798	
	John Cortright Mary Clarke	Sarah, b. Aug. 18, 1798	
	Richard West Elenor Green	John, b. Sept. 15, 1798	
	Nicholas McCarty Helena Decker	John, b. Feb. 4, 1798	
	John Kyte Leah Van Demark	Esther, b. April 9, 1798	
	Peter Brink Lydia Brink	Elizabeth, b. Nov. 3, 1798	
	Henry Westval Peggy Brink	Peter, b. June 3, 1798	
	Daniel B. Westfal Mary Westbrook	Jacobus, b. July 3, 1799	
	Severyn Westbrook Blandina Westbrook	Maria, b. March 26, 1799	
	Thomas Van Etten Elizabeth Ennest	Maria, b. July 19, 1799	
	Cornelius Rosenkrans Janeka Decker	Catharine,	Peter Decker, sponsor
	Robert Killgon Rachel Kyte	Anne, b. June 20, 1799	

DATE	PARENTS	CHILD	WITNESSES
1807.			
Oct. 14.	Simeon Cole Grietje Van Auken	Jacobus Van Auken, b. Sept. 10, 1800	Jacobus Van Auken Catharine Westbrook
	Wilhelmus Ennist Maria Ennist	Elizabeth, b. Sept. 9, 1800	Joseph Ennist, Margret Van Etten
	Daniel W. Dingman Maria Westbrook	Andries, b. Dec. 25, 1803	
	William I. Cortright Catrina Myers	Susannah, b. Aug. 12, 1803	
	Simeoh Cole Margret Van Auken	William, b. Jan. 10, 1804	
	Solomon Westbrook Margaret Dewitt	Severyne, b. Feb. 25, 1804	
	Benjamin Westbrook Magdalena Ennest	Daniel Ennist, b. Dec. 14, 1803	
	Henry Marvin Anne Van Auken	Caty, b. Aug. 12, 1803	
	Josaphat Westbrook Elizabeth Kortright	Simeon, b. July 11, 1803	
	Daniel Westfall Polly Maccabe	William, b. March 26, 1803	
July 18.	Abraham Rosekrans Hannah Hoff	Rachel, b. Aug. 23, 1805	
	Aaron Thomas Belchry Davis	Daniel, b. -- 25, 1799	Lidia Middag, sponsor
	Aaron Thomas Lidia Middag	Betchry, b. June 7, 1804	
	Soverins Horenbeek Hannah Decker	John, b. Feb. 3, 1805	
	Hermanus Van Aken Hannah Wood	Caty Westbrook, b. June 27, 1806	

DATE	PARENTS	CHILD	WITNESSES
1807.			
July 18.	George Westbrook Alty Cortright	Mehaly, b. Sept. 7, 1805 Joannes, b. June 11, 1807	
	Benjamin Westfall Hannah McCavy	Simeon, b. Dec. 12, 1804 Gilbert, b. June 27, 1807	
	Philip Decker Magdalen Hornbeek	Elizabeth, b. Jan. 18, 1805	
	Andrew Decker Maria Dewitt	Peter, b. April 6, 1806	
	Moses Crawford Rebeka Cole	James, b. June 28, 1807	
	Isaac Everet Mary Davis	Jane Westbrook, b. Aug. 24, 1804 Marian, b. Feb. 26, 1807	
	Marshal Everet Caty Van Garden	Hannah, b. June 18, 1804 Elizabeth, b. Sept. 14, 1806	
	Simeon Westfall Esther Brinck	Jane, b. July 26, 1806	
	William Anes Hannah rawford	Jacob, b. Nov. 1, 1802 Moses, b. Nov. 12, 1804 Elizabeth, b. Jan. 22, 1807	
	Elexander Ennes Roanny Rosekrans	Diana, b. Oct. 5, 1802	

DATE	PARENTS	CHILD	WITNESSES
1807. July 18.	Elexander Ennes Roanny Rosekrans	Daniel, b. Jan. 21, 1804 Lidia, b. Sept. 20, 1806	
	Abraham Hogtel-ing Lena Wook (wood)	Caty, b. July 6, 1804	
		Sarah, b. Feb. 5, 1807	
	James Fisher Charity Tilman	Maria, b. Jan. 26, 1807	
July 26.	William Looder Mary Fisher	Elizabeth, b. Oct. 6, 1806	
Aug. 8.	Abram Depew Sarah McKavey	Maria, b. March 19, 1804 Dirk, "in November," 1806	
	Josaphat Westbrook Elizabeth Cortregh	Lydia Cort-reght, b. Aug. 12, 1806	
	Wilhelmus Hoogteeling Susannah Cortregt	Josaphat, b. Feb. 18, 1805	
		Samuel, b. Feb. 11, 1807	
	Daniel Kortright Plony Westfall	Simeon, b, Jan. 8, 1804	
	Abraham Westbrook Jenny Van Auken	Wilhelmus, b. Dec. 18, 1804	
	Andrew Decker Maria Dewitt	Cornelius Dewitt, b. Jan. 31, 1804	

DATE	PARENTS	CHILD	WITNESSES
1807.			
Sept. 5.	Elias Patterson Russia Brink	Lydia, b. Oct. 20, 1800	
Sept. 6.	Zepharine Westbrook Blandina Westbrook	Hester, b. March 17, 1805 Catharine, b. July 31, 1807	
	Jacob Myers Sarah Cortright	Jacob, b. April 10, 1805 Sally, b. Aug. 13, 1807	
Sept. 20.	Mary Ellis, wife of M. Van Nest	Matthew Clark, baptized by Rev.	
	John Van Norman Sarah Depuy	Abraham, b. June 8, 1802	
	Gideon Van Etten Blandina Botrun	Sarah, b. July 15, 1804 Christina, b. May 1, 1806	
1808.			
May 7.	Job Westbrook Sarah Annes	Wilhelmus, b. Nov. 6, 1807	
Nov. 27.	John J. Van Etten Catherine Kykendall	Daniel, b. Jan. 22, 1808	
	John Fisher Mary Dewitt	Maria, b. — 21, 1808	
Dec. 11.	Thomas Van Etten Elizabeth Ennes	Levi, b. Sept. 6, 1805 Jonathan Dexter, b. June 15, 1807	
	Benjamin Westbrook Lenah Ennis	Cornelius, b. Aug. 20, 1806	
	Isaiah Van Alten Dinah Westbrook	Maria, b. Sept. 17, 1808	

DATE	PARENTS	CHILD	WITNESSES
1808.			
Dec. 12.	Peter Decker Lydia Westbrook	Lany, b. Oct. 27, 1808	
1809.			
Feb. 4.	Daniel Westphall Polly McAbey (Cahey)	John, b. Feb. 9, 1806 Solomon, b. Oct. 6, 1807	
Feb. 6.	Jacob Kite Mary Courtright	William, b. Feb. 17, 1807	
June 12.	George Everett Elizabeth Van Gordon	Erastus Stark-weather, b. Feb. 4, 1809	
July 23.	Alexander Annes Ariantie Rosekrans	James Rose-krans, b. Dec. 29, 1808	
	Josephas Westbrook Elizabeth Cortright	Jannitie, b. March 12, 1809	
	Benjamin Van Noey Hannah Decker	Sarah, b. Nov. 1, 1808	
	Jacob Westbrook Elizabeth Shimer	Blandena, b. Dec. 2, 1808	
	Andrew Decker Mariah Dewitt	Hester, b. Sept. 21, 1808	
	Peter Cortright Caty Hebler	Samuel, b. Sept. 20, 1807 Hannah, b. July 1, 1809	
Sept. 10.	Abraham Rosekrans Polly Williams Abraham I. Westbrook Pheby Annis	Hannah, b. Aug. 23, 1807 Hester Hoor-beck, b. April 4, 1809	

DATE	PARENTS	CHILD	WITNESSES
1809.			
Sept. 10.	Benjamin Westfall Hannah McCavy	Abraham, b. Feb. 26, 1809	
1810.			
May 6.	Simeon Westfall Hester Brink	Lydia Anne, b. July 11, 1809	
	Joseph Westbrook Sarah Annis	Hester, b. Oct. 13, 1809	
	George Westbrook Altie Cartright	Cornelius, b. April 22, 1810	
June 26.	Isaac Evert Mary Davis	Hannah, b. Oct. 10, 1809	
	Wilhelmus Hogtaling Susannah Cortright	Ledy, b. Feb. 25, 1809	
	Abraham Hogteling Lena Wood	Jacob, b. Nov. 27, 1809	
	George Brinck Dorcas Duelittle	Ledy, b. Oct. 20, 1807	
		Phebe Jane, b. Aug. 16, 1809	
Feb. 16.	William Loder Mary Fisher	Anny Culver, b. Dec. 22, 1808	
	Benjamin Westbrook Elizabeth Westbrook	Lena, b. Feb. 20, 1811	
Feb. 10.	Benjamin Van Noey Hannah Decker	Soevryn, b. July 30, 1810	
	Jacob Westbrook Elizabeth Chymer	Lidy, b. Dec. 10, 1810	
	Aaron Thomas Ledy Maddag	Joseph, b. June 15, 1810	
	Benjamin Westbrook Lena Annes	Blandina, b. Dec. 17, 1809	

DATE	PARENTS	CHILD	WITNESSES
1811.			
March 10.	Arthur Buchanan Polly, his wife	Ollive, b. July 14, 1806 Polly, b. July 21, 1808	
June 12.	Lydia Westbrook (deceased)	Severyne, L., b. Jan. 3, 1810	
	Nehemiah Westbrook Blandina Kittle	Simeon Kittle, b. Aug. 1, 1810	
June 16.	Daniel Cortright Plony Westfall	William, b. Dec. 2, 1808	
	Jacob Kyte Mary Cortright	Peter, b. Jan. 31, 1810	
	Simeon Cole Margaret Van Auken	David Finch, b. Nov. 6, 1810	
	Solomon Kittle Mary Rosekrans	Betsy Van Auken, b. Nov. 16, 1810	
July 16.	William Brink Nancy Haggerty	Lydia, b. July 14, 1808 Caty Jane, b. July 11, 1810	
	Isaiah Van Netten Blandina Westbrook	Henry, b. Jan. 13, 1811	
	Polly Foster	Ann Eliza, b. April 29, 1810	Julius Foster, Eliza Hedges, his wife
	William Loder Mary Fisher	Phebe, b. Jan. 1, 1811	
Oct. 22.	John Peiddis Leah Van Auken	Caty Jane, b. Dec. 31, 1809	
Dec. 22.	Peter Young Jane Brink, his his wife	Andrew Brinck, b. Sept. 10, 1810	

DATE	PARENTS	CHILD	WITNESSES
1812.			
May 27.	George Everet Elizabeth Van Garden	Marian, b. July 27, 1811	
	Moses Crofford Rebecka Cole	John, b. Nov. 21, 1811	
July 26.	Daniel Westfal Mary McCaby	Altie, b. July 24, 1809	
	Benjamin Westfall Hannah McCaby	Dennis, b. Aug. 21, 1811	
1813.			
Aug. 22.	Alexander Ennis Roanny Rosekrans	Alexander, b. Nov. 25, 1812	
	Peter Cortright Catharine Cebler	Jane Young, b. Feb. 19, 1813	
	Colomon Kittle Mary Rosekrans	Belindy, b. April 22, 1813	
Oct. 15.	Peter Young Jane Brinck	George Everet, b. Sept. 18, 1813	
Nov. 17.	Simion Cole Margret Van Auken	Caty Van Aucan, b. March 21, 1813	
	July Taylor, mother	Josephus Westbrook, b. May 6, 1813	Josephus Westbrook—"evidence" ("evidence is written sometimes in place of sponsors or witnesses in this book.)
Nov. 18.	Jacob Kyte Mary Cortright	Thomas, b. May 12, 1813	
	George Westbrook Alche Cortright	Julian, b. Feb. 25, 1811 Samuel Cortright, b. Oct. 27, 1813	

DATE	PARENTS	CHILD	WITNESSES
1813.			
Nov. 18.	Ruben Cortright Deborah Bedel	Peter, b. Nov. 1, 1809 Pheby, b. Jan. 11, 1811 Isaac Bedell, b. April 18, 1813	
1815.			
Nov. 14.	Joseph Westbrook Sally Ennes	Lydia Ennes, b. Sept. 20, 1814	
	Jacob Kyte Mary Courtright	Elizabeth, b. June 13, 1815	
	Jesse Loder Lanah Mapes	Elisha Mapes, b. April 14, 1814	
1816.			
Jan. 7.	Moses Crawford Rebecca Cole	Susan Mariah, b. Dec. 7, 1815	
Jan. 28.	Benjamin Westbrook Elizabeth Westbrook	Catharine, b. Jan. 26, 1815	
	Peter Keator July Anne, his wife	Elizabeth Westbrook, b. Dec. 7, 1815	
Feb. 25.	James B. Armstrong Mary D. Foster	Susan Eveline, b. Dec. 13, 1813 Julius Foster, b. Sept. 7, 1815	
	John Relyer Margaret Ennes	Joseph Ennis, b. April 7, 1811	
	Isaac Everet Mary Davis	Allon, b. July 24, 1814	

DATE	PARENTS	CHILD	WITNESSES
1816.			
Feb. 25.	John Ennes Mariah Seely	Simon Cortright, b. Jan. 28, 1813	
	Gesse Loder Lenah Mapes	Susannah, b. March 15, 1813	
	Daniel Ennes Susannah Renyer	Hiram, b. Nov. 3, 1811 Margaret, b. Sept. 13, 1813	
	John Relyer Margaret Ennes	Philip, b. Aug. 9, 1813	

BAPTIZED BY REV. CHARLES HARDENBERGH

Oct. 26.	Moses Craford Rebecca Cole	Hannah, b. June 24, 1816	
	Josephus Westbrook Margaret Middag	Noomi Decker, b. Dec. 26, 1815	
	Solomon Kittel Maria Rosekrans	Richard, b. Aug. 24, 1816	
	George Everett Elizabeth Van Gorden	Christine, b. Nov. 16, 1814	
	William Loder Mary Fisher	John Worth, b. April 24, 1813	
	John Loder Anny Culver	Matilda, b. March, 1807	
	Isaiah Van Etten Blandina Westbrook	Peter Westbrook, b. Feb. 14, 1814	
	Isaih Cortright Miriam Wilson	Jane, b. March 2, 1816	

Elizabeth Longstreet, adult
Peggy Dogety, adult

Book 2 of Original Records

DATE	PARENTS	CHILD	WITNESSES
1803.			
June 19	Peter Decker / Seeletje Decker	Simeon, b. March 16,	
	John Van Vliet / Catharina Westfall	Margaret, b. March 12	
	Isaac Decker / Maria Decker	Jacomeyntje, b. Jan. 31	
Sept. 11.	Jonas Schoonhoven / Ezube Patterson	Deborah, b. Oct. 27, 1802	
	Daniel Decker / Catharine Rosegrant	James Rosegrant, b. May 6, 1803	
	Charity Middagh wife of William Donally	Robert, b. —— 16, 1801	
	Tunis Osterhout / Pride Quick	Solomon Middagh, b. June 13, 1803	
	Abraham Van Imwegen / Elizabeth Sammons	Lenah, b. July 31, 1803	
Oct. 24.	Johannes Van Aken / Leah Cuykendal	Antje, b. Aug. 18, 1803	
	Cornelius Middagh / Jenneke Westbrook	Engeltje, b. July 21, 1803	
Oct. 28.	Solomon Decker / Lenah Schoonhoven	James, b. Nov. 12, 1802	
Oct. 30.	William Cuddebeck / Annatje Van Imwegen	Levi, b. Oct. 2, 1803	
	Josephus McCarty / Jane Van Aken	Maria, b. June 16, 1801	Levi Van Aken / Maria Dewit
1804.			
April 8.	Jacob Cuddeback / Dina Van Etten	Naomi, b. Feb. 17	
May 6.	Henry Cuddeback / Esther Gumaer	Benjamin, b. Feb. 22	
	John Van Etten / Sarah Vernooy	James, b. March 13	

DATE	PARENTS	CHILD	WITNESSES
1804.			
May 6.	David Wynkoop Elizabeth Smith	John, b. Feb. 28	
	Benjamin Gumaer Pateence Thomas	Thomas Lewis, b. March 3	
May 20.	John Neerpass Sarah Squirl	William, b. March 14	
	Isaac Van Strander Susanna Oosterhout	Rachel, b. March 27, 1803	
	Samuel Lambert Esther Kettle	James Newkirk, b. Oct. 11, 1803	
	William Little Caty Middagh	Henry, b. Aug. 11, 1803	
	John Decker Sarah Lambert	Huldah, b. March 29	
	Elizabeth Hoff wife of Joel Whitlock	Joseph Hoff, b. Oct. 27, 1803	
	Joshua Vredenburgh Elizabeth Van Aken	Caty, b. Jan. 13, 1803	
	Roman Elmendorf Helena Middagh	Richard, b. Jan. 16	
June 17.	Solomon Davis Margaret Daily	Daniel, b. May 1	
Aug. 12.	Jacob Quick Ellenor Van Garde	Ellenor, b. June 9	
	Isaac M. Decker Heyetje Westbrook	Abraham, b. Dec. 30, 1803	
1805.			
Jan. 13.	Joshua Van Aken Elizabeth Hoornbeek	Helena, b. Sept. 26, 1804	
	Cornelius Cuddeback Margery Van Aken	Caty, b. June 25, 1804	
	Henry Case Caty Neerpass	William Neerpass, b. April 14, 1804	

DATE	PARENTS	CHILD	WITNESSES
1805.			
Jan. 13.	Benjamin Neerpass Anna Lott	John, b. April 30, 1804	John Neerpass Sarah Squirl
Feb. 10.	Reuben Westfall Charity Cuykendal	Margaret, b. July 12, 1804	
April 21.	Gerardus Gumaer Eunice Patterson	Hannah, b. Oct. 20, 1804	
1805.			
May 5.	Peter Vernooy Hannah Concklin	Aaron, b. March 10,	
June 14.	Elias Cuykendal Elizbeth Gumaer	Wilhelmus, b. June 13	
	Elias Gumaer Mary Lewis	Martha, b. Oct. 26	
1806.			
May 18.	Elizabeth Van Vliet wife John Van Inwegen	Jacobus, July 11, 1804	
July 13.	Maria Westfall wife Henry Van Etten	Antje, b. May 16, 1805	
1807.			
Aug. 13.	David Vininwagen Anna Swartwout	Margret, b. Dec. 11, 1805	
	David Cutright Elezebeth Damport	Sarah, b. March 6, 1807	
	David Winekoop Elebath Smith	Jane, b. Nov. 27, 1805	
	Solomon Daves Margreth, his wife	James, b. May 17, 1806	
	Willem Cuddeback, Junior Hannah Wininwagen	Salay, b. Jan. 16, 1806	
	John Wininwagen Elizebeth Van Vlet	Mary, b. Aug. 2, 1806	
	Isaac M. Decker Hilthe Westbrook	Jane, b. Nov. 16, 1805	

DATE	PARENTS	CHILD	WITNESSES
1807.			
Aug. 13.	Peter Decker Salata Decker	Lana, b. May 8, 1805 Peter, b. Feb. 28, 1807	
	Samuel Patison Charity Bragan	Josep Maker, b. March 21, 1805	
	Oliver Whitehead Sala Lambert	Matilda, b. Aug. 8, 1806 Benjemin, b. April 15, 1800 Jane, b. July 21, 1806 Oliver	
	Cornelius Van Imwegen, Jr, Deborah Westbrook	Mary, b, June 12, 1806	
	Solomon Decker Jane Schonhoven	Mary, b. Dec. 9, 1806	
	Cornelius Rosecrans Jane Decker	Mary, b. March 12, 1795	
	Jacob Gumaer Sara Van Garden	Daniel, b. Aug. 10, 1804 Hannah, b. Nov. 23, 1806	
	William Cuddeback Hannah Van Imwegen	Lewes, b. Jan. 16, 1807	
	Geremy Paterson Elizabeth, his wife	Benjamin, b. Sept. 15, 1805	
	Isaac Decker Mary Decker	Jane, b. Oct. 26, 1805	
	Solomon Vanetten Gemine Gumaer	John, b. Nov. 20, 1806	

DATE	PARENTS	CHILD	WITNESSES
1807.			
Aug. 13.	Henry Cuddeback Peter Gumaer	Simeon, b. Oct. 6, 1806	
	John Van Etten Saly Vernoy	Peter, b. May 7, 1806	
	Gerardus Gumaer Eunice Paterson	Cornelius, b. Oct. 21, 1806	
	Abraham Van Imwegen Elizabeth Sammons	Jane, b. Oct. 18, 1805	
Aug. 15.	Jeremiah Van Aken Mary Westbrook	Rachel, b. June 2, 1804 Moses, b. Aug. 13, 1806	
	Abram Van Garden Rebecca Bevier	Abram Westbrook, b. Sept. 18, 1804	
	Cornelius Meddagh Cate Van Aken	Maria, b. Sept. 7, 1806	
	Richard Dekker Cate Brink	Roanney, b. March 1, 1805	
	William Dowley Ganehje Middagh	Henry, b. Jan. 8, 1804 Pegge, b. Dec. 25, 1805	
	Jacob Neerpass Cate Cuddebeck	William, b. Feb. 17, 1807	
	Peter Q. Patterson, deceased Elizabeth Brink	Blandina, b. Dec. 28, 1805 Peter, b. April 8, 1807	
	Solomon Brink Phebe Winfield	Yannetye, b. March 1, 1807	
	William Little Cate Middagh	Jene, b. Sept. 6, 1805	

DATE	PARENTS	CHILD	WITNESSES
1807.			
Aug. 15.	John J. Sammons, Sarah Dekker	Peter, b. Jan. —, 1806	
		Lilley Skner, b. July 2, 1795	
	Daniel Howey Jenne Quick	Daniel, b. Sept. 6, 1803	
	Cornelius Middagh Jenne Westbrook	Thatje, b. Nov. 20, 1804	
		Lydia, b. Oct. 12, 1806	
	Richard Shimer Ruthe Annest	Jacob, b. Nov. 30, 1806	
	Abram Van Aken Elizabeth Davis	Abram, b. June 26, 1806	
	Jacob Kuddebeek Dinah Van Netten	Jakem-eyntje, b. Oct. 30, 1805	
	Henry Bennet Sarah Vernoy	Sarah, b. Nov. 19, 1803	
		Petrus, b. July 18, 1807	
	Tunis Osterhout Ploney Quick	Sally Shepherd, b. May 26, 1805	
	Isaac Vanstrander Susannah Oosterhout	Lydia Van Vliet, b. Sept. 20, 1805	
	Roman Elmendorf Lena Middagh	Teunis, b. Dec. 26, 1805	
	Nathan Van Aken Hester Patterson	Reuben, b. March 23, 1806	
	John Osterhout Pegge Quick	Nelly, b. May 22, 1804	

DATE	PARENTS	CHILD	WITNESSES
1807. Aug. 15.	John Osterhout / Pegge Quick	Jeremiah Quick, b. 4, —	
	Joel Westbrook / Elizabeth Hoff	Alfred, b. Nov. 12, 1806	
	Benjamin Cuddebeek / Dina Van Etten	Levi Van Netten, b. March 3, 1807	Levi Van Netten, Jean Westbrook
	Isaiah Van Netten / Dina Westbrook	Cornelius Westbrook, b. Jan. 24, 1804; Elizabeth, b. March 23, 1806	Cornelius R. Westbrook, Mary Westbrook
	John B. Quik / Jeanna Rosecrans	Jacob, b. July 9, 1806	
	David Clark / Estor Shymer	Jacob, b. Nov. 20, 1804; "Marcy," b. Feb. 12, 1806	
	Henry Van Camp / Phebe Dewitt	Caty, b. Aug. 30, 1805	
	Sarah Quick	Isaac, b. July 27, 1801; Hannah, b. June 10, 1804	
	Frances Smith / Margret Quick	Hannah, b. April 7, 1803	
	John Decker / Mary Siddles	Joshua, b. May 9, 1805; Thomas, b. Jan. 14, 1807	
	Johannes Decker, as Godfather / Caty Rosekrans	Caty, b. June 16, 1805	

DATE	PARENTS	CHILD	WITNESSES
1807.			
Aug. 16.	Benjamin Carpenter Margret Decker	——, b. Jan. 20, 1807	
	Cornelius Cuddeback Margery Vannaaken	Peter, b. Nov. 13, 1806	
	Abraham T. Westbrook Mary Van Keuren ("Venkearn")	John, b. Dec. 24, 1806	
	David Camfield Mary Shamons	Jacob, b. Sept. 17, 1806	
	Benjamin Gumaer Patien Thomis	Samuel, b. Sept. 28, 1806	
	Garret Damport Caty Oosterhout	Samuel, b. Sept. 12, 1805	
	Samuel Lambert Ester Kittle	George, b. March 20, 1806	
	Ester Chimers	Polly, b. March 29, 1806	Polly Shimer, witness
Sept. 13.	Joshua Van Aken Elizabeth Hoornbeek	Daniel, b. Aug. 22, 1807	
	Hezekiah Vredenburgh Cathrine Shimer	Wilhelmus, b. Jan. 5, 1805 Havilah, b. Aug. 30, 1807	
	George Brink Dorcas Dolittle	Eliza, b. Oct. 1, 1802 Abbe, b. Oct. 1, 1802 twins Sherlott, b. Oct. 11, 1804	
	Martin Devenport Cathrine Cortregt	Alanson, b. Dec. 30, 1806	

DATE	PARENTS	CHILD	WITNESSES
1807.			
Sept. 13.	Thomas Decker Jenny Case	Absolam Case, b. July 25, 1804 Peter, b. June 18, 1806	
	Henry Case Cate Neerpass	George, b. June 21, 1806	
	John Quick Pegge Van Aken	Pegge, b. April 29, 1807	
	Samuel D. Westfal Jane Westbrook	Mary, b. Aug. 19, 1805	
	Benjamin Vredenburgh Mary Case	Aaron, b. March 8, 1807	
	—— Hester Chambers	Myram, b. Feb. 15, 1805	
	Bernardus Titcherd Hannah Mosher	Simon Middagh, b. Dec. 25, 1804 Nancy, b. May 24, 1807	
	James Decker Gloriannah Case	Mary, b. March 17, 1804 Jean, b. May 17, 1806	
	James Bennet Lydia Hoornbeek	Jacobus, b. April 16, 1804 Zephine, b. Aug. 16, 1806	
	Joshua Vredenburgh Elizabeth Van Aken	Levi, b. March 27, 1805	
	Elias Cuikendal Elisabeth Gumaer	Hannah, b. Aug. 13, 1807	

DATE	PARENTS	CHILD	WITNESSES
1807.			
Sept. 13.	Levi Van Aken Mary Dewit	Solomon Westbrook, b. Nov. 4, 1803	Solomon Westbrook Peggy Dewit
	John Van Vliet Catherine Westphal	Abraham, b. Sept. 20, 1807	
1808.			
June 5.	Peter Swarthout Jane Westfall	Deborah, b. March 29, 1808	
	Jacob Cuddebeek Dinah Van Nette	Abram, b. Jan. 30, 1808	
	Jacob Van Enwegen Sarah Paterson	Catherine, b. July 7, 1807	
	Lewis Van Sickle Syche Van Vleet	Jacobus, b. Aug. 20, 1807	
	Absalom Van Naken Magdalen Van Naken	Jane, b. Aug. 23, 1804 Coert, b. Aug. 23, 1807	
	Lewis Mapes Mary Play	Catherine, b. Dec. 29, 1807	
	Joshua Cole Leah Cole	Sarah, b. May 14, 1808	
	Cornelius Medack, Jun., Catharine Van Naken	Elenor, b. Dec. 14, 1807	
	Jacob Van Enwegen Sarah Sammons	Hannah, b. April 28, 1808	
July 31.	David Canfield Mary Sammons	John, b. April 8, 1808	
	Josiah Vanenwegen Majorey Van Aken	Hester, b. March 19, 1808	
	Samuel D. Westfal Jane Westebrook	Diana, b. May 26, 1808	

DATE	PARENTS	CHILD	WITNESSES
1808.			
July 31.	James Hovenbeck Elizabeth Dewitt	Benjamin, N. A., b. Dec. 21, 1807	
	Tunis Osterhout Prude Quick	Catey, W. B., b. Dec. 30, 1807	
Nov. 6.	Joseph Van Noey Mary Conklin	Jacob, b. July 25, 1808	
	James Cole Lidy Van Noey	William, b. Aug. 26, 1807	
	Jacob Quick Elenor Van Garden	Caty, b. July 12, 1808	
	Solomon Kittle Mary Rosecrans	Herman Rosekrans, b. Aug. 2, 1808	
	Henry Case Caty Neerpass	Jacob, b. June 11, 1808	
	Roman Elmendorf Leenty Meddag	Isaac, b. July 30, 1807	
	Henry Van Etten Mary Westfall	Jesse, b. Aug. 17, 1808	
	Isaac N. Decker Hetty Westbrook	Isaac, b. Sept. 1, 1808	
	Cornelius Van Emwegen Deborah Westbrook	Margaret, b. Sept. 18, 1808	
Nov. 27.	Simon Brink Phebe Winfield Peter G. Swartwoud Elizabeth Vernooy	Henry, b. July 26 MaryAnn, b. Sept. 7	
1809.			
Jan. 30.	Benjamin Westfall Syntje Gumaer	Margery, b. Jan. 30, 1809	

DATE	PARENTS	CHILD	WITNESSES
1809.			
Jan. 30.	Solomon Van Etten Jemima Gumare	Jane, b. Feb. 5, 1809	
	John J. Sammons Sarah Decker	Mary, b. March 6, 1809	
	Oliver Whitehead Sarah Lambert	Esther, b. April 9, 1809	
	Isaac Decker, Junior Mary Decker	Daniel, b. April 14, 1809	
	Joel Whitlock Elizabeth Huff	Joseph, b. Dec. 13, 1808	
	Martin Decker Huldah Cuykendal	Eleanor, b. Dec. 31, 1808	
	Jacob Neerpass Catharine Kuddeback	Anne, b. Nov. 7, 1808	
June 4.	Daniel Quick Rachel Osterhout	John, b. Aug. 20, 1808	
	Jacob Gumare Sarah Van Garden	Abraham, b. Aug. 15, 1808	
	Jeremiah Van Aaken Mary Westbrook	Catharine, b. Oct. 24, 1808	
	Richard Sheimer Ruth Ennis	Sarah Anne, b. July 30, 1808	
	Josiah Van Ninwegen Margery Van Aaken	Hermanne, b. May 4, 1809	
	Daniel Vredenburgh Eleanor Hopkins	Juliana, b. Nov. 26, 1805	
	Charack Van Nimwegen Jane Van Etten	Anthony, Jan. 11, 1809	
	John Van Nimwegen Elizabeth Van Vliet	Martinus, b. March 22, 1809	

DATE	PARENTS	CHILD	WITNESSES
1809.			
June 4.	Cornelius Middag Jane Westbrook	Jacob, b. April 19, 1809	
July 9.	Benjamin Cuddebeck Diana Van Etten	Catharine, b. June 6, 1809	
	James Bennet Ledy Hoovenbeck	Blandina, b. Jan. 30, 1809	
Oct. 1.	Henry Cuddenbeck Easther Gumaar	Catharine, b. June 28, 1809	
	Abraham Van Garden Rebecka Bovie	Martinus, b. June 10, 1809	
	Benony Maps Mary Nearpass	Anny, b. March 18, 1809	
	John B. Quick Diana Rosecrans	Martin Cole, b. Sept. 29, 1808	
1810.			
April 15.	Jacob Cuddebeck Dinah Van Etten	Isaac, b. June 30, 1810	
	Joshuah Cole Lea Cole	Josias, b. Nov. 23, 1809	
	Sarah Shegrave	Caty Cuddeck, b. Sept. 20, 1809	
	Moses Crofford Rebecca Cole	Sarah Wells, b. Aug. 6, 1809	
	John Bodle Cheziah Parmer	Jemima, b. Feb. 17, 1809	
	Elias Cuikendal Elizabeth Gemaar	Hester b. March 11, 1810	
	Alexander Westbrook Sarah Cole	Wilhemus, b. March 11, 1810	

DATE	PARENTS	CHILD	WITNESSES
1810.			
April 15.	John Van Ellen Sarah Van Noey	Daniel, b. Feb. 12, 1810	
	Peter Q. Howel Hester Cortright	JenyQuick, b. Sept. 26, 1809	
	Cornelius Meddag Caty Van Aken	Solomon V., b. July 6, 1809	
	Benjamin Glimps Margaret Windfield	Moses, b. Jan. 7, 1810	
May 27.	David Canfield Mary Sammons	Elizabeth, b. Sept. 1, 1809	
	Peter Decker Charlotte Decker	Thomas, b. April 29, 1810	
	William Little Catherine Middagh	Esther, b. Oct. 13, 1807 Peggy, b. Aug. 11, 1809	
	Aaron Dewit Jane Sammons	Aaron, b. Oct. 8, 1809	
	Lewis Mapes Mary Pray	Benoni, b. March 15, 1810	
	Abraham Van Inwegen Elizabeth Sammons	John, b. March 30, 1810	
	William Middagh Huldah Kaskey	Henry C., b. Dec. 11, 1809	
	Martin Kaskey Jane Middagh	Sarah, b. Sept. 28, 1809	
	Margaret Middagh	CharityD., b. March 18, 1810	
Aug. 12.	Jacob Quick Ellenor Van Gardon	Dan. Dimmick, b. April 24, 1810	

DATE	PARENTS	CHILD	WITNESSES
1810.			
Aug. 12.	Gerardus Gomaar Eunice Patterson	George, b. Sept. 23, 1808	
	Hezekiah Fredenburgh Catharine Shymer	Esther, b. May 18, 1810	
	Benjamin Carpenter Margaret Decker	Margaret, b. Dec. 20, 1809	
	Peter E. L. Gumaer Mary Van Inwegen	Jacob, b. Dec. 18, 1809	
	Joshua Van Akin Elizabeth Van Hornbeek	Richard, b. June 12, 1809	
	Nathan Van Aken Esther Patterson	Isaiah, b. May 29, 1810	
	William Kuddebeck Hannah Van Inwegen	Samuel, b. Oct. 14, 1808	
Sept. 9.	Frances M. Smith Margaret Quick	John Q., b. March 17, 1810	
	Morin Van Garden Jane "Gigge"	William, b. Oct. 17, 1809	
	Samuel D. Westfall Jane Westbrook	Sarah, b. June 28, 1810	
	James Osterhout Elizabeth Quick	John, b. May 22, 1810	
1811.			
May 19.	Benjamin Horenbeek Mary Schimer	Jacob, b. Dec. 24, 1809	
	Nathaniel Van Aken Jane Van Etten	Elizabeth, b. April 26, 1811	
	Daniel Van Etten Margaret Cuddebeck	Hannah, b. Jan. 24, 1811	
	Henry Van Etten Mary Westfall	Levi D., b. Oct. 9, 1810	
June 3.	Jeremiah Van Auken Mary Westbrook	Benjamin, b. Jan. 22, 1811	

DATE	PARENTS	CHILD	WITNESSES
1811.			
June 3.	Samuel Lambert, the second Esther Kittle	Alpheus and Alphred, b. Aug. 25, 1810	
	David Campfield Mary Semmons	Henry Titus, b. Oct. 26, 1810	
	Benjamin Westfall Cyne Gumeere	Simon, b. Nov. 27, 1810	
June 9.	Absalom Van Auken Magdalen Van Auken	Jacob Hoornbeek, b. Aug. 13, 1810	
June 12.	David Van Inwegen Ann Swartwout	Margery, b. May 2, 1808 Jane, b. July 22, 1810	
	Jacob Gumaar Sally Van Garden	Ezekiel, b. Oct. 8, 1810	
June 11.	Benjamin Gumaar Patience Thomas	Margaret, b. Sept. 3, 1808 Martha, b. Sept. 14, 1810	Elias Gumaar Margaret De Puy
June 16.	Ruth Enes, wife of Richard Shimer	Catharine Jane, b. Aug. 30, 1810	
	Catharine Brinck, wife of Richard Decker	Lydia, b. March 16, 1810	
July 3.	Abraham Van Aaken Elizabeth Davids	Catharine, b. Aug. 10, 1809	
Oct. 20	Joel Whitbeck, Elizabeth Hoff	Henry, b. July 1,	

BAPTIZED BY REV. JOHN DURYEA, V. D. M.

Dec. 15.	Henry Wingfield Deborah Westbrook	Mariah, b. Sept. 13, 1811	
	Benjamin Van Inwegen Charity Cole	Lewis, b. Nov. 23, 1811	

DATE	PARENTS	CHILD	WITNESSES
1812.			
Feb. 15.	Peter Van Noy, Junr. Mary Westbrook	William, b. Oct. 6, 1811	
Feb. 16.	John J. Sammons Sarah Decker	Martines, b. Nov. 9, 1811	
	Martines Decker Huldah Cuykendall	Catharine, b. July 12, 1811	
	Josiah Van Inwegen Marjory Van Auken	Jane, b. June 5, 1811.	
May 3.	Solomon Meddag Margaret Van Auken	Elshe, b. June 12, 1811	
	Martin Carpenter Mary Van Strander	Isaac, b. Feb. 9, 1812	
	Jacob Neerpas Caty Cuddebeck	Benjamin, b. June 10, 1811	
	Bennoney Maps Mary Nearpas	Elizabeth, b. Aug. 14, 1811	
	Joshuah Vredenburgh Elizabeth Van Auken, deceased	Elijah, b. April 25, 1808	
	Joshua Cole Leah Cole	Elizabeth, b. Aug. 11, 1811	
	Alexander Westbrook Sarah Cole	Maria, b. Oct. 4, 1811	
July 5.	Jacob W. Van Netten Charity Gumaer	Huldah, b. April 3,	
	David Canfield Mary Sammons	Jesse, b. Jan. 10,	
	Jacob Van Inwegen Sally Sammons	Margaret, b. Sept. 12, 1811	
	Isaac Decker, Junr. Mary Decker	John, b. June 20, 1812	
	Corns. Middag, Junr. Catharine Van Aken	Elias, b. Aug. 21, 1811	

DATE	PARENTS	CHILD	WITNESSES
1812.			
July 5.	Peter E. L. Gomaer Mary Van Enwegen	Cornelius, b. Aug. 22, 1811	
	Abm. Cuddeback Catharine Cuykendaal	James, b. April 12, 1812	
	William Cuddeback, Junr. Hannah Van Enwegen	Jane, b. July 4, 1811	
	Aaron De Witt Jane Sammons	Abrm., b. May 28, 1812	
	Cornelius Middag Jane Westbrook	William, b. June 14, 1811	
July 26.	William Little Catharine Middag	Levi, b. Jan. 26, 1812	
Aug. 16.	Jacob Cuddeback Dinah Van Etten	Joseph, b. April 22, 1812	
	Benjamin Cuddeback, Junr. Catharine Cuikendal	Elias, b. July 30, 1812	
	Benjamin Cuddebeck Dinah Van Etten	Jane, b. Dec. 22, 1811	
Aug. 15.	Samuel Lambert Esther Kettle	Daniel, b. May 31, 1813	
	Daniel Whitlock Sarah Westfall	Levy, b. July 5, 1812	
	Solomon Van Etten Gemima Gumaer	Sally, b. July 22, 1813	
1813.			
Aug. 15.	Levy Van Etten, Junr. Elenor Carpenter	Margaret, b. March 11, 1813	
	Josiah Van Inwegen Marjory Van Aken	Anne, b. May 17, 1813	
	Jacob Cuddebeck Dina Van Etten	Naomy, b. Aug. 31, 1813	
Oct. 31	James R. Cole Jane Cuddebeck	Maria, b. Sept. 25, 1812	

DATE	PARENTS	CHILD	WITNESSES
1813.			
Oct. 31.	Samuel D. Westfall Jane Westbrook	John, b. Feb. 11, 1813	
	Benjamin Westbrook Elizabeth Westbrook	Willhelmus, b. June 23, 1813	
	Benjamin Vradenburgh Mary Case	Mary Conckling, b. Sept. 12, 1812	
	Peter Q. Howel Esther Cortright	Caty, b. June 9, 1812	
	John Westfall, deceased Easter Westbrook	John, b. March 11, 1813	
	Abraham Westfall Maria Van Aeeken	Jemimy, b. Feb. 12, 1813	
Nov. 21.	Benjamin Carpenter Margaret Decker	Hannah, b. Aug. 15, 1812	
	Alexander Westbrook Sara Cole	Aaron, b. Aug. 26, 1813	
	John Van Inwegen Elizabeth Van Vliet	Solomon, b. June 12, 1812	
	Hezekiah Vredenburgh Catharine Sheimer	Daniel, b. Sept. 18, 1812	
Nov. 22.	Levy Van Garden Amey Davis	David, b. Sept. 8, 1812	
	Benjamin Van Noy Hannah Decker	Elias, b. Aug. 17, 1812	
	Martin Van Garden Jane Gegy	Silas, b. Feb. 25, 1812	
Nov. 8.	Cornelius Cuddebeck Marjory Cuddebeck	Sally, b. Jan. 26, 1811 Maria, b. Aug. 4, 1813	
	Abraham Van Enwegen Elizabeth Van Enwegen	Esther Gumaer, b. Oct. 20, 1812	

DATE	PARENTS	CHILD	WITNESSES
1813.			
Nov. 8.	Jacob Gumaer Sally Gumaer	Simeon, b. April 1, 1813	
1814.			
Feb. 14.	Benjamin Van Enwegen Charity Cool	George, b, Dec. 11, 1813	
	Cornelius Middag Meriam Van Aken	Edmund, b. May 7, 1813	
July 31.	Henry Windfield Deborah Westbrook	Jane, b. Dec. 15, 1813	
	David Glimps Mary Middag	Sally, b. Jan. 3, 1812	
	Solomon Middag Margaret Van Auken	Lydia, b. May 13, 1813	
	Benjamin Westfall Syntie Gymaer	Catharine, b. Jan. 6, 1814	
	Peter Van Noy, Junr. Mary Westbrook	Sally, b. Dec. 20, 1814	
	James Sawyer Catharine Neerpas	Hannah, b. Nov. 10, 1813	
1815.			
Mar. 26.	Levy Van Etten, Junr. Elenor Carpenter	John, b. Feb. 4, 1815	
	Daniel Van Inwegen Mary Cuykendall	Rachel, b. Nov. 1, 1813	
July 16.	Joel Whitlock Elizabeth Hoff	Eliza Ann, b. Nov. 27, 1813	
	Catharine Westfall, widow of John Van Vliet	John, b. Nov. 19, 1814	
	William Geegge Elizabeth Winner	Hiram, b. Oct. 16, 1814	
	John Van Inwegen Elizabeth Van Vleet	Sally, b. Feb. 15, 1815	
	Samuel Vaninwegen Caterina Rosecrans	Peter, b. April 13, 1815	

DATE	PARENTS	CHILD	WITNESSES
1815.			
July 16.	Benjamin Cuddeback, Junr. Catharine Cuykendall	Levy, b. July 2, 1814	
	Abraham Westfall Mariah VanAken	Elizabeth, b. July 19, 1814	
	Jacob Nearpass Caty Cuddeback	George, b. Oct. 6, 1814	
	Peter E. Gumaer Esther Cuddeback	Morgan, b. Jan. 27, 1815	
	James R. Cole Jane Cuddeback	Elenor, b. Jan. 27, 1815	
	Benjamin Cuddeback Dianna Van Etten	Senea, b. May 13, 1814	
	Isaac Decker Mary Decker	Benjamin, b. Apr. 2, 1815	
	Isaac Van Aken Elizabeth Courtright	Benjamin Westbrook, b. Oct. 21, 1814	
	Mary Van Strander wife of Martin Carpenter	Levy, b. March 8, 1814	
Dec. 3.	David Glimpse Mary Middag	Benjamin, b. June 21, 1815	
	Harmanus Van Inwegen Hannah Cole	David, b. Oct. 22, 1815	
Dec. 5.	Henry Cuddeback Esther Gumaer	George, b. Aug. 10,	
	Jacob Gumaer Sally Van Garde	Eleanor, b. July 2, 1815	
	David Canfield Mary Sammons	Sally, b. Jan. 13, 1815	
1816.			
Oct. 13.	Daniel Van Vliet Hester Westbrook	James, b. May 14, 1816	James Van Vliet Mary Westbrook
	Henry Winfield Deborah Westbrook	Aaron, b. Dec. 13, 1815	

DATE	PARENTS	CHILD	WITNESSES
1816.			
Oct. 13.	Moses Brass Jane Windfield	William, b. Nov. 4, 1813 Stephen, b. Nov. 27, 1815	
	Samuel D. Westphall Jane Westbrook	Jane, b. Aug. 4, 1815	
	Peter Van Noy Mary Westbrook	Jane, b. July 9, 1816	
	Cornelius Cuddeback Margere Van Aken	Martha, b. Aug. 26, 1815	
	George Nearpas Mary Westbrook	Anny, b. June 21, 1815	
	Benjamin Westfall Sinche Gumaer	Rusiller, b. April 14, 1816	
	Jeremiah Van Auken Mary Westbrook	Lea, b. Aug. 5, 1813 Thomas Clarke, b. Dec. 12, 1815	
	Daniel Van Inwegen Mary Cuikendall	Betsey, b. May 22, 1816	
	Benjamin Van Inwegen	Eli, b. April 27, 1816	
	Abm. Glimpse Jenny Glimplse	Maria, b. Oct. 30, 1815	
Oct. 28.	Joseph Bennet Polly Van Noy	William, b. Aug. 24, 1814 Lydia, b. Oct. 7, 1816	
1817. March 2.	David Wynkoop Elizabeth Smith	Jacobus Swartwout, b. Jan. 22, 1817	

DATE	PARENTS	CHILD	WITNESSES
1816.			
—	Graudus Swartwout Matilda Whitehead	Sally Ann, b. Dec. 22, 1813	
		Jane Hoornbeek, b. March 14, 1816	
1817.			
March 16.	Abraham Cuddeback Caty Cuykendall	William Abraham, b. Sept. 6, 1815	
April 10.	Solomon VanVleet, Jr. Sally Carpenter	Benjamin, b. March 13, 1823	Joel Whitlock, David Canfield, Betsey Buckley, Easter Corsa(?), Titus a blackman(?) } adults
April 13.		Lenah Hopkins	
May 4.	Joel Whitlock Elizabeth Hoff	Aaron, b. Nov. 19, 1816	
	David Canfield Mary Sammons	William Baldwin, b. Nov. 23, 1816	
	Benjamin Cuddeback Catherine Cuykendall	Rosetta, b. Oct. 19, 1816	
	Samuel Van Inwegen Catherine Rosekrans	Benjamin, b. April 5. 1817	
	Samuel Lambert Easter Kittle	Catherine, b. Nov. 24, 1815	
	James R. Cole Jane Cuddeback	Martin, b. April 9, 1817	
May 25.	John J. Sammons Sarah Decker	Huldah, b. Dec. 29, 1813 Cornelius, b. March 17, 1817	

DATE	PARENTS	CHILD	WITNESSES
1817.			
May 25.	Martin Decker Huldah Cuykendell	Nelson, b. Dec. 4, 1814	
	Isaac Van Stronder Sarah Van Stronder	Matthias, b. March 19, 1816	
June 8.	James D. Swartwout Naomi Cuddeback	Peter, b. April 1, 1817	
June 22.	Peter E. Gumare Easter Cuddeback	Ezekiel, b. May 10, 1817	
July 6.	Isaac Decker, Junr. Mary Decker	Levi, b. May 22, 1817	
	Benjamin Vredenburgh Mary Iase—deceased	Glorana, b. May 5, 1816	
July 20.	James Sawyer Catharine Nearpass	John Nearpass, b. April 6, 1817	
Aug. 31.	Titus Westbrook, a blackman of Lidia Westbrook Phillis Van Auken, a black woman of James Van Auken	Enis, b. April 14, 1808 Philis, b. April 30, 1810 Titus, b. Dec. 12, 1813 Anson, b. June 11, 1817	
Sept. 11.	Marcus Stickney Betsey Buckley	Eliza Maria, b. March 25, 1807 William Franklin, b. May 27, 1809 Washington, b. April 25, 1811	
Dec. 21.	Phillip Swartwout Esther Westbrook	Peter, b. May 25, 1817	

DATE	PARENTS	CHILD	WITNESSES
1818.			
April 26.	Samuel D. Westfall Jane Westbrook	Esther, b. Aug. 31, 1817	
	Samuel Lambert Esther Kittle	John, b. March 9, 1818	
June 7.	Abraham Cuddebeck Caty Cuykendell	Jane, b. Dec. 1, 1817	
June 8.	Anthony Van Etten Jane Cuykendell	Elizabeth, b. Dec. 19, 1817	
1814			
Jan. 2.	Salomon Van Auken Margaret, his wife	Leah, b. May 31, 1813	
1816.			
May 26.	Salomon Van Auken Margaret, his wife	Harrison, b. Dec. 29, 1815	
1818.			
June 21.	Salomon Van Auken Margaret, his wife	Maria, b. May 3, 1818	
	Henry Winfield Deborah Westbrook	Phebe Caroline, b. March 10, 1818	
	Cornelius Middag, Junr. Catherine Van Auken	Eli, b. Aug. 28, 1816 Hannah, b. May 22, 1818	
	Martin Decker Huldah Cuykendall	Peter, b. April 23, 1818	
	Cornelius Westfall Huldah Cuddeback	Jemina, b. June 21, 1817	
	Charity Middaugh, wife of William Dowley	Huldah, b. Feb. 20, 1812 John, b. Feb. 23, 1814	
July 19.	Cornelius Hornbeck Rachel Vernoy	Eliza, b. Dec. 22, 1817	
	John D. Carpenter Catherine Carpenter	Sarah, b. June 20, 1817	

DATE	PARENTS	CHILD	WITNESSES
1818.			
July 19.	Henry and Caty Case	Anne, b. March 20, 1816	bap. on the presentation of Anna, widow, Wm. Nearpas, guardian of the child
Aug. 2.	William and Mary Cuddebeck	Margaret, b. April 10, 1818	
Aug. 16.	Benjamin Cuddebeck Blandina Van Etten	Elting, b. Oct. 10, 1816	
	Hermanus Van Inwegen Hannah Cole	Evalina Swartwout, b. Dec. 11, 1817	
	Wilhelmus Westfall Mary Cole	Cornelius, b. July 12, 1818	
	Jacob Cuddeback, Junr. Elizabeth Van Auken	Diana, b. July 10, 1818	
Sept. 10.	David Canfield Mary Sammons	Abraham, Van Inwegen, b. July 15, 1818	
Sept. 13.		Mrs. Mary Bloomer, adult Lieshe ⎫ Dinah ⎬ servants of Van Auken	
Nov. 15.	Jacob Vaninwagen Sarah Vaninwagen	Isaac, b. Oct. 15, 1818	
Dec. 27.	Levi Van Etten, Jr. Eleanor Carpenter	Jacob, b. March 10, 1817	
	Benjamin Westfall Synche Gumare	Sally, b. July 14, 1818	
	Benjamin Cuddeback, Junr. Catherine Cuykendall	Jemima, b. Nov. 21, 1818	
1819.			
Jan. 10.	Daniel V. A. Vaninwegen, not present Mary Cuykendall	Jane, b. May 6, 1818	

DATE	PARENTS	CHILD	WITNESSES
1819.			
Jan. 10.	Solomon Van Fleet, Junr. Sarah Carpenter	Mary, b. March 26, 1819	
May 30.	Grandus Swartwout Matilda Whitehead	Mary, b. Aug. 16, 1818	
June 13.	Benjamin Cuddeback Blandina Van Etten	Hannah, b. April 12, 1819	
	John D. Carpenter Catherine Westfall	Senia, b. Nov. 25, 1818	
June 27.	Charles Gordon, not bap. Mary Rosecrans	Hannah, b. April 15, 1819	
Sept. 5.	Alexander Westbrook Sarah Cole	Jerusha, b. June 17, 1815 James, b. April 17, 1817 Henry, b. May 26, 1819	
	William Cortrigt Jemima Huff	David, b. July 18, 1819	
Sept. 26.	Samuel Vaninwagen Catherine Rosecrans	Jane, b. May 7, 1819	
Nov. 14.	James Sawyer Catherine Nearpass	Benjamin Carpenter, b. Sept. 17, 1819	
Dec. 12.	Isaac Decker Mary Decker	Anthony, b. Oct. 22, 1819	
	Jacob Cuddebeck, Junr. Elizabeth Van Auken	John, b. Sept. 29, 1819	
Dec. 26.	Philipp Swartwout Esther Westbrook	Jane, b. Sept. 6, 1819	
1820.			
Jan. 9.	Joseph Bennet Polly Vannoy	James, b. May 12, 1819	

DATE	PARENTS	CHILD	WITNESSES
1820.			
Feb. 6.	Nicholas Vannoy Sally Bennett	Joseph, b. Dec. 11, 1819	
April 23.	Jacob Vradenburgh Catherine Vanauken	Jacobus Vanauken, b. Jan. 15, 1820	
May 7.	David Vannoy Lenah Vanauken	Jacobus Vanauken, b. March 31, 1820	
June 11.	Peter Rosecrans, not present Sally, his wife	Mary Ann, b. Sept. 14, 1819	
June 25.	Henry Windfield Deborah, his wife	Hannah Smith, b. May 25, 1820	
	Cornelius Middaugh Catherine, his wife	Cynata, b. May 10, 1820	
Aug. 20.	Martin Decker Huldah, his wife	Chauncey, b. July 19, 1820	
Sept. 5.	Rev. John Iveson Jane, his wife	Sarah, b. June 28, 1820	
Nov. 19.	Levi Middaugh Margaret, his wife	Jane, b. Oct. 9, 1820	
Dec. 24.	Simeon Westfall Sarah	Ellenor, b. Sept. 11, 1820	
1821.			
Jan. 2.	Peter E. Gumare Hester, his wife	Jacob Cuddeback Elting, b. Oct. 18, 1820	
	Solomon Vanauken Margaret, his wife	Ezra, b. Nov. 13, 1820	
Jan. 22.	John D. Carpenter Catherine, his wife	James, b. Oct. 13, 1820	
	Jacob Cuddeback, Junr. Elizabeth, his wife	Washington, b. Dec. 21, 1820	

DATE	PARENTS	CHILD	WITNESSES
1821.			
Feb. 4.	William Cuddeback, Mary, his wife	Mary Van Keuren, b. Oct. 2, 1820	
Feb. 18.	Wilhelmus Westfall, Marjery, his wife	David, b. Jan. 16, 1821	
March 18.	Johannus Decker, Eleanor, his wife	Charlotte, b. Feb. 8, 1821	
May 20.	Joel Whitlock, Elizabeth, his wife	John Hoff, b. Nov. 12, 1820	
	Solomon Vanfleet, Jr., Sarah, his wife	Levi, b. March 14, 1821	
	Dinah, black girl of James Vanauken	Nelson, b. Oct. 6, 1816	
June 3.	Jeremiah Vanauken, Mary, his wife	Daniel, b. March 12, 1818 Mary, b. Aug. 23, 1820	
June 17.	Grandus Swartwout, Matilda, his wife	Cornelius, b. Aug. 31, 1820	
July 1.	James D. Swartwout, Naomi, his wife	Cornelius, b. Aug. 2, 1820	
	John W. Middaugh, Sally, his wife	Caty Jane, b. March 31, 1821	
	Benjamin Vaninwegen, Phebe, his wife	Charity, b. April 24, 1821	
	Hermanus Vaninwegen, Hannah, his wife	Iva, b. March 2, 1820	
Aug. 12.	Jacob Vaninwegen, Sally, his wife	Jemima, b. May 19, 1821	
Sept. 2.	James S. Vanfleet, Mary, his wife	Daniel Vradenburgh, b. Aug. 7, 1821	
Oct. 28.	Benjamin Cuddeback, Blandina, his wife	Thomas, b. Aug. 31, 1821	

DATE	PARENTS	CHILD	WITNESSES
1821.			
Dec. 23.	Benjamin Cuddebeek Catherine, his wife	Jacob, b. Sept. 9, 1821	
	David Vannoy Lenah, his wife	Oliver, b. Sept. 20, 1821	
	James Vanauken Jane, his wife	Garret, b. Oct. 9, 1821	
1822.			
April 14.	William Vannoy Esther, his wife	Sarah, b. Feb. 5, 1822	
June 2.	Garret Sullivan, not present Lenah, his wife	Jemima, b. March 3, 1822.	
June 23.	Jacob Vradenburgh, decd. Catharine, his wife	Lenah Hopkins, b. April 15, 1822	
	Hermanus Van Inwegen, not present Hannah, his wife	Josias, b. May 17, 1822	
July 21.	Phillip Swartwout Esther, his wife	Catherine, b. Aug. 7, 1821	
	Jacob Cuykendall Margaret, his wife	Jane, b. June 17, 1822	
Aug. 4.	Simon Cuddeback Marjery, his wife	John, b. Nov. 10, 1821	
	Jeremiah Gumare Charlotte, his wife	Isaac, b. Jan. 3, 1822	
Aug. 18.	Isaac Decker Mary, his wife	Sarah, b. April 21, 1822	
	Isaiah Decker, Junr. Eltse, his wife	Caty Jane, b. Feb. 26, 1822	
Sept. 1.	Joshua Cole Leah, his wife	Lidia, b. May 12, 1816	Presented by Josias Cole, Rosanna, his wife, Guardians.
Sept. 15.	James Sawyer Catherine, his wife	James, b. Feb. 28, 1822.	
	Isaiah Decker Hannah	Elizabeth, b. July 7, 1822	

DATE	PARENTS	CHILD	WITNESSES
1822.			
Nov. 10.	Nathan Vanauken Jane, his wife	Mirriam, b. Nov. 21, 1821	
	Joseph Bennett Mary, his wife	Burnett, b. Oct. 26, 1821	
	Peter Rosecrantz, not present Sarah, his wife	Abram Bross, b. June 17, 1822	
1823.			
Jan. 19.	Thomas Vanfleet Margaret, his wife	James, b. Nov. 19, 1822	
Feb. 16.	Martin Decker Huldah, his wife	Eliza, b. Dec. 11, 1822	
	Jacob Cuddeback, Junr. Elizabeth, his wife	Leah, b. Nov. 27, 1822	
April 27.	Solomon Vanfleet Sarah, his wife	Margaret, b. March 28, 1823	
	Henry Windfield Deborah, his wife	Abraham, b. March 30, 1822	
June 8.	Nicholas Vannoy Sally, his wife	Lanche, b. Jan. 8, 1823	
	John D. Carpenter Catherine, his wife	Eleanor, b. Oct. 22, 1822	
July 20.	Simon Westfall Sarah, his wife	Abraham, b. March 29, 1823	
Aug. 17.	Levi Middagh Margaret, his wife	James Nelson, b. June 24, 1823	
	Jacob Nearpass Catherine, his wife	John, b. Nov. 22, 1822	
Aug. 31.	Jacob Gumaer Sarah, his wife	Levi, b. Aug. 24, 1817 Mary Jane, b. Feb. 28, 1822	
Sept. 28.		Barret Sullivan, adult Jin, black woman of I. Swartwout	

DATE	PARENTS	CHILD	WITNESSES
1823.			
Oct. 12.	Phillip Swartwout Hester, his wife	Henry Brinkerhoff, b. April 19, 1823	
	James S. Vaninwegen Jane, his wife	Jemima Hornbeck, b. July 19, 1823	
	Frederick Westfall, not bap. Jemima, his wife	Nancy, b. May 11, 1822	
Feb. 1.	Cornelius Middagh Catherine, his wife	Margaret, b. Oct. 22, 1823	
1824.			
Feb. 29.	Benjamin Vaninwegen Phebe, his wife	Joseph, b. Sept. 11, 1822	
April 25.	Isaiah Decker, not present Ethe, his wife	Jacob Vradenbergh, b. Feb. 12, 1824	
May 23.		Eleanor Drake, an adult	
June 6.	Samuel Vaninwigen, Catherine, his wife	Herman, b. June 28, 1821	
		Joseph Hornbeck, b. Nov. 30, 1823	
July 4.	Cornelius C. Elting, Anna Maria, his wife,	Phillip Bevier, b. March 26, 1824	
	Solomon VanAuken, Margaret, his wife	Elizabeth, b. May 8, 1824	
	David Vannoy Lenah, his wife	Caty, b. March 22, 1834	
	Wilhelmus Westfall Marjery, his wife	Jacob Gumaer, b. Feb. 2, 1824	
Aug. 29.	Jacob Cuykendall Margaret, his wife	Wilhelmus, b. July 7, 1824	
Sept. 12.	James D. Swartwout Naomi, his wife	Sarah, b. Sept. 7, 1823	

DATE	PARENTS	CHILD	WITNESSES
1824.			
Oct. 10.	William Vannoy Hester, his wife	George, b. May 22, 1824	
	Elizabeth, wife of Banjamin Cole Van Auken	William, b. Aug. 18, 1824	
Dec. 19.	Jacob Cuddeback, Junr. Elizabeth, his wife	Jane, b. Sept. 24, 1824	
1825. Feb. 13.	James Sanger Catherine, his wife	William Stone, b. March 31, 1824	
March 13.	Solomon Van Etten Jemima, his wife	Peter Gumare, b. July 30, 1824	
March 27.	Sally, wife of John Middagh	Eli, b. Nov. 1, 1824	
	Elizabeth, wife of Abram Vanenwegen	Peter Gumare, b. Feb. 27, 1821	
May 8.	Mary, wife of Isaac Decker	Marjery, b. Oct. 1, 1824	
	Jemima, wife of Frederick Westfall	Mary, b. Oct. 10, 1824	
June 19.	Hannah, wife of Hermanus Van Inwegen	Margaret, b. Dec. 15, 1824	
July 17.	Senia, wife of Benjamin Westfall	Jemima, b. Dec. 5, 1820 Peter Gumare, b. March 23, 1824	
Nov. 6.	Huldah, wife of Martin Decker	Abigail Ann, b. Jan. 29, 1825	
Nov. 20.	Benjamin Cuddeback Blandina Van Etten	Jemima, b. April 1, 1825	
1826. March 26.	Garret D. Sullivan Lenah, his wife	John, b. March 4, 1826	

DATE	PARENTS	CHILD	WITNESSES
1826.			
	Baltiss Nearpass Sarah, his wife	John, b. Nov. 20, 1824	
May 21.	Benjamin Vaninwegen Phebe, his wife	Samuel, b. Aug. 27, 1824	
		Solomon, b. Feb. 20, 1826	
	Mary, wife of Joseph Bennett	Peter, b. July 20, 1824	
	Cornelius C. Elting Anna Maria, his wife	David, b. March 23, 1826	
June 18.	Marjery, wife of James Horton	William Denton, b. April 28, 1826	
July 16.	Elizabeth, wife of Benjamin C. Van Auken	Catherine, b. April 29, 1826	
Sept. 10.	Elizabeth, wife of Jacob Cuddeback	Maria, b. March 28, 1826	
1829.			
Jan. 28.	Solomon Van Auken Margaret, his wife	Jacob Westbrook, b. Dec. 24, 1826	
1827.			
Feb. 11.			Isaac Middagh, Adult
March 25.	Wilhelmus Westfall Marjery, his wife	Charles Hardenberg, b. Jan. 20, 1826	
	Thomas Van Fleet Elizabeth, his wife	Benjamin, b. May 21, 1826	
April 9.	Sarah, wife of Jacob Gumare	Jacob, b. July 18, 1824	
May 20.	James D. Swartwout Naomi, his wife	Abraham, b. May 13, 1826	
July 15.	Lena, wife of Benjamin Westfall	Levi, b. April 13, 1827	

Marriage Record—1737-97.

[Taken from a pamphlet by Rev. J. P. Ten Eyck, printed 1877.]

Marriage ceremonies performed by J. C. FRYENMUTH unless otherwise stated.

1738—March 5.* Johannes Westbroeck, jun., young man, born at Nytsfield, to Magdalena Westbroeck, young woman, born at Horly, and both dwelling at Manissinck, married by Anthony Westbroeck, Justice of the Peace, the last day of March.

1738—March 26. Jan van Netten, young man, born at Nytsfield, to Maritje Westfael, young woman, born at Menissinck, and both living there, married by Anthony Westbroeck, Justice of the Peace, April 13.

1742. Joh: Casparus Fryenmuth, young man, born in Switzerland, to Lena van Etten, young woman, born at Nytsfield, married with a license from Governeur Morris, in Jersey, by Justice Abram van Camp, the 23d July, 1742.†

1742—July 25. Jacobus Quick, young man, born at Rhocester, dwelling in Smithsfield in Bucks County, to Maria Westbroeck, young woman, born at Rhocester, dwelling at Menissinck, married the 22d of August.

1743—March 13. Simon Westfael, young man, born in Dutchess County, dwelling in Smithsfield in Bucks County, to Jannetje Westbroeck, young woman, born at Mormel, dwelling at Menissinck, married the 17th of April by Pieter Kuyckendal, Justice of the Peace.

1743—August 21. Johannes Bogaert, young man, born in Dutchess County, to Sarah Hoogteeling, young woman, born at Rochester, both dwelling at Menissinck, married the 9th November ditto, by Abraham van Aeken, Justice of the Peace.

1741—July 19. Abram Middagh, young man, born at Menissinck, to Lena van Aken, young woman, born at Rochester, both dwelling here, married August 18.

1745—March 24. Johannes Kuykendal, young man, born at Syndiaquai, to Elizabeth Decker, young woman, born at Shippegonck, both dwelling there, married April 19th.

1745—May 12. Salomon Decker, young man, born on the Caetsbaen (Katsbaan), to Lena Quick, young woman, born at Metschepekonck, and both dwelling at Metschepekonck, married June 8th.

1745—June 2. Benjamin Westbroeck, young man, born at Nytsfield, dwelling at Menissinck, to Catharina Westbroeck, young woman, born at Nepanach and dwelling at Namenack, married the 28th ditto.

1745—July 21. Johannes Kortrecht, young man, to Catharina Kortrecht, young woman, both born at Rochester, and both living in Bucks County in Pennsylvania, married August 27th.

---

* Date of first publication of banns.
† Joh: Casparus Fryenmuth, J. M., geboren in Switzerland, met Lena van Etten, J. D., geboren op Nytsfield, getrouwt met een Licence van Governeur Morris in Jersey, door Justice Abram van Camp, den 23 July, 1742.

1746—January 19. Benjamin Thomson, young man, born in Nieuw Engelant, to Lizabeth Westfael, young woman, born at Machackemech, and both dwelling there, married February 9th.

1746—February 23. Cornelis van Etten, young man, born at Nytsfield and dwelling at Namenack, to Heltje Westbroeck, young woman, born at Menissinck and dwelling there, married March 26th.

1746—March 24. Jacob Westbroeck, young man, born at Gilsford, dwelling at Menissinck, to Lydia Westfael, young woman, born in Duytsches County and dwelling at Sheppekonck, April 11th.

1746—June 15. James McCarty, young man, born in London, to Lisabeth Mey, young woman, born in Hooghduytschlant, both dwelling in Bucks County, married the 13th of July.

1747—March 1. Abram van Aken, jun., young man, born at Nepenack, to Margriet Westfael, young woman, born at Menissinck, the first living in Bucks County, and the last at Menissinck, married the 29th ditto.

1747—July 26. Dirk Rosenkranz, young man, born at ——, and dwelling in Bucks County, to Catharina van Aken, young woman, born at —— and dwelling at Machackemech, married the 21st of August ditto. Mach:

1747—July 5. James L'ove, widower of Mary Barren, to Marya Cole, young woman, born at —— and both dwelling at Walpeck, married the 2d of August by Abram van Kampen, Justice of the Peace. Men:

1747—August 30. Pieter Roet, widower of Meerte Berns, to Sara van Garden, widow of Leendert Cole, both dwelling in Walpeck, married the 9th of October. Men:

1747—September 13. Jacob van Campen, young man, born at Nepenack, to Rachel Decker, young woman, born at Neskotack, both living in Bucks County, married the 9th of October. Mach:

1747—October 11. Cornelis Westfael, young man, born at Machackemech, to Lisabeth Westfael, young woman, born at Sineaquan, and both dwelling there, married the 20th of November. Mach:

1747—November 22. Cornelis Kortrecht, young man, born at Mormel, to Tjaetje Kortrecht, young woman, born at Rochester, and both dwelling at Smithsfield, married the 25th of December. December 6th, Men:

Jacobus Rosenkranz, widower of Sara Decker, to Catharina Cole, young woman, born at Rochester and both dwelling at Machackemech, married the 13th of January, 1747-8. Mach:

1748—March 20. Daniel Westfael, young man, born at Machackemech, to Maria Westbroeck, young woman, born at Gilsford, and both dwelling at Menissinck, married the 8th of April ditto. Mach:

1748—October 30. Abram van Aken, widower of Margriet Westfael to Catharina Rosenkranz, young woman, born at Rochester, and both dwelling at Theeshacht, married the 1st of December.

1748—November 6. Johannes Westbroeck, young man, to Maria Westbroeck, young woman, both born at Wawarssinck, and dwelling at Namenak, married the 4th of December.

1748—November 6. Daniel Kuykendal, young man, born at Machackemech and dwelling there, to Lisabeth van Aken, young woman, born at Wawarssinck and dwelling at Theeshacht, married the 2d of December.

1748—December 11. Benjamin Westbrock Vernoy, young man, born at Wawarssinck and dwelling at Namenak, to Lydia Westfael, young woman, born at Machackemech and dwelling there, married the 8th of January, 1749.

1748—November 19. Benjamin Quick, young man, born at Metschpeconk and dwelling at Theeshacht, to Hanna Joons, young woman, born at Black River and dwelling at Metschpeconck, married the 6th of January, 1748-9.

1749—January 8. Joseph Westbroeck, young man, born at Wawarssinck and dwelling at Namenak, to Lizabeth Kuykendal, young woman, born at Machackemech and dwelling there, married the 27th of January.

1749—February 5. Abram Chambers, young man, born at Shippack, to Lena Westbroeck, born at Neshotack and both dwelling at Menissinck, married the 3d of March.

1749—July 2. Joseph Wallon, young man, born in Nieuw Engellant, to Neeltje Decker, widow of Jacobus Kuddebeck, both dwelling at Metschepeconk, married October 19th.

1749—August 27. Joris Kimber, young man, born at Long Eylant and dwelling on the verdroncken lant (Drowned Lands), to Sara Westfael, young woman, born at Machackemech and dwelling there, married the 5th of October.

1750—January 7. Isaac Middagh, young man, born at Menissinck and dwelling in Theeshact, to Femmetje Decker, young woman, also born at Menissinck and dwelling at Shippeconk, married the 16th of February.

1750—March 4. Manuel Gonsales, widower of Rachel Louw, dwelling at Memmekatting, to Jannetje van Etten, young woman, born at Nepenack and dwelling at Namenack, married the 23d ditto.

1750—April 8. Petrus Brinck, young man, born at Shippekonk, to Sara van Aken, young woman, born at Rochester, and both dwelling at Shippekonk, these banns are forbidden (literal, stopped) the 9th ditto, first by Catharina Hooghteeling and afterwards by Sara van Aken herself in the presence of me, J. C. Fryenmuth, and Antony Westbroeck, elder.

1750—April 13. Jacobus van Sickel, young man, born in Readingtown and dwelling there, to Sara van Aken, young woman, born at Rochester and dwelling at Shippekonk, married the 15th ditto.

Johannes Bruyn, young man, to Maria Schoonmaker, young woman, married the 21st of June with a license from his Excellency, the Governeur Clinton, of New York.

1750—May 13. Cornelis Westbroeck, young man, born at Nepenack, to Lisabeth Kittel, young woman, born at Mormel and both dwelling at Menissinck, married the 7th of June.

1750—July 8. Antony van Etten, young man, born at Nepenack and dwelling at Namenack, to Annatje Decker, young woman, born at Machackemech and dwelling there, married the 3d of August.

1750—July 15. Jacobus Quick, widower of Marys Westbroeck, to Jannetje van Aken, young woman, born at Shippekonk, and both dwelling in Bucks County, married the 10th of August.

1750—June 16. Daniel Consales, young man, born in Ulster County and dwelling at Memmekatting, to Elizabeth van Vliet, young woman, born in Ulster County and dwelling at Machackemech, married the 10th of July.

1750—December 2. Jan van Sickelen, young man, born upon the Raretan and dwelling there, to Margriet Dewitt, young woman, born at Rochester and dwelling in Bucks County, married the 14th of January, 1751.

1751—January 6. Jacobus Middagh, young man, born at Wackonck, in Ulster County, to Sara Decker, young woman, born at Machackemech, and both dwelling there, married the 29th ditto.

1751—April 14. Jan Kermer, young man, born in Kingston, and dwelling among (onder) Walpeck, to Lisabeth van Campen, young woman, born in Upper Smithsfield and dwelling there, married the 15th of May.

1751—May 12. Abram Codebek, young man, born at Pienpeck and dwelling there, to Hester Swartwout, young woman, born at Sindiachquan and dwelling there, married the 29th of May.

1751—July 3. Joel Quick, young man, to Christina Middagh, young woman, both dwelling at Machackemech, married the 3d of September.

1751. Alexander Ivory, young man, born in Irelant and dwelling at Skippekonk, to Maria Cole, young woman, widow of James Love, dwelling among Walpek, married December 24th.

1751—November 23. Salomon Kuykendal, young man, to Sara Cole, young woman, both dwelling at Machackemech, and both born there.

1752—February 9. Abraham Westbroeck, young man, born at Wawarsinck and dwelling at Namenack, to Blandina Rosenkranz, young woman, born at Skippekonk and dwelling at Machackemech, married the 6th of March.

1752—March 8. Jacob van Aken, young man, born at Rochester, to Margriet van Garden, young woman, born at Shippekonk and both dwelling there, married the 10th of April.

1752—April 5. Evert Roos Westbroeck, young man, born at Namenack, to Marya Kortrecht, young woman, born at Menissinck, and both dwelling at Namenack, married the 24th ditto.

1752—May 24. Cornelis Quick, young man, born at Shippekonk and dwelling in Upper Smithsfield, to Marya Westfael, young woman, born Menissinck and dwelling there, married the 14th of June.

1752—July 5. Samuel Fench, young man, born in Goshen, to Lena Bosenkranz, widow of Cornelis Kortrecht, both dwelling in Mechackemech, married the 26th ditto.

1752—August 9. Johannes Osterhout, young man, born at Rochester and dwelling there, to Jannetje Swartwout, young woman, born at Machackemech, and dwelling there, married the — September, by Johannes Westbroeck, Justice of the Peace.

1752—December 17. Petrus Kuykendal, young man, born at Machackemeck and dwelling there, to Catharina Kittel, young woman, born at Wawarsinck and dwelling at Menissink, married the 12th of January, 1753.

1752—October 28. Samuel van Vliet, young man, to Tjaetje Cole, young woman, both born at Machackemech and both dwelling there, married the 26th of November.

1752—November 12. Daniel van Vliet, young man, to Sara Codebek, young woman, both born at Machackemech and both dwelling there, married the 8th of December.

1752—December 16. Jan Middagh, young man, born at Aukwagkonk, to Elisabeth Kortrecht, young woman, born at Machackemech and both dwelling there, married the 12th of January, 1753.

1752—December 31. Jacobus Gunsales, young man, born at Mammekatting and dwelling there, to Sara Westbroeck, young woman, born at Namenack, and dwelling there, married the 28th of January, 1753.

1753—March 4. Cornelis Westfael, young man, born at Machackemech and dwelling there, to Grietje Decker, young woman, born at Menissinck and living there, married the 6th of April.

1753—May 27. Cornelis Middagh, young man, born at Rochester and dwelling in Upper Smithsfield, to Elisabeth Bunschoten, young woman, born in Kingstown and dwelling at Menissinck, married the 15th of June.

1753—June 24. Jacobus Devoor, widower of Evje Dingenman, to Lisabeth Prys, young woman, born in N. Engellant and both dwelling at Palingskill, married the 5th of July.

1753—July 15. Francis McGee, young man, born in Irelant, to Cathrina Quick, young woman, born at Metshippekonk and both dwelling in Upper Smithsfield, married the 10th of August.

1753—July 8. Joseph Bacor, young man, born in Trentown, to Sara M'Carty, young woman, born in Bucks County, and both dwelling in Lower Smithfield, married the 31st ditto.

1753—July 22. James Risla, young man, born in N. Jersey, to Cathrina Hoogteeling, born at Rochester and both dwelling at Menissink, married the 26th of August.

1753—August 5. Jeremias Bacorn, young man, born in Philipsburrough and dwelling in Lower Smithsfield, to Margriet Middagh, young woman, born at Memmekatting and dwelling at Menissink.

1753—November 11. Daniel van Aken, young man, born at Machackemech and dwelling there, to Lea Kittel, young woman, born at Wawarsink and dwelling at Menissink, married the 15th of December.

1753—December 2. Jeremias Kittel, young man, born at Horli, to Lea Davis, young woman, born at Menissinck and both dwelling there, married the 4th of January, 1754.

1753—December 16. Johannes van Aken, yonng man, born at Nepenack and dwelling at Upper Smithsfield, to Maria van Garden, young woman, born at Shippehonk and dwelling among Menissink, married the 18th of January, 1754.

1754—February 17th. Thomas Wells, young man, born in Philadelphia and dwelling at Menissink, to Elisabeth Dewitt, young woman, born at Rochester and dwelling in Upper Smithsfield, married the 14th of March.

1754—March 31. Petrus Kortrecht, young man, born at Namenak, to Maria Westfael, young woman, born at Teeshact and both dwelling at Menissink, married the 19th of April.

1754—June 2. Mattheus Brink, young man, to Sara Terwilge, young woman, both born at Shippekonk and dwelling there, married the 28th of June.

1754—June 2. James Everingame, young man, born in Croswicks and dwelling at Shippekonk, to Anna Quick, young woman, born at Shippekonk and dwelling in Upper Smithsfield.

1754—July 14th. Cornelis Brink, young man, to Lisabeth van Garden, young woman, both born at Shippekonk and both dwelling there, married the 9th of August.

1754—July 14. William Vredenburgh von Garden, young man, born in Upper Smithsfield, to Jenneke Terwilge, young woman, born at Rochester and both dwelling at Shippekonk, married the 9th of August.

1754—July 14. William Custard, young man, born in Philadelphia County, to Sara Swartwout, young woman, born in Upper Smithsfield and both dwelling there, married the 5th of August.

1754—August 4. Abram Kittel, young man, born at Wawarsink, to Christina Westfael, young woman, born at Menissink and both dwelling there, married the 30th ditto.

1754—August 25. Petrus Westfael, young man, born at Machackemech and dwelling there, to Arriaentje Rosenkranz, young woman, born at Teeshachtee and dwelling there.

1754—September 15. Mattheus Terwilligen, young man, born on the Walkill, to Lisabeth Latier, young woman, born at Smithsfield, and both dwelling at Shippekonk, married the 24th of October.

1754—September 29. Juriaen Westfael, young man, born at Machackemech, to —— Terwilligen, young woman, born on the Walkill, and both dwelling at Machackemech, married the 25th of October.

1754—October 13. Ezeckiel Decker, young man, born in Smithsfield, to Johanna van Tilburgh, young woman, born in New

Hanover, and both dwelling at Walpeck, married the 8th of November.

1754—October 13. Isaac Van Aken, young man, born at Wawarsink, to Margriet Hoornbeeck, young woman, born at Machackemech, and both dwelling at Shippekonk, married the 22d of November.

1754—December 22. James Perry, young man, born in Wallis (Wales), to Sara Conley, born in Yerlant (Ireland), and both dwelling at Shippekonk, married the 15th of January, 1755.

1755—January 26. Alexander Ivory, widower of Marya Cole, to Jenneke Decker, born at Menissink and both dwelling at Walpeck, married the 21st of February.

1755—February 16th. Johannes Bevier, young man, born at Nepenack and dwelling there, to Anna Juliana Decker, young woman, born at Shippekonk and dwelling there.

[This closes the marriage record in the handwriting of Rev. Mr. Fryenmoet. The number was 86.]

MARRIAGES BY ANTHONY VAN ETTEN, J. P.

1756—December 9. Salomon Kortregt, young man, born at Maggemeken, and dwelling there, to Cueliya Cool, young woman, born there.

1756—December 4. Daniel Decker, born at Maggemek and dwelling there, to Blandina Vredenburg, young woman, born in Penselvene, and dwelling at Sekepko.

1757—January 9. Josep Wesbroek, w. e. m., born at Wawasink, to Debra Krom, young woman, born at Sindeyaequan, and both residing at Manissink.

1757—January 22. Robbert Simon, young man, born in Penselvene, to Leya Meddag, young woman, born at Memekaten, and both dwelling at Cindeyaequan.

1757—January 22. Willim Macklinnin, young man, born in Irlant, to Sara Van Aken, young woman, born in Penslvene, and both dwelling at Maggagmeck.

1757—January 22. Byrn Hemmel, young man, born in Irlant, to Blandina Van Aken, young woman, born at Maghagmek, and both dwelling there.

1757—January 1. Jacob Helm, young man, born at Wawasink, to Helena Van Etten, young woman, born at Manissink, and both dwelling at Manissink.

1757—March 7. Johannis Decker, w. m., born at Mombackus, to Debora Van Vliet, young woman, born at Maggemek, and both dwelling there.

1757—April 16. Benjamen Van Vliet, young man, born at Pinpek, to Johanna Wesval, young woman, born at Sidneyaequan, and both dwelling there.

1757—May 19. Jan Van Vliet, w. m., born at Mormel, to Leya Decker, w. v., born at Sidneyaequan, and both dwelling there.

1757—July 3. Daniel Cooper, w. m., and Janneke Wesbroek, w. v., married by me with a license from his excellency, Jonathan Belcher, Esqr.

1757—June 17. Anthony Wesbroek, jr., young man, born at Manissink, to Schusanna Kettel, young woman, born at Wawasink, and both dwelling at Manissink, married August 5th.

1757—July 23. John Lyde, young man, born in Penselvene, to Arriyantie Rosekrans, w. d. v., born at Tyscbag, and both dwelling there, married August 19.

1757—July 16. Johannis Wesval, widower of Ploni Cortregt, to Marigrita Queck, widow of Johannis Van Gardn, both born at Manissink, and dwelling there, married September 2d.

1757—August 6. Helmus Vredenburgh, young man, born at Cepksbrrie to Elisabet Van Garden, young woman, born at Schibbeconk and both dwelling there, married September 16.

1757—August 20. Joseyas Cool, young man, born at Maghagkemeck, to Marrigrit Mollen, young woman, born at Maghagkemeck, and both dwelling there, married September 23.

1758—March 4. Johannis Cool, w. m., born at Maghagkemeck, to Helena Queck, w. v., born at Rosvesten and dwelling at Tycbag, married March 31.

1758—March 12. Gorgh More, young man, born in Irlant, to Helena Rosekrans, widow, born at Schebekom, and both dwelling at Maghagkemeck, married April 3.

1758—February 29. Elisa Middag, young man, born at Wesyester, to Maryte Cimber, widow, born on Lang Eyland, and both dwelling at Maghgemek, and married May 1.

1758—April 29. Martynus Kuykendal, young man, born at Maggemek, to Catrinte Kool, young woman, born at Maghemek, both dwelling there, married June 2.

1758—July 6. Dirck Van Etten, young man, born at Namenock, to Rusye Westvael, born at Pekeepsingh, and both dwelling here, married August 11.

1758—July 8. Jacob Figels, young man, born in Hoge Duyst Lant, to Bebte Dawets, young woman, born in Upper Smithfild, and both dwelling at Maggehemek, married July 28.

1759—February 2. Abraham Cuddebeck, young man, born at Pinpeck, to Hester Gumar, young woman, born there, and both dwelling there, married March 9th.

1759—January 5. Jacobus Van Aken, young man, born at Tyscbag, to Elisabet Bunscoten, widow, and both dwelling there, married February 10.

1759—February 28. Jacob I. Dewit, young man, born in Niew Engelant, to Leya Kortregt, young woman, born at Magghemeck, and both dwelling there, married March 30.

1759—January 26. Huged Sorrad, young man, to Enne Quek, widow, married January 2.

1759—May 20. James Patran, young man, to Elizabet Wesbroek, young woman, married May 20.

1759—June 2. John Dawets, w. e. m., born in the Raretans, to Elonara Wesval, w. e. v., born at Maggemek, and married July 20.

1759—August 19. Hermanus Van Enwegen, young man, born at Pinpek, to Marrigrita Kool, young woman, born at Maggemek, married the 21st.

[The record of the above marriages is in the handwriting of Anthony Van Etten, Justice of the Peace (Vredrichter). The names of persons and places are given as spelled by him.]

MARRIAGES BY REV. THOMAS ROMEYN.

1762—November 19. Abram Cool, young man, born in Northampton, and dwelling at Wantage, to Henetje Dekker, young woman, born and residing at Wantage.

1762—November 30. Johannis Cortregt, young man, born and dwelling at Naamanack, to Susanna Kittel, widow of Antony Westbroek, also born and dwelling there.

1763—January 2. Benjamin Van Vliet, widower, married to Grietje Dekker, widow.

1763—January 13. Jacob van Etten and Jannetje Low were married.

1763—April 30. Alexander Poole and Divertje Dekker, widow, were married.

1763—May 29. Jacobus van de Merken and Catrina Schoonhoven.

June 26. Tuines Sluiter and Sytje Terwilligen.

August 22. Alexander van Gerder to Lydia Kermer.

1764—December 7. Petrus Hoogtaling and Sarah Westvaal.

December 14. Leendert Brink to Rachel Cortregt.

1765—January 17. Abram Laan and Lena van Campen.

January 17. Jacob Dekker and Grietje Tilberg.

February 19. Hendrick Bross and Catrina Cool.

October. Josua Taylor and Hester ——.

1766—October. These in the marriage state were confirmed: Gedevie Middag, son of Aert Middag, to Garretje Cortregt, daughter of William Cortregt.

Nov. 30. These in the marriage state were confirmed: Joseph Hoornbeck, son of Evert Hoornbeck, and Blandina Westbroek, daughter of Jacob Westbroek.

Dec. 10. Is in the marriage state confirmed: Johannis Westbroek, son of Jonannis Westbroek, to Engeltje Davids, young woman.

1766—Dec. 18. Is in the marriage state entered: Jacobus Hoornbeck, young man, to Grietje Ennes, young woman.

December 26. Is in the marriage state entered: David Ennes to Gentje (?) Hoornbeck.

List of names of those who were married by me in the year 1767:

Oct. 8. Is by me married after last publication: Jan ver Wye to Mary Shinny, daughter of Luvonia Shinny.

Oct. 15. Is by married after last publication: Josias W. Cortregt to Cornelia Cool, widow of Johannis Van Gordon.

Oct. 19. Is by me married, Luvonia Shinny, junior, after last publication, to Mary Cool, daughter of Cobus Cool.

1768—Aug. 12. Is married, Stuffel Dekker to Maria McCarty, after last publication.

Dec. 2. Is married, Joseph Drake to Maragriet Hoogteling.

1768—Nov. 1. Thomas Welsh, young man, married to Gonda Krom, daughter of Rebeca Krom.
Nov. 7. Abram Johson, young man, to Elizabeth Devoir, young woman.
Nov. 9. Daniel Van Campen to Maria Dekker, daughter of Johannis Dekker.
Dec. 7. Joseph Drake to Maria Hoogtaling.
Dec. 27. Salomon Dekker, jun., to Mary Thomas.
1769—Jan. 3. Cornelis Dekker to Grietje Brink.
Jan. 8. Jurian Hoogtaling to a daughter of Abram Middag.
Jan. 18. Johannis B. Westbroek to Lydia Horenbeek.
Feb. 13. Charles Fleming to Christina Chambers.
April 13. Elias Gomaer to Grietje De Pui, daughter of Benjamin De Pui.
April 20. Samuel Williams to Lydia Cortregt, daughter of Arie Cortregt.
July. John W. Wye to Mary Ennes.
August. Benjamin Ennis to Lena Van Etten.
1770—Feb. E. Rundle, widower, to Rebacca Fakes.
March. Nicolaas De Pui to Elsje Van Campen.
February. Johannis Chambers to Hanna Clover.
April 9. Samuel Van Garden to Jenneke Swartwout.
Dec. 29. Is married, Salomon Dekker, junior, to Mary Thomas.
1770—April 19. Is married, Jacobus Roosekrans to Maria Hoornbeck.
April 20. Is married, Derik Westbroek to Mary Wilson.
April 22. Is married, John Curren to Jimentje Hoornbeck.
May 8. Is married, Lodewyck H—— to Hester van Gordon.
May 12. Is married, Jacobus Swartwout to Jenneke Davids.
June 22. Is married, Joseph Ennes to Grietje van Etten.
June 27. Is married, Ezechiel Gomaar to Naomi Low.
August 26. Is married, Daniel Middag to Maria Bunschoten.
Nov. 29. Is married, Samuel de Pui, young man, to Anna Swartwout, young woman.

MARRIAGES BY REV. D. ROMEYN.

1771—Nov. 30. Johannes Rosenkrants, young man, born in Magagkamek, to Maria Rosa, young woman, born at Minisink, and both residing there.
Nov. 30. William Bemer, young man, born in Germany, to Elizabeth Cool, young woman, born at Shepenagh, and both dwelling in Upper Smithfield.
Dec. 1. Joel Dekker, young man, born in Wantage, to Jenneke Cortregt, young woman, born in Mountague, and both dwelling there.
Dec. 1. Daniel Dekker, young man, born in Delaware township, to Rachel Williams, young woman, born in the same place and both residing there.

Marriages by Salomon Coykendal, J. P.

1771—May 1. Salomon Coykendal, junior, and Maria Wesbroek.
1775—June 1. Joseph Sawas and Eliesabeth Kortrecht.
June 1. Samuel Quick and Jenneke Kortrecht.
August 31. Jacobus Quick, jun., and Johanna Peltin.
1776—May 16. Jacobus Decker and Asseltie Vanaken.
Sept. 12. Joseph Job and Aeltie Wesbroek.
Oct. 27. Levy Decker and Eliesabeth Decker.
Oct. 28. Andries Dingeman and Catrine Cole.
Nov. 8. Gerret Brink and Catryntie Kortrecht.
Nov. 8. Benjamin Rashel and Geertie Dason.
1784—July 9. Proclamation of Joseph van Noey to Marey Cainlen.

Marriages by Rev. E. Van Bunschooten.

On proclamation the following persons were married by Elias Van Bunschooten, V. D. M., beginning July 9th, 1785:

1785—Sept. 25. William Gige and Lea Davis.
Oct. 27. Benjamin Rosekrans aud Hannah Travis.
Nov. 7. Jacob Quick and Rachel Wood.
Nov. 15. Moses Cuambers and Rhoda Riggs.
Nov. 24. Gedeon Cortreght and Rachel Decker.
Dec. 21. Daniel Westfaal and Maria Westbroeck.
1786—March 14. Petrus Gemaar and Majery Decker.
March 19. Thomas Brink and Sarah Bartron.
March 19. Daniel Lebar and Elizabeth Chambers.
March 23. Daniel Swartwout and Cathrina van Aken.
April 6. James Westfall and Caty van Campen.
April 6. George Bush and Mary van Campen.
April 27. Gedion van Etten and Nelly Deshea.
May 7. James Westbrook and Geertie Brink.
May 7. Soferyne Westbrook and Blandina Westbroek.
May 14. Josias Cooll and Rosina Westfall.
May 17. William Cuddeback and Annatje Van Emwegen.
May 21. David Litch and Mary Decker.
May 31. Daniel V. Garden and Maragrieta Middag.
June 1. Matthew Clarck, Anny V. Dyck.
Sept. 14. David Van Garden, Mary Emmans.
Aug. 23. Valentine Davids, Sarah Hofman.
Oct. 24. Jacob Wymant, Eleanor Delong.
Nov. 13. Peter Dingman, Gusche Stoffelbeen.
Dec. 6. Samuel Seeley, Abigail Wynans.
Dec. 13. Robert Sylsbee, Abigail Niemen.
1787—Jan. 10. George Quick, Catrina Meddag.
Feb. 8. John Decker, Cattrina Cortreck.
Feb. 11. Jonathan Van Garden, Ledea Van Sickel.
Jan. 29. Jacob Decker, Maria Terwelliger.
March 11. Moses Brinck, Anny Cortrecht.
March 19. Joannes Neerpas, Sarah Squrrel.*

---

* The proper name of Squirrel in Low Dutch is Inkhorn. The banns were published under the latter name.

1787—March 19. Casparus Middag, Lidea Shipperd.
April 9. Benjamin Carpenter, Margaret Decker.
May 5. Henry Westfal, Margret Brinck.
May 29. Symon Westfal, jun., Syntie Cuddebeck.
May 29. Valentine Smith, Helena Depuy.
May 31. David Dills, Rachel Broadhead.
May 31. Jacob Krass, Anna Depuy.
June 5. Joseph Swartwood, Nelly Schoonhoven.
July 3. Matthew Winans, Mary Van Garden.
July 15. Benjamin Depuy, jun., Ariaantie Van Aken.
July 23. Alexander Swartwout, Caty Schoonmaker.
Aug. 2. Bill Cortrecht, Cattrina Helm.
Sept. 11. Jacob Decker, jun., Tempy Marth.
Oct. 23. Cornelius Depuy, Susanna Chambers.
Oct. 13. Henry Quick, Sarah Quick.
Dec. 27. Elisha Decker, Sarah Carmer.
Oct. 29. Verdenant Van Etten, Sarah Westbrook.
1788—Jan. 1. Jacobus Kuikendal.
Jan. 22. Philip McCarty, Polley Van Demerck.
Jan. 24. Petrus Swartwout, Jannite Westfaal.
Jan. 31. Henry Poh, Jemima Halbart.
Feb. 23. Jacob Arneld, Anne Mullen.
March 2. Chareck Rosekrans, Sara Cortrecht.
May 12. Solomon Rosekrans, Cattrina Van Garden.
June 16. Calvin Clark, Polly Barker.
June 22. David Van Emwegen, Rachel Van Aken.
July 17. Thomas Van Etten, Elizabeth Ennes.
Sept. 14. John Coolbaugh, Susannah Van Campen.
Sept. 21. Gedeon Cole, Maria Van Etten.
Sept. 25. Samuel Quick, Maria Dinnis.
Oct. 6. William Barnet, Elizabeth Nyce.
Nov. 3. Joseph Cortrecht, Elizabeth Sly.
Oct. 10. David Westfal, Jacamyntic Cuddeback.
Nov. 9. Manuel Van Etten, Maria Shimer.
Nov. 23. Benjamin Decker, Rachel Cortright.
Dec. 16. John Brooks, Bethiah Goodspeed.
Dec. 18. John Clarke, Elizabeth Smith.
1789—Jan. 27. Broer Decker, Mary Van Campen.
Feb. 1. Gysbert Carmer, Peggy Decker.
Feb. 8. Samuel Westfall, Anny Lane.
Feb. 16. Martinus Kuikendal, Antie Cole.
Feb. 19. Jacobus Van Aken, Cattrina Westbrook.
Mar. 5. Jacob Myers, Sarah Cortright.
Mar. 18. Nathanael Van Aken, Maria Westbrook.
June 15. Jacobus Van Vliet, Maria Westbrook, widow of Salomon Kuikendal, Jun.
June 16. John Van Aken, Grietie Westfall.
July 14. Cornelius West: Cole, Annatie Geemaar.
Nov. 1. Alexander Sutherland, Sarah Schoonhoven.
Dec. 21. Stephen Munroo, Phebe Cortright.
Dec. 24. Abraham Swartwout.
Feb. 16. Geo. Sprigal, Sofya Lebar.

1789—Feb. 28. Petrus Decker, Selitee Decker.
July 26. Abraham Westbrook, Jannitee Van Aken.
1790—Mar. 31. Levi Cortrecht, Sarah Decker.
May 24. George Luths, Mary Evvens.
June 5. Benjamin Westbrook, Lena Ennes.
Sept. 7. Joseph Rosekrans, Jamima Emmes.
Sept. 16. William Edwards, Caty Wells.
Sept. 13. Daniel Kittle, Cattrina Crow.
Oct. 11. Benjamin Decker, Maria Cole.
Oct. 24. James Campbel, Margaret Stewart.
Oct. 28. Corneilus Tailor, Caty Brinck.
Nov. 20. Richard Decker, Caty Brinck.
Dec. 19. Thomas Caskey, Lidia Hopkins.
Dec. 19. Cornelius Meddag, Jane Westbrook.
Dec. 28. Samuel Gonsalis, Heyltie Dewitt.
Dec. 30. Luther Clark, Susannah Ross.
Dec. 16. Nathanael Meed, Mary Burrell.
1791—Jan. 10. Elias Kuykendall, Elizabeth Gumaar.
Jan. 13. Mosis Van Campen, Ann Riggs.
Jan. 20. Benjamen Nearpass, Anny Lott.
Jan. 30. William Kuykendal, Elizabeth Westbrook.
Feb. 7. David Van Emwegen, Antie Swartwouwt.
Feb. 17. Martynus Cole, Lena Rosekrans.
May 15. Jacob Swartwout, Cattrina Van Etten.
May 19. Charles Dutcher, Margaret Cortrecht.
Aug. 5. Manuel Westfal, Helenah Decker.
Aug. 7. Benjamin Depuy, Maria Depuy.
Sept. 11. William Mapes, Cathrina Decker.
Sept. 5. Abraham Van Aken, Elizabeth Davids.
Nov. 16. Derick Sutfin, Caty Van Dick.
Dec. 7. Even Bevans, Caty Carmer.
Dec. 8. Abraham Carmer, Sarah Carter.
Dec. 19. Ruben Westfal, Tyatie Cuikendal.
Dec. 2. John Decker, Sarah Lamberd.
Dec. 22. Martin Van Dyck, Mary Beagal.
Dec. 31. Matthias Clark.
1792—Jan. 1. John Curtis, Polly Munroe.
Jan. 1. Jacobus Bennet, Ledia Hornbeck.
May 20. Peter Quick, Lucy Lane.
May 21. Benjamin Gumaar, Maria Depuy.
June 7. Joseas Titchsord, Mary Van Garden.
Sept. 13. Jacobus Cole, Rachel Wells.
Oct. 25. —— Wintfield, —— Bennet.
Nov. 4. —— Nyse.
Nov. 18. Daniel Van Aken, Jr., Sarah Van Vliet.
Dec. 6. Abraham Decker, Maria Cortrecht.
Dec. 6. James Van Demeck, Sarah Hoornbeck.
Dec. 25. John Van Demerk, Jeny Annest Curtright.
1793—Jan. 17. Daniel Vredenburg, Lena Hopkins.
July 7. Peter Cuddeback, Elizabeth Helm.
Aug. 11. John Nice, Lena Westbrook.

1793—Oct. 28. John Buckbee, Lena Beemer, widow of Peter Decker, deceased.
Nov. 25. Evert Horenbeck, Jun., Jane Van Aken.
1794—Feb. 27. John Louw, Rushe Van Demerck.
March 3. Sephaniah Drake, —— Shans.
Apr. 27. Daniel Cortrecht, Plomy Westfall.
July 24. William Dutcher, Sarah Fuller, widow of William Cole.
Oct. 9. Jacob Kunbell, Anny Ansley.
Oct. 9. Powel Carpenter, Lucy Kellam.
Oct. 26. Joshua Van Aken, Elizabeth Horenbeck.
Nov. 16. Samuel Cortright, Anny Kyte.
Dec. 18. Levi Meddag, Elshe Van Garden.
1795—Jan. 4. Cornelius Cuddeback, Sarah Van Etten.
Jan. 8. John Kyte, Lea Van Demerck.
Jan. 18. Henry J. Brinck, Nealy Emmens.
Jan. 15. Daniel Westbrook Dingman, Mary Westbrook.
Feb. 5. Jacob Horenbeck, Lea Van Aken.
March 8. Charles Tyler, Ezable Young.
1795—March 8. Timothy Tyler, Rachel Meddag.
May 22. Thaddeus Caperon, Ledia Ennes.
Aug. 2. Moses Decker, Margaret Cuddeback.
Sept. 13. Solomon Cuddeback, Margaret Yan Etten.
Sept. 20. Jonathan Jones, Sebily, wife of John Mushback, dec'd.
Dec. 15. John Middagh, Maria Decker.
Dec. 20. Henry Van Etten, Maria Westfal.
Dec. 17. David Clark, Ester Chambers.
Dec. 23. Jacob Westbrook, Jenneca Decker.
1796—Jan. 10. Jacob Quick, Leentie Van Garden.
March 27. George Deusenbury, Cherity Flemen.
Sept. 29. Sovereign Horenbeck, Annatie Decker.
Oct. 6. Benjamin Vredenburgh, Mary Case.
Dec. 25. Bastian Myers, Sarah Van Garden.
Dec. Wilhelmus Ennes, Maria Ennis.
1797—Jan. 17. Jacob Smith, Margaret Smith.
Jan. 22. Joseph Cole, Lidea Middag.
Jan. 22. Simeon Cole, Grietee Van Aken.
July 28. Henry Wood, Cattrina Kittle, widow of Samuel C. Brink.
Aug. 3. Josaphat Westbrook, Elizabeth Cortright.
Aug. 26. John Van Vliet, Cattrina Westfall.

[Continued from original record.]

1804—Feb. 8. Gerardus Van Imwegen, Maria Demarest.
April 1. William Compton, Mary Depuy.
May 6. Joel Schoonhoven, Mary Holden.
June 20. Daniel G. Finch, Lydia Van Aken.
Aug. 10. Marinus Chambers, Lydia Van Garden.
Aug. 19. Peter Quick, Jr., Elizabeth Brink.
Nov. 24. John Johnson, Phebe Cuykendal.
Nov. 27. John Sammons, Sarah Decker.

1804—Dec. 6. John Decker, Mary Siddales.
1805—None.
1806—Jan. 9. Richard Shiner, Ruth Ennes.
May 25—Lewis Lambert, Mary Cashey.
June 5. John Middagh, widower, Mary Decker, widow.
July 9. John Faulke, Margaret Heiner, wid. of George Stahl. By me John Demarest, V. D. M.
1807—Aug. 16. Alexander Westbrook, Sarah Cole. Confirmed by me, Rynier Van Nest.
1808—June 16. Lewis Allen, Sarah Bugsbee. By me, J. Demarest, V. D. M.
1817—May 17. Cornelius Hornbeck, Rachel Vannoy. By Rev. E. C. Elting, in Montague, Sussex Co., New Jersey.
July 26. Wilhelmus Westfall, Marjery Cole. In Minisink, Orange Co.
Aug. 9. Anthony Van Etten, Jane Cuykendall. In Minisink.
Nov. 24. Isaac Van Standen, Catharine Ranette, widow. In Montague, Sussex County.
1818—April 4. Aldert Stearns, Elizabeth Quick. In Montague, Sussex Co.
Dec. 19. Samuel Swartwout, Jemima Whitlock. Married in Minnisink.
1819—Jan. 21. William Campbell, Hannah Johnson, colored.
May 1. Nicholas Vannoy, Sarah Bennet. Montague, Sussex Co., N. J.
June 12. Joseph Neely, Catharine Vredenburgh. Montague, Sussex Co., N. J.
June 19—Jacob Vredenburgh, Catharine Van Auken. Montague, Sussex Co., N. J.
Sept. 25. David Vannoy, Lenah Van Auken. Montague, Sussex Co., N. J.
Oct. 30. Simeon Westfall, Sarah Cuddeback.
Dec. 4. William Vannoy, Esther Westfall. Married in Upper Smithfield, Pike Co., Penn.
1820—Jan. 1. James C. Decker, Rachel Van Strander, Minnisink.
Feb. 2. Stroud J. Hollingshead, Jannet Labar.
May 6. John W. Middagh, Sally Van Auken. Upper Smithfield, Pike Co., Penn.
June 17. Jacob Cuykendall, Margaret Decker. In Minnisink.
July 1. James S. Vanfleet, Mary Vredenburgh. Montague, Sussex Co., N. J.
July 8. Benjamin A. Westbrook, Mary Nearpass, Montague, Sussex Co., N. J.
July 8. Johannes Decker, Eleanor Quick. Minnisink.
Sept. 16. Samuel Van Auken, Hannah Vannoy. Montague.
Sept. 16. David Swartwout, Synche Cuddeback. Peenpack.
Dec. 30. Peter Westbrook, Eltsie Westbrook. At Basher Kill, N. Y., by C. C. Elting.

1821—Jan. 13. Garret Van Auken, Nancy Butter (or Butler). At Sheholy, Penn.
Jan. 25. James Van Auken, Jane Vannoy. Montague, Sussex Co.
April 14. Jeremiah Gumar, Charlotte Cuddeback, at Peenpack, Orange Co., by C. C. Elting.
June 16. Frederick Westfall, Margaret Cuddeback, Peenpack.
June 17. Thomas Vanfleet, Margaret Cuddeback, Peenpack.
Aug. 11. Daniel Hilferty, Catharine Westfall, Minisink.
Oct. 20. Isaiah Decker, Jr., Eltse Vredenburgh, Montague, Sussex Co., N. J.
Nov. 17. Isaiah Decker, Hannah Vradenburgh, Montague, Sussex Co., N. J.
Nov. 24. John Van Strander, Hannah Carpenter, Minisink.
Dec. 1. Abraham Ackerman, Leah Cuykendall, Minisink.
Dec. 8. James Dilly, Margaret Vanimwegen, Peenpeck.
1822—Aug. 10. Benjamin Cole Van Auken, Elizabeth Vredenburgh. Montague.
1823—Feb. 22. John Adam Morrison, Catharine Nyce, Montague.
June 7. Edward Dilly, Hylah Decker. Minisink.
June 14. James Cuddeback, Jemima Cuddeback, Peenpack.
Dec. 3. Jacob C. Wilson, Parmelia Patterson.
1824—Feb. 21. Thomas H. Johson, Marjery Case. Basher Kill.
March 20. James Horton, Marjery Cuykendale. At Minnisink.
July 10. Jacob Westfall, Mary Westfall. Montague, Sussex Co.
Aug. 7. Henry Scott, Anna Doxy. Minisink.
Sept. 8. James S. Phillips, Mary Amanda Wallace. Minisink.
Sept. 1. William Doxy, Clary Schoonhoven. Minisink.
Sept. 8. John H. Broadhead, Louisa Ann Ross.
Sept. 25. Pompey Swartwout, Anna Gumaer. Minisink.
Dec. 4. Samuel B. Smith, Hilah Caskey. Minisink.
1825—Jan. 4. George T. Lambert, Julia Reed. Minisink.
May 14. Lewis White, Elizabeth Middaugh. Deerpark.
May 14. Henry Little, Jane McDonald. Deerpark.
May 30. George Cop, Rachel Kittle. Montague.
July 16. Levi Cuddeback, Maria Van Imwegen. Deerpark.
Oct. 15. Philip Holden, Huldah Westfall.
Oct. 27. Charles Sidgrieves, Jane Depue.

Church Members—1745-67.

[Copied from a pamphlet by Rev. J. B. Ten Eyck, printed in 1877.]

The following is the record of members of the Churches of Machackemeck and Mennisinck under the ministrations of Revs. J. C. Fryenmuth and Thomas Romien:

Register of Church members who from time to time by confession and by the exhibition of sufficient credentials were received as brothers and sisters in the Church.*

1745—April 11. These upon representation of satisfactory certificates in presence of Jan Van Vliet and Johannes Westbroeck, elders, were received:

Madlena Decker, Antjen Rosa, wife of Johannes Westbroeck.

The following were received upon a confession of faith in the presence of the above named elders:

Hendrick Kortrecht and his wife Gerretje van Bunschoten, Derrick Westbroeck and his wife Jenneke van Keuren, Jacob van Etten and his wife Antjen Westbroeck, Cornelis Westbroeck and his wife Antjen Rosa, Jan van Etten, Willem Kortrecht, Magdalena van Etten wife of J. C. Fryenmuth, Benjamin Westbroeck, Cornelis van Etten, Johannes Cornelis Westbroeck, Cornelis Westbroeck, jun., Antony van Etten, Catharina Westbroeck, Heltje Westbroeck, Maria Westbroeck, Jannetje van Etten.

1745—April 12. In the presence of the reverend Consistory of Menissinck, having beforehand laid aside the Roman Catholic religion (Roomsch Catholycke Religie), on satisfactory confession of our Christian Reformed faith as a member of our Reformed Church is received Hermanus van Nimwegen.

April 14. In the presence of the same Consistory and Pieter van Aken, elder of Walpeck, upon the exhibition of satisfactory certificates as members of our Church were received:

Hermanus Decker and his wife Antje Keyser.

June 19. In the presence of Hendrick Kortrecht and Dirk Westbroeck, elders of Menissinck, upon confession of faith and life, as members of our Low Dutch Reformed Church, the following persons were received:

William Ennes and his wife Lisabeth Quick, Johannes Westfael and his wife, Apollonia Kortrecht, Arie Kortrecht, Aeriaentje van Etten wife of Aert Middagh, Maritje Westfael wife of Jan van Etten, Rachel De Witt wife of Isaac van Aken, Dievertje Maul wife of Andries Decker.

June 23. Upon the representation of satisfactory certificates, in presence of Niclas Du Puy, elder of the Church of Smithsfield, as a member of the above named Church was received Christina Rosenkranz wife of Cornelis Kortrecht.

Sept. 19. In the presence of Hendrick Kortrecht and Dirk Westbroeck, reverend elders of Menissinck, upon satisfactory confession of faith and life, as members of the above mentioned Church were received:

---

* Register van Ledematen, die van tyt tot tyt door belydenisse & vertooninge van genoeghsame getuyghschriften als Broeders & Susters in dese Gemeentens zyn aengenomen.

Margriet Jansen wife of Willem Kortrecht, Annatje van Aken wife of Benjamin Westfael, Naemi Kuttebeck, Margriet Westfael.

As also upon the presentation of a satisfactory certificate Sara Schammers wife of Abram Kermer.

Sept. 20. These in presence of William Cole, reverend elder of Machackemech, upon confession of faith and life, as members of our Low Dutch Reformed Church were received:

David Cole and his wife, Alleonora Westfael, Jacob Westfael.

Dec. 20. In the presence of Dirk Westbroeck elder, and Cornelis Westbroeck, deacon, of Menissinck, on representation of a satisfactory certificate, as member of our Low Dutch Reformed Church, was received Aeltjen van Etten wife of Antony Westbroeck.

1746—March 27. These in presence of the respected elders of Menissinck on satisfactory confession of faith and life were received as members of our Reformed Low Dutch Church:

Antony Westbroeck, Johannes Westbroeck, Maritje Westfael.

Sept. 18. These in presence of Jacob Westfael, respected elder of Machackemech, upon sufficient confession of faith and life, were received as members of our Reformed Low Dutch Church:

Thomas Decker and his wife Jenneke van Nimwegen, Jacobus Rosenkranz, Antje Quick, Beeeltje Quick, Maria Koddebeck.

As also upon representation of a satisfactory certificate to the respected Consistory is received Pieter Lammertse Brinck.

1747—April 16. These in presence of Jacob Westfael and Dirk Westbroeck, elders of Machackemech and Menissinck, upon satisfactory confession of faith and life, to our Reformed Church were received:

Johannes Westbroeck, jun., and his wife Lena Westbroeck, Jacobus Swartwout, Pieter Gemar, Mattheus Brinck.

Sept. 10. These in presence of David Cole, elder of Machackemech, as members of our Low Dutch Reformed Church, upon satisfactory confession of faith and conversation, were received the following:

Johannes Decker and his wife, Lisabeth de Witt, Tjaetje de Witt, Femmetje Decker, Salomon Kuykendal.

1748—April 7. These in presence of the respected elders of Menissinck as members of our Low Dutch Reformed Church upon satisfactory confession of faith and life, were received:

Andries Decker, Jacobina Bernhardin.

October 16. These in presence of the respected elders of Machackemech upon satisfactory confession of faith and life, as members of our Low Dutch Reformed Church were received:

Gerardus van Nimwegen and his wife Jannetje de Witt, Antje Westbroeck wife of Jacobus Swartwood, Jesyntje Swartwood wife of Jan van Vliet.

As also in presence of the same elders upon certificate were received, October 19:

Jan Alderse Rosa and his wife Catharina van Etten.

1749—Sept. 21. In the presence of the reverend elders of Machackemech upon satisfactory confession of faith and conversation as a member of our, according to God's word, Reformed Church, was received Willem Cole.

1750—April 12. These in presence of the reverend elders of Machackemech, upon satisfactory confession of life and doctrine, as members of our Low Dutch Reformed Church, were received: Rachel van Etten wife of Dirk Kittel, Catharina Kittel.

October 11. These in presence of the reverend elders of Machackemech, upon satisfactory confession of faith and life, as members of our Low Dutch Reformed Church, were received: Benjamin Depuy and his wife Lisabeth Swartwout, Philip Swartwout and his wife Antje Wynkoop, Lisabeth Gemaer wife of Samuel Swartwout, Lisabeth Westfael, wife of Cornelis Westfael, Annatje Decker wife of Antonie van Etten, Johanna Westfael.

1751—April 4. Upon satisfactory confession of faith and conversation, in the presence of Jacob van Etten, reverend elder of Menissinck, as a member of our, according to God's word, Reformed Church, was received Daniel Cole.

November 16. These upon satisfactory confession of faith and life, in the presence of Jacob Westfael, elder of Machackemech, were received as members of our Church: Jacobus Middagh and his wife Sara Decker, Debora Schoonhoven wife of Joris Davis.

1752—March 26. In the presence of Jacob van Etten, elder, on satisfactory confession of faith, as a member of our Church was received Alidagh Middagh.

October 20. These in the presence of Johannes Westbroeck, elder of Machackemech, upon satisfactory confession of faith and life, as members of our Reformed Church were received: Josias Cole and his wife Marya Kimmel, Lea Decker widow of Salomon Davis, Jaetje Cole.

1753—August 30. These in presence of Thomas Decker, elder of Machackemech, upon satisfactory confession of faith and conversation, as members of our Reformed Church were received: Arriaentje Oosterhout wife of Herman Rosenkranz, Sara Cole wife of Salomon Kuyckendal.

1754—April 11. In the presence of the reverend elders of Menis: upon confession was received Sara van Etten.

1755—March 27. These in presence of Thomas Decker and Johannes Westfael, respective elders of Machackemech and Menissink, as members of our Low Dutch Reformed Church, received in confession:
Arie Vredenburg and his wife Sara Rosenkranz, Symon Westfael and his wife Jannetje Westbroeck, Daniel Gonsales and his wife Lisabeth van Vliet, Jacobus Gonsales and his wife Sara Westbrock, Joseph Westbroeck and his wife Lisabeth Kuykendal, Abram van Aken, Pieter Kuykendal, Joris Davis, Jacobus Westbroeck.

March 29. Also upon confession in presence of Thomas Decker respected elder of Machhackemech, is received Hester Swartwout wife of Abram Kodebek.

[This closes the record of members in Mr. Fryenmuth's handwriting.]

These by me (T. ROMIEN) are received as members:

1762—April 9. In presence of William Ennes, elder of the Church of Jesus Christ, were received on confession:

Hendrick Williamse Cortregt, Derick Romien, Susanna Romien, born van Campen, wife of Do. Romien.

Sept. 26. These in presence of Arie Vredenburgh and Philip Swartwout, elders, by confession were received:

Abram Cornelis van Aken, Hermanus van Nimwegen and Margrieta his wife, Catrina widow of Martinus Kuikendal.

1764—April 18. These by satisfactory confession to the Church of Namanach, were received in presence of Johannis Westvael, elder:

Gysbert Van Gorden and his wife Maria van Gorden, Debora Westbroek wife of Joseph Westbroek.

August 15. These in presence of Arie Vredenburg and Syman Westvaal, elders of Machagkemech, as members of the Low Reformed Dutch Church, were received on confession:

Maragrites van Vliet wife of Benjamin van Vliet, Catrina van Aaken widow of Dirk Roosekrans, Lea van Aaken wife of Daniel van Aaken.

Also upon presentation of satisfactory certificates as members of the Low Dutch Reformed Church, were received:

Jacob Rutscher Dewit, Annetje Westbroek widow of Major Jacobus Swartwout.

By satisfactory confession of faith these are received in presence of Jacob Westvaal and Hermanus van Nimwegen, elders of Machagemek, January 17, 1767:

Ephraim Middag, Helmus Cool, Lea Cool wife of Helmus Cool.

Record of the members received by me in the year 1767:

1767—September. These upon satisfactory confession of —— the godly truth, in presence of William Ennes and Hendrick Cortregt, respective elders of Naamnach, were received:

Maragrita Westvaal wife of Johannis Westvaal, Josias W. Cortregt and Susanna W. Cortregt son and daughter of William Cortregt, Jurian Westvaal son of Johannis Westvaal, Maria Westvaal wife of Daniel Westvaal.

[This closes Mr. Romien's record.]

[Continued from original record.]

1785—Dec. 10. James D. Westbrook and wife Maria Brinck, Samuel Westbrook and wife Catrina Vredenburg, Salomon Lane, Marareitee Berkelo wife of Johannes Van Etten, Maria Berthron wife of Benjamin Fisher.

1786—Feb. 11. Abraham Dutcher, Elizabeth Cole wife of William Beemer.

May 6. John Van Etten, Benjamin Fisher, Amy Rimer wife of John Steermand, Lena Westbrook wife of Solomon Lane.

May 6. Gilbert Sutfin and wife Geertie Sutfin, Johannis I. Westbrook and wife Hester Chimer, Lena Van Etten wife of Jacob Helm, William Crawford.

Sept. 27. Jeremiah Van Demark and wife Hester Cortrecht.

Dec. 31. Jonathan Clarck, Lewis Meed, Johannes Van Etten and wife Rachel Williams, Abraham Westfall and wife Antie Westbrook, John Steward, Ledia Westfall widow of Jacob Westbrook, Maria Decker wife of Cornelius Cole, Jannitee Van Etten wife of Jacobus Van Garden, Rushe Westfall wife of Samuel Kettle, Maria Westfal wife of Petrus Cortrecht, Mary McGee wife of Joannes Van Etten, Jr., Jerushe Bromesun wife of Abram Dutcher, Lidia Brinck wife of Cornelius Dewett, Lidia Vredenburg wife of Petrus Westbrook, deceased.

1787—May 19. Mattheus Brinck and wife Mary Adams, Seene Walker wife of Jurian Brinck.

July 11. Petrus Van Etten.

Aug. 18. Sarah Windfield wife of Hu Depuy, Grietie Van Etten wife of Joseph Ennes.

Sept. 28. Joseph Ennes, John Evens, Gideon Cole.

1788—June 20. Cornelius Cole, John Lounsberry, Maria Westbrook wife of Daniel Westfal, Ledy Drake wife of Matthew Williams, Esther Kidder widow of John Herris.

1789—May 8. Maria Van Etten wife of Gideen Cole.

July 8. Philip Jacson admitted to membership and baptized at Wyoming, was born 29 March, 1766.

1790—June 4. Jannatie Pouleson wife of Gysbert Sutfin.

1791—June 3. Derick Sutfin, Henry Openhuis and wife Annatie.

INDEX

A

Ackerman, Abraham, 280
Adam, Hans, 121
Adams, Mary, 285
Adkins, Sarah, 71
Aersen, Jan, 14
Aerson, John, 14
  Petrus, 14
Akle, Sarah, 70, 79
Aken, Sarah, 73
Allen, John M., xxix
  Lewis, 279
  William, xiv
Allvord, Sarah, 185
Allward, Sarah, 188, 198, 209
Amy, Mary, 62, 63; 70, 73, 90
Andriesse, Glaasje, 101
Anes, Elizabeth, 222
  Jacob, 222
  Moses, 222
  William, 222
Annes, Alexander, 225
  James Rosekrans, 225
  Lena, 226
  Sarah, 224, 226
Annis, Pheby, 225
Annest, Ruth, 236
Ansley, Anny, 278
Aptsepack, Jacob, 184
  John, 184
Aray, Adam, 187
  David, 187
  Elisabeth, 187
  Lydia, 187
  Isaac, 186, 187
  Jonathan, 187
  William, 186
Armstrong, James B., 229
  Julius Foster, 229
  Susan Eveline, 229
Arneld, Jacob, 276
Arnold, Delilah, 196
  Lois, 196
  Persela, 196
  Stephen, 196
Arnot, Martha, 188
Ase, Susannah, 90
Asherly, Rachel, 22
  William, 22
Atkins, Sarah, 66, 67, 77, 82
Atos, Ater, Jupe, 156
Aulin, Amy, 38
Avarts, Avants, Vernits, Maragriet, 157
  Hendrik, 157
Ayers, Samuel B., xxvii
  Samuel B., Rev., ix
Ayres, Elizabeth, 77, 84
Ayrs, Anna, 176

B

Baaty, Nancy, 36
Bacor, Joseph, 269
Bacorn, Jeremias, 269
Baen, Catharina, 13
  Geertje, 13
Baker, Abraham, 33
  Daniel, 46
  Helena, 46
  Henry, 35, 39
  Jane, 46
  John, 36
  Jonathan, 33, 35, 36
  Nancy, 39
  Sarah, 191, 193
Barker, Polly, 276
Barnet, William, 276
Barraber, Lisabeth, 169
Barren, Mary, 266
Barret or Bayert, Hendrik, 156
  Neeltje, 156
Barten, Benjamin, 44
Barthran, Maria, 188
Barthron, Blandina, 203, 208, 210
  David, 213
  Hyltie, 213
  James, 208
  Jenneke, 214
  Maria, 214
  Sarah, 41
Bartran, Mary, 177
Bartron, Daniel, 33, 65
  Elizabeth, 65, 67, 68, 84
  James, 24, 33, 68
  Lidia, 24, 42
  Maria, 196, 202, 216
  Mary, 180
  Richard, 65, 68, 84
  Sarah, 275
  Sarah Depuy, 67
Barttron, Elizabeth, 42
  Daniel, 42
Baseter, Charles, 146
  Elizabeth, 146
Basetis (Baxter), Charles, 149
  Maria, 149
Bash, Johannes, 94
Beagal, Mary, 277
Beakar, Sarah, 36
Beaker, Anny, 41
  Hannah, 42
  Henry, 37
  Jonathan, 37, 39
  Mary, 39
  Rachel, 37
  Sarah, 37
Beale, Joseph R., xxix
Beamer, Ann, 166
Bearch, Eliza Jane, 62
  Mary, 62
  William, 62
Becker, Anna, 49
  Joh. Dan., 12
  Maria Christina, 12
Bedel, Deborah, 229
Bedell, Jane, 89
  John, 79, 89
Beegle, S. D., Rev., xix
Beemer, Adam, 144
  Ann Elisabeth, 146
  Catrina, 146
  Elisabeth, 146, 149, 152
  Hendrick, 149
  Henry, 146, 156
  Johannis, 146, 149, 153
  John, 146
  Lena, 278
  Peter, 146, 157
  Petience, 156
  Petrus, 152
  Rebekka, 157
  Sarah, 149
  Thomas, 146
  William, 153, 284
Beemis, Mary, 22
Beer, Peter, 155
  William, 155
Begel, Esther, 214
Begly, Susannah, 200
Behm, Maria Barbara, 14
Behmin, Barbara, 112
Bel, Abigail, 98, 100, 102, 106, 114-116
  Ebbegken, 103
Belcher, Gov., 94
  Jonathan, 271
Bell, Abigail, 107, 109, 119, 120, 125, 128, 132, 136, 179

Bemer, Peter, 149
 William, 274
Bemis, Mary, 25
Bennet, ——, 277
 Abraham, xviii
 Blandina, 243
 Cobus, 148
 Cornelia, 172
 Hendrick, 172
 Henery, 172
 Henry, 148, 236
 Jacobus, 239, 277
 James, xviii, 198, 239, 243, 257
 Joseph, 252, 257
 Lydia, 252
 Maria, 172, 181
 Petrus, 236
 Sarah, 236, 279
 Susanna, 172
 William, 252
 Zephine, 239
Bennett, Abraham, xix
 Burnett, 261
 Henery, 172
 Joseph, 261, 264
 Mary, 172, 261, 264
 Peter, 264
 Sally, 258
 Sarah Van Etten, 172
Benschooten, Antony, 21
 Cornelius, 17
 Elisabeth, 21
Benschoten, Antje, 100
 Anthonie, 100
 Antonie, 105
 Elisabeth, 150, 155
 Gerretje, 100, 102
 Jenneke, 105
Bensley, Adam, 68, 71
 Anna, 68
 Catharine, 71
 Caty, 68
 Israel, 68, 71
 Jacob, 68
Berck, Catharine, 55
 Diterich, 55
Berg, David, 60
 Hontetrick, 60
 Marjory, 60
Bergstracer, John, xxiii
Berk, Cornelia Van Etten, 82
 Cyrus, 77
 Elemanda, 83
 Honteter, 73
 Hontiter, 84
 Margaret, 74, 77, 83, 89
 Mary Magdalen, 82
 Peter, 82
 William, 77, 83
 William Smith, 84
Berkelo, Marareitee, 284

Berklow, Margaret, 183
Bernhard, Catharina, 14
Bernhardin, Catharina, 9, 112
 Christina Elisabetha, 5, 14
 Christina Elizabeth, 102
 Christina Lis., 11
 Christina Lisabetha, 4, 10
 Jacobina, 14, 282
 Johanna M a r g r e t a Elisabetha, 111
 Margareta, 9
Berns, Meerte, 266
Bertbr——, Elisabeth, 33
Bertholf, J. H., Rev., xxii
Berthron, Blandina, 204
 Daniel, 46
 David, 46
 Ledy, 45, 47
 Maria, 284
 Sarah, 46
Betran, Blandina, 217
 Daniel, 45
 David, 45
Bertrand, Sarah, 48
Bertron, Blandina, 220
 Sarah, 44
Besetis, Charles, 156
 John, 156
Best, Margareth, 104
 Nicolas, 104
Bevans, Bethey, 209
 Evan, 71, 209, 213
 Even, 74, 277
 Jacob, 71
 James C., xxi
 James Carmer, 213
 John, 74
 Sally, 86
 Sarah, 90, 91
 Sydney, 74
Beven, Even, 42, 43, 212
 John, 43
 Moses, 42
 Nicholas, 212
Bevier, Annatie, 4
 Annatje, 3
 Hester, 117, 120, 124, 127-130, 132
 Jesse, 124
 Johannes, 271
 Marytje, 124
 Rebecca, 235
Bicker, Cattrena, 35
Bight, John, 122
Bill, John, 151
Binckner, Mary, 51
Birk, Elizabeth, 70
 Peter, 70
Birney, Ann, 174
Bishoff, Maria, 122

Blair, Elizabeth, 45
Blake, Margaret, 87
 Susannah, 68
 Thomas, 68
Blenkenberg, Lena, 149
Blizard, Rachel, 170
Blizzard, Elizabeth, 74
Bloomer, Mary, 256
Blysard, Rachel, 174
Bodine, Abraham Van Campen, 71
 John, 68, 71
 Lena, 51
 Lenah, 63
 William, 68
Bodle, Jemima, 243
 John, 243
Bodly, John, 151
Boel, xxiv
Boen, Marytje, 12
Bogaert, Antje, 97
 Benjamin, 125
 Hannatje, 109
 Hannes, 109
 Jacob, 108, 112, 113, 118, 125
 Johannes, 265
 Lizabeth, 108
 Sara, 113
Bogard, Antje, 101, 102
 Ezechiel, 99
 Gysbert, 99
 Jacob, 101
 Jesintje, 101
Bogardes, Jenneke, 4
Bogardus, Jenneke, 125
 Evert, 10
Bogart, Jacob, 104
 Sara, 104
Bogert, N. I. M., xxx
Bolett, Cattrina, 189
 James, 189
Bolton, Peggy, 49
Boman, Eva, 188
 George, 188
 John, 112
Bomen, Jan, 103
 Margarit, 103
Bons, Johanna, 30
Bonschote, Gerretje, 136
Bookstaver, Jacob, xxviii
Boom, Elisabeth, 146
Boorten, Tabitha, 189
Borck, John, 106
 Julick, 106
Borgh, Julick, 106
Bortrah, Dirck, 31
 James, 31
Bortron, James, 29
Bos, Antje, 17
 Cobus, 20
 Dina, 13
 Hendrick, 13

Bos, Jacobus, 17
  Marytje, 13
  Rachel, 20
  Sara Elisabeth, 13
Bosch, Cathrina, 15
  Dina, 7
  Johannes, 15
  Maria, 101
Bosenkranz, Lena, 269
Bosh, Angonietje, 6
  Dina, 12
  Hendrick, 6
  Lena, 10
  Marytje, 6
Botrun, Blandina, 223
Bouman, Hanna, 106
  John, 106
Bovie, Rebecka, 243
Bowman, Maria, 106
Boyd, Benne, 211
  John, Rev., xiv
  Samuel, 211
Bragan, Charity, 234
Brandt, ix
Bras, Peter, 216
  Sarah, 216
Brass, Hendric, 176
  Hendrick, 179
  Henericus, 179
  Maria, 176
  Moses, 252
  Stephen, 252
  William, 252
Breffert, Edtward, 168
  Mary, 168
Breffoert, Edtwort, 166
  Rebecca, 166
Brenck, Cornelis, 170
  Jen, 168
  Mateues, 140
  Lideia, 169
  Yuerrean, 140
Brencke, Russe, 170
Brenk, Lendert, 169
  Cathrynte, 169
Breslar, John, 134
Brinck, Andrew Dingeman, 211
  Areantie, 216
  Art, 187
  Benjamin, 12, 28, 52,216
  Boudewyn, 199
  Catharine, 246
  Cathrena, 207
  Cathrina, 12
  Caty, 187, 211, 277
  Cornelia, 12, 25, 94
  Cornelis, 5, 103, 109, 113, 114
  Cornelis, Jr., 126, 133
  Cornelius, 133, 185
  David, 27

Brinck, Dennis, 210
  Derick, 47
  Elesabet, 27
  Elisabeth, 133
  Elizabeth, 44, 123, 189 205, 214
  Emanuel, 207
  Ester, 200
  Esther, 222
  Fanny, 188
  Garret, 4
  Geertie, 186, 189, 199
  Geertje, 8, 120
  George, 216, 226
  Gerret, 5, 6
  Gertie, 32, 46
  Greitee, 209
  Hannah, 197
  Har., 211
  Harmanus, 205
  Henry, J., 278
  Hermanus, 103, 114
  Hester, 4, 128
  Isaac, 1
  Jacobus, 41, 107, 115, 190, 204, 209
  James, 188, 197, 200,211, 216
  Jan, 103, 114
  Jane, 46, 51, 228
  Janitie, 204
  Jannitie, 28
  Jenneca, 189
  Jenneke, 5
  Johanna, 1, 3, 6, 8, 12, 100, 113
  John, 12, 52, 209
  John McCaby, 214
  Joseph, 189
  Jurian, 285
  Lambart, 104
  Lambert, 6
  Lammert, 104
  Ledia, 209
  Ledy, 226
  Lena, 5, 27, 32, 106, 205
  Lenart Cole, 109
  Lidia, 216, 285
  Lidya, 205
  Lisabet, 2, 3, 15,94, 116, 120, 123
  Lydia, 246
  Manuel, 52
  Maragriet, 37, 199
  Maregreta, 169
  Margaret, 41, 44, 46,200, 205, 216
  Margret, 276
  Maria, 133, 284
  Marrigrit, 30
  Mary, 125
  Matheus, 116

Brinck, Mattheus, 103, 107, 107, 109, 114, 115, 119, 120, 123, 125, 128, 129, 190, 282, 285
  Matthew, 47
  Moses, 189, 275
  Niclaes, 11, 12, 27
  Peter, 52, 167, 203, 205, 214
  Peter, Jr., 210
  Peter V., 209, 216
  Peter W., 205
  Petrus, 116, 133, 185, 267
  Phebe Jane, 226
  Pieter Lammertse, 282
  Polly, 203
  Rachel, 2, 200
  Roelof, 1
  Rusha, 212
  Salmon, 167
  Samuel, 109, 197, 199
  Sara, 3
  Sarah, 38, 41, 52
  Stephanus, 1
  Susannah, 197, 209
  Thomas, 2, 3, 5, 8, 12, 41, 44, 46
  William, 41
Brink, Abbe, 238
  Abigail, 179
  Aert, 137
  Ann, 56
  Anna, 21
  Antje, 17, 20
  Arie, 103
  Beniaman, 30
  Benjamin, 64, 173
  Benjn., 31
  Cate, 235
  Catharine, 48, 56
  Catherine, 47, 60
  Cathrena, 29
  Cathrina, 179
  Caty Jane, 277
  Charity, 179
  Clara, 215
  Corneleja, 16
  Cornelia, 16, 18, 24
  Cornelis, 99, 100, 131, 167, 270
  Cornelis, Jr., 134
  Cornelius, 139, 160, 164, 173, 183
  Cornelius, Jr., 164
  Daniel, 52, 58, 65, 68
  Dereck, 166
  Derick, 56
  Dina, 102
  Elanah, 31
  Elibeth, 28
  Elinar, 30
  Elisabeth, 18, 19, 20, 58, 136, 177

Brink, Eliza, 238
  Elizabeth, 55, 68, 136, 162, 201, 220, 235, 278
  Ephraim, 180
  Eva, 13, 17, 20
  Femetje, 152
  Garret, 174
  Geertie, 15, 275
  Geertje, 17, 18, 48, 98, 162
  Geertye, 27
  George, 215, 238
  Geretie, 177
  Gerit, 176
  Gerret, 98, 101, 105, 132, 275
  Gerrit, 1
  Gerty, 158
  Grietje, 274
  Harmanus, 141, 150
  Helena, 5
  Hendrickje, 20
  Hendricus, 179
  Hendrik, 144
  Hendrikje, 22
  Henry, 52, 58, 202, 241
  Hester, 226
  Ionathan, 31
  Jacob, 179
  Jacob Kuikendal, 158
  Jacobes, 166
  Jacobus, 13, 19, 141, 161, 179
  James, 56, 60
  Jams, 38
  Jane, 50, 53, 65, 68, 227
  Janekie, 180
  Jannatje, 171
  Jenneke, 99
  Jenny, 60
  Jini, 38
  Johannes, 5, 13, 20, 134
  Johannis, 17, 30, 171, 180
  John, Jr., 198
  Jonas, 161
  Jose, 215
  Joshua, 64
  Jure, 167
  Lambertus, 99, 101, 103
  Lanah, 64
  Leendert, 152, 273
  Lena, 98, 141
  Lenah, 24
  Leonard, 161
  Levi, 47, 48, 56, 58
  Lidia, 161, 162, 202
  Lisabet, 19, 131
  Lovisa, 65
  Lydia, 105, 220, 227
  Manuel, 31, 64
  Maragrita, 139
  Maregrietje, 179
  Margareth, 50, 60, 183

Brink, Margreta, 33
  Margriet, 35
  Margrietje, 134
  Margrita, 16
  Maria, 16, 94, 100, 101, 143, 148, 161, 166
  Mary, 56, 179
  Marya, 137, 180
  Mateus, 136
  Matheus, 100, 102, 132, 164, 270
  Mattheus, Jr., 134
  Moses, 179
  Mosis, 147
  Necholas, 24
  Niclaes, 13, 93
  Nicolaes, 136
  Nicolas, 29
  Nicolaus, 16
  Nelly, 202
  Peggy, 220
  Peter, 141, 179, 202, 220
  Peter, Jr., 183
  Petrus, 100, 131, 134, 137, 140, 144, 147, 150, 183
  Petrus, Jr., 137
  Petrus Van Garden, 150
  Rachel, 18, 20-22, 150, 183
  Ruben Westfael, 180
  Russia, 224
  Samuel, 31, 55, 160, 164, 167, 174
  Samuel C., 278
  Sara, 15
  Sarah, 18-21, 30, 47, 56, 60, 215
  Sherlott, 238
  Simon, 241
  Solomon, 176, 235
  Stephanus, 17
  Thomas, xi, 29, 31, 47, 48, 52, 56, 60, 275
  Thomis, 38
  William, 29, 35, 38, 198, 227
  Yannetye, 235
Brison, Sary, 217
Bristol, John Decker, 79
  Leavitt B., 79, 83
  Mariah, 83
Britin, Betcy, 45
Broadhead, Abraham Coolbaugh, 85
  Cornelia, 36, 64, 66, 68, 69, 75, 77, 82, 86, 90
  Effe, 77
  Effy, 79
  Garret, 36, 50
  Garret, Jr., 85
  Gerret, 34, 37
  Hannah, 63, 66, 70, 74, 80

Broadhead, Joannah, 79
  Johanna, 34
  John, 13
  John H., 280
  Nicholas, 37, 77, 79
  Rachel, 83, 276
  Sarah, 66, 70, 72, 77, 84
Broca, Abraham, 33
  Judica, 33
Brocau, Jane, 56
Brodhead, C. W., xviii
  W. F., xxi
Brokaw, Abraham, 37, 38, 43
  Jane, 48, 51, 61, 76, 79, 85, 86
  Judith, 58, 65
  Margery, 38
  Maria, 37
  Mary, 53, 77, 81
  Sally, 43
Bromesun, Jerushe, 285
Brooks, Betsey, 71
  Elizabeth, 54, 65, 74, 80
  Elizabeth (Betsie), 58
  Gorge, 170
  Hannah, 79, 84
  John, 170, 174, 276
  Sarah, 174
Bross, Abram, 155
  Hendrick, 273
  Henry, 155
Brown, Benoni, 14
  Cornelia, 58
  Daniel, 36
  David Decker, 74
  Ebenezer, 14
  Elias, 66
  Henry, 153
  Henry Marvin, 80
  Jacob Hufty, 63
  Johanna, 35
  John, 58, 63, 66, 70, 74, 80
  Joseph, 38
  Martha, 171, 173
  Natan, 35
  Nicholas Broadhead, 70
  Rachel, 38
  Reuben, 35
  Walter, 35, 36
Bruyn, Johannes, 267
Brynck, Gertje, 168
  Lambart, xiii
Brynoek, Greetje, 172
Buchanan, Arthur, 227
  Ollive, 227
  Polly, 227
Buckbee, John, 278
Buckley, Ann, 213
  Anne, 219
  Betsey, 253, 254
Buckly, Anna, 216
Bugsbee, Sarah, 279

Buk (Cuk), Mary, 144
Bulbungh, Dereck, 166
Bull, Chrisse, 76
  Elizabeth, Maria, 76
  Hannah Rogers, 76
  Rosenkrans Chrisse, 76
Bunel, Jacob, 214
  James, 214
Bunnel, James, 184, 208
  Lena, 184
  Matth., 34
  Pheby, 208
Buncehoten, Jacob, 27
  Jacobus, 27
Bunschooten, Rev. Mr., xvii
  Antje, 17
Bunschoten, Abraham, 25
  Agnietje, 32
  Anthony, 176, 181
  Antje, 158
  Antoni, 13
  Antony, 6, 109
  Cobus, 141
  Cornelia, 11, 13
  Cornelius, 181
  Elisabeth, 141, 180, 269
  Elizabeth, 182
  Gerretje, 129
  Gerritje, 130
  Isaak, 25
  Jakobus, 25
  Jenneke, 176
  Jesyntje, 109
  Lena, 176
  Maria, 167, 274
  Lisabeth, 129, 137
Buntschote, Elizabeth,135
Bunscoten, Elisabet, 272
Buril, Mary, 202
Burrell, Mary, 277
Burtron, Sarah, 52
Bush, Anny, 206
  Benjamin, 204, 206
  George, 275
  Henrik, 15
  Johannes, 15
  Lena, 15
  Mary, 204
  Rebekka, 15
Buss, George, 69
  Jacob, 66, 69, 74
  John, 74
  Polly, 66
Buth, John, 59
  Mary Littesua, 59
Butter (Butler), Nancy, 280
Buttler, Sara, 2
Butts, Fanny, 60
  Jacob, 59
  Jane, 59, 60
  John, 59, 60

Buzzard, Elizabeth, 70

C

Caanan, Sarah, 34
Cainlen, Marey, 275
Caler, Magdalena, 52
Camfield, David, 238
  Jacob, 238
Cammers, Christina, 28
  Susana, 28
  Welhelmis, 28
Campbel, James, 277
Campbell, William, 279
Campfield, David, 246
  Henry Titus, 246
Cancalis, Jannitie, 28
  Manuel, 28
Caneda, Cattrina, 200
Canfield, Abraham Van Inwegen, 256
  David, 240, 244, 247,251, 253, 256
  Elizabeth, 244
  Jesse, 247
  John, 240
  Sally, 251
  William Baldwin, 253
Cannady, Cattrina, 37
  (Kennedy), Caty, 196
Cansalis, Sara, 28
Cape, Elizabeth, 62, 72
  Sarah, 39, 43, 72
Caperon, Thaddeus, 278
Caress, Elizabeth, 58
  Leonard, 59
  Susannah, 59
Carman, Charlothy, 190
  Deborah, 189
  John White, 199
  Joseph, 189
  Patty, 190
  Roberd, 189
  Robert, 189, 190, 199
  Sarah, 190
  Susannah, 190
Carmen, Abraham, 198
  Daniel, 198
Carmer, Abraham, 185, 188, 204, 209, 212, 277
  Asa Baldwin, 49
  Catharina, 24
  Catharine, 71, 74, 209, 213
  Cattrina, 43
  Caty, 212, 277
  Daniel, 209
  Elijah, 212
  Elizabeth, 38
  Gilbert, 39, 49
  Gysbert, 276
  Isaac, 72, 73
  Isaac, Jr., 62

Carmer, Jacobus, 24, 185
  Jemime, 188
  Johanna, 34
  John, 39
  Lena, 44
  Luther, 72
  Nichols, 209
  Peter, 204
  Sarah, 62, 276
  Susannah, 73
Carpenter, Benjamin, 238, 245, 249, 276
  Catherine, 255, 258, 261
  Eleanor, 256, 261
  Elenor, 248, 250
  Hannah, 249, 280
  Isaac, 247
  James, 258
  John D., 255, 257, 258, 261
  Margaret, 245
  Martin, 247, 251
  Powel, 278
  Sally, 253
  Sarah, 88, 255, 257
  Senia, 257
Carr, Mary, 189
Carson, Rachel, 39
Carter, Sarah, 204, 209, 212, 277
Cartright, Altie, 226
Case, Anne, 256
Caty, 256
  George, 239
  Gloriannah, 239
  Henry, 232, 239, 241,256
  Jacob, 241
  Jane, 213
  Jenny, 239
  Marjery, 280
  Mary, 212, 239, 249, 278
  William Neerpass, 232
Cashey, Mary, 279
Caskey, Hilah, 280
  Thomas, 277
Caski, Martin, 181
  Samuel, 181
Cass, George, 58
  Jacob, 58
Caster, William, 29
Castnor, Maria, 27
Catee, Lea, 209
Cator, Susannah, 184
Cattington, Christophel, 143
  Joseph, 143
Cebler, Catharine, 228
  Catherine, 219
Cermer, Abram, 16
  Christina, 16
  Grietie, 16
  Jacobus, xii
  Lena, 28

Cermer, Ludija, 16
  Lydia, 141
  Sara, 16
Cettel, Chelly, 188
  Cornelius, 188
Chaimber, Cloudean, 29
  Sarah, 29
  Wm. Helmis, 29
Chaimbers, Mary, 30
Chamber, Peter, 195
  Moses, 195
Chambers, Abraham, 163
  Abram, 117, 443, 267
  Benjamin, 25
  Catrien, 28
  Caty, 47
  Christoffel, 21
  Christina, 24, 274
  Elizabeth, 275
  Ester, 278
  Helmes, 21
  Hester, 239
  Jacob, 164
  Johannis, 274
  John, 23, 28, 47
  Lena, 143, 190
  Margaret, 79, 81, 87
  Maria, 23
  Marinus, 278
  Mary, 30, 190
  Moses, 47
  Myram, 239
  Neeltje, 164
  Polly, 47
  Susanna, 276
  Wilhelmus, 25, 190
Chaortrecht, Susanna, 165
Chandlar, Hester, 123
  John, 123, 130
  Samuel, 130
Chandler, Antje, 126
  John, 126
Chasnor, Margaret, 43
Cheat, Adam, 136
Cheiners, Hester, 166
  Jacob, 166
Chesly, Jenny, 162
Chesner, Ann, 53
Chesney, Margriet, 34
Chesnon, Margaret, 36, 39
  Mary, 30
Chesnor, Margaret, 46, 49
  Margariet, 41
  Mary, 29, 195
Chestnor, Anna, 57
  Anne, 31
  James, 31
Chettel, Johaenna, 166
Chidister, Massa, 83
Chimer, Elizabeth, 189
  Hester, 285
  Jacob, 214
  Margaret, 214

Chimer, Neeltie, 203
Chimers, Ester, 238
  Jacob, 167
  Lena, 167
  Polly, 238
Chitister, Merey, 80
Choertrecht, Gerte, 165
  Jantet, 165
Choertrect, Hendrick W., 165
Chollins, Barbary, 41
  Thomas, 41
Chram, Johannes, 25
  Necholas, 25
Chress, Christian, 140
  John, 140
Christopher, Nicholas, 175
Chymer, Elizabeth, 226
Cimber, Maritje, 154
  Maryte, 272
Cimmer, Joris, 142
  Sarah, 142
Cinney, Rachel, 28
Citel, Elizabeth, 136
  Jan, 136
Cittel, Cornelius, 136
  Jeremia, 136
Cittle, Elizabeth, 136
Clarck, Jonathan, 285
  Matthew, 275
Clark, xviii
  Abraham, 172
  Calvin, 276
  Catharina, 101
  Catrina, 151
  Daved, 166
  David, 237, 278
  Elisabeth, 140
  Elisah, 186
  Elizabeth, 66
  Elizabeth, Smith, 73
  Isaac, 172
  Jacob, 237
  Jacobus, 153
  James, 140, 151, 153
  Janetie, 181
  John, 39
  Jonathan, 172, 173, 186, 197
  Jonnethan, 166
  Luther, 277
  Marcy, 237
  Mardochia, 101
  Matthew, 223
  Matthias, 277
  Roger, 183
  Samuel, xviii, 28
  Thomas, 28
  William, xx, 39, 73
Clarke, John, 276
  Mary, 220
Clavonsher, Sara, 112

Cleck, Jacob, 173
  Jarnton, 173
Clevensher, Sara, 2
Clevins, Sara, 130
Clifford, Henry W., 85
  Mary Green, 85
Cline, Elizbeth, 59
Clinton, Gen., ii
  Gov., 267
  De Witt, ii
  James, Gen., ii
  William, 133
Clover, Hanna, 274
Cock, Anna, 113
Cockrum, Susanah, 31
Cocks, Cathrina, 39
  Joseph, 39
Coddebak, Abram, 139
  Abram, Jr., 139
Codebek, Abram, 123, 124, 128, 268
  Jacobus, 124
  Petrus, 128
  Sara, 269
Coel, Harmans, 26
  Marrigrit, 26
  Rachel, 26
Col, Leendert, 168
  Marey, 168
Cole, Abraham, 113
  Abram, 51, 155
  Andries, 6-8, 12, 14, 94, 114, 122
  Andris, 189
  Anna, 22
  Antie, 276
  Benjamin, 118, 181
  Catharina, 106-108, 113, 124, 127, 266
  Catrena, 167
  Catrina, 169
  Catrine, 275
  Cattrina, 198
  Caty Van Aucan, 228
  Charity, 246
  Cornelia, 7, 180
  Cornelis, 116, 119, 129
  Cornelis Westbroeck, 119
  Cornelius, viii, 172, 485
  Cornelius West., 276
  Daniel, 283
  David, 109, 111, 113, 116, 118, 120, 124, 125, 282
  David Finch, 227
  Dina, 7
  Dorethy, 217
  Elener, 209
  Elenor, 251
  Elisabeth, 8, 107, 113, 123

Cole, Elizabeth, 247, 284
Famatie, 178
Femmetje, 108
(Foly), Femmetje, 144
Gedeon, vii, 276
Gideon, 197, 198, 208, 217, 219, 285
Hanna, 10, 12, 93
Hannah, 251, 256
Helena, 3
Hermannes, 7
Hermanus, 3, 10
Heyltje, 129
Jacob, 12, 50, 51, 111, 116, 178
Jacobus, 7, 10, 13
Jacobus Van Auken,221
Jaetje, 283
James, 241
James R., 248, 251, 253
Jane, 65, 67
Jannitie, 197, 198
Jesse, 179
Joannes Van Etten, 208
Johanna, 6
Johannes, 111, 113, 118, 125, 128, 132
John, 219
Joseph, 189, 278
Josephas, 178
Joshua, 240, 247, 260
Joshuah, 243
Josias, 107, 108, 113,116, 124, 130, 137, 178, 243, 260, 283
Knelia, 184, 198
Lea, 243
Leah, 240, 247, 260
Leendert, 7, 13, 266
Lena, 3, 5, 6, 8, 12, 13, 198
Leonard, 3, 180, 189
Lidia, 260
Lisabeth, 4, 6, 7, 10, 12, 13, 108, 109, 111, 112, 114, 115, 117, 118, 126, 131, 137
Margaret, 181
Margret, 180
Margrietje, 113, 131
Maria, 5, 22, 109, 111, 113, 125, 128, 129, 137, 248, 268, 277
Marjery, 279
Martin, 253
Mary, 155, 256
Marya, 6, 7, 112, 114, 117, 266, 271
Martynus, 277
Nelly, 205
Nenzi, 6
Peter, 211
Petrus, 116, 178

Cole, Rachel, 22, 78, 87, 208
Rebecca, 188, 229, 230, 243
Rebecka, 228
Rebeka, 222
Rosanna, 260
Samuel, 124, 181
Sara, 14, 109, 111, 118, 127, 137, 243, 249, 268, 283
Sarah, 13, 50, 174, 179, 181, 240, 247, 257, 279
Sary, 29
Sarte, 167
Simeon, 211, 221, 227, 278
Simion, 228
Tjaetje, 125, 269
Tjatje, 127
Thomas, 199
Wilhelmus, x, 107, 113
Willem, 108, 118, 124, 125, 132, 283
Willem, Jr., 109
William, 107, 110, 113, 188, 189, 199, 205, 221, 241, 278, 282
Wm., 179
Coles, Phebe, 76, 82
Coll, Maregreetje, 170
Compen, Elisabeth, 18
Cornelius, 18
Compton, William, 278
Comstac, Rody, 168
Comstack, Deborah, 183
Comstock, Debera, 164
Debora, 165, 169
Phebe, 149, 152
Roedy, 166
Comstok, Debora, 159
Phebe, 145
Conckel, Christina, 34
Concklin, Hannah, 233
Conger, Willard, xxix
Conklin, Elias, 175, 183
Ellsabeth, 183
Esther, 177
Helena, 175
Jannetje, 177
John, 177
Nicholas, 175, 177
Mary, 177, 183, 241
Wm., 177
Conkling, Hannah, 184, 189, 199
Mary, 199
Conclin, Hannah, 175
Conley, Sara, 271
Consales, Elisabeth, 121
Daniel, 118, 121, 124,268
Johanna, 118, 123

Consales, Joseph, 100
Manuel, 12, 121, 124
Maria, 12, 118, 120, 121, 123
Sara, 100
Consalesduk, Lena, 2
Consalis, Manuel, 28
Consalus, Maria, 140
Mary, 43
Samuel, 43
Consolis, Lena, 34
Samuel, 44
Sarah, 44
Conterman, Anna Maria, 122
Pieter, 94
Contriene, Maria, 22
Contriman, Maria, 22
Contryman, Maria Elisabeth, 11
Cooke, Sylvester, Rev., xvii
Cool, Abram, 16, 140, 146, 156, 273
Andrew, 16
Andreas, 103
Andries, 3, 17, 19, 22, 100, 146
Catrina, 16, 140, 145-147, 152, 153, 273
Catryntje, 99
Charity, 250
Catharina, 100, 102, 165
Cobus, 273
Corneles, 140
Cornelia, 3, 19, 134, 144, 158, 273
Cornelis, 99, 102, 134,153
Cornelius, 136, 140, 144, 151, 154
Cornelius Westbroek, 151
Cueliya, 271
Daniel, 145, 151
David, 99, 102, 107
Elisabeth, 139, 146
Elizabeth, 274
Femitje, 154
Gideon Westbroeck,143
Grietje, 134, 153
Grietye, 168
Gritje, 140
Harmanus, 17, 18
Hejltje, 142
Helmus, 284
Hendrik, 18
Isaac, 19
Jacob, 22, 151
Jeseos (Jacob), 148
Johannes, 1, 102, 106
Johannis, 146, 272
Josephat, 106
Josephus, 145, 154

Cool, Joseyas, 272
Josias, 102, 142, 154
Lea, 284
Leendert, 18
Lena, 1, 100, 140
Lenert, Jr., 100
Leonard, 1
Lisabeth, 99, 103, 105
Maragriet, 142, 144
Margriet, 17
Margrietje, 107
Margrita, 182
Maria, 98-100, 103, 105, 134, 140, 144, 146, 151, 154
Martinus, 144
Mary, 273
Mosis, 17
Petrus, 102, 143, 150, 154, 156
Rachel, 19, 100
Sara, 102, 134
Sarah, 145, 147, 150, 171
Simion, 150
Wilhelmus, 148, 151
Willem, 100, 102
William, viii, 104, 145, 154
William, Jr., 108
Coolbaugh, Abraham, 84
Abm., 77
Andrew Jackson, 80
Hannah, 73, 78, 81, 86, 90
James, 83
John, 80, 276
John V., 84
Moses, 83
Moses W., 80
Sarah, 71, 80, 84, 88
Susannah, 77
William Findley, 80
Coole, Catrinty, 168
Catryntye, 168
Jacob, 168
Josias, 168
Samuel, 168
Sara, 168
Cooll, Josias, 275
Cooly, Mary, 185
Cooper, Daniel, 271
Isaac, 24
Coon (Boom), Elisabeth, 142
Cop, George, 280
Cornell, William, xxviii
Corthreght, Elizebeth, 35
Corthregt, Abraham, 28
Cornelia, 28
Corthright, Cornelius, 29
Elizebeth, 29
Henrey, 29
Stoffel, 29

Corthright, William, 29
Cortrecht, Aaron, 187
Abraham, 27
Abraham Decker, 27
Abraham P., 31
Annie, 27
Anny, 189, 275
Are, 166
Bill, 276
Catrina, 169
Cattrina, 37, 201
Caty, 200
Cornelius, 200
Cristefol, 27
Daniel, 208, 278
Debora, 199
Elesabet, 34
Elias, vii, 164
Elizabeth, 41, 45
Febe, 164
Hendrick, 27, 211
Hendrick Wm., vii
Hester, 189, 201, 285
Jacobus, 27, 187
Jannitie, 32
Jesias, vii
John, 166, 200
Joseph, 276
July, 208
Lena, 27
Levi, 277
Margaret, 277
Maria, 199, 277
Rachel, 38
Resyna, 31
Petrus, 285
Reuben, 199
Samuel, 199
Sara, 276
Sarah, 136, 201
Thomas, 27
William, 189, 201, 211
William, Jr., 201
Cortregh, Elizabeth, 223
Cortreght, ——, 176
Aaron, 184, 194
Andriss, 198
Ante, 176
Aron, 169
Blandina, 166
Cathrina, 172, 174
Cornelis, 106
Daniel, 106, 175, 181
Deborah, 180
Dorothy, 184
Elias, 169, 183
Elisabeth, 171, 175, 177
Elizabeth, 200, 216
Elsabth, 167
Esther, 184
Garetie, 180
Gedeon, 275
Gideon, 184

Cortreght, Hendrick W., 172, 180
Isias, 198
Jacob, 176
Janneke, 171, 175
Jannete, 169
Johannes, 169, 173
John, 177
John, Jr., 26
Jonas, 175
Jones, 167
Josias, 166, 184
Lea, 175
Ledea, 169
Lidea, 166
Lydia, 173
Maria, 178, 179
Maria Dor, 177
Mary, 177
Marya, 169
Marya Dewitt, 183
Moses, 171, 178
Nicholas, 177
Petres, 167
Petrus, 179, 194
Rachel, 26
Safferyn, 171
Samuel, 167, 173, 192, 194, 214
Sarah, 176
Simon, 179
Solomon, 176, 181
Susanna, 169
Sylvester, 171, 174, 180
Wilhelmus, 174
William, 183, 192, 194
Yennek, 166
Cortreck, Cattrina, 275
Janntie, 43
Cortregt, Abraham, 23
Abram, 17, 19, 23, 154
Abram P., 19
Anna, 20
Annatie, 17
Annatje, 158
Anne, 152
Anthony, 23
Arie, 138, 274
Benjamin, 17, 20, 22
Billinest, 16
Catharina, 162
Cathrine, 238
Catrina, 16, 17, 19, 141, 144, 148, 153, 157
Christina Elisabeth, 23
Christoffel, 23
Cobes, 23
Cornelia, 20, 21, 146, 147
Cornelus, 17
Daniel, 18, 141, 143, 146, 158, 164
Derik, 18
Elias, 140, 152, 159

Cortregt, Elisabeth, 23, 144, 148, 149, 151
Eliza, 21
Garretje, 273
Gedion, 158
Gerritje, 150
Gideon, 141
Gisbert, 144
Hendrick, 22, 94, 138, 146, 159, 284
Hendrick Jansen, 159
Hendrick Johnson, 140
Hendrick Williamse, 144, 284
Hendrik, 136, 140, 143, 144, 150
Janitje, 150
Janneke, 18, 143
Jannetje, 24, 143, 164
Jannitje, 150
Jenneke, 16, 274
Jesaias, 158
Johannes, 21, 136
Johannis, 144, 273
John, 18, 20, 136, 140, 141, 146, 150
John, Jr., 20
Joseph, 18
Josias, 150
Josias W., 273, 284
Lea, 146
Lydia, 21, 149, 158, 274
Maragriet, 144, 159
Margriet, 146
Maria, 140
Maria DeWit, 136
Mosis, 158
Petrus, 138, 147, 158, 164
Ploni, 272
Rachel, 18, 19, 152, 273
Rebecca, 19
Salomon, 138, 146
Samuel, 21
Sarah, 23, 149
Silvester, 151
Solomon, 147
Sophryn, 158
Susanna, 159
Susanna W., 284
Susannah, 223
Symon, 147
William, 94, 144, 273, 284
William Johnson, 158
Ysaac, 154
Cortright, Aaron, 192
Abraham, 25
Abraham P., 25
Abraham Peter, 72
Abram, 42
Alche, 228
Alty, 222
Antony, 42
Cortright, Benjamin, 25, 196
Blandina, 210
Caty, 63, 64
Cornelia, 25
Cornelius, 37, 70, 196
Daniel, 72, 206, 210, 214, 227
Deborah, 206
Elizabeth, 211, 219, 225, 278
Esther, 249
Hannah, 192, 194, 196, 225
Henry, 30, 219, 244
Isaac, 30, 72
Isaac Bedell, 229
Isaih, 230
Jacob Evrit, 219
Jane, 48, 51, 230
Jane Young, 228
Janntie, 210
Jenny, 45
Jentie Ennes, 25
Joannes, 206
John, 220
John Drake, 69
Lidia, 192, 194
Maria, 215
Mary, 37, 48, 52, 63, 67, 189, 206, 227, 228
Peter, 219, 225, 228, 229
Petrus, 192, 220
Phebe, 276
Pheby, 201, 229
Rachel, 276
Rosanna, 214
Ruben, 229
Sally, 69
Samuel, 214, 220, 225, 278
Sarah, 70, 208, 210, 214, 218, 220, 224, 276
Susannah, 51, 72, 216, 218, 219, 221, 226
Thomas, 72
William, 206, 227
William I., 69, 214, 221
William Johnson, 210
William Johnston, 215
Cortrigt, David, 257
William, 257
Corsa, Abram, 16
Banjamin, 30
Benyamin, 32
Easter, 253
Dennis, 16
Dinis, 30
Pecke, 32
Pieter, 32
Corsan, Hannah, 37
Rachel, 36, 37
Corso, Hannah, 35
Corso, Peter, 35
Corua (Corsen), Benjamin, 158
Petrus, 158
Coss, Catharine, 84
Daniel, 91
George, 64, 77, 84, 91
James Foree, 77
Maryanne, 73
Samuel, 64
Costerd, William, 20
Costor, Abraham, 19
William, 19
Cotregt, Gerritie, 141
Maragriet, 158
Cottenton, Christoffel, 148
John, 148
Cotton, Peggy, 52
Counterman, Peter, 12
Course, Benjamin, 168
Maria, 168
Courtright, Amanda, 83
Beniaman, 30
Catrina, 30
Cornelius, 76, 78, 83, 87
Daniel, 87
Eleyebeth, 29
Elisha, 31
Elizabeth, 251
Elizebeth, 31
Jane, 87
Mariah, 78
Mary, 225, 229
Nelly, 76
Susannah, 66
Counsoles, Mare, 164
Countryman, Hendrick, 7
Rachel, 7
Cova (Fero), Anna, 156
Coykendal, Salomon, 275
Salomon, Jr., 275
Craan, Johannes, 32
Crafford, Elizabeth, 188
Moses, 183
William, 183, 188
Craford, Hannah, 230
Moses, 230
Cral, John, 139
Samuel, 139
Cran, Elizabeth, 36
Joannes, 36
Crasman, Jacob, 214
Mary, 214
Crawford, Amy, 202
James, 222
John, 202
Moses, 222, 229
Susan Mariah, 229
William, 202, 285
Credmore, Abraham, xviii
Cregan, Peter, 38
Rachall, 38

Cressman, Daniel, 54
  George, 54, 59
  Ira, 59
  John, 54
  Sally, 59
  Sarah, 54
Crinkel, Christeenne, 28
Crisman, Elesabet, 34
  George, xxiii
  Johan, 34
Croeck, Geertruyd, 10
Croel, Antje, 143
  John, 143
  Lea, 143
Crofford, John, 228
  Mary, 185
  Moses, 228, 243
  Sarah Wells, 243
  William, 185, 198
Crom, Sarah, 151
  William, 151
Crook, John, Jr., xix
Crosman, Febe, 169
  Jacob, 165
  Samuel, 165, 169
Croswell, Esther, 52
Crouse, George, 86
  George Wintamute, 86
Crow, Cattrina, 277
Crub, Andries, 142
  Petrus, 142
Cuambers, Moses, 275
Cuck, Mary, 29
  Ruben, 29
Cuddeback, Abm., 182, 248
  Abraham, 181, 182, 197, 253
  Abram, 178
  Benj., 170
  Benjamin, xviii, 170, 230, 231, 251, 253, 257, 259, 263
  Benjamin, Jr., 248, 251, 256
  Blandina, 259
  Caty, 232, 251
  Charlotte, 280
  Cornelius, 197, 232, 238, 252
  Cornlius, 278
  Diana, 256
  Easter, 254
  Elias, 248
  Elizabeth, 258, 261, 263, 264
  Esther, 174, 178, 251
  Esyntje, 178
  George, 251
  Geradus Swartwoud, 175
  Hannah, 257
  Henry, 230, 231, 235, 251
  Hesther, 182

Cuddeback, Huldah, 255
  Jacamyntie, 276
  Jacob, iii, 230, 231, 248, 264
  Jacob, Jr., 256, 258, 261, 263
  Jacobus, 175
  James, 248, 280
  Jane, 248, 251, 253, 263
  Jemima, 256, 263, 280
  John, 260
  Joseph, 248
  Leah, 261
  Lewes, 234
  Levi, 280
  Levy, 251
  Margaret, 278, 280
  Maria, 264
  Marjery, 260
  Martha, 252
  Mary, 259
  Mary Van Keuren, 259
  Moses, 175
  Naomi, 230, 231, 254
  Peter, 174, 238, 277
  Petrus, 175
  Rosetta, 253
  Salay, 233
  Samuel, 177
  Sarah, 279
  Senea, 251
  Simeon, 235
  Simon, 260
  Solomon, 278
  Synche, 279
  Thomas, 259
  Washington, 258
  Willem, Jr., 233
  William, 181, 234, 259, 275
  William Jr., 248
  William Abraham, 253
  Wm., 177, 178
Cuddebeck, Abraham, 252, 272
  Catharine, 243
  Cate, 235
  Caty, 247
  Cornelius, 249
  Elting, 256
  Isaac, 243
  Jacob, 243, 248
  Jacob, Jr., 257
  Jane, 248, 255
  John, 257
  Lena, 110, 113
  Levi, 230, 231
  Margaret, 245, 256
  Maritje, 110
  Marjory, 249
  Mary, 256
  Marya, 113, 116
  Naomy, 248

Cuddebeck, Sally, 249
  Syntie, 276
  Willem, 113
  William, 230, 231, 256
Cuddebeek, Abram, 240
  Benjamin, 237, 260
  Catherine, 260
  Jacob, 240, 260
  Levi Van Etten, 237
Cuddebek, Abram, 144
  Catrina, 152
  Heyltje, 156
  Jacob, 144, 156
Cuddenbeck, Catharine, 243
  Henry, 243
Cuikendal, Andrew, 186
  Catharine, 248
  Elias, 239, 243
  Elisabeth, 186
  Hannah, 239
  Hester, 243
  Sarah, 186
  Tyatie, 277
Cuikendall, Mary, 252
Culver, Ann, 58
  Anna, 47, 48
  Anny, 230
  Hannah, 42
Curren, John, 274
Cursan, Benjamin, 195
  Elizabeth, 195
  Mary, 195
Curtis, John, 277
Curtregh, Elezebath, 38
Curtright, Alasabeth, 43
  Jeny Annest, 277
Curtwright, Isaac, 49
  Leah, 49
Cursaw, Isaac, 43
  Jane, 43
  Peter, 43
Cushing, David, xxix
Custard, Benjamin, 54
  Cyrus, 85
  Elizabeth, 85
  John Van Camp, 85
  Mary, 161
  Mason, 85
  Sarah, 56
  Susanna, 31
  Susannah, 56
  William, 54, 56, 59, 85, 161, 270
Custerd, Rebeca, 72
Cutright, David, 233
  Sarah, 233
Cuttebeck, Benjamin, 107, 113, 243, 248, 256
  Lena, 107
  Maria, 107, 249
  Willem, 107

Cuttenbeck, Elsje, 104
Lena, 106
Maria, 104
Cuykendaal, Catharine, 248
Cuykendael, Catelyntje, 178
Cathrina, 178
Jacobus, 178
Salomon, 178
Cuykendal, Charity, 233
Cornelius, 163
Elias, 233
Huldah, 242
Jonathan, 178
Leah, 230, 231
Phebe, 278
Samuel, 163
Solomon, 171
Wilhelmus, 233
Wm., 178
Cuykendale, Marjery, 280
Cuykendall, Catharine, 251
Catherine, 253, 256
Caty, 253
Huldah, 247, 255
Jacob, 260, 262, 279
Jane, 260, 279
Leah, 280
Margaret, 260, 262
Mary, 250, 256
Wilhelmus, 262
Cuykendell, Caty, 255
Huldah, 254
Jane, 255

D

Dacker, Eliner, 39
Sarah, 34
Daily, Charles, 15
Margaret, 232
Margareth, 50
Willjam, 15
Daley, Daggy, 41
Margaret, 56
Daly, Jane, 188
Jannetje, 33
Dami, Russie, 109
Damport, Elezebeth, 233
Garret, 238
Samuel, 238
Danels, Eva, 38
Danmark, Benardus, 34
Christina, 34
Daniel, Anna, 3, 5
Darbishire, Lois, 196
Dason, Geertie, 275
Davens, Mary, 26
Timothy, 26
Daves, James, 233
Margreth, 233

Daves, Solomon, 233
David, Catrina, 167
Davids or Daniels, Maritje, 152
Ann, 151
Beeletje, 149
Beletje, 98
Belitie, 136
Belletje, 144
Catrina, 141, 147
Cobus, 158
Daniel, 103
Debora, 135
Elisabeth, 158
Elizabeth, 246, 277
Engeltje, 144, 155, 273
Eva, 139, 154
Jacobus, 147, 151
Janneke, 151
Jenneke, 147, 274
John, 144
John, Jr., 154
Joris, 102
Lea, 136, 143, 149
Leonora, 144
Lesabeth, 167
Maria, 141
Maritje, 156
Oseltje, 141
Petrus, 158
Salomo, Jr., 103
Salomon, viii
Salomon, Jun., 98
Solomon, 158
Valentine, 275
Davies, Jane, 212
Leah, 164
Mary, 212
Davis, Mr., xiv
Amey, 249
Anatje, 171
Angeltje, 171, 174
Annatie, 180
Annatje, 124, 161, 174
Belchry, 221
Beletje, 137
Catharina, 114
Cathrina, 179
Catlyntje, 24
Daniel, 232
Elisabeth, 116, 175
Elizabeth, 161, 217, 236
Engeltje, 115, 161
Jacobus, 132, 137, 164
(Jaems), Joris, 106
Jan, 134
Janny, 168
Jany, 134
Jenneke, 118, 161
J. Kirby, Rev., xiii
John, 135
Joel, 108
Jonas, 109

Davis, Joris, 108, 112, 115, 118, 124, 125, 130, 283
Lea, 130, 159, 270, 275
Maria, 130, 170
Mary, 213, 217, 222, 226, 229
Petrus, 119, 135
Polly, 164
Salomon, 114, 116, 119, 125, 283
Salomon, Jr., 108, 109
Samuel, 108
Solomon, 232
Dawets, Bebte, 272
John, 272
Dayis, Saloman, 98
Dayly, Margaret, 52
Margarit, 46
Paggy, 44
Susannah, 72
Deary, Susannah, 49
De Camp, Elisabeth, 175
Deckker, Annatie, 136
Grietie, 135
Janneke, 168
J. H., 136
Johannes, 135, 136
Johannis, Jr., 168
Joseph, 168
Lea, 136
Nancy, 168
Tomas, 136
De Dutscher, Margariet, 107
De Duyser, Margriet, 97
De Duyster, Margriet, 97
Deen, Sara, 3
Deenmark, Bernardus, 33
Jenneke, 33
Deenmarken, Femmetje, 166
Deenmerk, Barnardus, 190
Clouwdiana Sophia, 190
Fametje, 161
Femetje, 161
Lea, 190
De Grootvelt, Ann, 205
De Hooges, Claertje, 97
Decker, Aaron, 48, 51, 54, 56, 59-61, 76, 79, 85, 86
Abigail Ann, 263
Abm., 90
Abraham, 10, 26, 27, 30, 34, 45, 49, 51, 60, 63, 67, 78, 80, 84, 86, 87, 130, 202, 232, 277
Abraham D., 86, 91
Abraham Brokaw, 48
Abram, 4, 6, 7, 13
Abram H., 12
Abram Hendrickse, 4
Absolam Case, 239
Affe, 36

Decker, Affy, 50
  Alida, 108, 137, 114, 181
  Amanda, 60
  Amos Atkins, 77
  Andrew, 191, 193, 200, 215, 222, 223, 225
  Andrew D., 60-62, 77, 83, 87
  Andries, 108, 112, 113, 118, 120, 124, 130, 138, 160, 185, 281, 282
  Andries Dingman, 41
  Anna, 51, 55, 57, 58, 153
  Anna Juliana, 271
  Annatie, 214, 278
  Annatje, 108, 109, 112, 115, 123, 124, 126, 128, 131, 132, 137, 171, 174, 268, 283
  Anne, 28
  Anthony, 257
  Antie, 26, 31, 34, 36, 124
  Arie, 30
  Barbara, 3
  Beeletje, 12
  Beletje, 122
  Belinda, 61
  Bellinda, 79
  Benjamen, 164
  Benjamin, 7, 8, 30, 38, 104, 109, 114, 251, 276, 277
  Benjamin Cortright, 63
  Bernardus, 51
  Blandiena, 43
  Blandina, 52
  Broer, 25, 26, 104, 108, 110, 113, 115, 124, 127, 276
  Caleb, 61
  Calvin, 59
  Caroline, 87
  Casparus Freyenmoet, 118
  Catharina, 5, 12, 24, 33, 93, 119
  Catharina Mapes, 72
  Catharine, 36, 56, 83, 90, 247
  Catherine, 215, 218
  Cathrina, 11, 13, 105, 277
  Cathrine, 39
  Catrena, 169
  Catrina, 34
  Cattrina, 36, 184
  Caty, 39, 63, 73, 78, 213, 237
  Caty Jane, 260
  Cecilia, 77, 89
  Cecillia, 76, 82
  Celletie, 197
  Ceselia, 71
  Charlotte, 244, 259
Decker, Chauncey, 258
  Christoffel Maul, 108
  Christophel M., 169
  Christopher, 160, 172, 175, 215
  Clara, 191, 193
  Cobus, 218
  Coenrad, 200
  Cornelia, 27, 29, 33, 127, 178
  Cornelia Van Leuwan, 10
  Cornelis, 32, 108
  Cornelius Dewitt, 223
  Cornilia, 30
  Danel, 166
  Daniel, 25, 27, 30, 33, 54, 63, 81, 164, 230, 231, 242, 271
  Daniel, Jr., 90, 92
  David Van Garden, 51
  Efye, 34, 37
  Eleanor, 242, 259
  Eleonora, 2, 6, 10
  Elia, 35
  Elias, 24, 32, 36, 38, 104, 115, 176, 191, 193, 200
  Eliesabeth, 275
  Elijah, 49, 83, 90
  Elinor, 214
  Elisa, 26, 163, 184
  Elisabeth, 5, 112, 178, 182
  Elisha, 25, 28, 31, 36, 191, 193, 276
  Elisha, Jr., 36
  Eliza, 26, 261
  Elizabeth, 25, 35, 51, 58, 61-63, 170, 175, 205, 208, 222, 260, 265
  Elizebeth, 60
  Eltse, 260
  Ephraim, 46
  Esegiel, 34
  Ethe, 262
  Eva, 191, 193
  Ezechiel, 131
  Ezeckiel, 270
  Ezegiel, 37
  Femmetje, 8, 9, 97, 109, 110, 114, 119, 124, 130, 138, 267, 282
  Garret Broadhead, 50
  Garretye, 168
  Geertje, 97
  George Washington, 59
  Gerret, 3
  Gerrit, 97
  Gertje, 104
  Grietje, 3, 97, 128, 130, 131, 269
  Hanah, 44
  Hanna, 11
Decker, Hannah, 43, 47, 62, 72, 77, 84, 218, 221, 225, 226, 249, 260
  Hannah Anne, 67
  Hannah Miffin, 80
  Hannatje, 25
  Hannes, 108
  Helemus, 172
  Helena, 114, 220
  Helenah, 277
  Henderick, 41
  Hendericus, vii, 8, 213
  Henderikus, 24, 25
  Hend'k, 33
  Hendrick, 12, 30, 31, 97, 108, 114, 115, 168, 172, 176, 177
  Hendricus, 34, 93, 127
  Henry, 35, 38, 43, 45, 49, 51, 54, 56, 58, 61, 67, 80, 86
  Henry Shoemaker, 50
  Hermanus, 281
  Hester, 225
  Hiram, 85
  Huldah, 232, 258, 261, 263
  Hylah, 280
  Iemimi, 30
  Isaiah, 260, 262, 280
  Isaiah, Jr., 260, 280
  Isaac, 51, 214, 230, 234, 241, 251, 257, 260, 263
  Isaac, Jr., 242, 247, 254
  Isaac Cortright, 64
  Isaac M., 232, 233
  Isaac N., 241
  Isaac Steel, 88
  Jacob, 26, 46, 72, 97, 105, 113, 124, 213, 275
  Jacob, Jr., 276
  Jacob Vradenbergh, 262
  Jacobus, 107, 110, 111, 114, 124, 169, 172, 174, 275
  Jacomeyntje, 230, 231
  James, 28, 230, 231, 239
  James C., 279
  James Force, 79
  James Madison, 67
  James Rosegrant, 230, 231
  James Van Campen, 80
  James Washington, 61
  Jan, 2, 97, 98
  Jan, Jr., 3
  Jane, 36, 48, 54, 57, 59, 60, 61, 77, 82, 220, 233, 234
  Jane Mapes, 63
  Janeka, 220
  Janneke, 53
  Jannetie, 44

Decker, Jannetje, 8, 10-12, 122, 132, 163
Jannetjen, 93
Jannica, 41
Jason, 84
Jean, 239
Jenneca, 38, 278
Jenneka, 34
Jenneke, 8, 10, 12, 24, 33, 46, 83, 132, 271
Jennika, 38
Jennike, 32
Jenny, 210, 215, 219
Jesaiah, 175
Joannes, vii, x
Job, 61
Joel, 110
Johanes, 71
Johanna, 1, 2, 4
Johannes, 8, 10, 82, 94, 107, 110, 112, 118, 124, 130, 182, 197, 237, 279, 282
Johannes, Jr., 131
Johannes Van Aken, 112
Johannis, 26, 32, 35, 38, 271
Johannus, 259
Johans, 174
John, 25, 30, 35, 37, 51, 53, 54, 56, 58, 60, 61, 77, 81, 200, 232, 237, 247, 275, 277, 279
John, Jr., 76, 79, 82, 89
John Brown, 72
John Westbroek, 62
Johns, 174
Johonas, 67, 77
Johannas, 66
Jonathan, xxiv, 107, 114
Joseph, 132
Joshua, 237
Josias, 176
Jury, 35
Knelia, 185
Lana, 234
Lany, 225
Lea, 3, 8, 32, 33, 92, 97, 108-110, 114, 116, 119, 125, 131, 132, 283
Leah, 85, 89, 178
Leja, 166
Lena, 4, 5, 10, 13, 94, 104, 165, 217
Levi, 24, 50, 213, 254
Levi Van Etten, 92
Leya, 271
Levy, 72, 275
Liedeja, 15
Lisabeth, 12, 108, 110, 123, 129
Louwrenz, 12, 94

Decker, Lydia, 6, 8, 10, 12, 13, 93, 176, 182, 183
Madlena, 281
Magdalena, 202
Majery, 275
Manuel, 63, 64
Maragriet, 185, 189
Maregreet, 181
Maregreta, 176
Margaret, 49, 245, 249, 276, 279
Margaret Maria, 57
Margaret Westbrook, 213
Margret, 39, 176, 238
Margriet, 1, 5, 7, 109, 112, 116, 118, 124, 128
Margrietje, 1
Maria, 1, 4, 111, 119, 172, 175, 188, 191, 193, 197, 230, 231, 278, 285
Mariah, 67, 89
Marinda, 92
Maritie, 28
Maritje, 106
Marjery, 263
Marteinus, x
Martin, 181, 242, 254, 255, 258, 261, 263
Martines, 247
Mary, 54, 56, 58, 60, 61, 67, 76, 78, 174, 234, 239, 242, 247, 251, 254, 257, 260, 263, 275, 279
Mary, ——, 49
Marya, 11
Molly, 89
Moses, 72, 177, 278
Mercy, 66
Nancy, 60
Neelgje, 104
Neeltje, 108, 110, 111, 114, 119, 267
Nelson, 254
Paul, 76
Peggy, 276
Peggy Mariah, 90
Peter, 56, 220, 222, 225, 231, 234, 239, 244, 255, 278
Petrus, 107, 109, 114, 118, 277
Phebe, 172
Philip, 131, 222
Phillip, 218
Polly, 172
Rachel, 1, 3, 94, 109, 110, 112, 114, 117, 125, 130, 266, 275
Racheltje, 104, 114
Reggy Mariah, 87
Richard, 246, 277
Richard Fulk, 63

Decker, Rosse Vanaken, 32
Ruth Mariah, 71
Rymerick, 132
Saertje, 138
Salata, 234
Saliche, 65
Salita, 56
Sality, 55
Salomon, 104, 107, 110, 114, 115, 119, 124, 128, 132, 137, 265
Samuel, 24, 32, 72, 109, 118, 169
Samuel, 165
Sara, 2, 5, 9, 13, 14, 45, 94, 104, 107-109, 111, 114, 124, 125, 128, 131, 137, 266, 268, 283
Sarah, 15, 36, 38, 41, 44, 49, 61, 88, 111, 114, 132, 172, 173, 174, 181, 182, 242, 247, 253, 260, 277, 278
Sarah Anne, 79
Sarah Eveline, 91
Sary, 58
Seeletje, 231
Seleche, 79, 83
Seletje, 53
Selitee, 277
Selitie, 35
Simeon, 82, 230, 231
Simon I., 86, 88
Simon Ingles, 49
Solomon, 176, 230, 231, 234
Susanna, 3, 50
Thomas, 50, 52, 57, 59, 79, 107, 108, 114, 115, 118, 119, 123, 124, 128, 137, 213, 237, 239, 244, 282, 283, 284
Tomas, 27
Willem, 4, 114
William, 103
William Wayne, 86
Wilson Monroe, 80
Dekker, Alida, 147, 155, 159
Andreas, 103
Andries, 17, 100, 101, 103, 105, 133, 139
Annaatje, 105, 134
Annatie, 141
Annatje, 98, 145, 146, 150, 156, 159
Antje, 21, 23, 139
Antye, 27
Benjamin, 17, 20, 21, 22, 102, 155, 162
Blandina, 145, 159
Boudewyn, 144
Broer, 98, 100, 102, 150

Dekker, Catharina, 99, 105
 Catrina, 153, 154
 Catrine, 155
 Cornelia, 19
 Cornelis, 102, 274
 Cornelius, 19, 27, 143, 162
 Daniel, 21, 102, 134, 141, 159, 162, 274
 David, 145
 Debora, 105
 Divertje, 105, 273
 Elias, 18, 98, 154, 164
 Elies, 17
 Elisa, 17, 18, 100
 Elisabeth, 157
 Eliza, 19
 Evon, 18
 Ezakiel, 19
 Ezechiel, 23, 142
 Femmetje, 98, 99, 101
 Geestje (Grietje), 23
 Grietje, 138, 147, 273
 Gritje, 147
 Hans, Jr., 138
 Henetje, 273
 Henderikkus, 16
 Hendrik, 141
 Hendrikkus, 144
 Henrick, 98, 99
 Henrik, 100
 Hermanus, 101
 Jacob, 18, 23, 141, 143, 149, 150, 273
 Jacob, Jr., 102
 Jacob, Jun., 98
 Jacobus, 103, 105, 143
 Janache, 18
 Janatje, 133
 Janche, 146
 Janeche, 154
 Janneke, 17
 Jannetje, 134, 141, 143
 Jeneke, 155
 Jenneke, 21, 160
 Jennetje, 164
 Joel, 161, 274
 Johannes, 98, 99, 103, 105, 134
 Johannes, Jr., 141, 147
 Johannis, 101, 148, 155, 274
 Johannis, Jr., 146, 155, 160
 Johannis Broerschen, 21
 John, 142
 Jonecke, 144
 Joris, 102
 Josias, 102, 144, 152, 156
 Laurentz, 105
 Leaatje, 103
 Lea, 98, 103, 139, 143, 146, 149, 157

Dekker, Leentje, 152
 Lena, 17, 105, 140, 162
 Lenora, 100
 Levi, 134
 Lidea, 136
 Lisa, 148
 Lydia, 20, 21, 98, 153
 Magdalena, 150
 Magerie, 155
 Manuel, 164
 Maragritie, 139
 Mareitje, 101
 Margriet, 99, 101, 102, 103, 105
 Maria, 23, 140, 144, 148, 153, 162, 274
 Martinus, 140, 144, 146, 148
 Mary, 21
 Moses, 161
 Neeltje, 139
 Nieltje, 133
 Peter, 145, 155
 Petrus, 99, 102, 140, 152, 153
 Philippus, 133
 Rachel, 19, 20, 100, 102, 105, 134
 Richard, 235
 Roanney, 235
 Salomon, 99, 102, 141, 153
 Salomon, Jr., 153, 274
 Samuel, 152
 Sara, 98, 101, 102, 103, 134
 Sarah, 22, 141, 145, 146, 148, 149, 154, 156, 157, 236
 Stephanus, 139, 143, 157
 Stuffel, 273
 Symon, 156
 Theatie, 141
 Thomas, 98, 101, 102
 Wilhelmus, 103
 Willem, 133
Delang, Sara, 13
Delay, Prudence, 201
De Long, Arriaentje, 5
 Eleanor, 275
Demarest, J., 279
 John, xxvii, xxviii, 279
 John T., xxviii
 Maria, 278
Demarken, Femete, 176
Demerken, Cloudina, 28
Demmon, Elijah, 49
 Jesse, 49
 John, 49
Demund, Isaac S., xxix
Denemark, Dorothea, 2
Denemarken, John Christoffel, 4
Denemerken, Blandina, 18
 Christoffel, 4

Denemerken, Claudina Sophia, 4
 Joh. Christoffel, 4
 Margriet, 8
 Denis, Hester, 105
Denmark, Bornodis, 30
 Christofil, 30
 Cloudina, 25
 Cornelea Hover, 30
Denmarken, Dorothea, 12
Dennemaken, Christoffel, 10
Dennemarck, Antje, 3
 Christophel, 3, 92
Dennemark, Christoffel, 14
 Grietje, 2
 Margriet, 102
 Margrieta, 14
Dennemarke, Anna Dorothea, 6
 Christoffel, 6
 Dorothea, 6
 Margriet, 99
Dennemarken, Bernardus, 15
 Christoffel, 9, 11, 15
 Femmetje, 9
 Johan Christoffel, 5, 11, 102
 Margriet, 2, 10
Dennemerken, Blandina, 21
 Margriet, 4
Dennis, Adam, 175
 John, 175
Depew, Abram, 223
 Dirk, 223
 Maria, 223
Depu, Helena, 176
De Pue, Mosis, 17
 Nicolaas, 17
Depue, Aaron, 57
 Anna, 87
 Benj. 54
 Benjamin, 70, 74, 89
 Blandena, 44
 Caty Anne, 80
 Daniel, 87
 Daniel, Jr., 23, 25, 28
 Elesabeth, 43
 Elias, 25
 Elijah, 89
 Elisabeth, 23, 57
 Elisabetha, 54
 Elizabeth, 68, 83, 89
 Ensy, 82
 Hannah, 54, 88, 90
 James Van Campen, 74
 Jane, 81, 89, 280
 Johannes, 15
 John, 43, 44, 54, 57, 61
 John, Jr., 57, 61, 80
 Margaret, 91

303

Depue, Maria, 23, 26
Marretje, 105
Mary, 61
Melcher, 82, 89
Moses, 54, 57, 87, 91,105
Nathan, 91
Nicholas, 25, 57, 91
Nicolaas, 28
Nicolas, 54
Samuel, 89
Sara, 16
Sarah, 15, 61, 89
Sarah Overfield, 89
Susanna, 89, 105
Susannah, 69, 81
De Pui, Benjamin, 19,143, 144, 151, 274
Elisabeth, 144, 154
Grietje, 274
Hendrikkus, 152
Henry, 152
Janneke, 151
Johannis, 142
John, 143
Lena, 143
Maria, 17
Nicolaas, 274
Samuel, 274
Sarah, 18
Susanna, 142
Wyentje, 18
Depui, Benjamin, vii
Samuel, vii
Sarah, 211
Depuis, i
S., i, ii
Samuel, ii
De Puy, Benjamin, 161
Daniel, 59
Jacobus, 161
John, Jr., 59
Margaret, 246
Mary, 59
Depuy, Abraham, 169,213, 217
Anna, 276
Antie, 182
Benj., 170, 182
Benjamin, x, xiii, xxvi, 63, 81,207, 213,277,283
Benjamin, Jr., 276
Benjn., 174
Cornelius, 276
Daniel, 47
Eleanor Maria, 55
Elijah, 81
Elyah, 76
Elisabeth, 168, 170
Elizabeth, 63
Greetje, 170
Grietye, 168
Helena, 182, 276
Hester, 182

Depuy, Hu, 285
Isaac, 217
Jane, 55, 76
John, 35, 47
Jonetie, 217
Margaret, 68, 174
Margrietje, 159
Maria, 277
Martynes, 170
Mary, 278
Moses, xiii, 35, 63, 169
Moses, Jr., 170
Sam'l, 170, 178
Samuel, x, 55, 168, 170, 183
Samuel Swartwoud, 178
Sarah, 40, 42, 207, 214, 223
Susan, 76
Dery, Susanna, 35
Desbri, Martynus, 186
Desha, Caty, 187
Heyltie, 186
Morgan, 186
Nelly, 186, 275
William, 187
Deshea, Nelly, 275
Deusenbury, George, 278
Devans, Abraham, 24
Elizabeth, 24
Devenport, Alanson, 238
Henry, 200
Jacobus, 200
Martin, 238
Rachel, 192, 194
Devens, Hannah, 40
Leonard, 40
Devin, Abraham, 113
Antje, 106
Leendert, 12
Niclaes, 10
Terrenz, 10, 12, 93, 113
Terrins, 103, 106
Devince, Abraham, 31
Elizebeth, 31
Devins, Abraham, 19
Jacobus, 159
Devis, Jan, 138
Devoir, Benjamin, 154
Cornelius, 142
Daniel, 142
Elizabeth, 274
Helena, 142
Lena, 140, 154
Rachel, 142
Devoor, Abram, 1, 139
Adam, 3
Alida, 119
Andries, 5
Benjamin, 7
Brechie, 123
Cornelis, 2, 7, 100, 119, 130

Devoor, Daniel, 5, 120, 123, 130, 139
Daniel, Jr., 120
David, 100, 119, 123,139
Elisabeth, 120
Engeltje, 130
Hendrick, 7
Isaac, 139
Jacobus, 1-3, 5-7, 119, 120, 121, 269
Johannes, 119
John, 121
Lena, 2, 168
Lisabeth, 120
Mattheus, 119, 123
Rachel, 5, 120, 122
Sara, 7, 122
Wilhelmus, 119
Willem, 5, 7, 119, 121
Devor, Helena, 175
Devour, Antje, 153
Elias, 154
Heltje, 18
Jacobus, 147, 154
Tjaatje, 147
Devous, Antje, 160
Dewett, Cornelius, 285
Dewey, Joseph, 200
Pheby, 200
Rhody, 200
Sarah, 200
Susannah, 200
De Wit, Anna, 163
Blandina, 98, 101, 107
Cornelis, 169
Elcy, 44
Elizabeth, 101
Elsy, 43
Jacob, 169
Jannetie, 135
Jannetje, 99, 101, 106
John, 98
Lisabeth, 98, 99
Rachel, 99, 100, 104,106
Rener, 169
Tjaadje, 101, 105
Dewit, Aaron, 244
Andrew Cupes, 69
Andrus, 157
Catharina, 62
Cornelius, 62
Elizabeth, 69
Grietie, 143
Henry, 69, 77
Jacob, 157, 175
Jacob I., 272
Jacob Rutscher, 284
Jannetie, 103
John, 62, 69
John H., 69
Liedia, 163
Lovina, 69
Maria, 136, 230, 231

Dewit, Mariah, 77
　Mary, 240
　Peggy, 240
　Peter, 69
　Rachel, 69
　Sally, 69
　Sapherin (Severyn), 175
　Tjaadje, 103
De Witt, Abrm., 248
　Aaron, 248
　Ann, 154
　Andries, 112
　Anna, 137
　Anny, 207
　Annatje, 153
　Blandina, 108
　Bodwyn, 146
　Cornelis, 126, 129, 158
　Cornelius, 141, 148, 180
　Cornelius, Jr., 162, 192, 194
　Elisabeth, 110, 141
　Elizabeth, 192, 194
　Elshe, 41, 46
　Eyke, 6, 7, 10
　Eyken, 15
　Famatie, 18c
　Grietje, 11, 13, 18, 20, 126, 128
　Hanna, 171
　Heiltje, 138
　Henry, 112
　Hyltje, 138, 174
　Jacob, 129, 138, 141, 145, 146, 149, 151
　Janetje, 128
　Janneke, 175, 182
　Jannetje, 107-109, 112, 113, 116, 117, 282
　Johanes, 138
　J. R., vii
　Lisabeth, 11, 107, 108, 118, 137, 282
　Lodewyk Hoorbeek,162
　Maragreit, 194
　Maragriet, 189, 192
　Maragrita, 16
　Margaret, 175
　Maria, 119, 145, 149,158, 162, 180, 184
　Margriet, 124
　Margrita, 21
　Mary, 149
　Marya, 115
　Moses, 174, 175
　Paul, 122
　Rachel, 115, 122, 125, 126, 281
　Rynier, 141, 180,189,207
　Sara, 122
　Sarah, 148, 158
　Tjaati, 121
　Tjaatje, 109

De Witt, Tjaetje, 118, 282
Dewitt, Andrew, 204
　Cornelius, 163, 185, 210
　Egbert, 112
　Elisabeth, 270
　Elizabeth, 241
　Gretie, 25
　Hannah, 198, 199, 203, 214
　Hennah, 208
　Hester, 185
　Heyltie, 277
　Jacob, 120, 160, 188
　Jacob R., ix, 151, 154
　Jacobus, 204
　Janetie, 210
　Jenneke, 154
　John, 72
　Lisabeth, 130
　Maragriet, 184, 204
　Margaret, 221
　Margriet, 268
　Maria, 120, 142,148,183, 222, 223
　Mariah, 225
　Martin, 183
　Martinus, 120
　Mary, 177, 215, 219, 224
　Marya, 130, 180
　Moses, 204
　Mosis, 151
　Paul, 120
　Phebe, 237
　Pieter, 120
　Ryneer, 204
　Rynier, 183
　Samuel, 160
　Sarah, 72
　Susannah, 72
Dey, Maria, 140
Dieven, Jacobus, 101
　Therrens, 101
Dills, David, 276
Dilly, Edward, 280
　James, 280
Dimman, John, 31
　Sarah, 31
Dimon, Assa Budd, 53
　Elisabetha, 53
　Elizabeth, 67
　Hannah, 67
　James, 51
　John, 51, 53, 67
Dina, 207
Dinah, 256, 259
Dingeman, Adam, 16
　Andries, 275
　Eva, 163
　Kornelia, 213
　Maritje, 159
　Petries, 16
　Rachel, 92

Dingemans, Andries, 103
　Cornelia, 103
Dingenman, Adam, 1, 2, 4-8, 11, 12
　Alida, 2, 4, 6, 110, 121, 122
　Andries, 2, 5, 7, 110, 125, 127
　Cornelia, 7
　Eva, 1-3, 6, 7
　Evje, 5, 7, 119-121, 269
　Hendrick, 7
　Jacob, 5
　Jacobus, 11, 12
　Rachel, 1
Dingman, A., 41
　Adam, 93, 146
　Alida, 26
　Andres, 167
　Andrew, 92
　Andrew, Jr., 88
　Andries, 19, 143, 221
　Andries, Jr., xii
　Andris, 26, 35
　Caroline, 92
　Cornelia, 19, 85, 143,167
　Daniel, 66
　Daniel V. Campen, 36
　Daniel W., 62, 215, 221
　Daniel Westbroek, 26
　Daniel Westbrook, 278
　Elizabeth, 33
　Eva, 19, 26, 28, 146, 184, 191, 193
　Eve, 25, 31
　Evi Sayre, 92
　J., 41
　Jacob, 26
　Jacobus, 31
　James, 28, 36
　Jane, 62
　Johannis, 31
　Kornelia, 217
　Lea Elizabeth, 91
　Margaret, 77
　Margaret Jane, 86
　Martin W., 79, 82, 86,91
　Martinus Westbrook, 215
　Mary, 88
　Oladan, 31
　Peter, 191, 193, 275
　Priscilla Mariah, 79
　Ragel, 35
　Solomon Hornbeck, 82
　Susan Elizabeth, 92
Dingmanse, Alida, 21
　Andrew, 17
　Andries, 17, 21
　Cornelia, 21
　Elisabeth, 17
　Eva, 17
　Lydia, 17

Dinmark, Bornodis, 30
Leah, 30
Sarah, 30
Dinnis, Maria, 276
Ditschious, Sara, 104
  William, 104
Ditsoort, Anna, 99
  Annaatje, 98
  Bernhardus, 101
  Jacobus, 97, 98
  Maria, 1, 101, 105
  Neeltje, 103, 105, 107, 110, 114
  Sara, 98, 114
  Stephanus, 97, 101
  Willem, 101, 114
  William, 103, 107
Ditzoort, Maria, 4
Divans, Jacobus, 144
  Maria, 144
Divens, Abraham, 26
Josip, 31
Leendert, 31
Levey, 26
Divoor, Abram, 21
Divvins, Rachel, 22
  Terrens, 22
Dixon, Mary Ann, 91
  Thomas, 91
Dodesinck, Mally, 92
Doff, Elisabeth, 125
  Thomas, 125
Dogety, Peggy, 230
Dolittle, Dorcas, 238
Donally, William, 230, 231
Doolittle, Dorcas, 265
  Peter, 214
  Stephen, 214
Dorsius, Rev., xxiv
  Peter Henry, Rev., xxiii
Doty, Marinda, 90
Dowley, Henry, 235
  Huldah, 255
  John, 255
  Pegge, 235
  William, 235, 255
Doxy, Anna, 280
  William, 280
Drach, Elizabeth, 48
  Peter, 48
  Joh. William, 48
Drake, Eleanor, 262
  Ephraim, 65
  Evje, 11
  George, 191, 193
  John, 11
  Joseph, 156, 273, 274
  Joshua, 65
  Ledy, 285
  Ruth, 191, 193, 207
  Sephaniah, 278
  Thomas, 191, 193

Draper, John, 196
  Nathan, 196
Dravese, Marya, 26
Dreaper, Nathan, 192, 194
  Saly, 192, 194
Dreck, Joseph, 168
Du Bois, Cornelia, 159
  Josephat, 101, 106
Duelittle, Dorcas, 226
Duff, Thomas, 131
  William, 131
Duk, Lena Consales, 100
Duke, Elizabeth Consales, 110
Dunnum, Sarah, 47
Dupue, Lidia, 25
Dupuis, N., ii
  Nicholas, ii
Du Puy, Catharina, 3
  Hanna, 3
  Lisabeth, 3
  Maritje, 4
  Moses, 3
  Moses Nicolase, 3
  Nicolas, 3, 281
  Susanna, 2, 4
Dupuy, Benjamin, 6, 7, 116, 118, 121, 124, 128, 205
  Catharina, 122
  Catharine, 120
  Elizabeth, 128
  Hannah, 205
  Johannes, 6, 14, 120, 122
  Johannes, Jr., 10
  Margrietje, 128
  Maria, 124
  Maritje, 7, 8
  Moses, xiii, 124
  Samuel, 118
  Sara, 6, 10, 14, 94
  Sarah, 207
  Susanna, 8, 14
Du Puys, Samuel, 2
Duryea, John, Rev., 246
Duryee, Johannes, 211
Dutcher, Abraham, 284
  Abram, 285
  Charles, 277
  Scinthy, 208
  William, 208, 278
Dyckman, Rachel, 191, 193

E

Eager, i
Eakle, Sarah, 84
Earl, Ebenezer, 195
  James, 24, 195
  Martha, 26, 29
  Matha, 30
  Roberd, 195
  Suffiah, 24

Eastlich, Alexander, 45
Betcy, 45
Easterline, Susannah, 85, 90
Eberth, Cathrina, 180
  Christina, 165, 180
  George, 172
  Jacob, 165, 172
  Marshal, 165
Edgerton, Edward, 201
  James, 201
Edmond, Catharine, 204
  Catterina, 202
  Cattrine, 199
Edwards, Mahely, 208
  Sally, 205
  William, 205, 208, 277
Edwart, Catrina, 20
  Frederick, 20
Einans, Johan, 27
Elbertson, Engeltje, 156
  Nicholas, 156
Eldredge, Nathaniel, 89
  Sarah Elizabeth, 89
Eldrige, Hannah Nyce, 84
  Nathaniel, 84
Elie, Hester, 4
Ellis, Mary, 223
Elmendorf, Cornelis, 104
  Isaac, 241
  Richard, 232
  Roman, 232, 236, 241
  Teunis, 236
Elmer, N., xxviii
Elten (Eltinge), J a c o-mynte, 109
Jocomyntje, 111, 137
Elting, Anna Maria, 262, 264
  C. C., viii, 279, 280
  Cornelius, 264
  Cornelius C., xxvii, xxviii, 262
  Cornelius C., Rev., ix
  David, 264
  E. C., Rev., 279
  Jacomyntje, 99, 101, 106
  Phillip Bevier, 262
Elyea, Sally Ann, 89
Emans, Johan, 32
  Lena, 32
Emens, Anne, 167
  Caty, 40
  Elaneh, 35
  Eliesabeth, 16
  Jemima, 40
  Nicholes, 16
Emery, Cornelia, 69
  Cyrus, 64
  Elenor, 66
  Hannah, 70, 72
  Hannah Eliza, 90
  George, 72

Emery, James Hamilton, 82
  John Keen, 72
  Julia Anne, 68
  Nathan, 64, 66, 68, 69, 75, 77, 82, 86, 90
  Oliver Perry, 75
  Phebe Jane, 77
  Sarah, 72
  Susan, 86
Emins, Catharine, 36
Emmans, John, 24
  Mary, 275
  Nicolas, 24
  Rachel, 2
Emmens, Alexander, 7
  Catharina, 13, 32
  Cattrina, 37
  John, 5
  Lea, 18
  Lena, 42
  Marya, 11
  Niclaes, 7, 9, 10, 13
  Niclas, 7
  Nicolaas, 18
  Nicolaes, 5, 11
  Polly, 51
  Nealy, 278
Emmes, Jamima, 277
Emmins, Daniel, 21
  Nicolaas, 21
Emmons, John, 31
  Sarah, 31
Empson, Abraham, 40
  Ann, 45
  Benjamin, 40, 45
  Caty, 40
  Elizabeth, 40
  Joseph, 40
  Rachel, 45
  Sarah, 45
  William, 40
Emson, Anne, 71
  Bengamin, 43
  Roberd, 43
Enderes, Christian, 50
Enes, Catharine Jane, 246
  Ruth, 246
Enest, Cornelis, 39
  Elijah Clark, 58
  Isaac, 58
England, Tenty, 2
Engelar, Elisabeth, 200
Engler, Elizabeth, 185
English, John, 182
  Levy, 182
Ennes, Alexander, 8, 137, 160
  Benjaman, 167
  Benjamin, 105, 157, 160, 164, 180
  Catharina, 160
  Catharine, 75, 79, 89

Ennes, Cathrina, 179
  Catrina, 157
  Cattrine, 202
  Cobus, 151
  Cornelius, 133
  Danel, 167
  Daniel, 70, 75, 82, 110, 151, 159, 162, 163, 190, 203, 223, 230
  David, 273
  Diana, 222
  Elenor, 64
  Elesabet, 27
  Elexander, 222, 223
  Elisabeth, 16, 18, 19, 21, 94, 139, 157
  Eliza Maria, 67
  Elizabeth, 35, 66, 82,162, 192, 194, 202, 207, 210, 218, 224, 276
  Greetje, 176
  Grietje, 20, 143, 273
  Hannah, 64, 65, 67
  Hiram, 230
  Isaac, 64, 65, 67
  Joseph, vii
  Ledia, 278
  Leentje, 159
  Lena, 201, 204, 209, 210, 216, 277
  Lenah, 211
  Lidea, 167
  Lidia, 223
  Lisabeth, 13
  Loiza Seely, 66
  Jacob, 70
  Jacobus, 203, 208
  Jannetje, 2, 4-8, 15, 101, 110
  Jennica, 203
  Johannes, 164
  John, 66, 128, 170, 230
  Joseph, 123,162,170,185, 190, 202, 217, 274, 285
  Margaret, 64, 79, 86, 87, 229, 230
  Margriet, 116, 160
  Maria, 163, 167
  Mary, 210, 274
  Matilda Jane, 65
  Moses, 208
  Nicolaas, 157
  Peggy, 70, 76
  Ruth, 279
  Sally, 229
  Sarah, 203
  Simon Cortright, 230
  Wilhelmus, 210, 278
  Willem. 99
  William, vii, 105, 109, 110, 116, 123, 125,128, 131, 133, 137, 139, 157, 160, 162, 217, 281, 284

Enness, Bethey, 199
  Cornelia, 104
  Jacobus, 199
  William, 104
Ennest, Elizabeth, 220
  Jannetje, 6, 102
  Magdalena, 221
  William, 102, 136
Ennis, Alexander, 210,228
  Benjamin, 274
  Daniel, 150, 155, 183
  Elisabeth, 155
  Lenah, 224
  Maria, 210, 278
  Phebe, 183, 219
  Ruth, 242
Ennist, Elizabeth, 221
  Jannetje, 2
  Joseph, 221
  Maria, 221
  Wilhelmus, 221
Epson, Benjamin, 40
  Jane, 40
Erel, Martha, 38
  Matte, 27
Erl, James, 191, 193
  Martha, 40, 43
  Mathew, 191, 193
  Samuel, 191, 193
Ernel, Jacob, 38
Ernet, Martha, 197
Erwen, Catharina, 14
Etten, Jacomyntje,107,113
Evelandt, Antje, 16
Evelant, Antie, 17
  Frederick, 20
Evens, Elisabeth, 174
  John, 174, 285
Everet, Allon, 229
  Elizabeth, 222
  George, 228
  George Baxter, 217
  Hannah, 222
  Isaac, 217, 222, 229
  Jane Westbrook, 222
  Marian, 222, 228
  Marshal, 217, 222
  Moses, 217
Everett, Christine, 230
  Erastus Starkweather, 225
  George, 225, 230
Everigame, James,133,270
Everit, Aaron Westbrook, 206
  Abraham, 206
  Betsy, 213
  Christina, 163
  Cristion, 169
  Hanna, 153
  Isaac, 213
  Jacob, 153
  Maria, 163

Everitt, John D., xviii
Evert, Hannah, 226
  Isaac, 212, 226
  John Davies, 212
Every, Molly, 168
Evvens, Mary, 277
Eylenberg, George, 77
  Hannah Nyce, 92
  John, 77, 92
  Mary, 92
  William Nyce, 92
Eylenberge, Mary, 84
Eylenberger, James Nyce, 84
  John, 84
Eylenbergh, Elizabeth Jane, 80
  John, 80

F

Fairchild, John, 200
  Mary, 200
Fakes, Rebacca, 274
Fanstah (Van Etten), Daniel, 218
  Samuel, 218
Fansworth, Elizabeth, 195
Farletier, Clea, 137
  Moses, 137
Faulke, John, 279
Faulkner, Abraham, 190
  Cornelius Schoonmaker, 190
  Robard, 190
Feber, Martin, 122
Feltus, George Haws, xxix
Fench, Jacobus, 127
  Samuel, 127, 269
Feydlie, Adam, 144
  Jacob, 144
Figeli, Jacob, 136
  Syme, 136
Figels, Jacob, 272
Figly, Eva, 149
  Jacob, 149
Finch, Daniel G., 278
  David, 196
  Samuel, 196
Fish, Mary, 201
Fishcharrelt, Elisabeth, 123
Fisher, Benjamin, vii, 188, 196, 202, 212, 214, 284
  Benjn., 177, 180
  Elia, 202
  Elizabeth, 212
  Jacobus, 177
  James, 216, 217, 223
  Johannis, 180
  John, 219, 224
  Maria, 223, 224

Fisher, Mary, 216, 223, 226, 227, 230
  Permelia, 217
  Samuel, 196
  Sarah, 219
  Simeon, 188
Fishler, George, 85
  John Van Scoda, 85
  Nathaniel, 85
  Susannah, 85
Fitzgerald, Thomas, xxviii
Fleming, Charles, 27, 274
  Charls, 24
  Sarah, 27
  Thomas Whiting, 24
Flemen, Cherity, 278
Flemmen, Jeramia, 33
  Margaret, 33
Flimmen, Caarls, 28
  Cristina Cambers, 28
Follet, Martha, 213
  Marthah, 50
Mattha, 72
Forbis, Eleonora, 14
  Hanna, 143
Forbus, Elenor, 93
Force, Rev., 58
  Rev. Mr., xi
  James G., xxix
Forguson, Benjamin, 144
  Thomas or Hanna, 144
Fortner, Francke, 186
Forva (Corva), Ann, 152
Fortnor, Lewis, 45
  Margarit Kuikendal, 45
Foster, Ann Eliza, 227
  Julius, 227
  Luther, 205
  Mary D., 229
  Polly, 227
  Silas Howell, 205
Fountain, Elizabeth, 216
Fourman, Agnas, 191
  Agnes, 193
Frazer, Jane, 71, 90
  John, 63
  William, 63
Frazure, Jane, 74
Freebes, Mar. Cathrina, 15
Freeland, Eva, 1
Freeman, Rev., xxiii
  Sarah, 34, 36, 41
Fredenburg, Antje, 101, 105
  Arie, 103
  Catrina, 151
Fredenburgh, Aaron, 218
  Esther, 245
  Hezekiah, 245
  Jane, 218
Fredericks, Mary, 200

Freligh, Solomon, 181
Frelinghuysen, Dom., xxvii
  Rev., xxiii
Fremen, Sarah, 38, 44
French, Aaron, 212, 218
Caty, 52
Elizabeth, 56, 212
Ester, 218
Marie, 54
Moses, 59
Richard, 52, 54, 56, 59
Sarah, 56
Selitie, 52
Susy, 52
Freyenmuth, Johannes Casparus, 109
  Joh. Casp., 106
Friman, Sara, 32
Frink, Henry, 51
  John, 51
Fritche, Susan, 49
Fruche, Sevilla, 62
  Susannah, 62, 66, 77
Fruchey, Susannah, 83
Fryenmoet, xiii, xiv, xxiv, xxv, xxvi
  Dom., xv, xvi, xxvi
  Rev., xiv
  Rev. Mr., xi, 15, 94, 271
  Casparus, Rev., xxvii
  Heyltje, 116, 128
  J. C., 120, 121, 123, 128
  J. C., Rev., 132, 136
  Joh. Casparus, 116
  Joh. Dom., 163
Johannes Casparus, xxiii, xxvii
Johannes Casparus Dom., iii, iv
Johannis Casparus, 142
  Maria, 121
Fryenmout, J. C., 118
Fryenmuth, Mr., 284
  Antje, 111
  Dorothea, 106
  J. C., 93, 108, 265, 267, 281
  J. C., Rev., 281
  Joh. Casparus, viii, 1, 103, 111, 265
Frynmoet, Magdalena, 142
Fuller, Denis, 208
  Eli, xv
  Ira, 208
  James B., xv
  Sarah, 189, 208, 278

G

Gaeress, Abraham, 53
  Isaac, 53

Gaeress, Leendert, 53
Gamaer, Esther, 178
Grietje, 136
Ganis, Mary, 71
Gans, Elizabeth, 65
Garess, Caty, 61
  John, 61
  Susan, 61
Garis, Elizabeth, 75
  John, 75
  Peter, 75
Gariss, Barbara, 85
  Elijah, xi
  Isiah, xi
  Leonard, xxiii
Garretson, Gilbert S., xxix
  Gilbert S., Rev., xxii
Gates, Cornelius, xxviii
Geavins, Agnes, 156
Geegge, Hiram, 250
  William, 250
Geemaar, Annatie, 276
Gegy, Jane, 249
Gemaa, Hester, 138
Gemaar, Antje, 101
  Elizabeth, 243
  Ezechiel, 105
  Hester, 139, 144
  Jacob de Wit, 103
  Lisabeth, 103
  Peter, 105
  Petrus, 275
  Pieter, 101, 103
Gemaer, Elizabeth, 121
  Ezechiel, 153
  Grietje, 136
  Lisabeth, 109, 118, 283
  Margrieta, 131
  Pieter, 118, 121
Gemar, Lisabeth, 107, 113
  Maria, 109
  Pieter, 109, 282
Gemes, Matte, 27
Geres, Catharine, 55
  Jonas, 55
  Lohnhart, 55
Germer, Catrina, 136
Gibbons, Nancy, 147
Gibs, Ruth, 155
Gibson, John, 35
  Mary, 35
Gieter, Elizabeth, 203
  George, 203
  Peggy, 175
Gige, William, 275
Gigge, Jane, 245
Gillet, Eusebia, 156
Gladden, Temperenz, 94
Glimplse, Jenny, 252
Glimps, Abram, 147
  Benjamin, 244
  David, 250
  Moses, 244

Glimps, Sally, 250
Glimpse, Abm., 252
  Benjamin, 251
  David, 251
  Maria, 252
Goetschius, I. H., Rev., 138
  J. H., Rev., 133
  John Henry, xxiv
Golden, Bethuel, 82
  Elisha, 82
  George C., 82
  Isaiah, 82
  William Nyce, 82
Gomaar, Alida, 144
  Annatje, 155
  Elias, 159
  Elisabeth, 147, 159
  Ezechiel, 274
  George, 245
  Gerardus, 245
  Grietie, 141
  Jacob, 144, 147, 155
  Jacob De Witt, 159
  Maria, 141, 159
  Peter, 141
  Petrus, 147, 159
  Tiatje, 159
Gomaer, Alida, 21
  Cornelius, 248
  Elias, 154, 168, 274
  Elisabeth, 181
  Ezegeel, 169
  Hester, 151
  Jacob, 21
  Maria, 147, 154
  Peter E. L., 248
  Petrus, 181
  Samuel, 168
Gomar, Alida, 146
  Jacob, 146
  Maragietje, 146
Gonsales, Benjamin, 128
  Daniel, 128, 283
  Jacobus, 128, 283
  Manuel, 12, 14, 128, 129, 267
  Maria, 126, 129, 132, 137
  Rymerick, 132
  Samuel, 128, 132
  Sara, 14
Gonsalies, Maria, 15
Gonsalis, Benjamin, 152
  Elizabeth, 46
  Manuel, 25
  Maria, 25, 143, 160
  Samuel, 46, 152, 277
Gonsaly, Catharine, 41
  Lena, 40
  Manuel, 40
  Mary, 40
  Samuel, 41

Gonsolis, Sarah, 30
Goodspeed, Bethiah, 276
Goodwin, Sellie, 155
  William, 155
Gordon, Allener V., 34
  Charles, 257
  Hannah, 257
Gornel, Jacob, 38
Gornor, Hester, 197
Green, Elenor, 220
Grootvelt, Anna, 183
Grub, Andres, 132
  Sara, 132
Grull, John D., xxx
Guillot, P. J., xxii
Guimar, Peter, iii
Gumaar, Benjamin, 246, 277
  Easther, 243
  Elias, 246
  Elizabeth, 277
  Ezekiel, 246
  Jacob, 246
  Jacob D., vii
  Jacob Dewitt, ix
  Margaret, 246
  Martha, 246
Gumaer, Abraham, 181
  Anna, 280
  Benjamin, 232, 238
  Daniel, 234
  Charity, 247
  Cornelius, 235
  Eleanor, 251
  Elias, 170, 174, 233
  Elisabeth, 174, 239
  Elizbeth, 233
  Esther, 181, 230, 231, 251
  Ezekiel, 181
  Gemima, 248
  Gemime, 234
  Gerardus, 233, 235
  Hannah, 233, 234
  Jacob, 174, 181, 234, 245, 250, 251, 261
  Jacob Dewitt, 174
  Levi, 261
  Martha, 233
  Mary Jane, 261
  Morgan, 251
  Peter, 235
  Peter E., 251
  Peter E. L., 245
  Sally, 250
  Samuel, 238
  Sarah, 261
  Simeon, 250
  Sinche, 252
  Syntje, 241
  Teatje, 174
  Thomas Lewis, 232
Gumar, Hester, 272
  Jeremiah, 280

309

Gumare, Abraham, 242
　Charlotte, 260
　Ezekiel, 254
　Hester, 258
　Isaac, 260
　Jacob, 242, 264
　Jacob Cuddeback Elting, 258
　Jemima, 242
　Jeremiah, 260
　Peter E., 254, 258
　Sarah, 264
　Synche, 256
Gumeere, Cyne, 246
Gun, Christian, 53
　Susanna, 53
　Thomas, 53
Gunn, Elizabeth, 73
Gunsales, Jacobus, 269
　Maria, 12
Gunsalis, Anthony, 174
　Benj., 170
　Benjn., 174
　Elizabeth, 170
　Emanuel, 22
　Samuel, 22
　Sarah, 31
Gunsaly, Mary, 71
　Sarah, 69
Gunsaules, Catharine, 79, 81, 89
　Eliza, 82, 89
　Eelse, 56
　Manuel, 81
　Mary, 80, 90
　Samuel, 56, 81, 88, 90
　Sarah, 86, 88
　Susanna, 56
　William Overfield, 90
Gunsaulis, Sarah, 81
Gustin, Anthony, 81
　Thomas P., 81
Gymaer, Syntie, 250

H

H——, Lodewyck, 274
Hacate, Eleonora, 156
　George, 156
　Stephen, 156
Haccate (Maccate), Huwe, 147
　James, 147
　Maragriet, 147
　(Maccarte), Stephen, 147
Hage, Cattrina, 37
　Hannah, 37
　Henry, 37
Hagerty, Fina, 74
Haggerty, Nancy, 227

Hagle, Henry, 37, 39
　Jacob, 37
　Peter, 39
Halbart, Jemima, 276
Halbert, Joseph, 175
　Wm., 175
Haldrin, Henrick, 98
　Lea, 98
Halring, Henrick, 105
　Laurenz, 105
Hamel, Brient, 143
Hammen, Bryan, 135
　John, 135
Hanan, Ellenor, 29
　John, 29
　Richard, 29
Handickea, Hanna, 1
　James, 1
Handshaw, Hanna, 33, 41
　Hanne, 32
　James, 17, 94
　Marget, 29
　Sarah, 94
　Susanna, 17
Hang, Daniel, 88
　Joseph, 88
Hankinson, Mary, 47, 62
Hankes, Catrien, 28
Hanna, Benjamin, 88
　Jonas, 88, 90
　Mary, 88
　Philip, 88
　William, 90
Hannah, 207
Hanners, John, 71
　Jonas, 71
　Sally Anne, 71
Hanneschat, Elisabeth, 146
Hannison, Catrina, 26
　Peetrick, 26
Hanon, Johan, 27
Hanse, Catrin, 26
　Hendrick, 26
Hansen, Cathrina Heylwills, 15
　Joh. Hendrick, 15
Hanshaw, Hannah, 39, 46
Hanson, Henry, 34
　Martha, 34
Hantze, John G., 74
　John Gottlob, 74
Hany, Hannah, 72
Hardenberg, xxvii
　Jacob R., Dr., 25
Hardenbergh, Dr., 26
　Charles, vii
　Charles, Rev., vii, 230
　Jacob R., Revd., vii, x
　Johannes I. or G., 159
Harriot, Nathaniel, 47
　Samuel, 47

Harris, Sarah, 49, 52
Hasbrouck, John, 172
　Mary, 172
Haver, Elizabeth, 24
Hawndshaw, Hannah, 29
　Sary, 29
Hayn, Hoyn, Frederik, 153
Hayns, Benjamin, 177
　Benjemin, 18
　Johs Shawer, 177
　Joseph, Jr., 18
　Margaret, 174, 180
　Margret, 170
Haynshaw, Hannah, 35
Hazard, i
Headly, Lois, 149
Heator, Polly, 89
Hebler, Caty, 225
Heckerin, A. Lisabeth, 12
Hedger, Ruth, 205
Hedges, Eliza, 227
Heds, Rhody, 216
Heely, John, 123
　Thomas, 123
Heerenmans, Engelje, 104
Heeter, Antony, 21
　George, 21
　Maria, 158
Keeter George, 158
Heiner, Margaret, 279
Hekke, Feronica, 147
Hellem, Peter, 184
　Samuel, 184
Heller, Amos, 68
　Blandinah, 65
　Daniel, 65
　Elenor, 88
　Elizabeth, 62
　Jane Belinda, 62
　John, xxii, 65
　John M., xxii
　Mary Elizabeth, 83
　Michael, 62, 68, 83
　Sarah, 68, 83
　Simon, 68, 88
　Susannah, 68
Hellor, Blandina, 60
　Elezebeth, 59
　Hannah, 59
　John, 60
　Mikle, 59
　James Van Auken, 60
Helm, Abraham, 199
　Bethcy, 189
　Catrina, 152
　Cattrena, 206
　Cattrina, 192, 194, 201, 276
　Celette, 145
　Daniel, 202
　Elisabeth, 23, 143
　Elizabeth, 277

Helm, Hester, 170
Jacob, 23, 131, 134, 139-141, 145, 152, 164, 170, 175, 179, 188, 271, 285
Lena, 140
Maria, 125, 128, 129,131, 139, 141, 142, 148, 153, 167, 197
Mary, 175
Michel, 125
Peter, 143
Rymerig, 164
Samuel, 141, 188, 189, 199, 202
Seletta, 175, 183
Helms, Ragel, 164
Hemmel, Byrn, 271
Hempt, Caty, 85
Henderson, James, 24
John, 24
Patrick, 24
Hendreks, Johannes, 169
Joseph, 169
Hendrik, Mareja, 167
Hennischeth, Elisabeth, 149
Henneshit, Michiel, 123
Sara, 123
Hennishot, Elisabeth, 157
Henry, 207, 219
Clinton, 219
David, 87
Isaac, 67
John, 67, 69, 73, 77,87,91
John, Jr., 77, 82
John Michel, 132
Mary, 73
Simeon, 82
Thomas, 91
William, 69
Hensaw, Margarit, 44
Henshaw, Maragrit, 42
Henshew, Elisabet, 15
Herchsel, Maria, 209
Herlokker, Agnietje, 146
Herris, John, 285
Herrison, George, 11
Herry, 37
Hesson, Ann, 8
Thomas, 8
Hesued, Jannetje, 20
Hetsel, Jacob, 73
Peter, 73
Hetzel, Fanny, 75
Mary, 75
Heyns, Lydia, 14
Hide, Shereman, 58
Susannah, 58
Higgons, Henry, 8
Robert, 8
Hilferty, Daniel, 280
Hill, Abraham, 58
Andrew, 60, 61, 65, 75

Hill, Andries, 58
David, 62
Elizabeth, 61
Elizebeth, 60
Horatio, xvi
James, 60
John, 61
Margaret, 62
Margareth Elizabeth,62
Nehemiah, 62
Sarah, 75
William, 65
William J., xxviii
William Uriah, 62
Hilman, Syntha, 38
Hinkly, Lena, 205
Samuel, 205
Hisson, John, 5
Thomas, 5, 13, 15
William, 13
Hoeper, John, 122
Joseph, 122
Hoever, Mari, 132
Hoeverin, Maria, 136
Hof, Sarah, 146, 153, 156
Hoff, Elizabeth, 232, 237, 246, 250, 253
Hannah, 221
Hofman, Sarah, 275
Hogaling, Ephraim, 199
Jonathan, 199
Hogdeling, Jonathan, 171, 172
Petrus, 172
Saferyn, 172
Hoghdeling, Joseph Brass, 172
Sara, 172
Hoghtaling, Grietie, 194
Jonathan, 194
Simeon, 194
Hoghteling, Grietie, 192
Jonathan, 192
Sarah, 183
Simeon, 192
Hogtaling, Ledy, 226
Hogtelin, Abraham, 213
Peter, 213
Hogteling, Abraham, 223, 226
Caty, 223
Doritea, 205
Elizabeth, 211
Jacob, 226
Jonatan, 205
Lena, 205
Petrus, 187
Sarah, 223
Wilhelmus, 226
Hoksen, Cathrina, 97
Elizabeth, 97
Holden, Mary, 278

Holden, Philip, 280
Hollingshead, Stroud J., 279
Hommel, Abram, 148
Brient, 148
Honterberg, ——, 92
Jacob, 92
Marjory, 92
Hoogeling, Maria, 141
Hooghdeylen, Johannes, 104
Jonathan, 104
Hooghteeling, Catharina, 119, 135, 267
Cathrina, 269
Jacob, 119
Jonathan, 114, 158
Maria, 106
Maritje, 130
Sara, 109, 119
Hooghteling, Gertruy,178
Sarah, 178
Hooghteiling, Catharina, 130
Hoogtaling, Cornelius Brink, 216
John Cortright, 218
Jurian, 274
Maria, 274
Petrus, 273
Wm., 218
William, 216
Hoogteelen, Abraham,216
Ledy, 216
Hoogteeling, Johannes, 100, 106, 114
Johannis, 158
Josaphat, 223
Leenty, 148
Maritje, 158
Petrus, 100, 148, 165
Samuel, 223
Sarah, 265
Wilhelmus, 165, 223
Hoogteting, Abraham,161
Antje, 165
Jonathan, 165
Lena, 187
Maragriet, 273
Peter, 179
Petrus, 161
Sarah, 185
Hoogtelink, Jonathan, 162
Lena, 162
Hoorbeek, Elisabeth Ennes, 160
Jacobus, 160
Hoorenbeek, Rachel, 98
Hoornbeck, Benjn., 171, 176
Blandina, 214
Elizabeth, 232
Evert, 113, 182, 273

Hoornbeck, Gentje, 273
Helena, 203
Jacob, 168, 182
Jacobus, 176, 273
Jacos, 176
Janneke, 174
Jimentje, 274
Joseph, 171, 182, 273
Lydia, 182
Magdalana, 183
Maregreet, 171
Maria, 181, 274
Mary, 175
Rachel, 105
Sara, 129
Sarah, 277
Sovereiyn, 214
Hoornbeeck, Abraham, 178
Abram Hooghteeling, 122
Annatjen, 97
Elisabeth, 110
Evert, 106, 107, 110,122, 178
Jacob, 128
Jannetje, 122
Joost, 97
Judic, 97
Lena, 110, 163
Ludwig, 107
Lydia, 106
Margriet, 271
Maria, 107, 126
Maritje, 114
Sara, 97
Hoornbeek, Abram Van Aken, 118
Elisabeth, 154, 238
Evert, 165, 168
Jacob, 154
Jacobus, 147
Lena, 162
Lidia, 162
Lourance, 210
Lydia, 147, 159, 239
Maragriet, 147
Margaret, 182
Margrietje, 118
Maritje, 104
Sara, 126, 168
Sarah, 160, 174
Tobias, 210
Hoorrenbeeck, Maretje, 106
Hoovenbeck, Ledy, 243
Hoover, Hannah, 23
Hopkins, Eleanor, 242
Lena, 277
Lenah, 253
Lidia, 277
Horbeker, Agnietje, 149

Horenbeck, Elizabeth, 203, 278
Evert, 206
Evert, Jr., 278
Greitie, 206
Grete, 170
Jacob, 278
Sovereign, 278
Tobyas, 203
Horenbeek, Benjamin,245
Evert, 158
Jacob, 245
John, 221
Lena, 158
Lydia, 274
Margriet, 134
Maria, 156
Marretje, 100
Rachel, 102
Sara, 101
Soverins, 221
Horenbek, Benjamin, 101
Evert, 101
Horlikke, Horbekke, Angenetje, 152
Horlingen, I. M., Rev., 212
Hornbak, Benjamin, 148
Lena, 148
Hornbeck, Belinda,91
Bellinda, 79, 86
Benj., 172
Cornelius, 255, 279
Daniel, 220
Eliza, 255
Evert, 66, 220
Jacob, 66
Jacobus, 176
Jenny, 66
Joseph, 218
Ledia, 277
Lena, 176
Magdalen, 218
Margaret, 164
Maria, 171
Sarah, 218
Soverine, 218
Hornbeek, Bellinda, 82
Benjamin, 167
Cobus, 148
Elena, 167
Jacob, 66
Jannetje, 158
Joseph, 148
Ledia, 167
Lena, 155
Lydia, 148
Magdalen, 222
Mareyte, 167
Maria, 148, 158
Priscilla, 66
Sara, 167
Sarah, 155

Hornbek, Cobus, 151
Grietje, 151
Lydia, 151, 157
Hornebeck, Evert, 49
Leah, 49
Horton, Bethiah, 184
Henry, 184
James, 264, 280
Marjery, 264
Sarah, 184
William Denton, 264
Houser, Caty, 30
Houwel, Louwrenia, 3
Richard, 3
Houwy, John, 4
Hove, Emmanuel, 29
Hannah, 29
Hovenbeck, Benjamin, 241
James, 241
Hover, Aariantie Schoonmaker, 51
Anny, 201
Antje, 20
Benjamin Van Garden, 49
Catharin, 25
Catharina, 19, 94
Catrina, 17, 20, 22, 25, 31
Caty, 30
Cornelia, 17
Elesabet, 26
Elisabeth, 21, 35, 37, 39
Elizabeth Nice, 72
Elizebeth, 31
Emmanuel, 20
Gilbert, 87
Hanna, 20
Hannah, 28
Henderick, 17, 20, 34
Henry, 20, 25, 30
Jane, 66
Jenny, 196
John, 21
John Linderman, 87
Lisabeth, 19
Lodeweyk, 26
Lodewick, 52
Lodewyck, 34
Lodewyk, 31, 162
Mannuel, 24
Manual, 20, 28, 31
Mary, 66
Peter, 51, 66, 69, 72
Petrus, 26
Salomon, 52, 162
Samuel, 20, 21, 30, 38
Sara, 28
Sarah, 38
Solomon, 49
Susan, 87
Susannah, 24, 69, 70

Howel, Betchcy, 52
  Caty, 249
  Femitje, 156
  Jeny Quick, 244
  Laetitia, 5
  Peter Q., 244, 249
  Petrus, 152
  Richard, 5
  Sarah, 149
  William, 152, 156
Howey, Daniel, 236
Howke, Blandina, 201
  William, 201
Howy, Abraham, 61
  Catharine, 69
  Charaty, 74
  Charity, 55, 61, 64, 65
  Daniel Van Gorden, 65
  James Nyce, 74
  John, 69
  Jonathan Van Gorden, 64
  Mariah, 69
  Mary, 69
  Peter, 69
  Robart, 55
  Robert, 61, 64, 65, 74
  William, 55
Huber, Catharina, 12
Joh. Mich., 12
Johannes, 12
Juliana, 127
Maria Juliana, 5, 111, 115, 129
Huberin, Maria Juliana, 120
Huff, Elizabeth, 242
  Jemima, 257
Hull, Joseph, xx
Hunt (Kint), Jeruche, 147
Hydelberk, Christian, 45
  William, 45
Hydt, Gerretje, 119, 123
Hyndshaw, Elisabeth, 14
  James, xiii, xiv
  James B., xxix
  Sarah, 26
Hyne, Adam, 29
  Eve, 29
  Beniaman, 29
Hynshaw, Hannah, 40
Hyse, Anna, 177, 179

I

Ilenberger, Mary, 80
Immens, Alexander, 22
  Ann, 26
  Daniel, 22
Imson, Benjamin, 84
  Elizabeth, 84
  Mary, 77, 83
Inglet, Elizabeth, 191, 193

Iveson, Jane, 258
  John, Rev., 258
  Sarah, 258
Ivory, Alexander, 132, 268, 271
Jacobus, 132

J

Jackson, Anny, 194
  Asa, 196
  Philip, 194, 196
Jacson, Anny, 192
  Philip, 192, 285
Jagerin, Maria Barbara, 7, 10
Jamison, David, iii
  Mary, 218
Janse, Margriet, 102, 105
Jansen, Lena, 6, 10
  Margriet, 98, 108, 110, 111, 114, 116, 126, 130, 163, 282
Janson, Margrit, 103, 104
Jayne, Elizabeth, 89
Jemes, Margrit, 32
Jillet, Esaba, 168
Jin, 261
Jinnings, Daniel, 90
  Hannah, 85
  John, 80, 85
  John, Jr., 90
  Mehaly Maria Van Auken, 80
Job, Joseph, 275
Johns, Hannah, 116
Johnson, Abram, 142
  Ann, 12
  Caty, 187
  Edward, 10-12
  Geertje, 147
  Hannah, 279
  Henderikkus, 146
  Hendrick, 142, 147
  Hendrik, 146
  Henry, 10
  Johannis Batton (Baltus), 159
  John, 278
  Lea, 142
  Maragrit, 140
  Margriet, 132
  Mary, 15, 94
  Peter, 20
  William, 20, 159
Johnst, Johanna, 134
Johson, Abram, 274
  Thomas H., 280
Jonas, Jonathan, 48
Jones, Anne, 155
  D. A., Rev., xix
  David A., Rev., xii, xviii, xix

Jones, David Adkin, xxviii
  Joseph Addison, xxx
  Edward, 50
  Hanna, 157
  Hannah, 157
  Isaac, 196
  Jonathan, 47, 50, 278
  Mary, 196
  Nancy, 48
  Nathan W., xxix
  Perregrin, 196
  Sevila, 47
  Sivilla, 48
  William, 157
Jongbloet, Claesje, 116, 119, 129
Jonkbloet, Klasje, 136
Joons, Hanna, 102, 119, 267
  Hannah, 117, 125
  Johanna, 126
  Moses, 102
  Saertje, 120
Jorner, David, 160
  Johannis, 160
Jory, Maria, 4

K

Kane, Mary, 125
Kanneda, Jacobus, 155
  John, 155
Karick, Elenor, 63, 70
  Jacob, 63
  Frederick, 63, 70
  Mariah, 70
Karmer, Lidia, 162
Kaser, Beniaman, 29
  Nancy, 29
Kaskey, Huldah, 244
  Martin, 244
  Sarah, 244
Kasky, Mary, 182
  Samuel, 182
Keally, John, 4
Keater, Leah, 159, 170
  Susanna, 161, 164
Keator, Elizabeth, 164
  Elisabeth Westbrook, 229
  Jannetje, 173
  July Anne, 229
  Leah, 168, 172, 179
  Peter, 229
  Susanna, 177, 180
Keen, Abraham, 72
  Elizabeth, 72
  Mary, 72, 131
Keesbrei, Christiaen, 93
Keersbi, Christiaen, 8, 127
  Heyltje, 127

Keeter, Cornelia, 17
Elisabeth, 147
George, 17
Jannetje, 158
Jannitje, 154
Lea, 154
Susanna, 158
Yannetje, 154
Kehrns, Catharine, 50
Leonhard, 50
Keiser, Christina, 101
Lea, 15
Kelder, Lidia, 169
Kellam, Lucy, 278
Kelleam, Jeptha, 184
Peter, 184
Kember, Mareytie, 136
Kemmel, Mareitje, 102
Maria, 108
Kenedy, John, 178
Thomas, 178
Kentner, Mary, 62
Kepser, Jacomyntje, 11
Kerker, Rebecca, 160
Kermer, Abraham, 11, 26, 98, 100, 102, 105, 111, 115, 167, 212
Abram, 14, 16, 125, 282
Agnietje, 18
Andres, 169
Angenitje, 115
Angonietje, 115
Angonitje, 163
Angontje, 105
Annatje, 16, 24, 93
Catrina, 17
Christiena, 16
Christina, 1, 3, 8, 11, 12, 14, 19, 22, 94
Cornelia, 2, 3, 5, 7, 14, 17, 94, 103, 110, 124, 125, 127, 132
Derrick, 1
Dirck, 3
Dirk, 8, 11
Elesabeth, 167
Eliesabet, 16
Elisabeth, 17, 27, 100, 134, 141
Elizabeth, 21, 25, 103, 165
Grietje, 3, 6, 8, 10, 13
Gysbert, 21
Hanna, 127
Hannatje, 25
Isaac, 33
Isak, 6
Jacob, 17
Jacobes, 169
Jacobus, 16, 102, 141, 146, 165
Jan, 7, 8, 12, 14, 17, 18, 21, 33, 124, 268

Kermer, John, 21
Lena, 165
Lidia, 17
Lisabeth, 3, 6, 8, 14, 124, 132
Lydia, 19, 21, 98, 273
Margriet, 26
Marritje, 163
Sara, 14, 112, 163
Sarah, 16, 18, 146
Silas, 212
Kerrick, John D., 90
Ketel, Dirk, 118
Keter, Elisabeth, 151
Jacobus, 163
Jannetje, 150
Jannitie, 143
Maria, 163
Susanna, 170
Kettel, Abram, 141, 143
Elisabeth, 166
Jeremias, 143
Joseph, 143
Lea, 138
Rachel, 141
Richard, 141
Schusanna, 272
Kettle, Abraham, 167
Abram, 148
Anne, 174
Blandina, 185
Catrina, 147, 150
Cattrina, 197
Cornelius, 183, 203
Daniel, 141
Derik, 154
Elisabeth, 145, 149
Elizabeth, 150
Esther, 232, 248
Jacob, 75, 167, 218
Jan, 148
Janneke, 167
Jeremie, 141
Jeremias, 149
Joseph, 190
Lea, 154
Leah, 171, 173
Margery, 203
Maria, 159, 167, 190
Marjory, 84
Mary, 75
Mary Halbert, 75
Marya, 173
Petrus, 149
Plonea, 167
Rachel, 154, 183
Ragel, 167
Samuel, 185, 195, 218, 285
Simeon, 195
Susanna, 197
Keuikendal, Peter, viii
Keukendal, P i e t ernella, 104

Keyser, Antje, 281
Arriaentje, 7
Jacomyntje, 8, 11, 15
Lea, 7, 8, 15
Keyzer, Abram, 13
Dirk, 13
Kittle, Abram, 152, 164
Belindy, 228
Betsy Van Auken, 227
Blandina, 227
Catharina, 159, 164
Cattrina, 278
Colomon, 228
Cornelius, 208
Daniel, 277
Easter, 253
Elizabeth, 164
Engeltie, 152
Ester, 238
Esther, 246, 255
Herman Rosekrans, 241
Jacob, 173, 197
Jeremiah, 159, 220
Jerremy, 164
Johanna, 164
John, 203
Jurrian, 164
Lea, 150, 159, 208
Marjory, 73
Mattheus, 203
Peter, 197, 220
Petrus, 203
Pheby, 203
Rachel, 280
Saml., 173
Samuel, 164, 193
Simeon, 193
Solomon, 227, 241
Susanna, 21, 169, 173
Kidder, Esther, 285
Kiersbi, Christiaen, 93, 123
Josua, 123
Killam, George, 203
Jepthah, 190, 198, 203
John, 190
Killan, Pheby, 198
Killgon, Anne, 220
Robert, 220
Killgore, Polly Melford, 216
Robert, 216
Killman, Arie, 20
Elisabeth, 20
Kimbel, Casparus, 120
Joris, 120
Lena, 120
Marya, 113
Petrus, 120
Kimbell, Marytje, 124
Kimber, Casparus, 107, 150
Helena, 150
Joris, 127, 131, 137, 267
Margaret, 184

Kimber, Margriet, 131
Maria, 107, 130
Maritje, 150
Marya, 131
Marytie, 135
Petrus, 107, 137
Samuel, 181
Sara, 127
Sarah, 181
Kimmel, Joris, 115
Lisabeth, 116
Marya, 116, 283
Kimmer, Casparus, 128
Lena, 128
Lisabeth, 128
King, Jacob Walker, 196
John, 196
John, Jr., 196
Mary, 196
Kinne, Antje, 25
Hannatje, 25
Kinny, Catharina, 22
Lourence, 22
Kinte, Jeremiah, 218
(Kyte), John, 218
Kintner, Elisabetha, 53
Johann Georg, 53
Mary, 57
Phillip, 65
Rudolp, 53
Rudolph, 65
Kiphart, Susanna, 35
Kite, Jacob, 225
John H., 215
Maria Dingman, 215
William, 225
Kithaline, Mary, 83
Kithcart, Susannah, 36
Kittel, Abraham, 134
Abram, 130, 144, 270
Apollonia, 130
Appolonia, 163
Catharina, 127, 135, 269, 283
Cathrina, 138
Catrina, 133
Dirk, 120, 283
Elisabeth, 122, 133
Jacob, 134, 163
Jeremias, 130, 132, 270
Johanna, 120
Lea, 128, 132, 135, 145, 168, 270
Lisabeth, 129, 268
Mosis, 144
Rachel, 91, 130
Richard, 129, 130, 230
Salomon, 230
Samuel, 164
Solomon, 230
Susanna, 133, 136, 144, 273

Klearwater, Geertje, 97
Klein, Conrad, 50
Elizabeth, 50
Margareth, 50
Klerk, Jeams, 138
Kleyn, Antje, 2, 3, 5, 8, 12
Catharina, 5, 8, 13
Cathrina, 15
Johannes, 8, 13
Kneicht, Susannah, 78
Koddebeck, Abraham, 97
Jacobus, 97, 110
Maria, 282
Maritje, 97
Koddebeek, Maritje, 97
Kodebek, Abram, 129
Willem, 137
Koetebek, Elsje, 98
Koeper, Henne, 34
Koettebeck, Dina, 102
Elsje, 102
Naomi, 102
Koettebek, Benjamin, 101
Elsje, 101, 102
Jacobus, 100
Lena, 101
Mareitje, 98, 100, 102
Naomi, 101
Willem, 101
Kole, Cornelia, 166
Elsabeth, 167
Kool, Abraham, 104
Andries, 16
Benjamin, 24
Catharina, 24
Catrinte, 272
Catryntie, 135
Catryntje, 138
Cornelia, 138, 165
David, 138
Hanna, 26
Harmanus, 161
Jannetje Lena, 16
Johannes, 104
Josias, 138
Maria, 161
Marrigrita, 272
Rachel, 24
Samuel, 155
Sara, 133
Sarah, 24, 136, 161, 176
Wilhelmus, 161
Koole, Beulah, 154
Jonathan, 154
William, 154
Kortrecht, Abraham, 2, 10, 103, 107
Abram, 6, 13, 137
Abram P., 11
Abram Van Kampen, 8
Anna, 97
Annatje, 8, 10, 13, 93
Apolonia, 100

Kortrecht, Apolonie, 99
Aplony, 117, 122
Apollonia, 107, 109, 111, 114, 117, 118, 120, 123, 125, 126, 281
Antoni, 13
Arie, 99, 109, 111, 112, 117, 118, 281
Bastaien, 117
Bastiaen, 109, 110, 112, 114, 125, 130
Bastian, 100, 109, 114
Benjamin, 13
Catharina, 2, 3, 5, 6, 8, 10, 13, 114, 265
Catharine, 94
Cathrina, 11, 163
Catriena, 15
Catryntie, 275
Christina Elisabetha, 14
Cornelia, 8
Cornelis, 5, 98, 104, 114, 266, 269, 281
Cornelis Cool, 104
Cornelis H., 6, 10, 93
Cornelis Hendr., 7
Daniel, 8, 10, 12, 15, 16, 108
Daniel, Jr., 94
Elias, 98, 137
Eliesabeth, 275
Elisa, 4
Elisabeth, 10, 125, 269
Elizabeth, 129
Femmetje, 112
Geertje, 116
Gerretje, 116
Hannes, 2, 4
Hendrich, 129
Hendrick, viii, 2, 4, 7, 8, 11, 15, 124, 126, 130, 281
Hendrick Corn., 5, 7, 8
Hendrick Cornelise, 5, 6, 110
Hendrick H., 6, 112, 118, 128
Hendrick Hendrickson, 103
Hendrick J., 115, 116
Hendrick W., 163
Hendrik, 163
Henrick Henrickse, 99, 109
Henrick Janse, 100
Hester, 12
Jacob, 117
Jacobus, 6
Jannetje, 8, 15
Jenneke, 4, 124, 275
Josias, 104, 114
Johannes, 2, 3, 8, 10, 14, 99, 125, 265

Kortrecht, John, 99, 132, 163
Jonas, 112
Lea, 99, 130
Lena, 8, 104, 109
Levi, 16
Lidia, 103, 164
Lisabeth, 125
Lydia, 99, 112, 131, 163
Margriet, 163
Maria, 93, 100
Marya, 126, 268
Moses, 109
Petrus, 123, 126, 127, 129, 131, 163, 270
Rachel, 3, 4, 5, 8, 10, 14, 109
Salomon, 130
Samuel, 2, 109, 118
Sara, 2, 3, 5-7, 11, 14, 15, 98, 105, 109, 115, 118
Sarah, 15
Sebastian, 104
Susannetje, 110
Sylvester Symon, 116
Tjaetje, 6, 7, 109, 266
Tjatje, 4, 5, 93
Willem, 98, 108, 110, 111, 114, 116, 281, 282
William, viii, 104
Wm., 163
Kortrect, Ragel, 169
Kortreckt, Hendrick J., 117
Kortright, Daniel, 223
Elizabeth, 160, 197, 221
Hendreck W., 167
Johannes, 197
Simeon, 223
Kortreght, Elias, 165
Elisabeth, 179
Elizabeth, 33, 161
Esther, 26
Hendrick W., 160
Hendrik, 33
Jacob, 161
Jacobus, 26
Jenneke, 161
Josias, 165, 179, 180
Lidia, 165
Thomas, 26
Kortregt, Antje, 160
Apollonia, 104
Arie, 103, 105
Bastian, 102, 133, 134
Benjamin, 25
Catharina, 105
Catryntje, 134
Christoffel, 102
Daniel, 15, 24, 105, 140
Elisabeth, 103, 134, 140
Eliza, 26
Elizabeth, 161, 165

Kortregt, Eva, 26
Gerretje, 162
Helena, 102
Hendrik, 138
Henrich, 102, 105
Henrich, Jr., 101
Henrich Henrichse, 102
Henrick Cornelius, 102
Hester, 24
Jacob, 161, 166
Jan, 134
Johannes, 25, 102
Johannis, 26
Jonas, 161
Josias, 165
Laurent, 102
Lea, 135, 138
Leah, 160
Levi, 160
Leya, 272
Lidia, 160-162
Lisabeth, 138
Margrita, 138
Maria, 134
Moses, 15, 160
Petrus, 160
Rachel, 102, 161
Ragel, 133
Salomon, 134, 271
Sara, 101
Susanna, 162
Willem, 102, 105
William, 26, 103
William Ennest, 102
Kosenkranz, Lena, 6
Koster, Jacob, 21
William, 21
Kottebek, Abraham, 99
Noemi, 99
Willem, 99
Kotregt, Janneke, 136
Petrus, 136
Krandal, Nelly, 202
Krass, Jacob, 276
Kriss, Christian, 29
Mary, 29
Kroeg, Andries, 137
Lisabeth, 137
Krom, Annatje, 106, 161
Benoni, 140
Cornelis, 99, 106, 107, 111, 113
Cornelius, 17, 143
Debora, 134, 136, 140, 145
Debra, 271
Elisabeth, 111
Gonda, 118, 274
Henrick, 99
Johannes, 113
Lydia, 99, 135, 140, 145, 151
Maria, 107, 113

Krom, Rebeca, 274
Rebecca, 118, 127
William, 135, 143
Kuddeback, Catharine, 242
Kuddebak, Benjamin, 155
Jeryna (Jesysus), 155
Kuddebeck, Abram, 112, 114
Dina, 111, 114, 116
Elsie, 135
Elsje, 115
Hendricus, 111
Jacobus, 111, 267
Noemi, 114
Samuel, 245
Willem, 111
William, 245
Kuddebeek, Jacob, 236
Jakemeyntje, 236
Kuddebek, Abram, 151
Abram, Jr., 155
Benjamin, 152
Hester, 155
Jacobus, 151
Lena, 122
Sarah, 155
Kudebek, Abraham, 138
Jakemyntje, 138
Willem, 138
Kuikendaal, Salomon, 133
Kuikendal, Annatje, 139
Benjamin, 155
Catrina, 139, 140, 144, 157, 284
Catryntje, 99
Caty, 217
Cornelia, 146
Daniel, 103, 146, 152, 155
Elisabeth, 146, 152, 157
Elizabeth, 152
Emanuel, 157
Femetje, 143, 146
Femmetje, 157
Henderikkus, 139
Henderikus, 149
Henrich, 99
Henrick, 99, 139, 146
Hendrickus, 157
Hendrik, 146, 152, 157
Hendrikkus, 146, 157
Jacob, 98, 101, 149
Jacobus, 276
Johannes, 105
Jonathan, 157
Joseph, 100, 149
——ka, 107
Lea, 150
Lieur, 100
Marretje, 101
Martinus, 139, 147, 276, 284
Mosis (Moris), 149

Kuikendal, Nelletje, 101
Peter, 140
Pieter, 98, 101, 135, 147, 150
Salomon, 134, 141, 144
Salomon, Jr., 276
Sara, 99, 144
Sarah, 141, 151, 157
Soloman, 151
Solomon, x
Tatje, 139
William, 143, 146, 149, 157
Kunbell, Jacob, 278
Kuttebeck, Dina, 108
Jacobus, 108
Maria, 108
Naemi, 282
Roelof Elten, 109
Willem, 109
Kuttenbeck, Abraham, 106
William, 106
Kuychendal, Maria, 130
Daniel, 130
Kuyckendal, Abram, 4
Antje, 1
Catharina, 110
Daniel, 107, 109
Dina, 2, 3
Jacob, 97
Jacobus, 2, 4, 97
Johannes, 2, 108, 110
Lisabeth, 119, 128
Luer, 2
Nellie, 125
Nelly, 108
Pieter, 107, 119, 265
Petrus, 127
Salomon, 110, 115, 127, 283
Sara, 2, 128
Kuykendaal, Martinus, 138
Pieter, 283
Kuykendael, Cornelis, 97
Johannes, 97
Mattheus, 98
Petrus, 98
Kuykendal, Annatje, 123
Benjamin, 6, 118
Catrina, 139, 142
Catryntie, 135
Christina, 6
Christyntje, 138
Cornelis, 113
Daniel, 113, 119, 125, 130, 135, 267
Dina, 98
Elisabeth, 112, 123, 159
Famety, 181
Hendrick, 107, 108, 113, 115, 118, 123, 131

Kuykendal, Hendricus, 107, 113
Hermanus, 138
Jacob, 6, 98, 115, 123
Jacobus, 6, 122
Johannes, 121, 122, 123, 129, 265
Josias, 131
Lisabeth, 113, 115, 120, 126, 128, 129, 133, 283
Lizabeth, 267
Lydia, 121
Margriet, 103, 137
Maritje, 93, 106
Martynes, 135
Martynus, 272
Marya, 113
Nelli, 112, 118
Pieter, 109, 114, 119, 130, 138
Pieternella, 113
Petrus, 119, 124, 133, 138, 139, 269
Petrus, Jr., 159
Salomon, 112, 113, 115, 136, 137, 268, 282
Samuel, 125
Sara, 110
Solomon, 181
Willem, 108
William, 277
Kuykendall, Elias, 277
Kykendall, Catherine, 224
Kuyte, Mr., xvi
Kyte, Anna, 170
Anny, 278
Elisabeth Hoornbeek, 154
Elizabeth, 229
Esther, 220
Jacob, 227-229
Jacob Hoornbeeck, 168
Johannes Hardenbergh, 159
John, xviii, 220, 278
Lea, 151
Peter, 227
Rachel, 172, 216, 220
Thomas, v, vii, ix, 151, 154, 159, 168, 170, 172, 179, 228

L

Laan, Abram, 273
Labah, Daniel, 90
Philip Garis, 90
Labar, Henry M., xxii
Jannet, 279
Lady, Jan, 133
Laen, Abram, 163
Cathrina, 163
Elisabeth, 163

Lake, George Nyce, 70
Thomas, 70
Lakkerey, Robert, 23
William, 23
Lamberd, Sarah, 277
Lambert, Alphred, 246
Alpheus, 246
Catherine, 253
Daniel, 248
Elisabeth, 153
George, 238
George T., 280
James Newkirk, 232
John, 255
Lewis, 279
Sala, 234
Samuel, 232, 238, 246, 248, 253, 255
Sarah, 232, 242
Lambert, Havelent, John, 153
Lance, Susannah, 75
Lane, Abraham, 36
Anny, 199, 203, 276
Bethia, 173
Effy, 159
Efje, 159
Elisabeth, 177
Ezechiel, 184
Fanny, 187, 189, 199
George, 198
Gilbert, xxviii
Henderick, 36
James, 198
Lucy, 277
Majory, 184
Melesen, 186
Phene, 182
Salomon, 186, 284
Solomon, 173, 177, 187, 189, 284
Susanna, 53
Susannah, 49
Langevelt, Hannah, 172
Lisabeth, 169
Lase, Mary, 254
Latier, Barnardus, 145
Cleophas, 145, 149, 154, 183
Elisabeth, 154
Lisabeth, 137, 270
Petrus, 154
Wilhelmus, 149
Lattimore, Charles, 91
George Washington, 91
Hannah Mariah, 91
Hugh, 90, 91
John, 63, 65, 75, 83
John Craig, 83
Joseph Cortright, 91
Leah, 65
Mary, 65

Lattimore, Polly, 63
Solomon Van Etten, 75
William, 91
Layton, Abigail, 63
Abraham Brokaw, 54
Henry Schoonhoven, 58
Judith, 54
Lewis, 54, 58, 65
Peter Van Neste, 65
Lebar, Daniel, 275
Sofya, 276
Lee, Hannis, 16
Leentie, 17
Willem, 17
William, 16
Leed, Mally, 120
Lenes, Joseph, 166
Wilhelmus, 166
Lesch, Catharine, 50
John, 50
John Philip, 50
Lester, Susanna, 94
Letts, John, 48
Moses, 48
Leutie, Elizabeth, 195
John, 195
Josiah, 195
Rossanah, 195
William, 195
Lewis, Mary, 233
Leydi, Jacobus, 135
Johannes, 135
Leydy, John, 137
Lichert, John Jurry, 163
Margaret, 163
Lieshe, —, 256
Liker, Maregrita, 167
Linderman, Garret Brodhead, 92
Hannah, 83
John J., 83, 92
Line, Adriaan, 200
Caty, 200
Conrad, 200
Maritie, 200
Lineden, Willemtje, 134
Lions, Caty, 191, 193
Litch, David, 275
John, 52
Lits, Caty, 60
Jacob, 60
John, 60
Mary Anne, 60
William, 60
Littier, Clefus, 168
Josias, 168
Little, Caty, 181
Cornelius, 202
Esther, 244
Francis, 171, 176, 181
Henry, 232, 280
Jannekie, 176
Jene, 235

Little, Levi, 248
Peggy, 244
Salomon, 202
William, 171, 232, 235, 244, 248
Litts, Mary Anne, 86
Moses, 86
Livengood, Effy, 79
Susannah, 70, 76
Livingood, Catharine, 85
Eve, 76
Lockerby, Anda, 48
Benjamin, 39
John, 57
Mary, 48
Robert, 34, 37, 39, 53
Samuel, 36
William, 53, 57
Wm., 48
Loder, Anna, 65
Anny Culver, 226
Elisha Mapes, 229
Gesse, 230
Jepthah, 66
Jesse, 229
Joh., 65
John, 66, 230
John Worth, 230
Matilda, 230
Phebe, 227
Polly, 87
Sally, 70
Susannah, 70, 230
William, 226, 227, 230
Londi, Mary, 136
Longerfeld, Hanna, 165
Longevelt, Elisabeth, 175
Longstreet, Andrew, 212
Christopher, 212, 216
Elizabeth, 230
Lonsbery, John, 189
Looder, Elizabeth, 223
William, 223
Look, Alida, 200
Lot, Grietje, 155
Mary, 184
Peter, 155
Petrus, 142
Sarah, 142
Lote, Peter, 163
Sara, 163
Lott, Anna, 233
Anny, 277
Jeny, 208
Mary, 190, 198, 203
Petrus, 160
Louden, J. W., xxx
Lounsberry, John, 285
Louw, Abraham, 102, 108
Abram, 111, 114, 116
Jacobus, 11
Jannetje, 102, 160
Johanna, 125

Louw, John, 278
Margaret, 160
Margriet, 116
Noemi, 114
Rachel, 267
Sara, 111
Love, Elizabeth, 201
Hester, 7, 24, 26
James, 10, 266, 268
James Henderse, 7
Susanna, 10, 191, 193, 195
Susannah, 24
Low, Catrina, 16
Caty, 217
Elisabeth, 211
Grietje, 155, 164
Jacob, 16
Jannetie, 153
Jannetje, 273
Jeremia Van Demerck, 213
John, 211, 213
John C., 217
Maregreta, 169
Naomi, 181, 274
Naomie, 153
Noemmy, 169
Sara, 169
Sarah, 170
Lowe, Jannetje, 21
Lowis (Louw), Maragret, 186
Lowrie, Mary, 155
Luckinbill, George Albert, xxx
Lukens, J., i
James, i
John, i, ii
Lundy, Mary, 122, 126, 131
Luths, George, 277
Lya, 37
Lyde, Johannes, 143
John, 272
Maragriet, 143
Lydi, Henderikkus, 140
Johannis, 140
Lydie, Benjamin, 154
John, 154
Lydye, Jacob, 148
John, 148
Lyons, Catharine, 36

M

Mabe, Abraham, 30
John, 30
Maccabe, Polly, 221
Mack, John, 55
Lanah, 86
Lena Van Auke, 55
Lenah, 88
Margareth, 55

Mackensie, Thomas H.,
  xxix
Macklinnin, William, 271
Maddag, Ledy, 226
Magee, Mary, 217
Magh, Mary, 38
Mahon, Catherine, 25
Majerin, Elisabeth, 136
Man, Barbara, 88
  Barbary, 90
  Catharine, 82
  Caty, 70
  Elizabeth, 71
  Peter, 72
  Susannah, 72
Mancius, xxiv
  Dom, xxiv
  Rev., xxv
  Georg Wilhelm, iv
  George Wilhelmus, iii,
    xxvii
  George Wilhelmus,
    Rev., iv
  G. W. Dom., 98, 134
  G. W., Rev., xxiii
Manknigteside, Antje, 19
Mann, Barbary, 71
  Elizabeth, 81, 85
Manrow, Stephen, 201
  William, 201
Manzius, G. W., Do., 106,
  107
Mapes, Benoni, 244
  Catharine, 76
  Catherine, 240
  Eleasor, 78
  Elisha, 76, 86, 90
  George, 90
  Jane, 68, 71
  Lanah, 229
  Lenah, 230
  Lewis, 240, 244
  Mary, 78
  Philip, 86
  William, 277
Maps, Anny, 243
  Bennoney, 247
  Benony, 243
  Elizabeth, 247
March, Mary, 29
  Phebe, 51
Marenus, David, 176
Maring, George, 87
  Margaret, 87
Marrell, Patience, 206
Marsh, Jenny, 49
  Margaret, 49
  Mary, 31
  Simeon, 49
  Temperance, 213
Marth, Tempy, 276
Marven, Cornelia, 35
  Maria, 35

Marvin, Betsseb, 57
  Caty, 221
  Daniel, 20
  Henry, 51, 57, 221
  Rachel, 20, 51
Mash, Temperance, 46,72
Mason, Frank E., xxx
Masten, Elizabeth, 33
Masterson, Leah, 174
  Maria, 32, 185, 192, 194,
    201, 205
  Rebekah, 177
  Uriah, 174
Martesin, Maria, 31
Matanye, Rebekah, 36
Maticks, Elizabeth, 184
Mattanje, Joseph, 158
  Maria, 158
  Rebecca, 158
Mattoks, Catrina, 153
  Samuel, 153
Maul, Dievertje, 108, 112,
    118, 120, 124, 130, 281
  Divertje, 100, 101, 105
  Johannes, 108
  Lisabeth, 108
Maus, Elizabeth, 41
Mavin, Catharina, 24
  Daniel, 24
Maxfield, Antony, 1
  Maria, 1
McAbey (Cahey), Polly,
  225
McCaby, Hannah, 228
  Jackemyntie, 214
  Jackmyntie, 214
  Mary, 228
  Sarah, 213
McCane, John, 74, 75
  Sally Anne, 74
  Sharlotte, 75
McCann, Mary, 147
McCary, Jacamyntie, 210
McCarty, James, 129
  Maria, 150
  Philip, 129
McCartery, James, 110
McCartey, Elizabeth, 164
  John, 161, 164
  Necholaas, 161
McCarty, Abraham, 184
  Cornelius Van Etten, 87
  Daniel, 87
  Frederic, 78, 87
  Gideon, 78
  Jacob Van Auken, 80
  James, 78, 111, 116, 120,
    125, 169, 177, 266
  James, Jr., 80
  John, 78, 120, 170, 177,
    180, 184, 220
  Josephat, 180
  Josephus, 230, 231

McCarty, Lea, 217
  Lisabeth, 125
  Maria, 116, 230, 231, 273
  Mary, 81, 87, 172, 175
  Nelson, 78
  Nicholas, 217, 220
  Philip, 78, 276
  Philip, Jr., 87
  Sara, 269
  Willem, 111
  Willim, 170
  Wm., 177
McCavy, Hannah, 222,226
  Mary, 215
M. Charty, Elizabeth, 160
  William, 160
McCharty, Maria, 160
McClean, Alexander, 149
  Catrine, 152
  John, 149
  Robert, 149
  William, 152
McCoemac, Francis, 217
  Sary, 217
McCracken, Susanna, 36
McDonald, Jane, 280
McDool, Sarah, 192, 194,
  196
M'Gee, Francis, 129
  Mary, 129
McGee, Francis, 162
  Mary, 162, 165, 172, 179,
    203, 269, 285
McGomley, Debora, 14
McGomly, Nathan, 14
McGumly, Nathan, 13
McGuym, Alexander, 156
M'Hollen, Margriet, 4
McIntosh, Elizabeth, 206
McKaby, Sarah, 217
McKady, Mary, 218
McKarter, Mariea, 169
McKater, James, 139
  Maria, 139
McKavey, Sarah, 223
McKenzee, Daniel, 206
  Mary, 206
McLaren, Rev. Dr., xix
McMichel, Elsje, 11
  John, 11
McMickel, Annatje, 3
  John, 3
McQueen, Elk, 152
  Mary, 152
McSweeny, Daniel, 170,
  175, 182
  John, 175
  Rachel, 182
  Timothy, 170
McWilliam, Alexander,
  xxix
Mead, Christian, 186
  Leuwis, 186

Mead, Levina, 186
Mebe, Johannes, 28
 John, 28
Mebie, Johan, 26
 Marya, 26
Meckentesh, Hester, 127
 Jacobus, 127
Meclean, Elsje, 144
Medack, Elenor, 240
 Cornelius, Jr., 240
Medag, Elesabeth, 176
 Ragel, 167
Meddag, Catrina, 275
 Chatrein, 165
 Cornelius, 244, 277
 Elshe, 247,
 Gideyoen, 165
 Leenty, 241
 Levi, 278
 Leya, 271
 Rachel, 278
 Solomon, 247
 Solomon V., 244
Meddagh, Cornelius, 235
 Jannyte, 166
 Maria, 235
Medool, Jenny, 2
Meed, Daniel Burril, 202
 Nathanael, 277
 Nathaniel, 202
Megeaw, Ellenor, 33
 Margaret, 33
 Thomas, 33
Meguarde, James, 136
Meir, Bastean, 163
 Petrus Wilhelmus, 163
Mekkentash, Heiltje, 133
 Hester, 133
Meller, James, 193
 Semeon, 193
Mennes, Lisabeth, 12
Merckel, Johannes, 93, 115
 Lisabeth, 11
Merit, Charity, 90
Merkel, Hannes, 4
Merring, Jacob, 73
 John, 73
Mervin, Daniel, 22
 Hendrikkus Schoonhoven, 22
Meselis, Annatie, 28
Meser, James Gunsaules, 89
 John, 89
Metex, Migel, 166
 Samuel, 166
Metler, Elshe, 188
Metticks, Samuel, 164
Mey, Elisabeth, 129
 Lisabeth, 108, 110, 111, 116, 266
Meyer, Andrew J., xxviii
 Lisabeth, 120, 125

Meyers, Christian, 215
Michael, Anna, 75, 79, 86, 87
 Georg, 53
Michaels, Anne, 70
Midag, Martines, 166
Middach, Elias, 135
 Eliza, 136
 Hannah, 136
 Jannetie, 136
Middaeg, Regel, 166
Middag, Aard, 100, 145
 Abraham, 133
 Abram, 94, 274
 Aert, 273
 Alida, 133, 137, 140, 144, 150
 Anna, 103
 Annatie, 151
 Arianntje, 145
 Ariantje, 145
 Benjamin, 149
 Blandina, 198
 Casparus, 139, 276
 Catrina, 132, 136, 140, 144, 150, 158
 Catrine, 198
 Catharina, 159, 160
 Catharine, 248
 Cathrina, 184
 Chatreina, 165
 Christina, 133, 137, 140, 145, 151
 Cornelius, 154, 243, 248, 250
 Cornelius, Jr., 255
 Corns., Jr., 247
 Danel, 167
 Daniel, 145, 191, 194, 274
 Debora, 152
 Deborah, 154
 Dorethea, 158
 Doritia, 205
 Dorothea, 165, 199
 Dortea, 192, 194
 Edmund, 250
 Elias, 247
 Elisa, 139, 150, 154, 272
 Eliza, 135
 Elizabeth, 145
 Elpina, 150
 Emanuel, 133
 Ephraim, 99, 133, 142, 151, 161, 284
 Femetje, 140, 146
 Gedevie, 273
 Gideon, 150, 162
 Grietie, 187
 Hannah, 255
 Helena, 150
 Isaac, 140
 Jacob, 99, 145, 243

Middag, Jacobus, 132, 142
 Jan, 134, 138, 149, 161
 Jannetie, 184
 Jannetje, 134, 149
 Jennetje, 100
 Jonathan, 149
 Joris (Jan), 146
 Lea, 135
 Lena, 158
 Levi, 167
 Lidea, 278
 Lidia, 221
 Lydia, 250
 Maragrieta, 275
 Margaret, 197, 202, 230
 Maria, 204
 Martinus, 145, 149, 150
 Mary, 250, 251
 Peter, 152
 Petrus, 135, 142, 154
 Rachel, 150, 162
 Saferyn, 172
 Salomon, 160
 Samuel, 158, 187
 Sarah, 142, 146, 152, 154
 Seeletje, 138
 Seletta, 170
 Solomon, 250
 Tunis, 135
 William, 248
Middagh, Abraham, 97, 104, 113, 138
 Abraham Van Aken, 181
 Abram, 108, 112, 113, 119, 128, 265
 Aert, 104, 109, 110, 115, 118, 132, 281
 Alida, 130
 Alidagh, 283
 Benjamin, 122
 Blandina, 125
 Bostean (Roslean), 176
 Brechie, 123
 Bregje, 98
 Cate, 235
 Catharina, 125
 Catherine, 244, 262
 Cathrina, 172, 174
 Cathrina Garetje, 172
 Caty, 232
 Charity, 230, 231
 Charity D., 244
 Christina, 125, 129, 268
 Cornelis, 129, 269
 Cornelius, 181, 230, 231, 236, 262
 Daniel, 108
 Dorothea, 119, 162
 Dorothy, 171, 172
 Eli, 263
 Elias, 174, 181, 197
 Elias, Jr., 171

Middagh, Elisa, 129
  Elisabeth, 110, 171
  Engeltje, 230, 231
  Fametie, 183
  Ganehje, 235
  Gideon, 110, 180
  Hanna, 112, 122
  Hannah, 106
  Helena, 232
  Hendrick C., 172
  Hendrick Cor., 174
  Hendrik Kortrecht, 129
  Henry C., 244
  Isaac, 264, 267
  Jacob, 110, 128
  Jacobus, 110, 124, 125, 128, 129, 268, 283
  James Nelson, 261
  Jan, 97, 269
  Jane, 244
  Janetje, 177
  Jannetje, 137, 163
  John, 278, 279
  John W., 279
  Jonathan, 176
  Jsak, 124
  Lea, 137
  Lena, 181, 236
  Levi, 261
  Lydia, 236
  Malletje, 97
  Maregreet, 181
  Margaret, 244, 261, 262
  Margriet, 269
  Margrietje, 134
  Maria, 197
  Martinus, 104
  Martynus, 115
  Moses, 128
  Rachel, 118, 180
  Robert, 230, 231
  Sally, 263
  Salomon, 113
  Samuel, 104, 113, 171
  Seletta, 173
  Solomon, 171
  Souverign, 138
  Thatje, 236
  Wilhelmus, 174
  William, 244
  William Cortreght, 180
Middaugh, Catherine, 258
  Caty Jane, 259
  Charity, 255
  Cornelius, 258
  Cynata, 258
  Elizabeth, 74, 280
  Jane, 258
  John W., 259
  Levi, 258
  Levy, 74
  Marggret, 258
  Mariah, 75

Middaugh, Sally, 259
Miels, Jackkemintie, 28
  Jacobus, 28
Miers, Bastian, 169
  Jacob, 201
  Josias, 201
Migdool, Elisabeth, 3
  John, 3
Miler, Rob., 29
  Robert, 29
Miller, Ann, 91
  Anna, 87, 91
  Betsey, 66
  Catharine, 81, 85, 88
  Elizabeth, 69, 74
  Jacob, 79, 81, 89
  James, 191
  Jemimy, 36
  Manuel, 89
  Margaret, 81, 82, 84, 88, 196
  Mariah, 89, 91
  Martha, 23, 29
  Mary, 71, 76
  Matta, 27
  Philip, 81
  Samuel Gunsaules, 79
  Simeon, 191
Millett, Joseph, xxviii
Mills, Dr., xi-xiii
  Samuel W., xxviii
  S. W., Rev., xi, xx, xxii
Miner, Christina, 39
  John, 39
  Sarah, 39
Minor, Christina, 37
Mires, Abijah, 67
  Christian, 69
  Jonathan, 67
Mixter, Catharine Scoanover, 55
  Isaac, 55
  Isaiah, 51
  Mary, 51
Mixture, Isaiah, 53
  John, 53
Mollen, Antje, 19
  Benjamin, 31
  James, 19, 27, 31, 136
  Heyltje, 136
  Lea, 41
  Margaret, 133, 138
  Margriet, 137
  Maria, 37
  Marrigrit, 272
Mollener, James, 167
  John, 167
Mollhallon, Ellonar, 4
Mollin, Barent, 101
  James, 132
  Margriet, 101
  Margrita, 168

Molnier, Jackobeus, 166
  Naomey, 166
Moloney, Joseph, 30
  Mary, 30
Monday, Benajy, 36
  Maria, 36
Montanje, Abraham, 25
  Joseph, 25
  Rebecca, 20
Montanye, Rebecca, 30, 45
Mood, Samuel, 92
  Samuel Westbrook, 92
  Sarah, 92
Moor, George, 135
Moore, Elisabeth, 145
  George, 145
  Margaret, 206
  William S., xxviii
Mooren, David, 189
  William, 189
More, Cathrina, 186
  Gorgh, 272
  Susannah, 81
Morfi, John, 122
  Thomas, 122
Morphe, Mare, 136
  Tomas, 136
Morphy, Mary, 126
  Thomas, 126
Morris, Gov., 265
Morrison, John Adam, 280
Morrow, David, 182
  Lydia, 176
  Saml, 176
  Samuel, 182, 183
  Solomon, 183
Morse, James G., xxviii
Moser, Adam, 68
  John, 68
  Sarah, 68
Moses, 207
Mosher, Hannah, 239
Mosier, Dan, 71
  John, 71
Motani, Rebecca, 29
Mott, Margriet, 11
Moul, Dievertje, 113
  Divertje, 103, 133
Mulford, Phanny, 216
Mulin, Amy, 38
Mullen, Anne, 276
  Maria, 205
  Hannah, 208
  James, 28
  Maragriet, 142, 154
  Philip, 205, 208
Mullener, James, 180
  Joseph, 180
Muller, Charity, 33
  Heyltje, 33
  Mary, 33
Mullin, James, 24, 30
  Janneke, 24

Mullin, Thomas, 30
Mulliner, Navmi, 212
Munroe, Polly, 277
Munroo, Stephen, 276
Murphy, Timothy, 131
  Thomas, 131
Mushback, John, 278
  Sebily, 278
Mushbaugh, John, 34
Mushpuch, John, 35
Myers, Adam, 212
  Bastian, 212, 218, 278
  Bastian, Jr,, 213
  Belinda, 218
  Catrina, 221
  Christena, 214
  Christopher, 178
  Cobus, 218
  Cornelius, 178
  Daniel, 173, 177, 182
  Daniel Van Aken, 173
  Elizabeth, 213
  Jacob, 182, 208, 210, 214, 218, 224, 276
  Johannes, 212
  Mahala, 214
  Mary, 212, 218
  Rebeckah, 212
  Roger, 212
  Roxeny, 208
  Sally, 223
  William Johnson, 210
Mykreed, Catharina, 121
Myles, William Guthrie, xxx
Myres, Bastian, 175
  Elisabeth, 175
  Elizabeth, 65
  Jacob, 65
  John, 174
  Mary, 174
  Sarah, 65

N

Nagtigaal, Elisabeth, 149, 153
Nash, Phebe, 50
Nearpas, Anna, 256
  Anny, 252
  George, 252
  Mary, 247
  Wm., 256
Nearpass, Baltiss, 264
  Benjamen, 277
  Catharine, 254
  Catherine, 257, 261
  George, 251
  Jacob, 251, 261
  John, 261, 264
  Mary, 243, 279
  Sarah, 264
  W. H., vi

Neely, Joseph, 279
Neerbas, Jacob, 135
  Willem, 135
Neerpas, Benjamin, 247
  Catharine, 250
  Elisabeth, 177
  Jacob, 247
  Joannes, 275
  Johannis, 177
Neerpass, Anne, 242
  Benjamin, 233
  Benjn., 179
  Cate, 239
  Cathrina, 180
  Caty, 179, 232, 241
  Christina, 180
  Jacob, 177, 180, 235, 242
  John, 232, 233
  William, 232, 235
  Wm., 177, 179
Nefe, Lena, 171
Neffe, Helena, 176
  Lena, 181
Neffi, Helena, 127
  Rebecca, 124
  Thomas, 124, 127
Nelson, 259
Nerapas, Elisabeth, 145
  Jacob, 145
Nerapos, Mary, 154
Nerepas, Anna Maria,150
  Baltus, 159
  Benjamin, 150
  Catrena, 166
  Catrina, 159
  Jacob, 150, 166
  Maria, 166
Nethier, Hannes, 104
  Margaritje, 104
Nice, Catharina, 54
  Daniel, 51
  George, 51
  Helena, 54
  John, 46, 54, 75, 277
  Mary, 80
  William, 46
  William H., 75
Niecles, Benjamin, 29
  Joshep, 29
Niemen, Abigail, 275
Nince, Caty, 45
North, Elisabeth, 154
Nottingham, Ann, 13
  Brechje, 112
  Mally, 112
Nyce, Balinda, 92
  Catharine, 280
  Daniel, 92
  Elenor, 79
  Elizabeth, 276
  George, 52, 56, 57
  George W., 74
  Hannah, 74

Nyce, Jacob, xxii, 57, 67
  James, xxii
  John, 56, 63, 67, 75, 209
  John, Jr., 79
  John Westbrook, 209
  Lenah, 75
  Lydia, 63
  Mary, 83
  Sara Elizabeth, 92
  Solomon Westbrook,78
  William, 52
  Wm. H., 78
Nylen, Elisabeth, 139
  William, 139
Nyse, ——, 277

O

Oberfield, Sarah, 179
Ogden, Elizabeth, vii
  Hannah, 62, 72, 73
Onson, Elizabeth, 200
  Frederick, 200
Ooserhout, Arriaentje,109
Oosterhout, Annatje, 149
  Ariaentje, 126
  Arriaentje, 112, 116,119, 137, 283
  Caty, 238
  Eldert, 159
  Jacobus, 116, 120, 149
  Johannes, 138
  Leentje, 114
  Lena, 99, 109, 116
  Magdalena, 118
  Maria, 128, 143, 148
  Rachel, 159
  Susanna, 232
  Susannah, 236
Oostrander, Maria, 143
Opdegraf, Abraham, 179
  Isaac, 179, 181
  Jacob, 181
  Sarah, 179
Optehoms, Hendrick, 198
  Jacobus, 198
Openhuis, Annatie, 285
  Henry, 285
Openhouise, Hendrick, 184
  Jacob, 184
Optenhousen,Cattrina,204
  Hendrick Jatus, 204
Osterhoudt, John, 175
Osterhout, Aldert, 173
  Ariaantje, 102
  Arriaantje, 100
  Catey W. B., 241
  Jacobus, 134
  James, 245
  Jeremiah Quick, 237
  Johannes, 269
  John, 236, 237, 245

Osterhout, Magdalena, 99, 102
  Nathan, 173
  Nelly, 236
  Rachel, 242
  Sally Shepherd, 236
  Solomon Middagh, 230, 231
  Tunis, 230, 231, 236, 241
Otley, Antie, 176
  Asa, 171, 176
  Samuel, 171
Oute, Elesabet, 28
Overfield, Amiel, 84
  Benjamin, 25, 40, 42, 44
  Elizabeth, 71, 86
  Helena, 40
  Joseph Ritner, 88
  Manuel, 25
  Maria, 40
  Paul, 42
  Sarah Van Campen, 80
  Susannah, 71
  Washington, 80
  William, 71, 80, 84, 88
Overpeck, Adam, 60, 71, 85
  Caty Mariah, 85
  Elizabeth, 77, 83
  Elizebeth, 60
  George, 80, 83
  Samuel, 60
  Sarah, 84, 85, 90
  Sarah Anne, 71
  Susannah Van Campen, 80
Overpeek, Adam, 81
  Elizabeth, 87
  Philip, 81
  Sarah, 80
Oversheimer, Peter, 48
  Susanna, 48
Owens, Margaret, 77, 79
  Mary, 151

P

Paers, Jonathan, 168
  Sara, 168
Painter, Mary, 186
Palmatier, Maregreet, 182
Palmetier, Maregreet, 171, 178
  Margarita, 121
  Michiel, 121
Panborn, Edmond, 143
  William, 143
Park, Elisabeth, 170
Parkerton, Edward, 1
Parks, Experience, 190
Parmer, Caty, 209
  Cheziah, 243
Parrish, Stephen, 205
  Zebelon, 205

Paterson, Benjamin, 234
  Elizabeth, 234
  Eunice, 235
  Geremy, 234
  Sarah, 240
Patison, Josep Maker, 234
  Samuel, 234
Patran, James, 272
Patrik, James, 156
  Maria, 156
Patson, Blandina, 214
Patterson, Blandina, 235
  Elias, 212, 224
  Esther, 245
  Eunice, 233, 245
  Ezube, 230, 231
  Hester, 236
  Lydia, 224
  Parmelia, 280
  Peter, 235
  Peter Q., 235
  Sarah, 212
Peach, Lucretia, 74, 75
Peck (Pach), Johannis, 149
Pecker, Angenitje, 32
  Edward, 32
  Dilye, 32
Peeke, Rev. Mr., xxi
  Harmon V. S., xxix
  Harmon Van Slyke, Rev., xxi
Peer, Elizabeth, 191, 193
  Rachel, 190
Pegar, Mary, 55
Peiddis, Caty Jane, 227
  John, 227
Peiker, Edward, 27
  Rebecca, 27
Pelten, Hannah, 175
Peltin, Hannah, 168
  Johanna, 170, 275
Pelton, Hannah, 181
Penet, Benjamin, 191, 193
  Samuel, 191, 193
Penn, William, ii
Pepinger, Sarah, 156
Perry, James, 271
Peters, Charles Ridgeway, 81
  Daniel, 84
  Delinda, 81
  Elizabeth, 69
  Else, 81
  George, 81, 82, 84, 88
  Henry, xxii, 69, 81, 86
  John, 51, 82
  Maria Louiza, 86
  Mary, 51
  Sarah Anne, 88
Petron, Sarah, 47
Petterson, Esaba, 168
  Nehemyah, 168

Petteson, Hester, 156
  Nehemiah, 156
Petty, Juno, 14
Phenix, Andrew, 159
  John, 159
  William, 159
Phillips, James S., 280
Phoenix, Andrew, 159
  Hendrick, 159
Phresuer, John, 51
Pheby, 51
Pifer, Sarah, 91
Pitt, Mr., xi
Pitts, Robert, xxix
  Robert, Rev., xii, xix
Place, Benjamin, 69
  James, 69, 89
  Susannah, 89
Play, Mary, 240
Ploeg, Abraham, 165
  Aldert, 165
Ploegh, Aldert, 15
  Hendrick, 6
  Sara, 15
Plouegh, Jacob, 192
  Jenny, 192
Plough, Jacob, 194
  Jenny, 194
Plysser, Magdalin, 25
Poh, Henry, 276
Polhemus, Henry, 50
Pomp, Thos., 55
Pomry, Henne, 31
Poole, Alexander, 273
Potman, John, 34
  Peter, 34
Pots, Patience, 13
Pouleson, Jannatie, 285
Pray, Mary, 244
Preston, Saml., i
  Samuel, i
Price, Apolonia, 178, 182
  Elizabeth, 40, 45
Prize, Elizabath, 43
Probasco, Abraham, 211
  George, 65
  Jacob, 211, 214, 217
  Joseph, 65
  Margaret, 65
  Mary, 214
  Petrus Van Nest, 217
Prosser, Ellenor, 27
  Maragrita, 22
  Nelly, 33
Provoost, Margriet, 97
  Willem, 97
Prys, Anna, 3
  Apollonia, 111
  Appolony, 160
  Elizabeth, 116, 156
  Francasje, 145
  Hanna, 3, 11
  Johannes, 121

Prys, John, 111, 116, 121,
  126, 160
  Lisabeth, 269
  Philip, 126
Puder, Lanah, 57
Pue, Hue, 98, 102
  Margriet, 98
  Pieter, 102
Pugh, Hugh, 5, 106
  Isaac, 106
Puss, Elezibeth, 59
  Jacob, 59
  Peggey, 59
Putman, Moria, 59
  Victor, 59

Q

Qick, Marey, 166
  Samuel, 166
Queck, Helena, 272
  Marigrita, 272
  Rabacka, 31
Quek, Enne, 272
Quick, Abm., 177
  Abraham, 160
  Abram, 111
  Adrian, 92
  Ann, 26, 129, 165
  Anna, 23, 126, 133, 138, 270
  Antje, 98, 282
  Beeletje, 282
  Beletje, 137
  Benjamin, 97, 115, 117-119, 125, 126, 140, 149, 157, 267
  Catharina, 117, 122, 129, 162
  Cathrina, 178, 269
  Catrina, 149
  Cattarina, 203
  Cattrina, 195
  Cattrine, 207
  Caty, 179, 197, 210, 241
  Clara, 121, 122
  Cornelis, 122, 126, 130, 132, 268
  Cornelius, 133, 148, 181
  Dan. Dimmick, 244
  Daniel, 242
  David, 157
  Derick, 176
  Derrick, 104
  Dirk, 111, 117
  Divertje, 158
  Eleanor, 279
  Elisabeth, 109, 116, 123, 133
  Eliza, 136
  Elizabeth, 34, 37, 110, 136, 245, 279
  Ellenor, 232
  Quick, Elsey Jane, 75
  Geertje, 98
  George, 205, 207, 210, 212, 275
  Grietje, 132, 150
  Griette, 140
  Hannah, 237
  Henry, 205, 276
  Heyltje, 19
  Hiram, 70
  Isaac, 237
  Jacob, 133, 232, 241, 244, 275, 278
  Jacobus, 108, 112, 122, 124, 126, 133, 137, 154, 168, 170, 175, 181, 197, 265, 268
  Jacobus, Jr., 275
  James, 212
  Janche, 147
  Jane, 205
  Jannitie, 198
  Jenne, 236
  Jenneke, 137
  Joel, 108, 109, 114, 125, 129, 133, 137, 145, 151, 158, 268
  Johannes, 98, 108, 161
  Johannis, 171
  John, 70, 179, 200, 204, 239, 242
  John B., 66, 243
  John T., 75
  Joris, 125
  Joseph, 160, 179
  Jurian, 148
  Lea, 126, 133
  Leenah, 197
  Lena, 105, 110, 112, 115, 119, 124, 128, 132, 137, 153, 176, 205, 210, 212, 265
  Lisabeth, 125, 128, 131, 137, 281
  Liza (Lena), 207
  Lizabeth, 104
  Lydia, 137
  Maragret, 147
  Maragriet, 157
  Maregriet, 135
  Margaret, 245
  Margariet, 164
  Margret, 237
  Margreth, 133
  Margriet, 2, 112, 115, 117, 118, 123, 130
  Margrita, 97
  Maria, 129, 157, 200
  Mariah Elizabeth, 66
  Marya, 171
  Martin Cole, 243
  Mattheus, 119
  Neeltie, 17
Quick, Pegge, 236, 237, 239
  Peggy, 35
  Peter, 198, 214, 277
  Peter, Jr., 278
  Petrus, 112, 118, 123, 153, 171
  Philippus, 123
  Ploney, 236
  Polly, 168
  Pride, 230, 231
  Prude, 241
  Rachel, 104, 204
  Rebecca, 2, 17, 19, 25
  Reymerig, 97, 98
  Roger Clark, 214
  Rymerich, 128
  Rymerick, 124
  Salomon, 151
  Samuel, 130, 164, 175, 197, 275, 276
  Saperine, 176
  Sarah, 145, 161, 180, 183, 189, 204, 207, 237, 276
  Simeon, 177
  Simon, 207
  Susannah, 88
  Teunis, 97, 157
  Thomas, 2, 97, 115, 117, 123, 133, 170
  Tomas, 133, 136
Quik, Adrian, 99
  Anna, 143
  Antje, 140
  Beletje, 98
  Benjamin, 105, 106, 134, 157
  Cattrina, 187
  Cornelius, 133
  Dirk, 98, 106
  Elisabeth, 105
  Greetje, 144
  Grietje, 134
  Hannah, 140
  Jacob, 237
  Jacobus, 102, 105, 144
  Jenneke, 98
  Joel, 105, 140
  John B., 237
  Lena, 103, 106, 141
  Lisabeth, 99, 102, 133
  Maragrita, 139, 140
  Margriet, 99, 100, 102, 134
  Maria, 133
  Rachel Corregt, 157
  Rebecca, 154
  Thomas, 105

R

Rakien, Anna Maria, 135
Ralls, Elisabeth, 175

Ralls, James, 175
Ramsey, Lucretia, 111, 116, 121
Randall, Enos, 160
  Lenah, 160
Ranette, Catharine, 279
Range, Elisabeth, 156
Ransen, James, 135
  Ruth, 135
Ranson, Alonzo A., xxx
Rashel, Benjamin, 275
Rasor, Benyamen, 27
  Hanah, 25
  Hanne, 27
  Rachel, 27
Ratier, Elisabeth, 144, 149
  Lisabeth, 131
Rattier, Elisabeth, 140
Rawford, Hannah, 222
Ray, John, 93
  Susannah, 195
Rayman, George, 68
  Jacob, 68
  Rachel, 68
Reaser, Elizabeth, 78
Rechard, Nathaniel, 194
  William, 194
Redford, John, 177
Ree, John, 3
Reed, Benjamin, 196
  Catterine, 196
  Julia, 280
  Thomas, 196
Reifsmyder, Andries, 93, 120, 126, 131
Reifsnyder, Jacobus, 120
  Joseph, 131
  Maria, 126
Relie, Hester, 6, 11
Relje, Hester, 12, 100, 101
Rellie, Hester, 7, 11
Relyer, John, 229, 230
  Joseph Ennis, 229
  Philip, 230
Remsen, Lucretia, 126
Rendall, J. H., xxx
Rendle, Antje, 145
  ——nes, 145
Renyer, Susannah, 230
Resep, Rachel, 33
Resen, Elizabeth, 76, 90
  John, 76, 79
  Sarah, 79
Reser, Anthony, 70, 83
  Barbary, 90
  Catharina, 77
  Catharine, 63, 86
  Caty, 65, 73
  Daniel, 83, 90
  Elizabeth, 74, 76, 86
  Henry, 70
  Isaac, 83
  Jacob, 63, 74, 79, 85

Reser, James, 63
  Jemimah, 79
  John, 64, 70, 86, 87
  Joseph, 64
  Margaret, 90
  Mary, 66, 68
  Peter, 62, 63, 66, 68, 70, 73, 90
  Philip, 62, 87
  Rachel, 63
  Sarah, 73
  Susan, 70
  Susanna, 75
  Susannah, 82
  William, 66
Rex, Henry L., xxix
Reysly (Rigley), Anatje, 177
Rhodes, vii
  Chas., xii
Richardson, Maria, 15
Richerd, Nathaniel, 192
  William, 192
Rider, Cattrina, 186
  James, 186
Riggs, Ann, 277
  Rhoda, 275
  Rhody, 47
Right, John, 121
  William, 121
Rimer, Amy, 284
Risla, James, 130, 269
  Margriet, 130
Risly, Annatie, 184, 204
Ritt, Geeshi, 115
Roaki (Rohbek), Anna Maria, 145
Robert, Antje, 121
  Elisabeth, 121
  Lisabeth, 120, 121
  Margriet, 120, 123, 130
  Vincent, 121
Roberts, Margriet, 126
  Mary, 77, 80, 84
Rochel, Dirck, 3
  James, 3
Roef, Hans Michel, 121
  Jacob, 121
Roet, Pieter, 266
Rogers, E. P., Rev., xxii
  Hanna, 154
  Samuel J., xxviii
Romaine, Dom., 19
  Rev. Thos., 19
Romein, Nicolaas, 145
  Susanna, 142, 284
  Thomas, Do., 142
Romeins, Dom., 23
Romeyn, xiv
  Dom., 22
  Rev. Mr., xx
  D., Rev., 274
  Thomas, Rev., 273

Romeyn, Thos., Rev., 159
Romfeld, Cathrina, 137
Romien, Dom., 94, 284
  Dr., 22
  Mr., 284
  Derick, 284
  T., 284
  Thomas, 94, 145
  Thomas, Rev., 281
Romine, Rev., 16
  Thomas, Rev., xvii
Romvellen, Cathrina, 132
Roos, Antje, 124
  Catrina, 148
  Gisbert, 104
  Marytje, 120
  Neelgje, 103
  Neeltje, 4
  (Kool), Cornelia, 179
Roosa, Catrina, 150
  Marya, 179
Rooscrans, Arriantje, 211
Roosekrans, Ariaantje, 143
  Arriantje, 154
  Blandina, 146, 157
  Benjamin, 154
  Catrina, 18, 147
  Cherk De Witt, 18
  Daniel, 147
  Derk, 284
  Elia, 20
  Engeltje, 154
  Jacobus, 147, 158, 274
  Jacobus, Jr., 154
  Jannetje, 153
  Johannes, 20
  Johannis, Jr., 18
  Lena, 145
  Levi, 158
  Salomon, 147
Roosenkrans, Catrina, 139
  Cobus, 158
  Helena, 158
Root, Catherine, 190
  Elisabeth, 20
  Jefred, 190
  Lisabeth, 8
  Pieter, 8, 12
Rortrecht, Rachel, 5
Rosa, Antje, 98, 100, 103, 104, 106, 108, 110, 112-113, 115, 119, 120, 122, 124, 134
  Antjen, 281
  Elisabeth, 177
  Isaak, 125
  Isak, 117
  Jacob, 129, 177
  Jan, 120
  Jan A., 121, 122, 125, 129
  Jan Alderse, 117, 282
  Maria, 162, 166, 173, 191, 193, 274

Rosa, Mary, 177
Marya, 117
Neeltje, 114
Rebecca, 121
Wyntje, 3
Rosakrance, Lydia, 183
Rosakrans, Jane, 188
  John, 25, 42
Rose, William, 177
Rosecrans, Arejate, 166
  Caterina, 250
  Catherine, 257
  Cornelius, 234
  Diana, 243
  Jan, 166
  Jannete, 166
  Jeanna, 237
  Johannis, 166
  Mary, 234, 241, 257
  Mary Ann, 258
  Peter, 258
  Sally, 258
Rosecranse, John, 49
  Solomon, 49
Rosecrants, Hannah, 57
  Sallomon, 57
Rosecrantz, Abram Bross, 261
  Peter, 261
  Sarah, 261
Rosegrant, Catharine, 230, 231
Rosekrace, Har, 179
Rosekrance, Abraham, 173
  Anantie, 179
  Ariantie, 181
  Benj., 179
  Benjn., 172
  Blandina, 175
  Harme, 182
  Isaac, 177
  Jacobus, 173, 175, 181
  Jesaias, 182
  Johannes, 173
  Johannis, 179
  Johans, 177
  John, 173
  Lydia, 171, 175, 178, 179
Rosekrans, Alida, 152
  Antje, 100
  Areantie, 216
  Ariaantie, 200
  Ariaantje, 161
  Arianje, 204
  Ariaentje, 140
  Ariantie, 225
  Ariantje, 140, 148
  Arriantie, 190, 209
  Arriyantie, 272
  Aryantie, 135
  Benjamin, 40, 42, 45, 47, 148, 275

Rosekrans, Blandina, 136, 138, 142, 150, 196
  Catherine, 253
  Catriena, 16
  Catrina, 16, 144
  Caty, 207, 237
  Chareck, 276
  Christina, 98
  Cornelius, 143
  Coriany, 38
  Daniel, 98, 152
  David, 40
  Elizabeth, 207
  Evert, 47
  Francis, 207
  Geertje, 102
  Hannah, 225
  Harme, 100, 102, 132
  Harmen, 140
  Helena, 272
  Herme, 218
  Jacob, 191, 193
  Jacobus, 98, 102, 142, 144, 152, 191, 193
  Jannetie, 204
  Jannitie, 198, 204, 208, 210
  Jaremia, 198
  Jeremiah, 203, 208
  Joannes, 191, 193
  Johannes, Jr., 24
  Johannis, 16, 21, 152
  Joseph, 40, 148, 277
  Ledy, 208
  Lena, 16, 277
  Lenah, 24
  Levy, 21
  Margriet, 24
  Maria, 230
  Mary, 227, 228
  Nicholas, 45
  Petrus, 143, 148, 218
  Rachel, 40, 221
  Rebecca, 191, 193
  Reremiah, 203
  Roanny, 222, 223, 228
  Rosanny, 42
  Sara, 98, 103
  Solomon, 276
  Suse, 208
Rosekranse, Jacobus, 171
Rosekrantz, Helena, 93
Rosekrans, Alexander, xix
  Amanda, 66
  Ariantje, 133
  Arietta V. Campen, 64
  Asa, 65, 67
  Benjamin, 63, 66, 82
  Blandina, 160
  Catharine, 74, 76, 77, 83, 90, 220
  Catrina, 133

Rosenkrans, Caty, 63
  Charriek, 65
  Cornelia Winecoop, 75
  Cornelius, 220
  Cyrus Egbert, 62
  Daniel, 134
  Deborah Ann, 89
  Diana, 66
  Elizabeth, 64
  Elizabet Jane, 87
  Esther, 78
  Event, 82
  Evert, 89
  Frazure, 67
  Hannah, 89
  Herman, 7
  Horris, 65
  James, 72
  John, 63, 87, 89
  John, Col., xix
  John I., 75
  John J., 64
  Julia Mariah, 75
  Levi, 47
  Levy, 62
  Lidia, 133
  Margaret, 70
  Mariah, 69, 74, 76, 81, 83
  Peggy Mariah, 89
  Petrus, 133
  Rachel, 64, 73, 77, 80, 83, 91
  Sally, 63
  Samuel Shoemaker, 67
  Sara, 134
  Sarah, 74, 78, 81, 87, 89
  Simeon, 63, 65, 67, 70, 75, 89
  Solomon, 72, 78
  Susannah, 87
  William, 47
Rosenkrants, Benjamin, 162, 165
  Catharina, 160, 162
  Catherina, 161
  Francis, 162
  Johannes, 274
  Johannes, Jr., 162
  Petrus, 161
Rosenkrantz, Alexander, 4
  Catharina, 5, 161
  Catharine, 1
  Cathrina, 104
  Johannes, 1, 5
  Hermanus, 4
  Lena, 4, 5, 92
  Magdalena, 4
  Sara, 108
Rosenkranz, Alexander, 8
  Alida, 124
  Anna, 10
  Ariaentje, 131

Rosenkranz, A r r iaantje, 127
Arriaentje, 127, 131, 137, 270
Benjamin, 116
Blandina, 125, 126, 130, 132, 268
Catherina, 7, 9, 10, 11, 13, 109, 118, 119, 126, 130, 266
Cathrina, 138
Christina, 281
Dirk, 109, 116, 119, 127, 131, 132, 266
Herman, 10, 12, 109, 112, 114, 116, 119, 122, 126, 137, 283
Hermanus, 7, 8
Jacob, 13
Jacobus, 107, 108, 109, 111, 113, 114, 116, 118, 124, 127, 266, 282
Jannetje, 116
Johannes, 10, 11, 13, 108
John, 11
Joseph, 12
Leentje, 10
Lena, 5, 7, 8, 109, 116, 127
Lydia, 132
Madelena, 13
Magdalena, 9, 11-13
Margriet, 112, 113, 115
Marya, 11
Petrus, 127, 137
Salomon, 107, 114
Sara, 107, 109, 114, 116, 120, 127, 283
Roskrans, Abraham, 166, 221, 225
Petris, 166
Ross, Louisa Ann, 280
Susannah, 277
Rouly, Samuel, 188
William, 188
Rozekrans, Daniel, 168
Jacob, 168
Rubart, John, 215
Margaret, 218
Peter, 215, 218
Rummerfield, H a n nah, 81, 84, 89
Rumvelt, Catrina, 142
Rundle, E., 274
Rusle, Annaatje, 135
James, 135
Russel, Davet, 16
Evje, 13
Isak, 6
James, 6, 8, 10, 13, 16
Mattheus, 10
Rutson, Blandina, 157
(Ratran), James, 157
Ruttenber, xviii
Ryan, John, 201
Sarah, 201
Ryker, Elisabeth, 153
Rymer, Ann, 176
Rys (Prys, Kyer, Ryer), Frederick, 145
Rysly, Hennah, 198
Ryt, John H. B., 209, 210
Rachel, 210
Thomas, 209

S

Sammons, Cornelius, 253
Elizabeth, 230, 231, 235, 244
Huldah, 253
Jane, 244, 248
John, 278
John J., 236, 242, 247, 253
Lilley Skner, 236
Peter, 236
Martines, 247
Mary, 240, 242, 244, 247, 251, 253, 256
Sally, 247
Sarah, 240
Sanders, Sarah, 155
Sanger, Catherine, 263
James, 263
William Stone, 263
Saunders, Sarah, 160
Sawas, Joseph, 275
Sawin, Charity, 14
Joseph, 14
Sawyer, Benjamin Carpenter, 257
Catherine, 260
Hannah, 250
James, 250, 254, 257, 260
John Nearpass, 254
Sayin, Joseph, 6
Sayre, Caroline, 88
Schaffer, Caspar, 9
Margareta, 9
Schamers, Lisabeth, 98
Samuel, 98
Schammers, Benjamin, 6
Cathrina, 11
Christina, 5
Helmer, 18
Maria, 33
Marya, 14
Mosis, 18
Petrus, 7
Samuel, 5-7, 11, 14, 101, 105, 115
Sara, 11, 14, 98, 100, 102, 111, 112, 125, 127, 282
Sarah, 105, 115
Wilhelmus, 101
Scheever, Christina, 159
Schembers, Hester, 166
Schenck, Catharina, 162
Garret C., xxix
Schendeler, Antje, 120
John, 120
Schermerhoorn, Neeltje, 119, 123
Lucas, 120, 123
Lisabeth, 123
Schenk, Catrina, 152
Schick, Adam, 33
Maria, 33, 193, 194
Schimer, Elizabeth, 195
Jacob, 195
Mary, 245
Schink, Adam, 18
John, 18
Schippard, Benjamin, 154
Lydia, 154
Schmidt, Daniel, 50
Jacob, 50
Susanna, 50
Schmitz, William, xxix
William, Rev., xxii
Schoemaker, Lena, 27
Schoenhoven, Henry, 158
Joseph Mattanje, 158
Schoenover, James, 71
Mary, 71
Schoenwars, Mary, 166
Schnabel, Andries, 52
Susanna, 52
Schnauben, Anna Elizabetha, 93
Schnawbel, Magdalen, 50
Schomaker, Sara, 122
Schonauvel, Andrew, 50
Joseph, 50
Schonemake, Madelea, 16
Schonhove, Dolvus, 29
Dority Williams, 29
Elizabeth, 33
Evert, 33
Nicklaas, 33
Rudolphus, 33
Schonhoven, B e n yamin, 32
Catrina, 30
Esegel, 27
Henry, 30
Jan, 34
Jane, 234
Maria, 28, 34
Mary, 44
Niclaes, 27
Piternel, 27
Rachel, 27
Redalves, 32
Redolves, 30
Schonhover, Abraham, 24
Calheen, 27
Garret, 29

Schonhover, Henry, 29
Schonmaker, Benjamin, 27
Isack, 27
Elesabet, 30
Schonnover, Rudolph, 35
Susannah, 35
Schonover, John, 35
Joseph, 35
Schoohaven, Debora, 134
Schoohoven, David, 125
James, 54
Thomas, 125
William Smith, 54
Schoomaker, Sara, 8
Schoonhoove, Debora, 142
Schoonhooven, Christoffel, 142
Debora, 146
Joseph, 36
Lena, 39
Nelly, 39, 42
Nicholas, 36
Peter, 39
Rebbecka, 142
Schoonhovan, Nicholas, xi
Schoonhove, Benjamin, 142, 168
Benjn, 59
Cornelius, 135, 168
Elezebeth, 59
Jan Vyert, 136
John, 59
Joseph, 142
Josias, 142
Rabecka, 136
Sarah, 142
Thomas, 142
Schoonhoven, Abraham, 43
Adolphus, 20, 24, 33
Benjamin, 1, 22, 23, 46, 119
Benjn, 16
Catharina, 2
Catrina, 20, 23, 273
Cattrina, 36
Caty, 38
Clary, 280
Cobus, 22
Cornelia, 11, 14, 20, 22, 24
Cornelis, 99, 154
Cornelius, 139, 140
Daniel, 46
Debora, 105, 106, 108, 112, 113, 115, 118, 122, 124, 125, 130, 137, 161, 283
Deborah, 230, 231
Doloos, 39
Dorithy, 40

Schoonhoven, Dorothea, 1
Elisabeth, 22, 154
Elizabeth, 21, 41, 160
Ezechiel, 139
Ezekiel, 25, 37, 53
Ezekiel V., 37
Grietie, 40, 42
Handerecus, 38
Hanna, 22
Hendericus, 14, 94
Hendrick, 11
Hendricus, 1-4, 11, 14
Hendrikkus, 22
Henry, 20, 36, 45, 58
Isack, 122
Jacob, 49, 110, 160, 178, 182
Jacobus, 20, 21
James, 50
Jan, 2
Jannekie, 182
Joel, 278
John, 21, 22, 33, 38, 41, 43, 45
Jonas, 230, 231
Joris, 137
Joseph, 178
Jsaac, 139
Keety, 14
Lena, 139, 230, 231
Levi, 178
Levicia, 53
Maragriet, 22, 23
Margaret, 63
Maria, 4, 20-23, 37, 134, 140
Marrita, 27
Mary, 24, 40, 41, 58
Marya, 25
Nelly, 37, 41, 276
Nicholas, 38, 40, 41, 49, 52
Nickolas, 53
Nic'l, 33
Niclaes, 11
Niclaes, Jr., 27
Nicolas, 1
Nicolaus, 33
Pegay, 47
Peggy, 45
Peternella, 20
Petrus, 20
Rachel, 14, 41, 94, 178
Rebecca, 45, 99, 106, 107, 111, 113, 124
Redolphus, 20
Redolvus, 41
Rhodolvus, 51
Roedolfus, 1
Rodolfus, 212
Rodolvis, 39
Rodolvus, 40, 46
Rudolvus, 36

Schoonhoven, Samuel, 129
Sara, 105
Sarah, 21, 25, 46, 276
Thomas, 99, 102, 105, 106, 110, 113, 115, 119, 129, 134, 137, 140
Weyntje, 115
William, 46, 50, 51, 53
Schoonhover, Abm. Decker, 57
Cornelers, 175
Gertie, 16
Hendrickas, 29
Hendrikus, 16
Henry, 57
Jacob, 175
John, 29, 31
Margit, 29
Mary, 30, 31
Nicholas, Jr., 29
Sarah, 30
Schoonmaaker, Magdalena, 17
Schoonmaker, Abram, 18
Ann, 29
Ariaantie, 190
Benjamin, 3, 19, 155
Catharina, 5, 7, 100, 119, 121
Catrina, 20
Caty, 42, 276
Cornelius, 22
David, 19
Elisabet, 22
Elisabeth, 18
Elisebeth, 17
Elizabeth, 33, 51
Frederick, xix
Gerret, 3
Gerrit, 19
Hanny, 22
Isaac, 18, 20, 44, 100, 162
Jacob, 5, 162
Jacobus, 11
Jinneke, 155
Jochem, 1, 4, 5, 8, 100
Lea Kriss, 29
Lena, 20
Lenah, 24
Lisabeth, 1, 3, 4
Maria, 267
Martha, 44
Moses, 3, 22, 44
Mosis, 19
Petrus, 8, 178
Sara, 3, 6, 7, 94, 100
Susanna, 5
Schoonoven, James, 74
Susanna, 75
Susannah, 64
Schoonover, Benjamin, 67
Benjamin Franklin, 88

Schoonover, Bernardus
    Swartwood, 81
    Daniel, 67, 81, 88
    Elijah Parmer, 58
    Elizabeth, 67
    Ezekiel, 85
    Hannah, 85
    Hendrickus, Jr., 36
    Henry, 36
    Ira, 85
    James, 58, 65, 67, 80
    Leonard, 85
    Margaret, 66
    Rachel, 65
    Rodolvus, 80
    Sarah, 73
    Simeon, xxii
    Susannah, 67, 70, 83, 88
    William, xxii
Schouk, Hendericus, 27
Schouwers, Johannis, 139
    Maria, 139, 153
Schuymer, Abraham, 119
    Jsaak, 119
Scoot, Elizabeth, 49
Scot, Elilabeth, 67
    Elizebeth, 31
Scott, Elizabeth, 51
    Henry, 280
Scrosman, Easter, 52
Scull, N., i, ii
    Nicholas, i
Seafos, Elizabeth, 82, 92
Seaman, Daniel, 78
    Ira Kintner, 78
    Isaac Nelson, 78
Seaphos, Catharine, 86
Seeley, Samuel, 275
Seely, Cattrina, 34
    Cornelia, 206
    Hariott, 206
    Jonas, 34, 37
    Maria, 206
    Mariah, 66, 230
    Mary, 37
    Michael, 186
    Samuel C., 206
    Sharlott, 206
    Susannah, 186
Semlebarah, Cornelius, 39
    John, 39
Semmons, Mary, 246
Semon, Solomon, 187
    Walter, 187
Seymor, Abraham, 136
    Elizabeth, 136
Shafer, Christina, 165
    George, 85
Shammers, Christina, 27
    Johannes, 3
    Maria, 34
    Samuel, 2, 3, 15

Shamons, Mary, 238
Shans, ——, 278
Shaphaly, Barbara, 40
Shappee, Ashkenas, 185
    Kezia, 185
    Jene, 185
    Robert, 185
Sharrer, Andrew, 79
    Susannah Smith, 79
Shaubas, Johannes, 132
    Susanna, 132
Shauers, Mary, 164
Shaunts, David, 196
    Elizabeth, 196
Shaver, Christina, 169
    John Adam, 35
    Sary, 35
Shaw, John F., xxix
    John F., Rev., xxii
Shawars, Jacobus, 171
    Joseph, 171
    Susanna, 177
Shay, Joshua, xviii
Sheefer, Caspar, 112
    Valentyn, 112
Sheffard, Barbara, 155
Sheffer, Caspar, 14
    Maria Susanna, 14
Shegrave, Caty Cuddeck, 243
    Sarah, 243
Sheimer, Catharine, 249
    Richard, 242
    Sarah Anne, 242
Sheldren, Abraham, 55
    Benjamin, 55
    Catharine, 55
Shellet, Grietje, 138
    Hugh, 138
Shemmers, Jenneke, 15
    Samuel, 15
Shephaly, Barbery, 42
Sherred, Helen, 197
    Helena, 202
    Lena, 186, 188
Shever, Christina, 167
Shewmaker, Elizabeth, 57
Sheyger (Keyser), Frederick, 147
    Petrus, 147
Shick, Adam, 25
    Benjamin, 25
Shiffer, Barbara, 159
    Hannes, 159
    Lisa Margriet, 159
Shifly, Barbara, 35
Shimar, Elizabeth, 208
Shimer, Abraham, 170, 188
    Cathrine, 238
    Elizabeth, 184, 214, 225
    Hester, 170

Shimer, Isaac, 204
    Jacob, 188, 202, 204, 208, 214, 236
    Jacob, Jr., 208
    Ledy, 208
    Maria, 276
    Nelly, 197
    Polly, 238
    Richard, 236, 246
Shiner, Richard, 279
Shink, Adam, 16
    Maria, 16
Shinny, Luvonia, 273
    Luvonia, Jr., 273
    Mary, 273
Shipperd, Lidea, 276
Shirly, Catharina, 165
    James, 165
Shirrid, Hugh, 143
    Lena, 143
Shoemaker, Abraham Van Campen, 90
    Benjamin, 67
    Blandina, 71
    Catharine, 80
    Daniel, 67, 72, 75
    David, 185
    Elizabeth, 52, 74
    Elizebeth, 28
    Henrey, 32
    Henry, 79, 81
    Isaac, 28
    Johannes, 28
    John, 71, 80, 90, 91
    John Van Campen, 90
    Maria, 185
    Mary, 67
    Mary Anne, 79
    Moses, 75, 79, 90, 91
    Moses Chambers, 87
    Samuel, 71, 79, 81, 87
    Sarah, 63, 65, 67, 70, 75, 80
    Susanna, 52
    Susannah, 32, 59, 72, 79
    Thomas, 185
Shoff, John Nicholas, 85
    Michael, 85
    Sarah, 63
Shonoven, Anna, 47
    Johanna, 47
Shoonmaker, Doritia, 196
    Hanery, 44
Showas, Susanah, 29
Showers, Cattrina, 186
    Joseph, 175
    Mary, 175
Shurrah, Andrew, 61
    Elizabeth, 61
    William Hankinson, 61
Shuttz, Jacob, 90
    Sarah, 90

Shutz, Caty Anne, 85
Jacob, 85
Shuymers, Abram, 127
Hester, 127
Shyfre, Parabel, 34
Shymer, Abraham, 172
Abram, 122, 140
Catharine, 245
Cathrina, 175
Derick, 178
Estor, 237
Hester, 171, 172, 187
Jacob, 171, 175, 178, 183
Maragrit, 140
Marie, 122
Mary, 175
Susanna, 183
Shymers, Abram, 130
Hester, 130
Shymir, Elenor, 220
Sickle, Elizabeth, 204
John, 204
Grietie, 204
Siddales, Mary, 279
Siddles, Mary, 237
Sidgrieves, Charles, 280
Simon, Jacob, 182
Lea, 199
Robbert, 271
Walter, 182
William, 199
Simour, Jacomyntje, 137
Robert, 137
Simson, Gersom, 12
John, 12
Sinor, Robert, 135
Sara, 135
Skinner, Emy, 183
Hagge, 173
Magdelana, 173
Skirmer, Abraham, 214
Slausan, Hiram, xxviii
Slover, Abraham, 121
Isaac, 121
Isaak, 120
Sluiter, Abram, 151, 157
Elizabeth, 157
Geertje, 151
Tuines, 273
Sluyter, Cornelia, 15, 165
Elizabeth, 32
Janatje, 32
Wilhelmus, 32
Sly, Elizabeth, 276
Smit, Willm., 15, 60
Smith, Abraham, 50, 55, 62
Ana Maria, 46
Anna, 63, 73, 76, 83
Anna Maria, 53, 55
Anne, 219
Anny Mary ———, 47
Barbara, 53

Smith, Barbary, 56, 92
Benjamin, 2, 47, 88
Benjamin Schoenover, 54
Catey, 58
Catharina, 2, 53, 132
Catharine, 55, 78, 80, 84, 87
Catherine, 59
Cathrina, 183, 185
Catrina, 139
Catterine, 198
Cattrina, 188, 202
Caty, 60
Cecelia, 61
Charles, 62
Christian, 64, 66, 83
Christion, 56
Chrysparus Van Naken, 57
Coonrod, 62
Daniel, 92
David, 45
Doratha, 61
Dorothea, 47, 50, 53, 55
Elebath, 233
Elezebeth, 59
Elias, 62
Elijah, 60
Elisa. Cath., 17
Elisabeth, 50
Elisabetha, 54
Eliza, 55
Elizabeth, 39, 51, 56, 62, 64, 66, 77, 79, 84, 91, 232, 252, 276
Elizebeth, 60, 61
Frances, 237
Frances M., 245
Frederick, 49
George, 47, 52, 53
Han. George, 47
Hannah, 79, 237
Jacob, xi, 47, 49, 50, 51, 53-56, 58, 61, 62, 68, 278
Jacob, Jr., 62, 66, 69, 77, 83
James, 42, 45, 47, 82, 88
James Barnhart, 60
Jane Amanda, 61
Johannes, 53
John, 36, 50, 54, 57, 60, 61, 179
John Anderson, 59
John Philip, 47
John Q., 245
John S., xii, xiii, xxii
Jonah, 82
Jonas, 46, 47, 53, 55
Jonas Samuel, 92
Joseph, 36
Joshua, 54, 57, 59, 60

Smith, Julianna, 84
Laudewick, 51
Lena, 52
Lodawick, 62
Lodovick, 57
Lusy Ann, 64
Lydia, 82, 88
Margaret, 46, 278
Margareth, 50, 55
Margery, 60
Mariah, 75
Mary, 56, 60, 61, 64, 66, 73, 82, 83, 89
Michael, 50
Parmelia, 61
Philip, xxiii, 47, 50, 53, 55, 56, 61
Rodolvus, 42, 68, 70, 73, 79, 84
Samuel, 56
Samuel B., 280
Sarah, 50, 62, 68, 77, 186
Sevele, 50
Sibilla, 55
Simon, 82
Solomon, ix
Susanna, 52-54
Susanna Maria, 61
Susannah, 56, 62, 69, 70, 91
Toriteawe (Dorothea), 56
Valentine, 276
William, 14, 17, 54, 61, 91
Smook, Daniel, 186
John, 186
Snabel, Susannah, 91
Snauber, Anna Elizabetha, 115
Johannes, 111
Snedeker, Willempi, 135
Snel, Susanna, 24
Susannah, 40
Snell, Susanna, 32, 165
Snider, Jacob, 40, 44
Joseph Montonye, 40
Rebecca, 44
Snyder, Christina Lisabetha, 10
Johan Christoffel, 4
Valentyn, 4, 7, 10
Sorrad, Huged, 272
Sprigal, Geo., 276
Squerrel, Anna Barbara, 172
Squirl, Sarah, 232, 233
Squrrel, Sarah, 275
Staats, Frederick, 147
Sebella, 147
Stahl, George, 279
Staley, Magdalen, 86
Staly, Susannah, 62
Stearns, Aldert, 279

Steel, Abraham, 76, 79
　Belinda Hornbeek, 68
　Catharina, 87
　Catharine, 67, 69, 73, 77, 82, 91
　Catharine Reser, 85
　Caty, 58, 65, 69
　Elenor, 62, 76, 77
　Elizabeth, 73
　Eveline, 76
　Gilbert, 62, 65, 68, 72, 73, 77
　Hannah, 65, 68, 70, 73, 76, 78, 83, 87
　Hannah Jane, 84
　Henry, 34, 55
　Henry, Jr., 70, 76
　Isaac, 63, 65, 69, 73, 77, 85, 89
　Jacob, 34, 55, 58, 74, 77, 83, 89
　Leah, 73
　Margaret, 63
　Margareth, 55
　Mariah, 70
　Nicholas Livingood, 76
　Rachel, 77
　Sarah, 72, 77
　Simon, 83
　Solomon, 79
　(Stol, Slot), Jacob, 156
Steermand, John, 284
Stegs, Madlena, 12
Stendly, Janneke, 23
　Michel, 23
Stetler, Benjamin, 74
　Hannah, 74
　Susanna, 73
Steven, 207
Steward, Ann, 176
　John, 166, 176, 285
　Nicholas, 166
Stewart, Margaret, 277
Stickney, Eliza Maria, 254
　Marcus, 254
　Washington, 254
　William Franklin, 254
Stiel, Hendrick, 32
　Isack, 32
Stiles, Catrina, 21
　J., 21
　Sarah, 18
　Stephen, 18
Stillwell, John L., xxviii
Stoffelbeen, Gusche, 275
Stofflebeen, Creshe, 191
　Cresshe, 193
Stoley, Catharine, 62
Stoll, Albert S., xxi
　Frank, xxi
　James, vii
　Robert, xxi
Stone, Dirk, 13

Stool, Mr., vii
Stout, Maria, 4, 12
　Mary, 7, 8, 10, 12, 122
　Sarah, 153
Strader, Catrina, 153
　Elisabeth, 153
　John, 153
　William, 153
Straudes, Thys, 152
Stricklen, Sarah, 203
Stricklin, Sarah, 198
Strickling, Sarah, 208
Strouds, Strouder, Mathys, 146
Stuart, Ann, 157
　John, 157
Stull, Judge, v
　Esther, 64
Styvers, Osie, 205, 207
Sullivan, Barret, 261
　Garret, 260
　Garret D., 263
　Jemima, 260
　John, 263
　Lenah, 260, 263
Sutfin, Derick, 203, 209, 213, 277, 285
　Gertie, 285
　Gilbert, 285
　Gysbert, vii, 203, 285
　John Powelson, 209
　Nicholas Arrosmith, 213
Sutherland, Alexander, 276
Sutphen, Derick, 211
　Richard, 211
Suttin, Derick, 206
　Jacob, 206
Swart, Teunis, 6
Swarthout, Antye, 168
　Deborah, 240
　Peter, 240
Swartswelder, Anna Margaret, 87
Swartwood, Absalom, 42
　Alexander, 42
　Andrew Jackson, 88
　Antony, 4
　Barnardus, 38, 89
　Bernardus, 1, 3
　Blandina, 48
　Catriena, 38
　Caty, 30
　Charles Ridgeway, 83
　Clarissa, 83
　Cornelia, 70, 81, 88
　Daniel, 43, 58
　David, 43
　Elizabeth, 35, 72, 100
　Esaia, 41
　Hannah, 28, 64
　Jacob, 71
　Jacobus, viii, 282

Swartwood, James, 29, 30, 38
　Jesyntje, 107, 108, 282
　J. M., xxii
　John, 29, 41, 48, 49, 71, 89, 91
　Joseph, 276
　Lea, 3, 4, 92
　Manuel, 28
　Martha, 38
　Mary, 28, 30, 58, 61, 80, 86
　Natel, 28
　Neeltje, 4
　Oliver Perry, 88
　Peter, 28
　Philip, 91, 108
　Rimareth, 89
　Rimerick, 67
　Samuel, 107
　Sarah, 48
　Sary, 29
　Simeon, 58, 64, 67, 70, 75, 83, 88
　Susanna, 58
　Susannah, 75
　Thomas, 35
Swartwoot, Antony, 3
Swartwoud, Alexander, 18
　Antie, 178, 182
　Antje, 170
　Bernardus, 19
　Bernhardus, 101, 103
　Cornelius Wynkoop, 144
　Elisabeth, 21, 174
　Gerardus, 19
　Hester, 182
　Jeseintje, 101
　Jacobus, 101, 174
　Jacobus, Jr., 97
　Jannekie, 182
　Jocobus, 182
　Joseph, 19
　Lisabeth, 103
　Mary Ann, 241
　Peter G., 241
　Philip, 144
　Philipus, 174
　Samuel, 103
　Sarah, 177
　Thomas, 18, 21, 94
Swartwoudt, ——, 143
　Alexander, 16
　Jacobus, 97
　Jannetje, 175
　Maria, 24
　Neltie, 25
　Thomas, 16
Swartwout, Abraham, 264, 276
　Abram, 21
　Alexander, 276

Swartwout, Ann, 246
Anna, 233, 274
Annatie, 38
Annatje, 129
Anthony, iii
Antje, 155, 158, 161, 170
Antony, 5, 10, 13
Benjamin, 8, 9, 16, 41,94
Benyamen, 27
Bernardus, iii, 7, 15, 46, 94
Bernardus, Jr., 13
Catherine, 260
Catrina, 136
Cornelis, 125
Cornelius, 259
Daniel, 34, 36, 39, 275
David, 279
Ebenezer, 43
Elesabet, 30
Elias, 42
Elisabeth, 112, 121, 154, 170
Elizabeth, 116, 161, 191, 193, 206, 210
Esther, 260
Eva, 97
Gerardus, 10, 118, 128, 138
Graudus, 253, 257, 259
Hannah, 208
Henry Brinkerhoff, 262
Hester, 106, 118, 123, 124, 128, 129, 139, 262, 268, 284
I., 261
Isaac, 22
Jacob, 6, 8, 10, 12, 13,15, 20, 21, 36, 93, 136, 202, 210, 217
Jacobus, x, 26, 27, 40, 117, 121, 124-126, 161, 274, 282, 284
James, 37, 43
James D., 254, 259, 262, 264
Jane, 257
Jane Hoornbeek, 253
Jannetje, 10, 138, 269
Jenneke 8, 10, 12, 163, 165, 274
Jesyntje, 97, 113, 116, 118, 119, 127
Joannes, 38, 202
Johannes, 13
John, 34, 36, 44, 45, 76
Joseph, 37, 39, 41, 42
Knelia, 46
Lea, 6, 9, 11, 15
Lidia, 39
Lisabeth, 118, 124, 128, 283
Lydia, 20

Swartwout, Maragriet, 18
Margaret, 76
Margriet, 13, 17, 161
Margrieta, 13
Maria, 7, 19, 27, 136
Marie, 27
Marrigrit, 26
Mary, 26, 31, 44, 51,191, 193, 257
Matilda, 259
Minne, 16
Naomi, 259, 262, 264
Neeltie, 39
Neeltje, 23
Nieltie, 27
Permele Berton, 44
Peter, 191, 193, 254
Petrus, 6, 18, 22, 30, 36, 276
Philip, xviii, 121, 125, 126, 129, 138, 161, 283, 284
Philipp, 257
Philippus, 123
Phillip, 254, 260, 262
Pompey, 280
Sally Ann, 253
Samuel, 109, 113, 118, 283
Sarah, 19, 21, 161, 262, 270
Thomas, iii, 5, 12, 19, 39, 45
Tomas, 27
Swartwouwt, Antie, 277
Swortwood, Elizabeth, 35
Sylsbee, Robert, 275
Symers, Abram, 125
Jacob, 125
Symor, Abraham, 132
Mari, 132

T

Tack, Geertry, 34
Hannah, 88
Isak, 10
Geertruyd, 10
Sara, 115, 123
Sarah, 34, 37, 39
Tailor, Corneilus, 277
Tak, Isak, 6
Sara, 6
Sarah, 23
Talmage, Frank De W., xxix
Goyn, xxviii
Tamson, Benjamin, 139
Elisabeth, 139
Tappan, Christopher, ii
Juriaen, 93
Tappen, Jurian, 100
Tayler, Mary, 185

Taylor, Daniel, 37
Hester ——, 273
Jacob, 35
James, 199
Jane, 202
Jaspar, 199, 204
Jasper, 202
Jerred, 204
John, 35, 191, 193
Josephus W e s t brook, 228
Josua, 273
July, 228
Lidia, 191, 193
Livingston L., xxviii
Mary, 72, 75
Peter, 30, 37
Rachel, 30
Samuel, 35, 199
Teckworth, Sara, 176
Teehore (Titsoort), Jacobus, 176
Joel, 176
Teel, Benjamin Van Demerk, 45
Catharine, 55
John, 45, 55
Mary Ann, 55
Teeler, Philip, 101
Samson, 101
Tefft, Sarah, 199
Teler, Pieter, 34
Nellie, 34
Ridolves, 34
Teneik, Sara, 102
Ten Eyck, J. B., Rev., vi, 281
J. P., Rev., 265
Terwielger, Sara, 140
Terwilge, Annaatje, 134
Annatje, 120
Catharina, 135
Cathrina, 122
Jenneke, 124, 134, 270
Mattheus, 123
Sara, 123, 134, 270
Seitje, 135
Terwilger, Blandina, 131
Catharina, 118
Cathrina, 131
Mattheus, Jr., 131
Terwillege, Annatje, 116
Terwilleger, Greetje, 170
Terwilligen, ——, 270
Cathrina, 137
Cleophas, 154
Isaac, 140
John, 137
Matheus, 140, 144, 154
Mattheus, 119, 137, 270
Sarah, 164
Sytje, 273

Terwilliger, Blandina, 168
Cathrina, 173
Greetie, 182
Jacobus, 149
Margaret, 175
Maria, 144, 275
Matheus, 149
Terwyligen, Catrina, 139
Jenneke, 139
Mathew, 139
Sytje, 139
Teter, Sevilla, 50
Sibble, 35
Thiel, Cathrina, 48
Fred'k, 48
John, 48
Thom, Susanna, 3
Thomas, Aaron, 217, 221, 226
Betchry, 221
Daniel, 221
Duly, 156
Joseph, 226
Mary, 217, 274
Pateence, 232
Patience, 246
Susanna, 93
Thomis, Patien, 238
Thompson, Elias W., xxix
Thomson, Alexander, 5, 8
Benjamin, 121, 129, 144, 266
Catrina, 144
Joseph, 179
Margaret, 179
Tichort, Stephanus, 181
Wilhelmus, 181
Tiechean (Tietshoort), Greetie, 183
Tiehl, James, 51
John, 51
Tiel, Elizabeth, 48
John, 48, 53
Rosanna, 53
Tietsoort, Sara, 144
Sarah, 144
Stephanus, 144
Tiff, Polly, 189, 202
Tifft, Sarah, 189, 190
Tilberg, Grietje, 273
Tilburg, Abram, 17
Grietje, 150
Jacob, 18
Johanna, 19
John, 17, 18
Maria, 21
Sarah, 17-19
Tilburgh, Mary, 124
Tilbury, Sary, 38
Tillberg, Anna, 23
Maragrieta, 23
Tillburg, Johanna, 142

Tillburg, John, 142
Lena, 142
Tilman, Charity, 216, 217, 223
Timber, Maria, 139
Titcherd, Bernardus, 239
Nancy, 239
Simon Middagh, 239
Titchsord, Joseas, 277
Titer, Christina Septile, 34
Tithoor, Titsoort, Margriet, 168
Titman, Margaret, 86
Titsoort, Annatje, 114
Catrina, 157
Catrine, 149
Elisabeth, 139
Femitje, 157
Jacobus, 111
Leendert, 115
Maragretje, 145
Maragriet, 154
Margaret, 149
Margriet, 137
Maria, 5
Marya, 6
Neeltje, 111, 115
Sara, 115
Sarah, 152, 156
Stephanus, 149, 157
Willem, 111, 115
William, 145
Titsworth, Wallace W., xvii
Titus, 253
Tock, Hannah, 34
John, 34
Tomson, Margaret, 186
Trauger, Lewis, xxiii
Traver, Annatie, 185
Philip, 185
Travis, Hannah, 275
Turn, Samuel, xiv
Turner, Elisabeth, 144
Esaias, 153
Jacob, 144
Johannes, 153
William E., xxviii
Tvori, Alexander, 133
Wilhelmus, 133
Tyler, Charles, 278
Tys, Jan, iii
Tyse, Sara, 120, 123

U

Upinhuysen, Elisabeth, 177
Hendrick, Jas., 177
Utt, Jane, 59

V

Vadakin, Frederic, 73
Ira, 73
V. Aken, Abraham, 34, 39
Benjamin, 34, 36
Casparus, 34, 37
David, 40
Gerritie, 185
Harmanus, 36, 39
Jacobus, 34, 38
Lena, 35
Moses, 36
Rachel, 36, 40
Sarah, 39
Van ——, Antony, 145
Teunis, 145
Van Aak, Sara, 139
Van Aake, Catrina, 132
Van Aaken, Abraham, 99, 142, 246
Abraham, Jr., 133, 162
Abram, 139, 140, 148, 151-154, 158
Abram, Jr., 142
Abram C., 154, 161
Abram J. or Y., 148
Absolom, 150
Annaatje, 106
Annatje, 144
Blandina, 143, 148
Catharina, 135, 161
Catharine, 242, 246
Catrina, 143, 145, 151, 153, 154, 284
Cobus, 150
Cobus C., 155
Cornelis, 100, 101, 105, 106, 118
Cornelius, 139
Daniel, 135, 138, 140, 141, 145, 150, 154, 159, 284
David, 17, 19, 20
Eliphas, 23
Elisabeth, 146, 151, 152
Eliza, 138
Gideon, 100
Hannah, 48
Harmanus, 17
Helena, 20, 101
Isaac, 99, 100, 106, 134, 143, 147
Jacob, 17, 24, 134
Jacobus, 147, 151
James, 48
Janetje, 133
Janneke, 144
Jannetje, 22, 105, 148, 212
Jannitje, 154
Jenneke, 19, 118
Jeremiah, 242

Van Aaken, Jerremy, 164
Johannes, 118, 134, 138, 150, 155
Johannis, 146, 147, 150, 151, 155
Joseph, 100, 134, 152
Joshuah, 159
Lea, 140, 141, 150, 284
Lena, 19, 102, 133
Lizabeth, 103
Lydia, 99, 154
Maragriet, 143
Margery, 242
Maria, 146, 150, 152, 154, 155
Nathaneel, 145
Nelle, 23
Pieternella, 102, 106, 118
Rachel, 24, 142, 154, 158
Rusja, 143
Rusje, 18
Russe, 141
Russie, 164
Sara, 106, 133, 138, 139
Sarah, 140, 148, 151-153, 158, 212
Usseltje, 138
Yannetje, 154
Van Acce, Anatje, 136
Van Aeeken, Maria, 249
Van Aeke, Catrina, 135
Van Aeken, Abraham, 104, 107, 108, 265
Abraham, Jr., 109
Abram, 143
Annatje, 104
Blandina, 107
Catharina, 107
Cornelis, 4
Cornelius, 108
Eliphaz, 4
Isaeck, 104
Jesyntje, 4
Johanna, 104
Lea, 104
Lena, 108
Lisabeth, 104
Maria, 143
Pieter, 2, 109
Pieternella, 104
Russje, 2
Sara, 108, 109, 118
Van Ake, Abraham, 135
Blandientie, 135
Casparus, 135
Elizabeth, 135
Gideon, 33
Isack, 34
Jacob, 34, 135
Jacobus, 135
Margrete, 34
Maria, 33
Sarah, 135

Vanake, Casparus, 48
Davit, 16
Jinny, 49
Rachel, 33
Rusje, 16
Van Aken, ——, 188
Aaron, 47
Abm., 183
Abraham, 113, 126, 160, 277
Abraham, Jr., 114, 118
Abram, 112, 113, 115, 126, 128, 236, 266, 283
Abram, Jr., 119, 123, 130, 138
Abram C., 160
Abram Cornelis, 284
Abram Isakse, 111
Abram J., 130
Absalom, 182
Ann, 41
Anna, 113
Annatje, 110, 112, 117, 122, 127, 132, 282
Anthony, 185
Antje, 230, 231
Antony, 198
Aploney, 166
Ariaantie, 276
Benjamin, 39, 41, 43, 46, 131
Benjamin Westbrook, 251
Blandina, 38, 271
Casparus, 44, 45, 51
Cate, 235
Catharina, 114-116, 119, 266
Catharine, 247
Cathrina, 127, 131, 132, 171-174, 177, 179, 182, 275
Catrine, 198
Cattrina, 38, 39
Cornelis, 6, 7, 11, 12, 125, 127, 131, 137
Caty, 244
Caty Westbrook, 221
Cobus, Jr., 141
Cornelius, 27, 174, 182
Daniel, 39, 41, 128, 132, 168, 171, 173, 238, 270
Daniel, Jr., 277
David, 27, 32, 37, 51
Eliphay, 93
Eliphaz, 14
Elisabeth, 172, 180, 182
Elisah, 198
Elisha, 198
Elshe, 43
Elizabeth, 40, 175, 198, 232, 239, 245
Eliza Johnson, 53

Van Aken, Fametje, 174
Femmetje, 131
Garetie, 182
Genny, 45
Gerretje, 188
Gerritje, 141
Gretie, 211
Grietee, 278
Grietie, 46, 200, 204
Hannah, 64, 66, 68, 73, 184
Hannes, 110
Harmanus, 42, 44
Helena, 182, 232
Helmus, 172
Henry, 211
Herman, 47
Hermanus, 45, 221
Hester, 6
Isaac, 35, 40, 42, 164, 182, 251, 271, 281
Isaac I., 204
Isaak, 126
Isaiah, 245
Isak, 115
Jacob, 15, 26, 46, 118, 124, 126, 131, 268
Jacob J., 68
Jacobus, 15, 38, 41, 46, 116, 117, 126, 128, 132, 180, 182, 188, 272, 276
Jacobus, Jr-, 137
James, 44, 53, 211
Janake, 197
Jane, 178, 215, 230, 231, 278
Janetje, 172
Jannetie, 197, 206
Jannetje, 7, 268
Jannitee, 277
Jemima, 37
Jenneke, 110, 119, 122, 124, 126, 137
Jeremiah, 171, 235
Johannes, 112, 116, 130, 131, 230, 231, 270
Johannis, 141, 175
John, 44, 276
John, Jr., 172
John Emmons, 32
John W., 64
Josep, 166
Joseph, 32, 38, 178, 179
Joshua, 232, 238, 278
Jsaak, 125
Jsack, 122
Lea, 168, 278
Leah, 66, 67
Leah Naamy Jane, 61
Lena, 112, 113, 119, 128, 138, 265
Levi, 137, 184, 230, 231, 240

Van Aken, Levy, 180
Lidea, 202
Lisabeth, 113, 119, 125, 130, 267
Lydia, 113, 126, 128, 178, 278
Lodewyck, 185
Magdalena, 182
Majorey, 240
Maragreet, 35
Maregreet, 179
Maregretie, 179
Margaret, 67, 182
Margere, 252
Margery, 173, 232
Maria, 118
Mariah, 251
Marjory, 248
Mary, 45, 61
Mary Anne, 68
May, 42
Meriam, 250
Moses, 235
Nathan, 173, 236, 245
Nathanael, 276
Nathaniel, 61, 245
Nelli, 125
Osseltje, 172
Pegge, 239
Philip, 44
Pieter, 281
Pieternella, 111, 113, 128, 132
Rachel, 38, 41, 42, 180, 183, 187, 199, 204, 235, 276
Reuben, 236
Richard Westbrook, 64
Russie, 94
Russje, 12, 15
Sara, 111, 120, 126, 132, 267, 271
Sarah, 174, 178, 181, 183, 199, 205
Seletie, 164
Solomon, 67
Solomon Westbrook, 240
Sophia, 93
Sophya, 6
Usseltie, 164
Wilhelmus, 32, 141
Vanaken, Asseltie, 275
Benjamin, 49
Caty, 43
Elisabeth, 47
Elesie, 28
Hannah, 49
Jacob, 28
Mahala Mariah, 56
Marey, 57
Nathanel, 56
Nathaniel, 57

Vanaken, Rachel, 27
Vananker, Rachel, 29
Van Akin, Cornelius Brooks, 65
Hannah, 65
Jacob J., 65
Joshua, 245
Richard, 245
Van Alten, Isaiah, 224
Maria, 224
Van Arnom, Benjamin, 214
John, 214
Van Arnum, Elizabeth, 40
John, 40, 42
Susannah, 42
Van Auken, Aaron, 81, 87
Absalom, 246
Anne, 221
Anson, 254
Aram, 61
Benjamin, 245
Benjamin C., 264
Benjamin Cole, 263, 280
Calvin, 85
Catharine, 279
Catherine, 255, 264
Chrispaurus, 89
David, 36
Elijah, 87
Elizabeth, 51, 57, 81, 88, 218, 247, 256, 257, 262-264
Elizebeth, 28
Ensly Roy, 73
Eveson Wheat, 91
Ezra, 258
Garret, 280
Grietje, 221
Hanna Jane, 80
Hannah, 77, 82, 89
Harrison, 255
Jacob, 28, 36
Jacob Hoornbeek, 246
Jacob J., 79, 84
Jacob Westbrook, 264
Jacobus, 81, 84, 89, 221
James, 36, 254, 280
Jane, 78-80
Jane Elizabeth, 81
Jannetje, 220
Jenny, 223
Jeremiah, 245, 252
John, 83, 87
John W., 61, 73, 77, 80, 91
Joseph, 81, 85, 88, 160
Joseph McCarty, 87
Lea, 252
Leah, 227, 255
Lenah, 279
Lydia Mariah, 77

Van Auken, Magdalen, 246
Margaret, 74, 79-82, 227, 247, 250, 255, 258, 262, 264
Margariet, 76
Margret, 221, 228
Maria, 255
Marjory, 247
Persilly Margaret, 83
Philis, 254
Phillis, 254
Nathaniel, xiii
Rachel, 61, 160
Sally, 279
Salomon, 255
Samuel, 279
Sarah, 84
Solomon, 258, 262, 264
Thomas Clarke, 252
William, 263
Vanauken, Catherine, 258
Daniel, 259
Garret, 260
James, 259, 260
Jane, 260, 261
Jeremiah, 259
Lenah, 258
Mary, 259
Mirriam, 261
Nathan, 261
Van Benschoten, Rev. Mr., xi
Anthony, 104
Cornelis, 104
Cornelius, 19
Elias, xxvii
Gerretje, 115
Heyltje Van Aaken, 19
Van Bunschooten, Antony, 185, 189
E., Rev., 275
Elias, vii, ix, x, 275
Elias, Rev., vi, vii, x, xii, xvii
Elizabeth, 188
Kanelia, 38
Maria, 185
Thomas, 189
Van Bunshoten, Antony, 14
Antie, 203
Dom., 55
E., Rev., 211
Elias, Rev., 50
Elisabeth, 123
Gerretje, 116, 117, 281
Maria, 191, 194
Van Benschouten, Gerritje, 140
Van Camp, Aaron, 56, 59
Abm., 59
Abraham, 2

Van Camp, Abram, 72, 265
Anna, 48
Benjamin, 49
Blandina, 32
Catharina, 75
Catharine, 48
Caty, 237
Daniel, 28
Elijah, 59
Elisabeth, 54
Elizabeth, 85
Elizebeth, 59
Garret, 48, 49
Gerret, 32
Henry, 237
Isaac, 92
James, 59
Jannica, 28
Jinny, 50
Johan, 32
John, 50, 56, 72
Leanah, 56
Lanah, 59
Mary, 48, 59
Salicha, 59
Selecha, 59
Van Campen, Aaron, 57, 186
Abraham, 4, 23, 26, 33, 42, 46, 55, 87
Abraham, Jr., 2, 38, 39, 43
Abram, 4, 5, 14, 94, 142, 158
Abram, Jr., 10, 11
Alexander, 8
Andrew, 43, 70, 75, 79, 86, 87
Andries, 91
Benjamin, 13, 23
Bellinda, 89
Blandina, 15
Catharina, 13
Cathrina, 94
Catrina, 10, 17, 19
Caty, 52, 64, 275
Cobus, 23
Daniel, 23, 274
Elesabet, 26
Elijah, 65
Elisabeth, 1, 16, 20, 21, 57, 93, 186
Elizabeth, 41, 56, 82
Elshe, 186, 274
Emely, 86
Gerret, 42
Gerrit, 41
Gisbert, 17
Gysbert, 2
Helena, 20
Henry, 76
Isaac, vii, 2, 13, 18, 20

Van Campen, Isack, 4, 12
Isak, 5, 8, 11
Jacob, 3, 13, 15, 94, 266
Jacob S. Thompson, 86
Jacobus, 33
James, 65, 71, 76, 82, 89, 91
Jan, 10, 15, 17, 23, 94
Jannetje, 2
John, 14, 15, 18, 42
John Michael, 75
Lana, 36
Lena, 2, 18, 163, 273
Lisabeth, 3, 11, 93, 268
Lucas, 2
Margaret, 42
Magdalena, 5, 38
Marey, 57
Maria, 23
Mariah, 79
Maritje, 4
Mary, 70, 275, 276
Marya, 14
Moses, 26, 39, 71, 86
Mosis, 23, 277
Rachel, 142, 158
Sarah, 18, 23, 46, 79, 90, 91
Sarah Mariah, 86
Susan, 86
Susanna, 14, 145, 284
Susannah, 42, 88, 276
Titje, 17
William, 42, 86
Van Camper, John, 39
Maria, 39
Van de Barak, John, 39
Van de Marck, Elizabeth, 182
Lodewyck, 182
Van Demark, Benjamin, 52
Cathren, 27
Caty, 53
Henry, 52
James, 35
Jans, 27
Jeremiah, 285
Johanna Schoonhoven, 52
Johannah, 44
John, 35
Joseph, 44
Lea, 53, 209
Leah, 218, 220
Lode, 185
Mary, 35
Peter, 69
Susannah, 69
William Ennes Cortright, 52
Van de Mark, Banadiah, 54

Van de Mark, Benjamin, 50, 55
Catharine, 50
Elisabetha, 54
Henry, 54
Lea, 55
Mary, 50, 55
Sarah, 55
Vandemark, Anna Mary, 58
Benjamin, 58
Casparus, 48
Catharine, 51
Cathrina, 184
Elisabeth, 57
Henericus, 47
Henry, 50
James, 50
James, Jr., 48
Jenny, 48
Jeremiah, 184
Johanna, 48
John, 48
Leah, 51
Margaret, 48
Rachel, 47, 50
Susanna, 50
Van Demeck, James, 277
Van Demerck, Abraham, 51
Cattrina, 210
Cherk, 43
Derck, 43
Elias, 44
Frederick, vii
Hendericus, 43
Henry, 46
Jacobus, 46
Jeremia, 44
Jeremiah, vii
Johannah, 51
John, 43, 51
Knelia, 43
Lea, 210, 278
Mary, 46
Nancy, 46
Polley, 276
Rushe, 211, 213, 278
Samuel, 43
Van Demerck, Benjamin, 56
Benjamin Berton, 44
Cattherine, 45
Caty, 41
Hendericus, 44
Henry, 41, 56
Jacobus, 41, 44, 188
Jeremiah, 24
Johannah, 45
John, 45, 277
Lea, 56
Lodewyck, 188
Peter, 45

Van Demerk, Riese, 217
  Ruschje, 24
  Sarah, 41
Vandemerk, Elesebet, 27
  Elias, 28
  Handerecus, 38
  Jacobus, 30
  Johan, 28
  Mary, 38
  Lea, 30
Van de Merken, Benjamin, 18, 19
  Cobus, 23
  Elias, 162
  Elisabeth, 17, 18, 20
  Elizabeth, 162
  Hannis, 143
  Jacobus, 20, 273
  Jannetje, 143
  Johannis, 18
  John, 21
  Maria, 20
  Petrus, 21
  Stephanus Brink, 18
Vandemerken, Benjamin, 23
  Emanuel, 23
  Ezechiel, 23
  Henderikkus Schoonhoven, 22
  Peter, 22
Van den Berg, Goosen, 20
  Gysbert, 20
Van Denmark, Cathrina, 203
Van Denmerken, Jacobus, 37
  Johanna, 37
Van der Linde, 15
  Rev., 16
Van der Lip, Boudewyn, 2
  Dorothea, 2
  Frederick, 14
Van der Merck, Benjn., 15
  James, 8
  Jeremias, 8
  Maria, 15
Vandermerck, Jeremiah, 26
  Leah, 26
Vandermerk, Benjamin, 48
  Catharine, 48
  Elizabeth, 48
  Henry, 48
  Jacobus, 33, 48
  John, 48
  Leah, 215
  Nicholas, 48
  Petrus, 33
Van der Merckel, Benjamin, 14

Van der Merckel, James, 7
  Lisabeth, 14
Van der Merkel, Jeremias, 15
  Johanna, 93
Van der Merken, Elias, 165
Van Dick, Caty, 277
Van Ditmars, Elisabeth, 175
Van de Winkel, Alexander, 100
  Antje, 100
Van Dyck, Catherine, 206
  Martin, 277
Van Dyk, Aart, 162
  Catharina, 162
Van Dyke, Aard, 152
  Catherine, 213
  Cathrine, 209
  Cattrina, 203
  Caty, 211
Van Ellen, Daniel, 244
  Margaret, 214
Van Emwegen, Annatje, 275
  David, 276, 277
  Harmanus, ix, x
  Margaret, 241
Van Emwigen, Harmanus, vii
Van Enwegen, Abraham, 249
  Benjamin, 250
  Catherine, 240
  Cornelius, 241
  Elizabeth, 249
  Esther Gumaer, 249
  George, 250
  Hannah, 240
  Hermanus, 272
  Jacob, 240
  Mary, 248
Vanenwegen, Abram, 263
  Elizabeth, 263
  Hannah, 248
  Hester, 240
  Josiah, 240
  Peter Gumare, 263
Vanest, Abigal, 54
  Caty Ann, 54
  Elizebeth, 54
  Isaac, 54
  Peter, 54
  Rebecca, 54
Vanett, Margriet, 166
Van Ette, Antony, 141
  Cornelius, 136
  Derrik, 136
  Hendricus, 141
  Johanes, 217
  Johannis, 15

Van Ette, Kornelius, 135
  Magdalena, 135
  Majore, 217
  Tonie, 136
Van Etten, Aeltje, 110, 111, 117, 119, 121, 130
  Aeltjen, 282
  Alida, 137, 170, 174
  Amanda, 83
  Amos, xviii, xix, 63
  Anna, 64, 68
  Annatie, 181
  Annatje, 113, 121, 155, 178
  Anneke, 110
  Ant., 204
  Anthony, 69, 126, 145, 159, 171, 204, 207, 213, 255, 271, 273, 279
  Antie, 187, 193, 195, 210
  Antje, 22, 23, 108, 112, 115, 126, 145, 148, 154, 163, 171, 172, 178
  Antonie, 134, 283
  Antony, 6, 110, 123, 124, 128, 131, 132, 137, 150, 153, 155, 188, 268, 281
  Aeriaentje, 281
  Ariaentje, 109, 118
  Ariantje, 104
  Arriaentje, 110, 115, 132
  Blandina, 145, 171, 173, 175, 181, 256, 257, 263
  Catharina, 117, 120, 121, 125, 160, 162, 282
  Cathrina, 106, 129
  Catrina, 210
  Cattrina, 202, 277
  Caty, 64-66
  Caty Anne, 68
  Christina, 223
  Cornelia, 78
  Cornelis, 5, 106, 112, 116, 121, 128, 129, 137, 266, 281
  Cornelius, 63, 64, 68, 73, 75, 76, 83, 142, 148, 207, 219
  Daniel, 63, 65, 73, 78, 83, 104, 115, 148, 180, 192, 194, 215, 224, 245
  Daniel Dingman, 213
  David, 81
  Deborah, 182
  Derick, 141, 179
  Derik, 150
  Diana, 153, 243
  Dianna, 251
  Dina, 230, 231, 237, 248
  Dinah, 243, 248
  Dirck, 145, 272
  Dirk, 14, 137
  Dorothy, 74, 83

Van Etten, Dorothy, 63, 65, 75, 215
Elisabeth, 143
Elizabeth, 255
Ferdenandus, 148
Gedion, 275
Gideon, 129, 163, 177, 203, 204, 208, 210, 217, 220, 223
Grietie, 285
Grietje, 159, 274
Hannah, 90, 215, 245
Helena, 139, 141, 145, 164, 175, 180, 271
Henericus, 182
Hendricus, 175
Henery, 183
Henricus, 170, 178
Henry, 233, 241, 245, 278
Heyltje, 148
Hilay, 75
Hulda, 77
Isaiah, 230
Jacob, 111, 112, 116, 126, 129, 137, 139, 148, 153, 160, 171, 173, 256, 273, 281, 283
Jacobus, 140, 193, 194
James, 208, 230, 231
Jan, 104, 106, 110, 114, 116, 120, 125, 126, 141, 281
Jane, 242, 245
Jannitee, 285
Jannitie, 28, 40
Jannetje, 6, 12, 14, 22, 25, 121, 129, 148, 267, 281
Jemima, 263
Jenneca, 217
Jenneke, 128, 160
Jesaias, 175
Jesse, 241
Joannes, vii, 185, 202, 203, 208
Johannes, 12, 120, 121, 123, 126, 129, 132, 137, 140, 160, 178, 180, 192, 194, 284, 285
Johannes, Jr., 178, 285
Johannis, 143, 150, 154
John, 63, 65-67, 69, 74, 76, 89, 122, 128, 173, 183, 217, 230, 231, 235, 244, 250, 284
John, Jr., 79, 81, 83, 89
John J., 64, 224
Jonathan Dexter, 224
Joseph, 141
Joshua, 194
Josua, 193
Lanah, 76

Van Etten, Lena, 106, 134, 152, 157, 179, 265, 274, 285
Levi, 134, 171, 224
Levi, Jr., 256
Levi D., 245
Levy, 174
Levy, Jr., 250, 256
Lydia, 145
Mag., 204
Magdalena, 109, 111, 116, 118, 120, 121, 123, 128, 142, 160, 174, 188, 281
Magdalina, 213
Magdenina, 207
Manuel, 83, 129, 164, 276
Maragreit, 202
Maragret, 141
Maragriet, 190
Margaret, 76, 181, 248, 278
Margarita, 116
Margret, 221
Margriet, 162, 185
Margrieta, 126, 131
Maria, 110, 150, 154, 175, 178, 188, 197, 198, 208, 217, 220, 276, 285
Mariah, 67, 74, 89
Mary, 87, 174, 181, 213, 219
Mary Margaret, 79
Oliver Perry, 73
Peter, 179, 183, 235
Peter Gumare, 263
Peter Westbrook, 230
Petrus, 121, 145, 285
Phebe, 218
Polly, 64
Rachel, 63, 87, 118, 120, 129, 130, 219, 283
Robert Kenady, 73
Rymerich, 132, 163
Rymerig, 46, 164
Sally, 248
Saly, 207
Samuel, 120, 183
Sara, 14, 129, 137, 283
Sarah, 66, 150, 190, 223, 278
Simeon, 83, 213, 217
Soloman, 77
Solomon, 63, 64, 67, 74, 83, 90, 174, 192, 194, 234, 242, 248, 263
Thomas, 123, 192, 194, 207, 210, 215, 218, 220, 224, 276
Tomas, 153
Verdenant, 276
William, 210
Vanetten, John, 234

Van Fleet, Benjamin, 264
Daniel, Jr., 171, 173
Elizabeth, 264
Esyntje, 171
Jacobus, 171
Mary, 257
Marytje, 26
Rebeca, 173
Solomon, Jr., 257
Thomas, 264
William, 171
Vanfleet, Abraham, 261
Annatie, 181
Catharin, 170
Cornelius, 181
Daniel V r a denburgh, 259
Deborah, 182
Elisabeth, 182
Jacobus, 172, 182
James, 261
James S., 259, 279
Levi, 259
Margaret, 261
Mary, 259
Samuel, 181
Sarah, 259, 261
Solomon, 261
Solomon, Jr., 259
Thomas, 261
Van Flera, Mikel, 57
Samuel, 57
Van Fleren, Elesabet, 34
Samuel, 34
Van Fredenburg, Arie, 98
Blandina, 98
Van Gam, Gonda, 45
Van Garde, Arie, 33
Benjamin, 102, 169
Catharina, 32
Daniel, 169
Elisabeth, 139
Elizabeth, 135
Ellenor, 232
Harme, 98, 102, 135
Hester, 16
Jacobus, 15
Jenneke, 136
Joseph, 169
Lena, 169
Marietie, 16
Margariet, 135
Moses, 32
Petries, 15
Sally, 251
Susanna Maraja, 15
Van Garden, Abraham, 163, 200, 243
Abram, 16, 117, 235
Abram Westbrook, 235
Albartus, 23
Albert, 166

Van Garden, Alexander, 5, 10, 13, 93, 109, 162
Allexander, 17
Anny, 45, 191, 193, 197
Annatje, 144, 150
Antje, 23
Aplony, 111
Apollonia, 117
Apolonie, 106
Are, 39
Arie, 105
Benj., 175
Benjamin, 24, 45, 151, 155
Benjn, 171
Cary, 217
Catharina, 2, 6, 103, 114, 162
Catharine, 29
Catrina, 15, 143, 202
Cattrina, 52, 211, 276
Caty, 222
Charity, 187
Cobus, 22
Cornelis, 117, 159, 163, 166, 169
Cornelius, 158, 162, 164
Daniel, 104, 115, 144, 163, 165, 186, 187
Daniel, Jr., 197, 202
David, 51, 144, 249, 275
Elenor, 241
Elesabet, 32
Elia, 162
Elias, 162
Eliphas, 14
Elisabet, 272
Elisabeth, 99, 134, 151, 163
Elisabetha, 53
Elizabeth, 39, 160, 164, 165, 199, 228
Ellenor, 244
Elshe, 278
Elsje, 17
Ester, 34
Esther, 24
Geertie, 207
Gideon, 163
Gisbert, 103
Gisbert, Jr., 142, 144
Grietie, 198
Gysbert, 1, 3-5, 10, 18, 19, 52, 99, 100, 105, 111, 112, 114, 117, 125, 134
Gysbert, Jr., 5, 8, 14, 109, 150, 162
Hanna, 8, 11
Hannah, 207
Hannes, 2
Harmanus, 17
Harme, 102

Van Garden, Helena, 99, 179
Hendrick, 2, 6, 10, 11, 97
Henrich, 100
Herman, 104, 115
Hester, 10, 21, 101
Hesther, 162
Heylte, 184
Heyltie, 186, 187
Heyltje, 127
Hyltie, 192, 194
Isack, 23
Jacobes, 167
Jacobus, 8, 11, 13, 15, 16, 39, 94, 102, 134, 162, 163, 165, 172, 175, 187, 193, 195, 285
Jan, 6, 11, 14, 17, 18, 93, 162
Janche, 147
Janneke, 93
Jenneke, 99, 115, 127, 139
Jenneken, 123
Joannes, 197
Johanna, 10, 12
Johannes, 99, 100, 102, 112, 115, 117, 118, 123, 125, 130
Johannes Cortregt, 139
Johannis, 22, 144
John, 18, 23, 200
Jonathan, 17, 188, 198, 207, 210, 275
Joseph, 19
Knelia, 202
Lea, 165
Leah, 162
Leentie, 278
Lena, 19, 52, 100, 105, 150
Lente, 211
Levy, 249
Lidia, 165
Lisabeth, 15, 131, 270
Lydia, 171, 278
Maragrita, 16
Maragreta, 169
Maragrit, 17
Maratje, 146
Margareta, 8
Margarit, 24
Margriet, 15, 124, 126, 130, 131, 134, 268
Maria, 5, 27, 127, 134, 141, 145, 151, 163, 270
Maritje, 5, 7, 8, 11, 12, 93
Marretje, 3
Martie, 25
Martin, 249
Martinus, 243
Martynus, 186

Van Garden, Mary, 172, 196, 215, 276, 277
Marya, 10, 14, 130, 131
Morin, 245
Moses, 13, 53
Neele, 32
Peter, 16
Petrus, 10, 17, 18, 109, 111, 123, 188
Pheby, 210
Pieter, 1, 101
Plone, 104
Rachel, 1, 4, 5, 8, 19, 101, 103, 104
Sally, 246
Salomon, 188
Samuel, 112, 142, 163-165, 186, 274
Sander, 19
Sara, 1-3, 8, 12, 115, 167, 234, 266
Sarah, 213, 242, 278
Seletje, 162
Silas, 249
Souvregn, 163
Susannah, 39, 42
Teatje, 177
Willem, 101, 105, 123
Willem Vredenburgh, 134
William, 19, 22, 24, 186, 188, 197, 202, 245

Vangarden, Alexander, 31
Elisabeth, 17
Gouda, 17
Hester, 26, 27, 31
Jacobus, 17
Johanna, 26
Josip, 31
Margrietta, 26
Maria, 34
Marregrit, 28
Marritje, 26
Rachel, 16
Willem, 26

Van Gardn, Johannis, 272
Vangardon, Elizabeth, 46
James, 46
Rebecca, 46
Van Gargen, Abraham, 201
Isaac, 201
Van Gelder, Cornelius Timpson, 82
George, 82
Henry Owins, 76
John, 76, 82
John Jinkins, 76
Van Gerden, Annatje, 21
Alexander, 21
Van Gerder, Alexander, 273

Van Glien, Elisabeth, 146
Van Gorde, Apolonie, 98
  Gysbert, 98
  Maria, 138
Van Gorden, Amanda, 81
  Anne, 84
  Antje, 153
  Benjamin, 54, 57, 64, 84, 87
  Catharine, 49, 72, 78
  Catrina, 20, 138
  Cherick, 70
  Daniel, 153
  David, 19
  Diana, 84, 89
  Drusilla, 87
  Elisabeth, 139, 148
  Elisabetha, 54
  Elizabeth, 84, 87, 225, 230
  Elsey, 78
  Elsje, 165
  Gonda, 101
  Gysbert, 138, 149, 284
  Gysbert Gysbertse, 148
  Gysbert, Jr., 153
  Harme, 101
  Helmus, 148
  Henry, 54
  Heyltje, 148
  Isaac, 90
  Isaac P., 71, 74, 90
  Jacob Dewit, 64
  Jacobus, 19, 148
  James, 74, 78, 81, 84, 87, 89
  Jan, 20
  Jane Eveline, 64
  John, xxi, 57, 78, 81, 84, 212
  John Wilson, 71
  Joseph, 64
  Lena, 98
  Lenah, 89, 91
  Lucinda, 84
  Magdalen, 49
  Margriet, 28
  Maria, 149, 284
  Mariah, 81
  Mary, 51, 61, 78, 80, 81, 84, 212
  Moses, 49, 89
  Polly Reser, 70
  Rachel, 74, 79, 85, 99, 100
  Richard, 84
  Samuel, 84
  Sarah, 100, 145, 212
  Sary, 218
  Solomon Hornbeek, 74
  Solomon Rosenkrans, 74
  Susannah, 50
Van Gorden, Sytje, 139
  Willem, 101
  William V r e denburg, 139
Vangorden, Hannah Jane, 78
  Isaac P., 78
  Jemimy, 47
  Marey, 57
  Mary, 57
  Moses, 47
Van Gordon, Gideon, 210
  Hester, 275
  Jacobus, 210
  Johannis, 273
  Mary, 218
Vangordon, Aaron, 31
  Beniaman, 31
  James, 31
Van Horn, Ann, 57
  Anny, 51
  Caty, 47
  Cornelius, 42
  Elizabeth, 42, 81, 83, 88
  Simon, 47
Van Hornbeek, Elizabeth, 245
Van Imwege, Cornelius, 168, 169
  Gradus, 168
  Gretje, 168
  Harmus, 168
Van Imwegen, Abraham, 230, 231, 235
  Annatje, 230, 231
  Cornelius, Jr., 234
  Gerardus, 278
  Hannah, 234, 245
  Haremanus, 170
  Jacobus, 233
  Jane, 235
  Janetje, 170
  John, 233
  Lenah, 230, 231
  Margaret, 280
  Maria, 280
  Mary, 234
Vaninwagen, Isaac, 256
  Jacob, 256
  Jane, 257
  Samuel, 257
  Sarah, 256
Van Innewege, Janneke, 136
Van Inwege, Janneke, 168
Vanin Wegen, Annatie, 181
  Anntje, 181
  Cornelius, 181
  Haremanus, 182
  Jacob, 181
  Josias, 182
  Seletta, 181
Van Inwegen, Abraham, 244
  Anne, 248
  Benjamin, 246, 252, 253
  Betsey, 252
  Cornelius, 174
  Daniel, 250, 252
  David, 246, 251
  Eli, 252
  Evalina Swartwout, 256
  Grietje, 138
  Hannah, 260, 263
  Haremanus, 173
  Hermanus, 138, 251, 256, 260, 261
  Jacob, 173, 247
  Jane, 246, 247
  John, 174, 244, 249, 250
  Josiah, 247, 248
  Josias, 260
  Lewis, 246
  Margaret, 173, 247, 263
  Margery, 246
  Mary, 245
  Rachel, 250
  Sally, 250
  Samuel, 253
  Seletta, 177
  Solomon, 249
Vaninwegen, Benjamin, 259, 262, 264
  Catherine, 262
  Charity, 259
  Daniel V. A., 256
  Hannah, 259
  Herman, 262
  Hermanus, 259
  Iva, 259
  Jacob, 259
  James S., 262
  Jane, 256, 262
  Jemima, 259, 262
  Joseph, 262
  Joseph Hornbeck, 262
  Peter, 250
  Phebe, 259, 262, 264
  Sally, 259
  Samuel, 250, 262, 264
  Solomon, 264
Van Kampe, Benjin, 15
  Catharina, 24
  Isaac, 24
  Isack, 16
  Jacobus, 16
  Jan, 16
  Maria, 15
  Susanna, 15, 16
Van Kampen, Abraham, 105
  Abram, 13, 266
  Abram, Jr., 6, 8
  Catharina, 6, 13
  Daniel, 8

Van Kampen, Gysbert, 5, 9, 14, 101
  Isaac, 4, 5
  Isak, 6, 7, 9
  James, 55
  Jan, 4
  Lena, 7
  Lisabeth, 4, 14
  Madlena, 4
  Magdalena, 9
  Martinus, 101
  Moses, 105, 179
  Sara, 5, 9
  Susannah, 55
Van Keuren (Venkearn), Janneke, 8
  Jannetje, 3, 106
  Jenneke, 98, 100, 101, 105, 110, 126-128, 131, 281
  Mary, 238
  Rachel, 3, 4, 6-9, 12, 13
  Tjaadje, 101, 106
Van Kleef, Maria, 23
Van Leeuwen, Cornelia, 3
Van Leuven, Cornelia, 7, 13
  Hanna, 124
Van Leuwen, Cornelia, 10
Van Loon, Hannah, 190
  Nicholas, 190
Vannaaken, Margery, 238
  Russje, 15
Van Nak, Joseph, 167
Van Nake, Cornelius, 168
  Gerretye, 168
  Gretje, 168
  Isaac, 160
  Jannetje, 168
  Joseph, 160
  Lidea, 168
  Maria, 168
  Sartye, 168
Van Naken, Absalom, 240
  Coert, 240
  Cornelis, 166
  David, 24
  Gretie, 170
  Hester, 24
  Isack, 167, 170
  Jane, 240
  Jarmiah, 166
  Jeames, 57
  Joseph, 169
  Magdalen, 240
  Margaret, 218
  Ragel, 169
  Ruschje, 24
  Sarah, 218
  Seletta, 167
Vannaken, Elisabeth, 57
  Hannah, 58
  Jacob I., 58
Vannaken, Sollomon, 58
Vannalten, Gidean, 214
  Jacob, 214
Van Namen, Elisabeth, 127
  Sara, 127
Van Nanken, Henry Barnhart Wintermute, 60
  John, 60
  Rachel, 60
Van Nanker, James, 59
  Jane, 59
  Sarah, 59
Van Natte, Elizabeth, 49
Van Nette, Antje, 98, 160
  Dinah, 240
  Elizabeth, 32
  Jacob, 98
  Jacobus, 33
  Margaritje, 160
  Mary, 33
Van Netten, Antje, 104, 167
  Catharina, 54
  Cornelia, 53, 54
  Cornelius, 133
  Cornelius Westbrook, 237
  Dinah, 236
  Elizabeth, 47, 237
  Henry, 227
  Huldah, 247
  Isaiah, 227, 237
  Jacob W., 247
  Jan, 265
  Johannes, 164, 167
  John, Jr., 54
  Lena, 170
  Levi, 237
  Magdalen, 167
  Magdalena, 164
  Manel, 167
  Maregreta, 170
  Maria, 53, 167
  Semijon, 167
  Simeon, 53
Van Nest, Catrina, 20
  Isaac, 16, 20, 143
  Judica, 4
  Judick, 24
  Lea, 16
  Peter, 143
  Petrus, 24
  N., Rev., 223
  Rynier, 279
Vannest, Peter, vii
Van Neste, George, 70
  Ira Vredenbargh, 63
  Isaac Hankinson, 70
  Jacob Ross, 70
  Peter, Jr., 63
Van Nimwegen, Annatje, 112, 154
  Annetje, 153
  Anthony, 242
  Antje, 153
  Caletta, 144
  Cornelis, 106
  Elisabeth, 112
  Gerardus, 106, 107, 109, 112, 113, 140, 282
  Gradus, 161
  Grietje, 154, 161
  Gritje, 140
  Harmanus, 140, 141, 144, 153, 154
  Hermanus, 281, 284
  Jacob, 107, 113, 147, 153
  Jannetje, 107, 108, 114
  Jenneke, 115, 118, 119, 123, 124, 128, 282
  John, 242
  Margrieta, 284
  Margrietie, 141
  Martinus, 242
Van Ninwegen, Charack, 242
  Hermanne, 242
  Gerardus, 103
  Janneke, 102
  Josiah, 242
Van Niuwegen, Gerardus, 101
  Janneke, 102
  Jannetje, 101
  Jenneke, 98
  Tjaadje, 101
Van Noey, Benjamin, 225, 226
  Elias, 184
  Elizabeth, 217
  Jacob, 241
  Joseph, 241, 275
  Ledia, 189
  Lidy, 241
  Peter, 189
  Petrus, 184
  Sarah, 225, 244
  Sowryn, 226
Van Noj, Benjamin, 138, 142
  Sarah, 142
  Usselje, 138
Van Norman, Abraham, 223
  John, 223
Van Noy, Benjamin, 249
  Elias, 249
  Elisabeth, 169
  Jane, 252
  Peter, 252
  Peter, Jr., 247, 250
  Polly, 252
  Sally, 250

Van Noy, William, 247
Vannoy, Caty, 262
  David, 258, 260, 262, 279
  Esther, 260
  George, 263
  Hannah, 279
  Hester, 263
  Jacobus Vanauken, 258
  Jane, 280
  Joseph, 258
  Lanche, 261
  Lenah, 260, 262
  Nicholas, 258, 261, 279
  Oliver, 260
  Peter xvi
  Polly, 257
  Rachel, 279
  Sally, 261
  Sarah, 260
  William, 260, 263, 279
Van Noye, Joseph, 199
  Mary, 199
  Peter, 199
Van Oetten, Aaltje, 105
  Aeltje, 99
  Annetjen, 102
  Antje, 100
  Ariaantje, 100
  Dirk, 100
  Helena, 99
  Jacob, 100, 103, 105
  Jan, 99, 100, 103
  Lena, 99, 102
Van Orman, Johannes Depui, 211
  John, 207, 211
  Osee, 207
Vanoy, Benjamin, 133
Van Scoda, Johanna, 85
Van Sickel, Jacobus, 120, 267
  Johannes Casparus, 120
  Ledea, 275
Van Sickele, Cobus, 135
Van Sickelen, Cornelis, 126
  Jan, 124, 126, 268
  Jannetje, 129
  John, 128, 177
  Reynier, 124
Van Sickkle, Jacobus, 178
Van Sickle, Jacobus, 188, 240
  Janny, 206
  John, 188
  Ledy, 206
  Lewis, 240
  Lidia, 207, 210
  Lucy, 206
  Rynier, 206
Van Sikel, Jenneke, 210
  John, 198, 210
  Lidia, 198

Van Sikel, Maria, 198
Van Sikele, Andrew, 104
  John, 204, 208
  Sarah, 208
Van Sikelen, Abram, 143
  John, 143
Van Sikkelen, Janetje, 145
  Jannetje, 141, 157
Van Sikle, Lidia, 188
Van Strander, Isaac, 232, 236, 279
  John, 280
  Levy, 251
  Lydia Van Vliet, 236
  Mary, 247, 251
  Rachel, 232, 279
Van Stronder, Isaac, 254
  Matthias, 254
  Sarah, 254
Van Syckel, John Merit, 90
  Letitia Merrit, 90
  Samuel, 90
Van Tessel, Johannes, 12
  Theodorus, 12
Van Teesselen, Nicalaas, 153
Van Thuil, Catrina, 151
  Isaac (Simon), 151
Van Tilbur, Mari, 26
Van Tilburg, Jan, 17
  Margritha, 26
  Mary, 35
  Sary, 29
Van Tilburgh, Abraham, 2, 130
  Abram, 112
  Elisabeth, 25
  Grietje, 2
  Johanna, 131, 270
  John, 25
  Mary, 94, 130
  Sara, 112
Van Tilbury, Sarah, 41
Vantilbury, Sarah, 29
Van Tillburgh, Hendrikus, 150
  John, 150
Van Tuil, Walter, 139
Van Tuyl, Isaac, 173
Van Vleet, Benjamin, 253
  Elizabeth, 250
  John, 55
  Michael, 55
  Solomon, Jr., 253
  Syche, 240
Van Vlera, Elizebeth, 59
Van Vlet, Elizebeth, 233
Van Vliedt, Benjamin, 135
  Debora, 135
  Samuel, 135
Van Vliere, Cornelis, 24
  Cornelius, 40

Van Vliere, Daniel, 40
  Lena, 24
Van Vlieren, Catharina, 122
  Cornelius, 32, 165
  Hieronymus, 122
  Jeronimus, 165
  Susanna, 32
Van Vliet, Abraham, 240
  Abram, 155
  Anna Catharina, 6
  Annatje, 147
  Benjamen, 271
  Benjamin, 119, 125, 128, 147, 273, 284
  Catharina, 108, 161
  Catrina, 20, 139, 155
  Cobus, 139, 158
  Daniel, 138, 151, 155, 251, 269
  Debora, 125, 128, 134, 155, 197, 271
  Derick, 18
  Derick, Jr., 20
  Derrick, 4
  Dirck, 3, 6, 7
  Dirk, 4, 7-9, 12, 13
  Eegje, 97
  Elisabeth, 13, 116, 121, 128, 152
  Elizabeth, 233, 242, 249, 268
  Esyntie, 136
  Gerret, 4
  Gertruy, 178
  Jacobus, 127, 147, 155, 178, 276
  James, 251
  Jan, viii, 107, 108, 113, 116, 118, 119, 127, 136, 271, 281, 282
  Jenneke, 9
  John, 230, 231, 240, 250, 278
  Judic, 20
  Judica, 4
  Ledia, 42, 45, 46
  Lisabeth, 108, 112, 119, 124, 283
  Lizabeth, 108
  Lyntje, 160
  Maragrites, 284
  Margaret, 230, 231
  Maria, 18, 107, 139
  Maritje, 20, 155
  Marya, 113, 178
  Michael, 178
  Rachel, 6, 18
  Samuel, 108, 112, 116, 124, 127, 269, 277
  Sara, 138
  Sarah, 151
  Syntye, 175

Van Vliet, Tjerck Van Keuren, 3
Tjerk van Keuren, 8
Van Vliett, Jennica, 43
Van Wege, Aard, 16
Van Weye, Jonas, 25
John, 25
Van Weyen, Aert, 94, 132
Cathy, 6
Charles, 3, 6, 8, 103
Evje, 3
John, 1
Joseph, 6
Helena, 150
Hendricus, 1, 3, 132
Lena, 3
Van Wien, Lena, 25
Van Winkelen, Aron, 156
Cobus, 156
Wyntje, 152
Van Woert, Sarah, 211
Van Wyck, Geo. P., iv, ix
George P., xviii, xxviii
Van Wye, Susanna, 33
Varnoje, Benjn, 171
Elizabeth, 171, 175
Jannetje, 177
Joseph, 177
Petrus, 172
Oseltje, 177
Sartje, 172
Varnoye, Elisabeth, 175
Petrus, 175
Varway, Aert, 14, 124
Catharina, 14
Charles, 14
Hanna, 14
Hendricus, 124
Vas, xxiv, xxv
Petrus, 97
Petrus, Rev., iii, xxv
V. Bunschooten, Anganitie, 36
V. Bunschoten, Antony, 117
G., 45
Jacobus, 38
Maria, 38, 117
V. Campen, Jacob, 37
John, 35, 37
Sarah, 35
V. Demerk, Johanna, 37
V. D. Merk, Elizabeth, 33
Jacobus, 33
V. D. Merken, Annatie, 34
V. Dyck, Anny, 275
V. Garden, Aria, 36
Daniel, 275
Elizabeth, 37
Jacobus, 37
Jenneca, 37
Susanna, 36, 37
Susannah, 35

V. Noy, Benjamin, 183
Joseph, 183
Venauken, Leana, 43
Ven Campen, Blandena, 44
Vengarden, Catey, 43
Elizabeth, 43
Jems, 43
Vengorden, Elesa Bath, 44
Hannah, 44
Jems, 44
Vennema, Ame, xxix
Vernoi, Benjamin, 133
Joseph, 133
Vernon, Petrus, 160
Vernooy, Aaron, 233
Benjamin Westbr., 121
Benjamin Westr., 126
Elisabeth, 121
Elizabeth, 241
Peter, 233
Petrus, 126
Sarah, 230, 231
Vernoy, Benjamin, 158
Benjamin Westbrock, 267
Petrus, 158
Rachel, 255
Saly, 235
Sarah, 236
Verwey, John, 22
Mery, 22
Verweye, Aerd, 22
Charles, 22
Lena, 17
Ver Wye, Jan, 273
Viegli, Jacob, 137
Viervan, Cornelia, 104
Vigely, Jacob, 141
Zacharias, 141
Vigli, Jacob, 132
Vincent, Hanna, 8
Vininwagen, David, 233
Margret, 233
Visher, Minne, 16
Vlierden, Elizabeth V., 54
Vliedt, Jan, 136
Vliet, Jacobus, 101
Jan, 101
Vocht, Andries Madlena, 14
Valentin, 14
Valentyn, 112
Volckertse, Johannes, 92
Von Garden, William Vredenburgh, 270
Voorhees, Henry M., xxviii
Vradenburgh, Benjamin, 249
Catharine, 260
Hannah, 280

Vradenburgh, Jacob, 258, 260
Jacobus Vanauken, 258
Lenah Hopkins, 260
Mary Conckling, 249
Vredenberg, Lydia, 21
Vredenburg, Aaron, 212
Arie, 139, 283, 284
Benjamin, 151
Blandena, 30
Blandina, 27, 30, 33, 141, 271
Catharina, 165
Catrina, 148, 150, 159, 284
Daniel, 277
Helmus, 151
Lidia, 285
Lydia, 141, 145, 150, 159
Mattheus, 114
Sara, 139
Wilhelmus, 139, 148
Vredenburgh, Aare, 205
Aaron, 107, 114, 199, 239
Antje, 123
Arie, 108, 109, 116, 120, 127, 134, 284
Benjamin, 205, 212, 239, 254, 278
Blandina, 25, 131, 134
Catharina, 109
Catharine, 279
Catrina, 169
Caty, 232
Daniel, 242, 249
Elijah, 247
Elizabeth, 199, 212, 280
Elsche, 38
Elsie, 135
Elsje, 32, 165
Eltse, 280
Glorana, 254
Havilah, 238
Helmus, 199, 272
Hezekiah, 238, 249
Jacob, 279
Joshua, 232, 239
Joshuah, 247
Josua, 163
Juliana, 242
Levi, 239
Lidia, 201
Lydia, 107, 114, 172
Mary, 279
Mattheus, 107
Wilhelmus, 131, 163, 165, 238
Wilhels, 135
Vrelingbergh, Arie, 178, 183
Benjn, 178
Cathrina, 180
Caty, 178, 179

Vrelingbergh, L y d i a, xxiv, 179
Maria, 183
Wilhelmus, x

W

Waaker, John, 154
Petrus, 154
Waard, Hermanus Dekkar, 101
William, 101
Waarner, Frederick, 41
Wach, Caspar, 53
Wachman, Elizabeth, 48
Waerd, Benjamin, 155
Johannis, 155
Waert, Benjamin, 106
Jan, 103
John, 1
Lisabeth, 11
Rachel, 111
Willem, 111
William, 1, 4, 11, 106
Wagenaer, Elisabeth, 163
Wagener, Andries, 14
Wainwright, Jacob, xix
Waldrum, Jane, 205
Wales, Femmetje, 128
James, 128
Walker, Elizabeth, 200
Mary, 196
Sarah, 201
Seene, 285
Wallace, Francis Barton, 73
Isayas, 161
James, 73
John, 161
Margaret Matilda, 73
Mary Amanda, 280
William Alexander, 73
Wallen, Lisabeth, 119
Phebe, 175, 183
Pheby, 208
Susanna, 6, 126, 131
Waller, Corns, 181
Jannetie, 181
Susanna, 93
Walles, Joseph, 186
Sarah, 186
Wallin, Febe, 167
Wallis, John, 168
Wallon, Joseph, 119, 267
Phebe, 164
Pheby, 188, 202, 204, 214
Phiby, 195
Susanna, 120
Walter, Elenor Elizabeth, 91
Moses, 89
Peter, 89, 91

Warner, Adam, 39
An Catreen, 28
Catharine, 81
Catrine, 34
Christina, 34
Daniel, 41, 77, 84
Elisabeth, 157
Eliza Ann, 71
Frederick, 28, 34, 38, 39, 49, 71
Hannah, 84
Henry Arns, 88
Jacob, 36, 81, 83, 88
John, 49
Lewis, 77, 83
Lodewick, 34, 36, 44
Lodewyck, 41
Lodewyk, 38
Maragriet, 44
Sarah, 38
Warsbon, (Washburn),
Abeneser, 169
Nathannel, 169
Wasben, Rachel, 47
Wasbon, Elizabeth, 43
Wasborn, Marcia, 167
Noah (Nathaniel), 167
Wasburg, Nathaniel, 159
Patience, 159
Washboun, Elesabeth, 27
Noach, 27
Washburn, Anna Barbar, 165
Henry, 52
Nathaniel, 165
Nicholas Schoonhoven, 52
Washburne, Henry, 49
Noah, 49
Wass, Elizabeth, 49
Waus, Elisabeth, 39
Elizabeth, 38
Week, Margriet, 169
Weiss, xxv
Welbingt, Dereck, 166
Welfelt, Adam, 214
Peter, 214
Wells, Abraham, 164, 180
Ann, 211
Annatje, 137
Betick, 167
Caty, 205, 277
Esrael, 208
Isaac, 173
Israel, 180, 183, 187
James, 173, 183, 198
James, Jr., 164
Jesse, 187
John, 198
Margriet, 6, 13, 14, 109, 117
Mary, 109
Nathan, 208

Wells, Pheby, 208
Phenes, 167
Polly, 198
Rachel, 277
Reb., 188
Rebecca, 130, 185
Rebecka, 167, 171, 198
Rebekah, 176
Sara, 167
Sarah, 172, 173, 179, 188, 199, 205
Thomas, 130, 137, 270
Wels, Margriet, 100, 105
Margrita, 104
Salomon, 105
Welsch, Jacobus, 141
Maria, 107
Thomas, 141
Welsh, Thomas, 274
Weltvael, Bn., 136
Rusje, 136
Wert, Elizabeth, 65
Wesbroek, Aeltie, 275
Anthony, 272
Elizabet, 272
Janneke, 271
Magere, 49
Maria, 275
Petrus, 145
Sarah, 145
Wesbrook, Johannes, 152
Engeltie, 152
Wesfal, Christina, 152
Wessebrock, Anthonie, 99
Antje, 98
Cornelis, 98
Johannes, 98
Johannis, 99
Magdalena, 99
Maria, 105
Petrus, 98
Wessebroeck, Johannes, 100
Antje, 100, 103, 105
Antonie, 105
Benjamin, 105
Cornelis, 100
Dirk, 100, 101
Dyrk, 98
Heilje, 105
Jannetje, 100, 102
Johannes, 98
Jurk, 105
Lisabeth, 105
Tjerk Van Keuren, 101
Turk, 105
West, John, 220
Richard, 220
Westbook, Seletie, 57
Westbrock, Abram, 157
Annatje, 148
Antie or Lintie, 166
Antje, 158

Westbrock, Benjamin, 133, 155
Daniel, 159
Derick, 149
Dirk, 110
Catrina, 133
Cornelius, Jr., 133
Helmus, 159
Heyltje, 136
Jacob, 129
Johanna, 165
Johannis, 156
Johannis B., 159
Johannis J., 155
Lea, 142
Lena, 159
Levi, 158
Lidia, 133
Lydia, 110
Maria, 141, 149
Rachel, 159, 164
Saffrein, 129
Samuel, 142, 159
Sara, 283
Sarah, 156
Therk. 157
Tjerk Van Keuren, 137
Westbroeck, ——, 132
Abraham, 132, 268
Abraham, Jr., 120
Abram, 125, 128, 129-132
Abram Dirkse, 126
Aeltje, 124
Alida, 114
Anatje, 133
Annatje, 119, 131
Anthony, 265
Antie, 185
Antje, 108, 111, 112, 116, 117, 121, 124-126, 129, 163, 282
Antjen, 281
Antony, 110, 117, 119, 121, 130, 136, 267, 282
Arie, 126
Benjamin, 6, 104, 108, 111, 115, 117, 124, 129, 265, 281
Catharina, 111, 115, 265, 281
Cathrina, 106, 124, 129
Cherk Van Keuren, 153
Cornelis, 108, 110, 119, 120, 124, 163, 281, 282
Cornelis, Jr., 122, 129, 281
Cornelius, 106, 133
Derrick, viii, xv, 106, 281
Dirck, 3
Dirk, 8, 126-128, 130, 131, 281, 282
Elisabeth, 122
Evert Rosa, 126
Evert Roos, 119, 268

Westbroeck, Gideon, 129, 132
Hannes, viii, 104
Helltje, 108
Heltje, 266, 281
Heyltje, 5, 112, 116, 121, 128, 129, 137
Jacob, 113, 114, 117, 123, 125, 131, 166, 184, 266
Jacobus, 127, 132, 186, 283
Jannetje, 110, 114, 116, 122, 127, 131, 265, 283
Jannetje M., 132
Jenneke, 115, 126, 131
Jennetje, 122
Joel, 132
Johanna, 131, 163, 169
Johannes, 108, 111, 112, 115, 117, 121-123, 127, 132, 265, 267, 269, 281-283
Johannes, Jr., 9, 112, 114, 117, 282
Johannes, Sr., 113
Johannes C., 131
Johannes Corn., 112, 126
Johannes Cornelis, 281
Johannes Dirkse, 115
Johannes I., 166
Joseph, 116, 119, 120, 123, 126, 128, 131, 267, 283
Josephet, 132
Lena, 110, 112, 117, 119, 121, 122, 127, 130, 132, 163, 169, 267, 282
Levi, 128
Lydia, 120
Magdalena, 108, 114, 117, 122, 123, 127, 265
Mari, 132
Maria, 9, 104, 108, 110, 116, 117, 120, 121, 125, 126, 129-131, 136, 163, 265-267, 275, 281
Marie, 122
Martinus, 128
Marya, 6, 112, 113, 115, 117
Marys, 268
Michel, 125
Moses, 120, 129
Petrus, 133
Rachel, 129, 164
Salomon, 110, 120, 124, 127-130, 132, 184
Samuel, 110, 117, 186
Sara, 118, 120, 125, 127, 128, 130, 137, 269
Sarah, 153
Susanna, 133
Wilhelmus, 124
William, 132

Westbroek, Abraham, 136, 172
Abram, 138, 140-142, 146, 149, 150
Abram Joh., 152
Alexander, 149
Alida, 136
Annatje, 142, 162
Annetje, 284
Anthoni, 133
Annitje, 153
Antie, 184
Antje, 140, 151, 156, 158, 165
Antje B., 153
Antone, 136
Antonie, 135
Antony, 111, 146, 149, 156, 273
Benjamin, 115, 138, 140, 142, 159, 168
Benjamin Vernoi, 135
Blandina, 111, 140, 150, 185, 273, 275
Casia, 150
Catharina, 117
Cathrina, 129
Catrina, 21, 138, 140, 142, 157
Ceeletje, 33
Cherk Van Cuiren, 141
Cherk Van Keuren, 142
Cherk Van Kuiren, 148
Cobus, 138
Cornelia, 136, 138
Cornelis, 134, 153
Cornelius, 136, 138, 141, 151
Debora, 133, 143, 148, 284
Derick, 146
Derik, 140, 274
Elisabeth, 156, 158
Elizabeth, 24, 136, 157
Evert Roosa, 138
Evert Rosa, 134, 140
Gideon, 138, 158
Grietje, 146
Hannes, 103
Hans C., 133
Heiltje, 133
Helmus, 162
Hendrik, 146
Hester, 187
Heyltie, 136, 142, 161
Huyltie, 135
Jacob, 107, 111, 141, 151, 273
Jacobus, 134, 151, 165
Jaen, 166
Janche, 149
Janetje, 140

Westbroek, Janneke, 140, 142, 146, 148
Jannetie, 136
Jannetje, 108, 117, 136, 147
J. Dirikse, 136
Jenneca, 185
Jenneke, 23, 164
Jennike, 26
Johanes, 138
Johannes, 117, 135
Johannes, Jr., 103, 117, 161
Johannes B., 162
Johannes J., 187
Johannis, 141, 146, 148, 149, 273
Johannis B., 150, 151, 157, 274
Johannis J., 172
John, 82
Jonannis, 273
Josep, 271
Joseph, 128, 133, 134, 136, 140, 143, 145, 148, 284
Josua, 165
Lea, 141, 148, 151
Leah, 161
Ledea, 34
Leentje, 168
Lena, 132, 136, 140
Leonard, 136
Levi, 23
Louis, 117
Lydi, 141
Lydia, 23, 141, 148
Magdalen, 138
Magdalena, 103, 135, 186
Magdalene, 146
Majory, 35
Margery, 33
Maria, 26, 107, 138, 145, 146, 148, 149, 151, 152, 156, 162, 164
Maria dirks, 133
Martinus, 164
Meseri, 133
Petrus, 141, 150, 159
Saferyn, 185
Salomon, 33, 117
Samuel, 143, 151, 165, 168
Sara, 142
Sarah, 108, 146, 148, 149
Seletje, 133
Solomon, 82
Westbroet, Johanna, 186
Westbrok, Johannis, 26
Westbroock, Antie, 192
Maria, 195
Westbrook, Aaltje, 215
Aaron, 183, 249

Westbrook, Abm., 66
Abraham, 169, 170, 196, 197, 206, 212, 213, 215, 216, 219, 223, 277
Abraham I., 219, 225
Abraham M., 66, 219
Abraham T., 238
Abram, 160
Alchie, 183
Alexander, 189, 243, 247, 249, 257, 279
Alfred, 237
Altie, 187, 196
Anna, 66
Annatje, 23, 25, 28
Antie, 190, 194, 202, 210, 285
Antje, 172, 175, 180, 181
Are, 167
Arie, 177
Ary, 189
Benjamin, 174, 201, 204, 209, 211, 216, 221, 224, 226, 229, 249, 277
Benjamin A., 279
Blandena, 225
Blandina, 30, 179, 190, 197, 201, 203, 207, 216, 220, 224, 226, 227, 230
Catharine, 61, 221, 224, 229
Cathrina, 196
Caty, 60
Cattrina, 38, 189, 206, 276
Chark, 200
Cornelia, 177, 183, 188, 203, 208
Cornelius, 179, 224, 226
Cornelius B., 210
Cornelius D. or P., 197, 202, 205
Cornelius R., 237
Daniel Dingman, 66
Daniel Ennist, 221
Deborah, 234, 241, 246, 250, 251, 255
Dedion, 211
Dina, 237
Dinah, 224
Easter, 249
Elesabet, 31
Elisabeth, 55, 173
Eliza Hagerty, 219
Elizabeth, 29, 199, 204, 208, 226, 229, 249, 277
Eltsie, 279
Emy, 183
Enis, 254
Esther, 220, 254, 257
Evert Rosa, 177
Femmetje, 160
George, 222, 226, 228

Westbrook, Hannah, 72
Hannah Jane, 77
Helena, 46
Helmus, 196
Henry, 257
Hester, 187, 224, 226, 251
Hester Hoorbeck, 225
Hetty, 241
Heyetje, 232
Hilthe, 233
Hiram, 81
Hugh, 219
Hymen, 89
Jacob, 64, 66, 68, 70, 73, 77, 82, 89, 171, 190, 210, 215, 220, 225, 226, 278, 285
Jacobus, 177, 189, 199
James, 46, 48, 257, 275
James D., 284
Jane, 84, 239, 243, 245, 248, 249, 252, 255, 277
Janetje, 174
Jannetje, 171, 173
Jannetye, 219
Jannke, 167
Jannitie, 225
Jean, 237
Jenne, 236
Jenneke, 230, 231
Jerusha, 257
Joannes, 37, 192, 194, 222
Joannes C., vii
Joannes D., vi, vii
Job, 223
Jacob, 219
Joel, 237
Johannes, 167, 174
Johannes D., 94
Johannes Ja., 170
Johannis, Jr., 171
Johannis D., 180
Johannis I., 285
John, 66, 70, 72, 73, 77, 84, 219, 238
John Coolbaugh, 78
John I., xxi
Joseph, 207, 226, 229
Joseph Jobs, 183
Josephas, 225
Josephat, 211, 219, 221, 223, 278
Josephus, 228, 230
Joshua, 47, 51, 57
Josua, 55
Julian, 228
Kesia, 200
Knelia, 202
La Fayette, 86
Laffaryne, 82
Lana, 170
Lanah, 56, 63, 67

Westbrook, Lantie, 189
  Lena, 172-174, 181, 187,
    188, 216, 226, 277, 284
  Lenah, 79
  Lendert, 30
  Leonard, 200
  Levy, 68
  Lidia, 191, 193, 201, 203,
    254
  Lidy, 226
  Lina, 209
  Lydia, 172, 182, 225, 227
  Lydia Cortright, 223
  Lydia Ennes, 229
  Magdalena, 177
  Magdalena Winter-
    mute, 61
  Majory, 41
  Margret, 57, 60, 66, 73,
    75, 78, 88, 216
  Maria, 37, 48, 171, 181,
    187, 197, 201, 202, 204,
    205, 207, 210, 215, 220,
    221, 247, 276, 285
  Marie, 178
  Mariah, 64, 211, 213
  Marjory, 45
  Marory, 43
  Marten, 216
  Martines, 169
  Martinus, 160
  Mary, 62, 174, 179, 218,
    220, 235, 237, 242, 245,
    247, 250-252, 278
  Mehaly, 222
  Moses W. Coolbaugh,
    90
  Nancy, 56
  Nehemiah, 227
  Noomi Decker, 230
  Peggy, 201
  Peter, 46, 203, 279
  Petrus, 172, 180, 205,
    211, 285
  Rachel, 51
  Ragel, 166
  Richard, 201
  Richd Broadhead, 77
  Ruben Buckley, 219
  Sally, 215
  Salomon, 192, 194, 204
  Samuel, 55, 169, 180, 284
  Samuel Cortright, 228
  Sara, 171
  Sarah, 47, 176, 201, 209,
    212, 276
  Seletie, 38, 43
  Severyn, 220
  Severyne, 221
  Severyne L., 227
  Simeon, 221
  Simeon Kittle, 227
  Soferyne, 275

Westbrook, Soforyne, 88
  Solomon, 60, 61, 62, 66,
    86, 90, 91, 174, 215,
    219, 221, 240
  Solomon, Jr., 73, 78, 81
  Souweruyn, 203
  Soverine, 216
  Soveryn, 190, 201, 207
  Susannah, 219
  Susannah Maria, 62
  Titus, 254
  Welhelmus, 187
  Wilhelmus, 169, 183,
    215, 223, 224, 243, 249
  Zepharine, 224
Westebrook, Jane, 240
Western, Pellip, 169
Westervelt, Pellip, 169
Westes, Dina, 209
  Henry, 209
  Lize, 209
Westfaal, Abraham, 32,
    184, 185, 192
  Blandina, 171
  Daniel, 275
  David, 183
  Elizabeth, 160, 192
  Grietie, 183
  Grietyie, 214
  Christina, 164
  Jacobus, 32, 161
  Jannite, 276
  Jurrian, 164
  Maria, 160, 161, 185
  Rushe, 185
  Salomon, 184
  Symon, ix
Westfael, Abel, 97
  Abm., 175
  Abraham, 163, 171-173,
    181
  Abram, 117
  Aeltey, 173
  Aeltje, 110, 130, 131
  Alleonora, 282
  Altje, 172
  Altye, 174
  Annatje, 116, 173, 181
  Antony, 121
  Apollonia, 163
  Benj., 170
  Benjamin, 97, 104, 110,
    112, 113, 117, 122, 127,
    132, 172, 282
  Benjn, 173
  Blandina, 180
  Christina, 130, 270
  Cornelis, 106, 107, 109,
    112, 113, 116, 120, 127,
    130, 131, 266, 269, 283
  Cornelis Ab., 116
  Cornelis Van Aken, 127
  Cornelius, 135, 180

Westfael, Danel, 165
  Daniel, 104, 105, 108,
    115, 116, 117, 120-122,
    125, 130, 136, 163, 173,
    266
  David, 135
  Dievertje, 130
  Eleonora, 116, 118, 120,
    124, 125
  Eleonord, 118
  Elisabet, 166
  Elisabeth, 111, 121, 142,
    171, 178
  Elizabeth, 135, 178
  Elleonora, 111
  Geertje, 103, 104
  Hannatje, 109
  Hendrick, 117, 165
  Jackobus, 166
  Jacob, 97, 107, 110, 111,
    127, 128, 130, 135, 180,
    282, 283
  Jacobus, 6, 10, 11-13, 93,
    122, 132
  James, 179
  Jan De Witt, 122
  Jannetje, 98
  Johanna, 124, 127, 135,
    283
  Johannes, 104, 107, 109,
    111, 114, 117, 118, 120,
    122, 123, 125, 126, 130,
    135, 137, 183, 281, 283
  Johannis, xiv
  John De Witt, 170
  Jorian, 107
  Jory, 107
  Joseph, 123, 173
  Juriaen, 97, 115, 131,
    137, 270
  Jury, 108, 112, 116
  Lea, 104
  Leanora, 138
  Ledia, 184, 197
  Lena, 2, 7, 119, 130
  Leonora, 107, 109, 113,
    135, 142
  Levy, 11
  Lidea, 190
  Lisabeth, 107, 110, 112,
    113, 116, 120, 127-129,
    132, 163, 266, 283
  Lizabeth, 107, 266
  Lidia, 106, 107, 111, 113-
    117, 120, 121, 123, 125,
    126, 129-131, 171, 180,
    183, 266, 267
  Maregreet, 171
  Margareta, 115
  Margareta, 105
  Margariet, 164
  Margarita, 104
  Margret, 173

Westfael, Margriet, 104, 112, 114, 115, 117, 120, 125, 127, 131, 266, 282
Margrietje, 131
Maria, 97, 104, 106, 110, 120, 142, 163, 164, 179, 270
Maritje, 97, 104, 106, 110, 113-116, 120, 122, 125, 126, 128, 265, 281, 282
Marya, 113, 115, 119, 125, 126, 129-131, 137, 179, 268
Nicael, 97
Pieternella, 1, 11
Petrus, 125, 126, 131, 179, 270
Petrus Brink, 183
Rushie, 183
Rusie, 173
Russia, 164
Russie, 137
Salomon, 136
Samuel, 117, 163, 170
Sara, 97, 98, 110, 111, 120, 127, 131, 137, 267
Sarah, 173
Simeon, 117, 174
Simon, 108, 110, 171, 265
Solomon, 170
Syme, 136
Symon, 116, 117, 122, 127, 131, 283
Wilhelmus, 127, 174, 180
Westfal, Abby, 209
Abraham, vii, 190, 194, 202, 205, 215
Abraham, Jr., 201
Abraham Westbrook, 201
Allie, 202
Altie, 186, 197, 228
Annatie, 184, 199
Benjamin, 195
Bethiah, 199
Busche, 203
Cathrina, 170
Cherk, 187
Daniel, 187, 195, 201, 207, 215, 228, 285
Daniel, Jr., 204
Daniel B., 220
David, 276
Diana, 240
Elizabeth, 40, 194, 207
Gretie, 199
Hannah, 188, 203
Hendrick, 199, 209
Henry, 205, 276
Hester, 187
Jacobus, 187, 195, 203, 207, 220
Janneca, 207

Westfal, Jannitie, 201
Jennika, 195
Johannes, 199
Joshuah, 205
Jurean, 199
Lidia, 190, 202
Manuel, 277
Maragriet, 187
Maria, 278, 285
Mary, 239
Plony, 214
Ruben, 277
Russie, 195
Rushe, 193
Samuel, 199, 203
Samuel D., 239, 240
Sarah, 204
Simeon, x
Simion, 205
Symon, Jr., 276
Wilhelmus, 170
Westfall, Abraham, vii, 87, 226, 249, 251, 261, 285
Antje, 233
Benjamin, 222, 226, 228, 241, 246, 250, 252, 256, 263, 264
Catharina, 230, 231
Catharine, 250, 257, 280
Cattrina, 278
Charles Hardenberg, 264
Cornelius, 211, 255, 256
Daniel, 211, 218, 221
David, 259
Dennis, 228
Elisa, 163
Elizabeth, 251
Ellenor, 258
Esther, 255, 279
Frederick, 262, 263, 280
Gilbert, 222
Grietie, 276
Henry, 216
Huldah, 280
Jacob, 131, 280
Jacob Gumaer, 262
Jacobus, 163
James, 275
Jane, 222, 240
Janey, 218
Jannetie, 210
Jemima, 255, 262, 263
Jemimy, 249
John, 216, 249
Ledia, 285
Lena, 264
Levi, 264
Lydia Anne, 226
Margaret, 233
Margery, 241
Maria, 233

Westfall, Marjery, 259, 262, 264
Mary, 241, 245, 263, 280
Matthew, 218
Nancy, 262
Peter Gumare, 263
Plony, 210, 223, 227, 278
Reuben, 233
Rosina, 275
Rushe, 285
Rusiller, 252
Sally, 256
Samuel, 276
Samuel D., 245, 248, 255
Sarah, 245, 248, 258, 261
Sarah Jane, 87
Senia, 263
Simeon, 222, 226, 258, 279
Simon, vii, 246, 261
Wilhelmus, 256, 259, 262, 264, 279
William, 221
Westfalls, Jacobus, 15
Westpertus, Diana, 215
Dina, 215
Harry, 215
William, 215
Westphaal, Hendrik, 159
Lidia, 133
Maria, 133
Westphal, Catherine, 240
Jurge, 98
Westphall, Daniel, 225
Jane, 252
John, 225
Solomon, 225
Samuel D., 252
Westvaal, Abram, 139, 143
Annatje, 147, 151
Antje, 157
Benjamin, 140, 141, 144, 147
Blandina, 140
Catrina, 139
Christina, 141, 144
Cornelis, 145, 147, 155, 157
Cornelius, 161
Cristina, 148
Daniel, 141, 143, 144, 158, 284
David or Daniel, 144
Divertje, 155, 158, 161
Elisabeth, 140-142, 144, 145, 147, 152, 155, 157
Hannatje, 141
Helmus, 160
Hendrik, 162
Hendrik Cortregt, 150
Jacob, 161, 284
Jacobus, 141, 143
Jannetje, 150

Westvaal, Johannes, 144
  Johannis, 132, 140, 142,
    147, 158, 284
  Juriaan, 139
  Juriaen, 139
  Jurian, 139, 145, 148, 150,
    284
  Jurry, 168
  Leonora, 140, 161
  Lidia, 133
  Lydia, 139, 142
  Maragriet, 142, 144, 148,
    151, 158
  Maragrita, 284
  Maragritje, 159
  Margrita, 145
  Maria, 138, 139, 143, 144,
    147, 148, 158, 165, 284
  Petrus, 145
  Rosyna, 147
  Ruben, 147
  Russia, 141
  Russie, 145, 150
  Sara, 139
  Sarah, 143, 147, 273
  Simion, 168
  Simon, 140
  Syman, 284
  Symion, 150
  Symon, 147, 150
  William, 162
  Zacharias, 155
Westvael, Aeltye, 168
  Daniel, 136
  Elesabet, 31
  Grietje, 22
  Johannis, 284
  Leida, 166
  Lidja, 142
  Lydia, 138
  Maria, 136
  Rusje, 136
  Rusye, 272
  Yuerrean, 140
Westval, Abel, 101, 102
  Abram, 158
  Benjamin, 99, 106
  Catrina, 167
  Christina, 134
  Cornelis, 106
  Daniel, 132
  Eleonora, 102
  Geertje, 102
  Hanna, 167
  Hannah, 167
  Henry, 220
  Jacobus, 134
  Johannes, 98-100, 102, 134
  Joseph, 134, 135
  Jure, 167
  Jurge, 98
  Jurian, 100, 135
  Jurye, 101

Westval, Lena, 100
  Lenora, 99
  Leonora, 99
  Lisabeth, 99
  Lydia, 101, 135
  Margrietje, 220
  Maria, 99, 102, 105, 158
  Marretje, 99, 100
  Marrietje, 103
  Peter, 220
  Phony, 208
  Samuel, 167
  Sara, 99, 102, 105
  Sarah, 23
  Simon, 102
Westvale, Abraham, 166
  Altie, 166
  Catrena, 166
  Cornelis, 166
  Cristena, 167
  Elisabeth, 169
  Gretie, 167
  Jacob, 166
  Jacobus, 170
  James Ma Carte, 167
  Lidia, 166
  Rusce, 167
  Russe, 170
  Sara, 167, 170
  Semyon, 167
Westvall, Elizabeth, 160
Westviel (Wintviel),
  Derick, 151
  Femmetje, 151
  Lydia, 151
  Maragriet, 158
Westvoel, Abraham, 31
Wesval, Elonara, 272
  Johanna, 271
  Johannis, 272
Wever, Elisabeth, 186
Whitaker, Charles H.,
  xxix
John P., xviii
Whitbeck, Henry, 246
White, Elisabeth, 177
  Lewis, 280
  Thos., 170, 177
Whitehead, Benjemin, 234
  Esther, 242
  Jane, 234
  Matilda, 234, 253, 257
  Oliver, 234, 242
Whitlock, Aaron, 253
  Daniel, 248
  Eliza Ann, 250
  Elizabeth, 259
  Jemima, 279
  Joel, 232, 242, 246, 250,
    253, 259
  John Hoff, 259
  Joseph, 242
  Joseph Hoff, 232

Whitlock, Levy, 248
Wickham, William, x
  Wm., x
Wildfield, Abraham, 107
  Abram, 109
  Abram, Jr., 114
  Grietje, 128
  Neeltje, 109
  Sophia, 128
  Thomas, 107
Willer, Catherine, 42
Williams, Cate, 152
  Ezechiel, 131, 191, 193
  Greetje, 172
  Grietie, 216
  Jacobus, 165
  James, 172, 216
  Johannes, 110
  John, 3, 8, 92, 110, 131,
    152, 211, 216
  Lea, 191, 193
  Lidia, 211
  Lydia, 216
  Margeree, 173
  Matthew, 285
  Polly, 225
  Rachel, 8, 178, 180, 192,
    194, 202, 208, 274, 285
  Sammuel, 165
  Samuel, 3, 160, 173, 274
  Sarah, 216
Williamse, Femmetje, 107
  Johannes, 158
  John, 158
  Rachel, 158
  Samuel, 158
Williamson, Rachel, 162
  Samuel, 162
Willims, Ledeja, 166
  Ragel, 166
  Samuel, 166
Wilson, Hannah, 92
  Jacob, 174, 181
  Jacob C., 280
  John Westbrook, 92
  Mary, 274
  Mierom, 181
  Miriam, 230
  Thomas, 174
  William, xvi
  Wm. T., 92
Winans, Elizabeth Depue, 68
  Matthew, 276
  Samuel, 68
Windemoedin, Anna
  Elisabetha, 111
Windemoet, Abraham,
  120
  Elizabeth, 132
  Johannes, 115
  Jory, 9

Windemoet, Jury Philip, 115, 120, 127
  Petrus, 127
  Philip, 129, 132
Windemout, Benjamin, 141
  Philip, 141
Windemuth, Johan Jory, 111
  Philip, 5
  Maria Juliana, 111
  Maria Margreta, 111
Windenmuth, Jory Philip, 111
Windfield, Deborah, 258
  Hannah Smith, 258
  Henry, 250, 258
  Jane, 250, 252
  Manuel, 183
  Margaret, 244
  Sarah, 285
Windle, James, 201
  John, 201
Winecoop, Cornelia, 69
Winekoop, David, 233
  Jane, 233
Winfield, Aaron, 251
  Henry, 251, 255
  Phebe, 235, 241
  Phebe Caroline, 255
Wingfield, Henry, 246
  Mariah, 246
Wininwagen, Hannah, 233
  John, 233
  Mary, 233
Winne, Hannah, 204, 206
Winner, Elizabeth, 250
Wintemaut, Leendert, 145
  Maria, 145
  Philip, 145
Wintemuth, Elizabeth, 136
  Johan Christoffel, 5
  Phillip, 136
Winteramute, David Hunt, 86
  George, Jr., 86
Wintermoet, Elisabeth, 148, 187

Wintermoet, Greitet, 169
Jeur (Jurry), 169
Jury, Jr., 148
Leonard, 136
Wintermout, Elisabeth, 149
  Johannis, 153
  Jurian, 153
  Jurry, 162
  Leendert, 149
  Lidia, 162
  Mary, 153
  Stoffel, 148
Wintfield, ——, 277
  Dyrck, 165
  Peggy, 165
Wintfiel, Derik, 152
  Elisabeth, 152
Wintviel, Abram, 154
  Derck, 146
  Derick, 140
  Derik, 144
  Elisabeth, 146
  Emmanuel, 140
  John or Josua, 145
  Joseph, 144
  (Windfield), Maritje, 145
Wiseborn, Elizabeth, 50
  Rachel, 50
Wittiker, John, 154
  Richard, 154
Woeltman, Sarah, 214
Woertman, Sarah, 217
Wolfe, Jacob, 34
  Jannitie, 34
Wolff, Jacob, 40
  Peter, 40
Wood, Benjamin, 159
  Benjn, 179
  Cathrina, 179
  Edward, 207, 211
  Emanuel, 207
  Hannah, 36, 39, 42, 44, 45, 47, 221
  Helena, 179
  Henry, 278
  John, 144

Wood, Lany, 211
  Lena, 213, 216, 226
  Lisa Margariet, 159
  Rachel, 178, 275
  Susannah, 216
  Tryntje, 173, 178
Wook (Wood), Lena, 223
Woolf, Caty, 40
  Jacob, 40
Wordly, Cornelis, 122
  Isack, 12
  John, 12, 122
Worner, Henry Arins, 32
  Lodewyk, 32
Wornes, Cristena, 163
  Mary, 163
Wright, James, 11
  Jeremias, 11
  Jonathan, 11
Wybrand, Dirck, 3
  Susanna, 3
Wyckoff, P. F., xxviii
Wydelig, Eva, 209
  Frederick, 209
  George, 209
  Hester, 209
Wye, John W., 274
Wymant, Jacob, 275
Wynans, Abigail, 275
Wyndfield, Abraham, 178
  Joseph, 178
Wynhoop, Antje, 129
Wynkoop, Antje, 121, 123, 125, 126, 138, 144, 283
  David, 232, 252
  Jacobus, 125
  Jacobus Swartwout, 252
  John, 232
Wyomy, 192, 194-196

Y

Yotter, Caty, 91
Young, Andrew Brinck, 227
  George Everet, 228
  Peter, 227, 228
  Susanna, 195

www.ingramcontent.com/pod-product-compliance
Lightning Source LLC
Chambersburg PA
CBHW050329230426
43663CB00010B/1788